THE POLITICS OF SECULARISM

Religion, Culture, and Public Life

RELIGION, CULTURE, AND PUBLIC LIFE
Series Editor: Katherine Pratt Ewing

The resurgence of religion calls for careful analysis and constructive criticism of new forms of intolerance, as well as new approaches to tolerance, respect, mutual understanding, and accommodation. In order to promote serious scholarship and informed debate, the Institute for Religion, Culture, and Public Life and Columbia University Press are sponsoring a book series devoted to the investigation of the role of religion in society and culture today. This series includes works by scholars in religious studies, political science, history, cultural anthropology, economics, social psychology, and other allied fields whose work sustains multidisciplinary and comparative as well as transnational analyses of historical and contemporary issues. The series focuses on issues related to questions of difference, identity, and practice within local, national, and international contexts. Special attention is paid to the ways in which religious traditions encourage conflict, violence, and intolerance and also support human rights, ecumenical values, and mutual understanding. By mediating alternative methodologies and different religious, social, and cultural traditions, books published in this series will open channels of communication that facilitate critical analysis.

For a complete list of books in the series, see page 359.

The Politics of Secularism

RELIGION, DIVERSITY, AND INSTITUTIONAL
CHANGE IN FRANCE AND TURKEY

Murat Akan

Columbia University Press
New York

Columbia University Press
Publishers Since 1893
New York   Chichester, West Sussex
cup.columbia.edu
Copyright © 2017 Columbia University Press
All rights reserved

Library of Congress Cataloging-in-Publication Data
Names: Akan, Murat, 1973– author.
Title: The politics of secularism: religion, diversity, and institutional change in France and Turkey / Murat Akan.
Description: New York : Columbia University Press, 2017. | Series: Religion, culture, and public life | Includes bibliographical references and index.
Identifiers: LCCN 2016053253| ISBN 978-0-231-18180-8 (cloth : alk. paper) | ISBN 978-0-231-54380-4 (e-book)
Subjects: LCSH: Secularism—Political aspects—France. | Secularism—Political aspects—Turkey. | Church and state—France. | Islam and state—Turkey.
Classification: LCC BL2765.F8 A58 2017 | DDC 322/.10944—dc23
LC record available at https://lccn.loc.gov/2016053253

Columbia University Press books are printed on permanent and durable acid-free paper.
Printed in the United States of America

Cover design: Chang Jae Lee

For Fethi, Sandrine, and Roza

Contents

Preface ix

I Traveling Through Analytical and Hermeneutical Approaches 1

II Accounting for Institutional Outcomes and Trajectories: Political Ends, Ideas, and Institutions 16

III The Institutional Politics of Laïcité in the French Third Republic 30

IV The Politics of *Laïcité Positive* and Diversity in Contemporary France 97

V The Institutional Politics of Laiklik in Kemalist Turkey 135

VI The Sincere Government (*Samimi Hükümet*), the Institutional Politics of Religion, and Diversity in Contemporary Turkey 209

Conclusion 277

Notes 287
Bibliography 325
Index 341

Preface

"The rise of sociology" wrote Antonio Gramsci in the *Prison Notebooks*,

> is related to the decline of the concept of political science and the art of politics which took place in the nineteenth century (to be more accurate, in the second half of that century, with the success of evolutionary and positivist theories). Everything that is of real importance in sociology is nothing other than political science. "Politics" became synonymous with parliamentary politics or the politics of personal cliques.[1]

In the study of secularization, either one theory of sociological determinism replaces another or Hegelian or Weberian ideational approaches present the most common alternatives to sociologism. To situate the current state of the art in researching secularism vis-à-vis Gramsci's remarks warning against limiting politics to parliamentary politics, our current knowledge of the politics of secularism can in fact benefit from restarting with the parliament today and in the nineteenth century. With the turn to ideas, studies of the place of religion in politics and society show increased theological tendencies in method. Thus they distance themselves slowly from Niccolò Machiavelli's simple and powerful lesson, supported by historical examples in *The Prince*, that even in analyzing the pope (or perhaps especially in analyzing the pope), we have to depart from the medieval tendency of focusing on ideas only and look also at action.[2]

Moreover, some approaches present themselves in thinned form; that is, disregarding fundamental aspects of their original formulations. For instance, many Weberians forget Max Weber's cautious remarks in *The Protestant Ethic and the Spirit of Capitalism* on studying the role of ideas: "We are concerned with the influence that *their* conduct [religious ethics of the classes which were the culture bearers of their respective countries] has had. Now it is quite true that this can only be completely known in all its details when the facts from ethnography and folklore have been compared with it. Hence we must expressly admit and emphasize that this is **a gap** to which the ethnographer will legitimately object."[3]

Weber's gap is often bridged with assumptions rather than filled with research material. Those who follow from Hegel with the currently popularized concept "imaginaries,"[4] which in my reading is simply the new term for "intersubjective meaning,"[5] often forget Judith Shklar's important call for an "example of how one might discover an 'intersubjective' meaning of political practices and beliefs" and her remark that "between an authoritative act of consciousness-raising and an interpretation that simply relates two areas of understanding, there can really be no compromise."[6]

This book originated with these preliminary observations, and from two concerns. Weberians, instead of taking Weber's gap seriously, often focus on *isomorphic relations* between sociology and action or ideas and action. Working on secularism in France and Turkey for almost two decades now, I kept noticing certain facts falling through the theoretical approaches and analytical frameworks appropriated in describing the politics of secularism and religion in these two critical cases. The most striking examples were exactly the kind of *nonisomorphic relations* that became invisible with sociologism and ideationalism. For example, in both France and Turkey some proponents of religion courses in public schools emerged from the ranks of opponents of the headscarf, and in Turkey defenders of state-salaried imams could be found among both proponents and opponents of the headscarf. Such facts were either ignored or explained away, but they were repetitive enough to be taken as a starting point for reflecting back on current theoretical approaches and analytical frameworks.

My second concern was the various hermeneutical turns that critical studies on modernity kept claiming in regular cycles in response to culturalist comparative accounts in general but still without success in cracking the codes of culturalism. What was at stake in these failed attempts was a *political field* that was within our reach but for some reason we just couldn't rest our eyes on. I hope that this book will at least partially rest our eyes and bridge some of the gaps between the analytical and hermeneutical schools in the social sciences.

This comparative project started with my work under Alfred Stepan at Columbia University. I never lost touch with Al after receiving my degree from Columbia. The many conversation-walks I took with him in New York and along the Bosporus in Istanbul were always illuminating and reinforced in me the idea that finishing a research project was only a beginning, and that sitting on a manuscript until you know you are done is difficult in today's academic environment of "publish or perish" but is still an option. By waiting I gained the opportunity to accumulate further primary sources and new conversation partners, and to appreciate the political struggles and people fighting for democracy in both France and Turkey at a depth beyond culturalist paradigms, a depth comparative research is in urgent need of.

Besides Al Stepan, I am grateful for the mentorship of Karen Barkey, Brian Barry, and Andrew Davison. I had graduated with a bachelor's degree in industrial engineering, and Brian directed the analytical capacity of an engineer to political philosophy. As my advisor before I met Al, Brian secured my funding at Columbia. It is still difficult for me that he passed away before I finished this book. Karen was always a meticulous reader; I still remember her entering my defense in 2005 and starting the conversation from footnote 614. Andrew Davison was always there for a good conversation and sharp comments on my work.

Anthropology and history contributed immensely to my formation. Sandrine Bertaux, a dedicated historian, taught me to appreciate history. The two anthropologists who have supported my research, writing, and thinking are Peter Geschiere of the University of Amsterdam and Peter van der Veer, director of the Department of Religious Diversity at the Max Planck Institute for the Study of Religious and Ethnic Diversity in Göttingen.

Peter van der Veer put his confidence in me to finish this book and invited me to the Max Planck Institute (MPI) for the 2012–13 academic year. The Scientific and Technological Research Council of Turkey International Post Doctoral Research Fellowship Programme (TÜBİTAK 2219) funded that sabbatical year at the MPI. I presented parts of chapter 6 in Peter's weekly seminar, where the critical comments by the seminar's participants were very helpful. I thank Steven Vertovec and Fran Meissner for engaging me with their workshop and giving me the opportunity to meet Ralph Grillo. I also thank the staff of the MPI for making the institute what it is, particularly Martin Kühn and Dagmar Recke.

Between 2009 and 2012 the Amsterdam School for Social Science Research of the University of Amsterdam offered me a nonresidential postdoctoral research fellowship with the project on Culturalization of Citizenship. I learned immensely from all the participants in this project, particularly Francio Guadeloupe and Peter Geschiere, director of the subgroup View from the South. I aired and discussed some of the ideas in this book in various workshops. I co-organized "Contextualizing Multiculturalism: Realities and Pitfalls" with Peter Geschiere at the 13th Mediterranean Research Meeting (MRM) in Florence in 2012 and "Secularization, Secularism, Secular: Democracy and Religious Minorities" with Sandrine Bertaux in 2008, again at the MRM. Under the Culturalization of Citizenship program, Peter, Sandrine, and I organized the workshop and conference series "Citizenship, Democracy and Diversity: Comparisons" at Boğaziçi University in 2012. Francesco Ragazzi and Frank de Zwart invited me to their workshop on State Categories/Social Identities at Leiden University in 2014. Ji Zhe invited me to the CNRS in 2015 for a workshop with Groupe Sociétés, Religions, Laïcités. Mirjam Künkler and Hanna Lerner, the two other participants in Alfred Stepan's first seminar on religion, have invited me to many conferences and workshops since I left Columbia in 2005. I thank them all. I also thank all the student participants and guests of my seminar at Boğaziçi University on Secularism, Democracy, and Religion.

Three of my projects funded by the Boğaziçi University Research Fund were crucial in providing me the opportunity to gather research material for this book: "The Politics of Secularism in France and Turkey" (project no. 12668), "Politics, Religion and Society Before and Through the 1980 Military Takeover in Turkey, 1975–1987" (project no. 6732), and "The Politics of Laiklik in the Writing of the 1961 Turkish Constitution" (project no. 5523). I advance a special thank you to my research assistants who worked on these projects, Ekin Kurtiç (now a PhD candidate at Harvard), Sumru Atuk (now a PhD candidate at CUNY), and Ezgi Murat (now a PhD candidate at Boğaziçi).

I conducted research at various libraries in France, Germany, Great Britain, the United States, and Turkey. I thank all the librarians for making the research life pleasant. Special thanks to Richard at Columbia's Lehman Library, and Hatice, Sema, Zeynep, Mustafa, Seyfi, and Kamber at Boğaziçi Library. Many thanks also to Cuma, Nevzat, Serap and Halil for all the tea-chats we had.

I thank Boğaziçi University dean Ayşegül Toker for taking the initiative to create and institutionalize a faculty book-editing fund for this book and for all future faculty books to come. I thank Boğaziçi University rector Gülay Barbarosoğlu for her exemplary dedication to an autonomous research university in changing and hard times.

I am grateful to the Akan family, Fügen Akan, Engin Akan, and Burcu Akan, for always being there, and to the Parla family for launching me on my academic path in the social sciences.

My wife, Sandrine Bertaux, and my kids, Dylan and Luka, were with me all through the research and writing of this book. They continuously supported, encouraged, and comforted me in difficult times. I would not have been able to finish without them. And their presence assures me that this book is just another beginning.

Turkey witnessed a radical escalation of police violence during the writing of this book. I live in a neighborhood that is considered to be one of the bastions of Turkey's democratic movements. I cannot count the times I had to rush to close my windows before police tear gas reached my sleeping kids. Late one evening I was walking to a friend's house when I was stampeded by a crowd of youth running from the police. As a reflex I also started a sprint but after five seconds remembered to ask myself, "Why am I running?" I stopped because dignity did not allow me to set an example to those youth to run; I stopped and sat on a bench while I watched the police on my left approaching the youth crossing in front of me. I thought of my grandfather, who was a respected police officer, and I am sure if he were alive today he would have resigned or picked a fight with the institution. He was ninety when he described to me how, right after the 1960 coup, when he was in his early forties, a high-ranking military officer told him "the neighborhood likes you" and offered to promote him into the regime. My grandfather said to me, "I told him, Officer, you lean against a wall, the wall one day crumbles; you trust a person, the person dies one day; thank you, but I prefer to stay in the square." Granddad started his police career in the street and ended in the street; to avoid corruption he refused to climb the ladder of state bureaucracy. This Turkish man who grew up in a diverse neighborhood apparently had a sense of institutional boundaries and duty. Today the police substitute for the military in Turkey. As I sat on the bench, a few young men stopped right in front of me. One of them turn to the other and asked, "Why are we running?" They looked at each other in silence and then sat near me while I embraced my seat, the gang of police on the left slowly approaching. This book is for those who are willing to sit and stay on their benches.

Kadıköy
May 2016

THE POLITICS OF SECULARISM

CHAPTER I

Traveling Through Analytical and Hermeneutical Approaches

Doing ethnography is like trying to read (in the sense of "construct a reading of") a manuscript—foreign, faded, full of ellipses, incoherencies, suspicious emendations, and tendentious commentaries, but written not in conventionalized graphs of sound but in transient examples of shaped behavior.
—CLIFFORD GEERTZ, *THE INTERPRETATION OF CULTURES*, 1967

Mr. Lerner shows that every encounter with another people is a confrontation with ourselves.
—DAVID RIESMAN, INTRODUCTION TO *THE PASSING OF TRADITIONAL SOCIETY*, 1964

Passions without truth, truths without passion.
—KARL MARX, *THE 18TH BRUMAIRE OF LOUIS BONAPARTE*, 1869

Is there the same deep chasm between the peasant and the literate class of each country? I don't know! But, the difference between a literate Istanbullite (kid) and an Anatolian peasant is greater than the difference between a Londoner English and a Punjabi Indian. While I write this, my hand shakes.
—YAKUP KADRI KARAOSMANOĞLU, *YABAN*, 1932

In the recent literature on politics and religion, "modes of secularism,"[1] "multiple secularisms,"[2] "alternative modernities,"[3] and "multiple modernities"[4] challenge the "secularization,"[5] "clash of civilizations,"[6] and "end

[1]

of history"[7] theses. Yet in this research movement toward *varieties* of secularism and modernity, a rigorous comparative analytical framework is becoming elusive.

Sociologists lead the way, tackling the modernization-secularization thesis by simply making a reverse Durkheimean "factual" claim. The "fact" of deprivatization of religion[8] is announced in the same way the fact of privatization of religion was announced some years ago, as a spontaneous "development, whose sole driving force seems to be the calendar."[9] Normative political theory follows sociology. Public space has to relax the boundary between obligations of citizenship and demands of faith; a "learning process" between secular and religious citizens has to be the new mode of deliberation.[10] While in the nineteenth century the religious were told that "secularism is not antireligious,"[11] today the secular are told that religionism is not antisecular. Meanwhile, it is unclear whether religion is a fact we have to face or a solution we have to seek. For instance, the report of the Alliance of Civilizations meeting in 2006 between Prime Minister José Luis Rodríguez Zapatero of Spain and Prime Minister Recep Tayyip Erdoğan of Turkey explicitly considered religion as one solution to "help build harmony" in the world.[12]

The post 9/11 literature on secularism and religion highlights one analytical distinction—moderate and radical religions—and dissolves another—the political and the theological. The distinction between moderate and radical religions demands attention to the particular content of each religious tradition and feeds into a rampant methodological move rendering "religion" a significant determinant of agency. The most common way to tackle the question of content is a selective kind of scriptural hermeneutics, treating religious texts as either univocal or multivocal.[13] Saba Mahmood underlines the politics of this "shared approach to scriptural hermeneutics," bringing together U.S. analysts and "self-identified secular liberal Muslim reformers" who assume that "the core problem . . . is not militancy itself but interpretation, insomuch as the interpretive act is regarded as the foundation of any religious subjectivity and therefore the key to its emancipation or secularization."[14] One exception to this tendency to rely on religion as a significant determinant of agency is Talal Asad's genealogical approach to religion and secularism, which calls for a focus on all the practices that go into making religion religion and secular secular.[15]

As for the analytical distinction between the political and the theological, this distinction is constantly worked on, crossed, relaxed, and sometimes collapsed. Political theologies, theo-politics, and theologico-political are among the emerging composite concepts.[16] In the *Letter Concerning Toleration*, John Locke underlined that "moral action belongs . . . to the jurisdiction both of the outward [civil government] and the inward [church] court. . . . Here therefore is great danger, lest one of these jurisdictions entrench upon the other."[17] This kind of analytical observation in nuance now becomes proof for how the political and the theological are immanently interwoven rather than a path for further research. On the one hand, the Enlightenment tradition of addressing religion formally and not in its claim to truth—captured by the common distinction between the utility and truth of religion[18]—is receding from current analytical frameworks; on the other hand, the engagement with its claim to truth has been reduced to the level of "lived experience / self-understanding" with little regard for the institutional mechanisms[19] that sustain the truth, practice, and the "lived experience" of religion.[20] It is not uncommon to hear the "distinction in rational credibility between religious and nonreligious discourse" as "without foundation."[21] What remains as an analytical framework is often religion as a "set of ideas," "discourse," "way of life," "worldview," "imaginary," "identity," or an aspect of subjectivity without its institutions.

Religion talk has become popular, while the conceptualization of secularism is multiplying with the lead of the multiple modernities approach. With this approach, from the debates around the secularization thesis[22] and principles of secularism,[23] there is a turn toward a focus on mapping and accounting for multiple institutions and practices of secularism in challenge of the idea of a single separation doctrine.[24] Upon a close look, one can notice right away that in fact the multiple modernities approach addresses the same benchmark question as the modernity and alternative modernities approaches: how does secularism *travel* outside its European context of origin?[25] Therefore it suffers from the same handicaps as its precursors—handicaps embodied in the very formulation of the question. This question assumes a single atemporal model of European secularism and puts aside the question of secularism *traveling to* and *within* Europe. Therefore the question keeps reproducing an academic field of discussion caught in between two types of answers. On the one hand, from an atemporal model of separation, analytical schools describe institutional deviations outside of Europe as *anomalies* and attribute them to sociocultural variables. On the other hand, critics *claim* a hermeneutical turn and document how secular political actors comprehend institutional arrangements in their specific contexts of production, asserting how the institutional differences the modernists qualify as anomalies make sense from the point of view of the actors who erected the institutions. The former displace anomalies to the outside of Europe; the latter encapsulate the anomalies in a specific understanding of secularism, and both produce a *deadlock* for comparative research by preempting the possibility of investigating political fields of secularism common to Europe and its outside. The multiple modernities approach coined in Shmuel N. Eisenstadt's article is just another hermeneutical turn, calling for a focus on the reinterpretations European modernity goes through in various contexts,[26] as a way to go beyond modernist-sociological "subtraction stories"[27] of modernity.

The objective of this book is to resolve this deadlock and explore the possibility of a shared political field that can account for trajectories of secularism across the boundaries of Europe, through diachronic and synchronic comparisons of France and Turkey. These two cases are critical for addressing this deadlock. Turkey is the longtime critical case of whether and how secularism can travel to a Muslim-majority country. In the seminal work on modernization, Daniel Lerner's book *The Passing of Traditional Society: Modernizing the Middle East* (1958); in Samuel Huntington's article "The Clash of Civilizations" (1993), and in Shmuel N. Eisenstadt's article "Multiple Modernities" (2000), the critical case is Turkey.[28] Eisenstadt lays out his argument for the "Multiple Modernities Approach" with the example of Turkey, which he reads through Nilüfer Göle's *The Forbidden Modern: Civilization and Veiling* (1996).[29] France is the key case in Europe, qualified as an exception in many respects but whose history has constituted many of the political ideals of Western modernity and has set an example for many countries. There is a strong claim in the literature that secularism in Turkey (*laiklik*) has followed French *laïcité*. Furthermore, in the recent literature on secularism and religion, the relation between rigid forms of secularism and challenges of diversity figures centrally.[30] Turkey and France again constitute the historical examples of rigid secularism in building the case for why challenges of diversity require more moderate forms of secularism.

This book locates the precise moments of *traveling* and the translations secularism goes or does not go through in each context at *moments of potential institutional change*. Both ideational and sociocultural arguments deny autonomy to the political field at moments of potential institutional change. The former sees institutions as an outcome of certain ideas of secularism and the latter as the outcome of certain sociocultural conditions. However, moments of potential institutional change are the precise moments when

[4] ANALYTICAL AND HERMENEUTICAL APPROACHES

relations among ideas (of secularism and religion), sociology, and institutions are discussed and negotiated comparatively. These are the moments where traveling either does or does not occur. These moments maximize the overlap between sets of political positions across countries and through time, because they include reasons for and against eliminated institutional options as well. Such overlapping sets of political positions allow for comparison in their scope, conceptions, argumentations, practical concerns, and contestation over meanings and sociology.

In fact, the current literature's determination that secularism in Turkey (laiklik) and in France (laïcité) are more similar than different in their historical origins is a starting point to underscore the limitations of existing attempts to resolve the deadlock and explore the possibility of an alternative common political field. Current comparative accounts have predominantly turned to the headscarf debates as a litmus test and have claimed that France and Turkey share a similar political field characterized by the historical struggle between two competing ideas of secularism: one for and the other against the public visibility of religious symbols.[31] The former, a liberal doctrine, won in Turkey with the removal of the ban on scarves in 2013; the latter, a comprehensive doctrine, won in France with the ban on religious symbols in 2004. However, Turkey has two major institutional differences from France that complicate this particular claim of a shared political field: in Turkey, imams are paid by the state, and there are required and optional courses on religion, morality, and ethics in public schools. These institutional differences have been attributed to different levels of sociological secularization, with the further claim that Islam has tamped down secularism in Turkey. The exclusive focus on the headscarf, instead of resolving the deadlock, completely excludes these institutional differences from the comparative description of the political fields in France and Turkey.

The Politics of Secularism: Religion, Diversity, and Institutional Change in France and Turkey takes an alternative comparative route to resolving the deadlock. As a starting point, the book (1) approaches institutional separation as a historically contingent and contested outcome, (2) takes the *relation* between ideas and institutions of secularism as open-ended rather than assuming a constitutive relation, and (3) focuses on this relation in multiple issue areas (headscarf, religion courses, state salaries for clerics/imams). These three methodological caveats document many contradictions found as much in France as in Turkey, such as proponents of religion courses in public schools emerging from the ranks of opponents of the headscarf in both France and Turkey, or proponents and opponents of the headscarf in Turkey both defending state-salaried imams and religion courses in public schools. I take these contradictions as the keys to an alternative description of the trajectories of French and Turkish secularism and to a remapping of the political fields that account for these trajectories.

The book identifies two historical and two contemporary empirical puzzles of potential institutional change to address the question of traveling: (1) The *Loi du 9 Décembre 1905 concernant la séparation des Églises et de l'État* passed the French parliament with a small margin of votes. How did this French parliament, which opposed separation in 1902 and maintained the status quo of state-salaried clerics, separate churches and the state in 1905? (2) During the debates over the headscarf in France in the 2000s, how did the proponents for religion courses in the public school curriculum emerge from the ranks of the opponents of the headscarf? (3) How in Turkey did state salaries for imams and religion courses on Sunni Islam in the public school curriculum continuously win over other alternative institutional arrangements of state and religions at various moments between 1923 and 1982? (4) Why did Turkey's governing political Islamist party, the Justice and Development Party (Adalet ve Kalkınma Partisi, AKP), which sometimes aired the idea of separation while in opposition, organize outreach meetings with religious minorities when in government and then recently strengthen the institution of state-salaried imams and triple the number of religion courses in public schools?

Neither modernist approaches nor prevailing hermeneutical critiques can account for these puzzles. The sociocultural variables that modernist approaches employ cannot fully account for the puzzles because these puzzles either address institutional change over a relatively short period of time or present similar institutional arrangements (in place or as proposals) across the two countries with different sociocultural conditions. Prevailing hermeneutical turns to ideas cannot fully account for them either, because the puzzles involve either significant variations through time in actions associated with an idea of secularism, coterminous multiple actions associated with the same idea, or different ideas associated with the same action. In other words, they all violate the necessary condition of an ideational approach: an *isomorphic relation* between an idea and an action. The multiple-issue focus of this book allows for a differentiation in nuance of the political positions on institutions that the ideational accounts cannot capture. The book answers its puzzles by taking traveling literally, documenting from primary sources the precise political calculations, arguments, and discussions of other country contexts by competing political actors. Primary sources include records of the French Parliament, the Turkish Parliament, and the Constituent Assembly; commission reports, records of state dialogue projects with civil society organizations, state statistics, court decisions, and many other state documents; memoirs, newspapers, civil society organization reports and public statements, and some interviews.

The book advances its arguments on two levels. First, it resituates the comparative trajectories and remaps the political fields in France and Turkey. All these moments in France and Turkey are struggles not between two but among three distinct institutionalist political currents: anticlericalism, liberalism, and state-civil religionism. The book fleshes out the third current—state mobilization of religion as the cement of society—which not only is left out of the existing comparisons of the two countries but is also largely ignored in the emerging literature on secularism and religion. Focusing on state-civil religionism not only is important for a fuller account of the institutional outcomes in France and Turkey; it is also theoretically significant because it has its own way of articulating the boundary between the secular and the religious. This articulation at times resonates with antisecular movements, and by fleshing it out it becomes possible to investigate the limits of secular politics.

On a second level, the book advances arguments built on certain elements present in all four empirical puzzles, giving birth to a new set of hypotheses addressing the more general question of traveling and politics: (1) The struggle over institutions is a multidimensional, transnational struggle of evaluating institutions in other countries. This book uniquely documents the discussions on Europe (France in particular) in Turkey during struggles over institutions, the United States in the French Third Republic, and Turkey in contemporary France. The book follows an approach that I call "mutually interactional modernities" as a critique of the multiple modernities approach. Modernity does not necessarily multiply out of one historical origin through reinterpretations but rather through mutual interactions. The interpretation of other countries varies across competing political interests in each country and also changes through history with changing political interests; therefore one cannot really talk about "being modeled after" but rather of "taking as a battleground of discussion." (2) Not all the arguments in debates on institutions *concerning* secularism are arguments *from* secularism. That is precisely why the struggles in France and Turkey cannot be reduced to a struggle over the meaning of secularism. There are also arguments on the importance of having a religious society, and some of the actors who advance such arguments make the effort to convincingly or unconvincingly redefine secularism; others do not even make an effort and simply argue from religion. The book finds this latter group only among the political Catholics in Third Republic France and among AKP parliamentarians in Turkey. (3) There is not necessarily an isomorphic relation between the set of institutional options and the set of ideas of secularism. For instance, both institutional separation and state participation in religious affairs can serve the purposes of mobilizing or demobilizing religion depending on the context and how the particular terms of the institutional arrangement are negotiated. (4) State-civil religionists can emerge from the ranks of anticlericals, as was the case with Kemalism in late 1940s, and with *Républicains progressistes* at the end of the nineteenth century in Third Republic France. They can also emerge from ex-monarchists, as was the case with political Catholics at the end of the nineteenth century in Third Republic France. At different degrees and with different arguments, they both demanded the state play a role in maintaining or promoting a majority religion as the cement of society as an end in itself or as a means to various ends of governance. In the case of these actors, studying anomalies takes on a new significance. How such political actors negotiate this anomalous position and what kind of new meanings they create to render the anomaly "normal" also becomes a part of the politics over secularism. These utilitarians are a transition point, a vessel for some religious actors. This path is visible in Turkish politics and with lesser intensity in contemporary France, and this utilitarian approach to institutions is precisely what was defeated in the separation of churches and the state in the Third French Republic.

Working with very rich research material and focusing on the "nuts and bolts"[32] of potential institution change, I have found it impossible to follow the "ideational" approach, in either its "Verstehen" (Weber) or its "imaginaries" (Taylor) forms, two currents quite widespread not only in the study of France and Turkey but more generally in the study of secularism and religion. Doubly committed to narrating in a way as detailed and as analytical as possible, I found it impossible to reduce ideas of secularism to "imaginaries" or "worldviews," for the primary sources I worked with uncover many nonisomorphic relations between ideas and actions, similar to the ones Clifford Geertz addresses in his article "Ritual and Social Change: A Javanese Example."[33]

Besides rampant nonisomorphic relations, working with the precise political calculations and arguments by competing political actors at these moments of potential institutional change uncovers another missing link in the current literature following the lead of the multiple modernities approach; namely, "interactional histories."[34] In this book I use the term to refer to an analytical focus on moments when actors in political action in a particular context discuss and evaluate various histories, institutions and policies in other contexts and engage in a "politics of comparison," both in conceptualizing and in institutionalizing a relation between the "secular" and the "religious." The book's analytical framework is inspired by various currents but also expands on them in quite a few novel directions. The focus on conceptualizations of "the secular" and "the religious" in a specific context recalls the genealogical approach articulated in Talal Asad's *Formations of the Secular: Christianity, Islam, Modernity* (2003). Its focus on these conceptualizations in the political agents' comparative articulations, fitting in the genre of "ideas across contexts," resembles Partha Chatterjee's *Nationalist Thought and the Colonial World: A Derivative Discourse?* (1986) or Peter van der Veer's focus on "interactional histories" in *Imperial Encounters: Religion and Modernity in India and Britain* (2001). The emphasis on potential moments of institution building and change presents the political life of sociological arguments and the politics of the creation of new comparative meanings vis-à-vis other countries, the multiple relations—including especially nonisomorphic ones—between ideas and institutions of secularism. At the same time it significantly shares the analytical tools and concerns of the (historical) institutionalist school, such as James Mahoney and Kathleen Thelen's *Explaining Institutional Change: Ambiguity, Agency, and Power* (2009), or Alfred Stepan's "The World's Religious Systems and Democracy: Crafting the 'Twin Tolerations'" (2001).

Chapter 2 defends an alternative comparative route with two cornerstones in order to account for institutional outcomes and trajectories: (1) a comparative historical analysis that takes "separation" not as a model but as a historically contingent outcome; and (2) a comparative contextual focus on the *precise political ends and arguments* by various competing political actors at moments of potential institutional change, rather than tracing institutions to sociology or ideas and tracing ideas to imaginaries or historically rooted ideologies.

Chapter 3 explores the making of the March 28, 1882, law on free public obligatory education and the December 9, 1905, law on separation in Third

Republic France. The chapter maps out the debates over the most contested aspects of these laws from the *Journal officiel de la République française*, Débats parlementaires, Chambre des députés; commission reports; and other primary sources. In the 1882 law the most contested issue was the question of religion courses in the public school curriculum, and in the 1905 law it was article 4 on the redistribution of church property. In 1882 monarchists opposed the entire law, anticlerical republicans wanted to exclude religious instruction from the curriculum and just provide a weekly time slot for those who would like to receive religious instruction outside of school hours and grounds, and state-civil religionist republicans demanded that schoolteachers teach, if not a particular religious tradition, one's general duties to God. The anticlerical republicans dominated the parliament; therefore their position passed. They defended voluntary religious instruction outside of school hours and grounds with a public argument premised on the societal condition of diversity as opposed to one premised on the prevalence of a societal majority religion. Some of these anticlericals had also argued for an end to state salaries for clerics when they were running for election at the dawn of the Third Republic, but once having consolidated their power in the mid-1880s, they moved toward state-civil religionism on this issue; that is, they wanted to maintain (not to demobilize) Catholicism as the cement of society. With rising competition from socialism, the end of the monarchists, and the rise of political Catholicism at the end of the century, some of these anticlericals looked forward to a coalition with the political Catholics who were defending a much stronger version of state civil-religionism against socialism; that is, they aimed to mobilize Catholicism.

This dynamic of changing positions among some anticlericals toward state-civil religionism was crucial in the battle over the 1905 law. The *Loi du 9 Décembre 1905* passed the French parliament with a very small margin of votes, which points to the insufficiency of the sociological explanations for the law. The battle was between political Catholics who wanted to mobilize Catholicism as the cement of society, civil-religionist republicans who did not want to demobilize Catholicism as the cement of society, socialists who wanted to take religion off the public agenda, and followers of Émile Combes, who had utilized the state salaries for clerics to contain and attack the church and now, convinced that the church was no longer a regime threat, wanted institutional separation to hit a final blow on it. The chapter documents that given such conflict of interests, a majority for the law could be established only by the socialists' push for secularism above comprehensive doctrines of anticlericalism and civil religionism toward a general liberal institutionalist principle, and they negotiated the terms of the separation accordingly. As was the case in the making of the 1882 law, socialists also built their arguments from the premise of diversity instead of from the premise of a majority religion, and the law put an end to both Combiste anticlericalism and state-civil religionism. The chapter also documents how the interpretation of secularism in the United States was a battleground for these political struggles.

Chapter 4 turns to contemporary France. The exclusive focus on the headscarf question to map out the political field of struggle over laïcité in France has mislocated the much more complicated trajectory laïcité entered with the passage of the 2004 law banning the donning of large religious symbols at public schools vis-à-vis the Third Republic. Such an exclusive focus has reduced the political field to a binary opposition between two understandings of laïcité, an "anticlerical" side favoring the ban and a "liberal" side opposing the ban, and has totally ignored the state-civil religionists in the field. The chapter argues that it was, in fact, the state-civil religionists who partially resolved and almost cashed in on the conflict between these two sides. The formulation of the question as laïcité versus the "new challenge" of diversity in France totally ignored what chapters 3 and 4 read together demonstrate: that diversity is neither new nor a challenge to laïcité. On the contrary, it was its constitutive premise in building public schools in 1882 and separating churches and state in 1905. As far as public school was concerned, the premise of a diverse student body was the common ground of almost all anticlerical republicans in 1882. "Diversity," rather than being a challenge to laïcité, in the Third Republic was the fundamental premise grounding neutrality at the institutional level.

Contemporary France has not experienced a reassertion of Third Republic laïcité but rather an institutional regression from it toward civil-religionism. In contemporary France as anticlericalism diverged from its premise of diversity (only some socialists could still hold on to this premise), state-civil religionists claimed diversity by turning it from a "premise" to a "sociological category" and by reducing it to religious diversity. They mobilized against neutrality through the headscarf affair and pushed religion as the cement of society. State-civil religionism was a tripartite movement only partially materialized and ossified around the governing party, the Union for a Popular Movement (Union pour un mouvement populaire, UMP). It consisted of (1) defending the legal ban on the scarf, (2) the rise in public Muslim infrastructure (building of Muslim high schools and the French Muslim Council), and (3) pushing religious infrastructure in general in public space. This included challenging the 1905 separation law, mobilizing the Catholic Church, and mobilizing for the teaching of religious facts in public schools.

Chapter 5 addresses the question of how in Turkey the institutional relation between state and religion became locked into the institution of state-salaried imams and religion courses on Sunni-Islam in the public school curriculum. The struggle in the French Third Republic between anticlericalism and state-civil religionism was resolved by liberalism. The pillars of state-civil religionism were the ideas of a majority religion and the utility of religion, and the political Catholics advanced the most explicitly utilitarian arguments on religion. In Turkey, most moments of institutional change were directly top down, and even when they were not, they excluded actors such as minorities and the left, who could at least potentially produce these liberal institutionalist arguments. The chapter argues that the institutions locked in because the struggle in Turkey remained encapsulated between anticlericalism and state-civil religionism, the former frequently joining the ranks of the latter, and the institution of state-salaried imams and religion courses could be used like a lever to mobilize as well as demobilize religion. After the coup d'état in 1980, the Kemalist military constitutionalized compulsory Sunni religion courses in the public school curriculum and redefined the constitutional role of state-salaried imams as serving national solidarity. The part of the literature that takes Kemalist laicism as anticlerical qualifies this moment either as mere contradiction or as "anticlericalism within the limits of Islam," which requires a different kind of secularism.

The chapter documents how at various critical junctures[35] the idea of a majority religion and utilitarian approaches to religion are a crucial part of the explanation for why Turkey got locked into its institutions. One critical juncture was when the Republican People's Party (Cumhuriyet Halk Partisi, CHP) moved away from its original anticlerical elements, reinvested in the institution of state-salaried imams, and reestablished optional Sunni religion courses outside class hours in state schools in 1949, four years after the transition to a multiparty system. A close analysis of the internal debates within the party at the time shows that this was not only to counter the critique of anticlericalism from its major challenger, the newly established conservative liberal Democrat Party (Demokrat Parti, DP), but very significantly to fight communism. However, such utilitarian politics of religion were not specific to the CHP of that time. The first parliamentary discussion in 1951 on the future of state-salaried imams during the DP government show that what framed the debate over separating or keeping the institution was a question of which option would provide a stronger religion to fight communism. This position of "separation for more religion" was also present in the French Third Republic but just as a few dissident voices within the political Catholics. In Turkey, the DP increased the budget for state-salaried imams even further, moved the optional religion courses within class hours, and changed the terms of being optional from "opt-in" to "opt-out." This institutional change was hotly debated in the Annual National Education Congress in 1953 among teachers and DP ministers, where many examples from European cases were laid on the table. The discussion focused more on institutional principles, but it was still framed by the idea of a Sunni Muslim majority country disregarding non-Muslims and non-Sunni Muslims, and it also exposed further vicissitudes of making liberal principles and *optional* religion courses during class hours compatible. In another critical juncture, the military coup of 1960, there were few non-Muslim, non-Sunni Muslim and liberal republicans in the Constituent Assembly of 1961, which inserted the institution of state-salaried imams into the constitution. Although they were unable to change the outcome, these marginalized groups ignited highly important discussions, bolstered by some petitions written by minorities to the Constituent Assembly.

The chapter concludes with an analysis of the Constituent Assembly debates in the making of the 1982 military constitution. The Constituent Assembly records from 1982 show that the military's institutional preferences came from an explicit interest in mobilizing religion (as the cement of society) against the leftist movement and had nothing to do with the "threat of Islam," and that the military reinterpreted some examples from Europe and particularly pushed a distinction between religion as such and religion as culture in order to normalize this anomaly.

Each time Kemalist laicists were challenged by political or social diversity, they turned to religion as the cement of society, and each time they sought to guarantee the support from religion at a higher level of institutionalization. Chapter 6 documents how the AKP is mobilizing religion by deepening and layering the Kemalist laicist institutions that already give religion a place at the constitutional level, appropriating a politics of diversity that advances religion even deeper as the cement of society.[36]

The exclusive focus on the headscarf in mapping the political field of struggle over laiklik and laïcité has collapsed the political fields of Turkey and France into each other and makes them look more similar than they in fact are. In the case of Turkey, it has for long made the AKP look like a "radical" critique of the Kemalist establishment from a "liberal" perspective. In 2013 the headscarf ban was removed in all state institutions, including for state employees and students starting in fifth grade (age ten). This has already changed the scope of the debate in the two countries. Wearing the scarf as a ten-year-old public school girl is not up for discussion in France.

The more significant change is at the institutional level, however. The already required course on religion in Turkey has now been supplemented by two optional courses: one on reading the Koran and the other on the life of the Prophet. The institution of state-salaried imams has also been restructured to enhance the hierarchies among imams. In all these restructurings, minorities have been totally ignored. What happened? Has the AKP changed? I show that the roots of the recent institutional restructurings by the AKP were already present in parliamentary records and other primary sources when it first came to power in 2002. The AKP always worked from the premise that Turkey is a Sunni Muslim–majority country. What has changed, however, is that the party's defense of institutions on the relation between state and religion issues less and less from arguments on laicism. I document this from parliamentary records and other primary sources on the party's politics around state-salaried imams from the time it took office in 2002 until the institution's final restructuring in 2010; its Democratic Opening: National Unity and Brotherhood/Sisterhood Project (Demokratik Açılım: Milli Birlik ve Kardeşlik Projesi), the party's failed project for writing a new constitution in 2013; and the reintroduction of the new optional religion courses in 2012. The chapter particularly zooms in on one aspect of the Democratic Opening Project, the Alevi Workshops, to assess AKP's politics of religious diversity.[37] I offer a close textual analysis of the approximately two thousand pages of state minutes and report on the seven workshops that took place between June 2009 and January 2010. Despite their anomalies and varieties, all Kemalists more or less took laicism as the battlefield. The parliamentary discussions show that AKP parliamentarians argue more and more from the point of view of religion as an end itself or as a means to some particular political goal; some of their arguments approach those of political Catholics in Third Republic France, and laicism is losing its place as the framer of the political field of discussion.

These trajectories become visible only when we precisely step aside from an exclusive focus on isomorphic relations between ideas and action and expand our framework to multiple-issue areas. The conclusion turns to a discussion of the general theoretical and methodological significance of the book's empirical material and argument.

CHAPTER II

Accounting for Institutional Outcomes and Trajectories

Political Ends, Ideas, and Institutions

Our politics, in the relations of the Republic with the Church, have been very resolutely anticlerical, it has never been an antireligious politics. (*Excitement from right.—Applause from center.*)
—JULES FERRY, CHAMBER OF DEPUTIES, 1881

The principle of the separation of religion and state should not imply the state's advocacy of being without a religion.
—İSMET PAŞA AND FRIENDS, TURKISH GRAND NATIONAL ASSEMBLY, 1928

The religion of Islam cannot be confined and practiced within the four walls of the mosque, because the religion of Islam puts rules on the whole life of the believer and asks him/her to practice them. Therefore, the Directorate of Religious Affairs has to diagnose all kinds of problems of our people and find solutions.
—AKP SPOKESPERSON, TURKISH GRAND NATIONAL ASSEMBLY, 2010

In two words, I stay resolutely concordataire, being a catholic and a French.... President Roosevelt said, "The future of our nation depends on the way we combine force with religion." Here it is! The mental state of American democracy. And ours?
—ALBERT DE MUN, *LE GAULOIS*, 1905

Ideas to Institutions: The Missing Links

Ideas matter, if one can reach them and situate them. A significant part of the current literature on secularism and religion *claims* to have taken a hermeneutical turn following the lead of the multiple modernities approach, putting a lot of weight on ideas and reinterpretations of secularism for an explanation of different institutional outcomes. However, we face a claim of either Charles Taylor's imaginaries or a Weberian Verstehen approach without a full exposition of ideas and how they relate to institutions. In this chapter I articulate why and in which respects focusing on the precise arguments by various competing political actors at moments of potential institutional change breaks with these ideational approaches and leads to an alternative comparative analytical framework. Charles Taylor has contributed to the theoretical debates on the question of whether secularism can travel outside its context of origin, as well as "alternative modernities" and "multiple modernities," and his book on Europe, *A Secular Age* (2007), guides the discussion on multiple secularisms.[1] In all these debates, even if Taylor defends a hermeneutical approach,[2] that is, taking ideas as constitutive of action, it is often missed that he grants *a precondition* for such an epistemology; power has not taken over all aspects of human life, including how subjects understand their own actions. The kinds of discussions over institutions that this book documents do not fulfill this precondition. I would like to spell out and situate this precondition in Taylor's own words in the precise dialogue that gives birth to it.

In "The Hermeneutics of Conflict," commenting on Quentin Skinner's work, Taylor criticizes the reductionism of the rise and fall of ideas to a context of conflict (materially defined), in his own terms, a claim to have found the right level from which to read the actions of our subjects. Even if ideas are outcomes of conflict, some stay and others do not; therefore "we may have to explain their rise at least partly in terms of their fit with what we have become, rather than explaining in the reverse direction, where what we become is a function of the language which has been imposed on us by strategies of power."[3]

Taylor sums up his critique of Skinner with the "thesis of hermeneutical theory": "Confronting one's own language of explanation with that of one's subjects' self-understanding. . . . We can meet it by asking what our language of explanation entails about the truth of our subjects' beliefs. Or we can get at the same issue via another route by asking how we ought to describe their action and thoughts." Taylor argues that the nonhermeneutical thesis would be granted "only if we could show that the relations of domination, and the strategies which create and sustain them, have totally invaded the world of everyday self-understanding. [Only then] could we . . . make all dominant ideas the outcome of conflicts which centre on war and the struggle for power." In other words, if "Michel Foucault['s] strong case for the invasion of everyday understanding by relations of power . . . could be made good." Taylor puts Clifford Geertz against Skinner in his defense to underscore how self-understandings cannot be factored out from an account of conflict.[4]

As for Max Weber, he is much more hesitant and critical than Weberians in pushing forward the role of ideas. As mentioned earlier, in *The Protestant Ethic and the Spirit of Capitalism*, where Weber correlates historically rooted ideas (as read from the texts of elites) and capitalist development, he drops a note for further research: "We are concerned with the influence that *their* conduct [religious ethics of the classes which were the culture bearers of their respective countries] has had. Now it is quite true that this can only be completely known in all its details when the facts from ethnography and folklore have been compared with it. Hence we must expressly admit and emphasize that this is **a gap** to which the ethnographer will legitimately object."[5]

This book objects to this gap in the study of institutions of secularism not with ethnography but with history and in-depth case analysis. It aims to explore the comparative trajectories of secularism through a focus on the "nuts and bolts" of institutional change without losing the significance of ideas.[6]

Clifford Geertz objected to this gap with ethnography. It is quite surprising that Charles Taylor seeks support in the work of Geertz, because, unlike Taylor, Geertz takes "meaning" and "action" as "independently variable mutually interdependent factors . . . capable of a wide range of modes of integration with one another, of which *the simple isomorphic mode* is but a limiting case."[7] This epistemological difference turns into an acute problem when put to the test of evaluation of concrete examples. For instance, Taylor qualifies laïcité as a social imaginary and comments on the French law banning religious symbols in public schools in 2004 as a reassertion of this social imaginary purifying public space of "religious difference" against the new challenges of diversity.[8] Such a description of what happened in France, first, overlooks the fact that the axis of struggle in France did not correspond exclusively to a laic subject and a Muslim subject. The contestation was internal, and not external, to laïcité, and the struggle was precisely over French history, particularly the Third Republic period. There were laic and Muslim subjects who were for the law, as well as laic and Muslim subjects against the law. Not to mention that the commonly assumed attribution of "increased" diversity of France to immigration completely overlooks the making of demographic categories.[9] Second, coterminous with the law there were three other movements—covered in detail in chapter 4—that, to the contrary, aimed at putting religion institutionally in the public space: (1) the establishment of the French Muslim Council and France's first new Muslim high school in the summer of 2003; (2) an emerging movement, including the governing political party UMP, to reintroduce "factual" teaching of religion in public schools; and (3) Minister of Interior Nicolas Sarkozy's mobilization of *laïcité positive*,[10] which for the most part resonated with the pope. Such complex, nonisomorphic developments fall to the margins and receive the status of anomalies with the imposition of the "imaginaries" approach as a master narrative on what went on in contemporary France in terms of laïcité vis-à-vis its own past and in comparative perspective.

Charles Taylor's comments on France are by a philosopher; however, recent in-depth anthropological and historical analyses of France also frame themselves in the very binary opposition, a specific French understanding of secularism versus the "challenges of diversity." In *Why the French Don't Like Headscarves: Islam, the State, and Public Space*, John Bowen takes "an anthropology of public reasoning" approach to present a detailed exposition of moments with nonisomorphic relation between laïcité and the action it entails through the complexity and diversity of subject positions over the headscarf question. However, after a hermeneutically committed exposition with rich ethnographical material on a multiplicity of positions on laïcité in the French public space on the question of the headscarf, Bowen concludes that laïcité remains an amorphous object, a field of some sort, a "narrative framework" from which each political actor in public debate remembers according to his or her politics. "The difficulty with this notion," Bowen writes, "is that there is no 'it.'" And, after all those intertwined narratives Bowen offers of moving subjects and articulations, scatterings, and regatherings of collectivities that cut across the French versus Muslim binary opposition, we are handed the *real* fears of the French: sexism, communitarianism, and Islamism, rooted in "distinct strands of French self-understanding." We are now asked to take an analytical turn and are served one more time, in softer form, the "multicultural challenge" against French "self-understanding," in other words, the French "imaginary." All the French whose public positions do not fit into this imaginary fall out of the conclusion and are cleared to the margins, the weight of *their* "self-understandings" reduced only to a proof that the dominant view exists and is real.[11]

Joan Scott, in *The Politics of the Veil*, poses the backbone of her narrative as "the requirement of assimilation has come under attack by groups demanding recognition of their difference," in other words, as the new multiculturalist challenge.[12] This pitting of laïcité against multiculturalism marks many other works as well.[13] In claims to clear the ground of reductionist binary oppositions, which are part not only of the French public debate but also of the major political philosophical discussions on secularism and diversity, again and again we are served the "dominant French view," a closure on a particular "self-understanding"; in sum, the "French exception."[14]

The contemporary struggles over Turkish laiklik have also been assessed using the headscarf question as the litmus test. The Kemalist laicist establishment opposing the scarf in public institutions has been understood as pursuing a comprehensive doctrine of secularism, and its challenger AKP has been presented as following a more liberal line of secularism.[15] While they have clashed on the headscarf, the AKP has totally embraced and restructured the institutions of state-salaried imams, a Kemalist laic institution in its historical origins. Similarly, it has never challenged the required courses on religion, culture, and ethics in the public school curriculum that were established by the Kemalist laic military coup in 1982. To the contrary, in 2012 the party started "institutional layering,"[16] introducing two new optional courses, one on the life of the Prophet and another on reading the Koran, despite resistance from opposition in the parliament and from some civil society organizations. Here again, an exclusive focus on the scarf disregards significant nonisomorphic relations between ideas and action.

A pertinent example of a Weberian Verstehen approach that overlooks Weber's caution on the "gap" is Ahmet Kuru's *Secularisms and State Policies Toward Religion: The United States, France, and Turkey*. Kuru as well primarily uses the headscarf question to compare the two countries and argues that different "policies toward religion" in Turkey and France are the result of historically rooted ideological struggles between assertive and passive secularists, in effect, arguing that the countries share the same political field.[17] "Assertive secularism is a 'comprehensive doctrine,' whereas passive secularism mainly prioritizes state neutrality toward such doctrines."[18] In the case of

Turkey, according to Kuru, "the debate between the Kemalists [defending assertive secularism] and conservatives [AKP, defending passive secularism]" is "not simply a conflict between Islamism and antireligionism, but rather it is a discussion over the 'true meaning and practice' of secularism."[19] However, for a book that claims to explain policy, the lack of a single reference to the debates in the main institution responsible for policy making, the parliament, is striking.[20] Instead, Kuru gathers his "historically rooted ideas" from selective past and present actions in the name of Kemalism and sometimes public statements in their defense, and for the AKP, from AKP leaders' public speeches, official party pamphlets, and party programs.[21] Parliamentary records since the AKP came to power in 2002 document anything but a concern with state neutrality toward religion. As politicians, both AKP leaders and representatives of Kemalism through history definitely qualify as part of a field of power, with strategies and domination of the sort that even Charles Taylor would question the sovereignty of their ideas. Kuru's different ideas of secularism cannot account for the convergences on policy and institutions between the two sides. Kemalists' major deeds, such as including required courses on religion in the 1982 Constitution, are presented as "inconsistent policies toward Islam,"[22] for it obviously contradicts the idea of assertive secularism that Kemalists are supposed to be defending.

In France, according to Kuru, again the struggle was between antiheadscarf assertive secularists opposed to the headscarf and passive secularists in favor of it. "Assertive secularism" corresponds to *laïcité de combat*, which, according to Kuru, has among its ranks contemporary public intellectuals like Régis Debray and Henri Pena-Ruiz, and Third Republic prime minister Émile Combes (June 7, 1902–January 24, 1905). "Passive secularism" corresponds to *laïcité plurielle* and has among its ranks contemporary public intellectuals Jean Baubérot and Jean-Paul Willaime, and Third Republican parliamentarian Jean Jaurès. Here Kuru's Weberian Verstehen approach misses even more realities. Kuru's assertive secularist Debray defended the teaching of religious facts in laic schools in a report he was commissioned to write in 2002 by the socialist minister of education, Jack Lang,[23] and Kuru's passive secularist Jean-Paul Willaime presented the Debray report as "a significant and major advance. It is striking that in our country, where the scientific, secular and multidisciplinary study of religious fact is so highly developed at institutes of higher learning, many universities, and the CNRS, such a gap should exist between higher education on the one hand and primary and secondary on the other."[24]

Kuru's passive secularists Baubérot and Willaime completely disagree on article 4 of the separation law of 1905. According to Baubérot, the *Loi du 9 Décembre 1905 concernant la séparation des Églises et de l'État* was the end of a civil religion tradition at the institutional level.[25] Jean-Paul Willaime contests this position in his analysis of the separation law and places the emphasis on what he interprets as the social recognition of religions in article 4.[26] Moreover, Willaime and Baubérot both opposed the headscarf ban, but Willaime argued from the position that wearing the scarf can be an act of individual preference, "an affirmation of liberty and to demonstrate . . . personal autonomy," whereas Baubérot opposed the ban because it was discouraging students from the public education system, historically the main pillar of laïcité.[27] Picking on the difference in argumentation may look like hair splitting. However, it points to a crucial part of the political field of secularism, and it is not possible to situate the politics of the socialists of the Third Republic, which this book covers in the next chapter, without attention to such detail. Nor could one uncover some of the overlooked positions in the current debate on secularism versus the challenges of diversity.

The major loss in working out a comparison from positions on the headscarf question is two significant institutional differences between France and Turkey. Turkey has an institution of state-salaried imams and religion courses in the public school curriculum, and France has institutional separation in both areas. How has the literature handled these institutional differences?

The differences have mostly been approached by qualifying the French case as a *standard* and the Turkish case as an *anomaly*, and this is only one instance of how the anomalies of the secular state have long been treated as an exclusive phenomenon of the non-Western world measured vis-à-vis an idealized atemporal Western model of separation.[28] The literature on secularism in Turkey (laiklik) presents numerous examples in this regard. At least since the 1950s, the major preoccupation of single-case analysis of secularism in Turkey has been to follow a modernist line of creating conceptual binary oppositions vis-à-vis an idealized atemporal Western model of separation in order to handle these anomalies, such as separation versus control,[29] separation versus union,[30] full laiklik versus half laiklik,[31] and policing (*zabıta*) of religion versus separation.[32] These works have all claimed that the meaning of laiklik differs in kind from "the Western model of separation," finding the reason for the difference in the lack of a societal secularization, and attributing this lack particularly to Islam. On the other hand, hermeneutical approaches have turned to the self-understanding of the political actors, the founding

Kemalist Republican People's Party in the 1920s and 1930s. For instance, Andrew Davison's *Secularism and Revivalism in Turkey: A Hermeneutical Approach* starts out from the premise of the alternative modernities approach,[33] critiquing those binary oppositions vis-à-vis Europe that narrate secularism in Turkey in terms of what it "lacks" rather than what it "has." Turning to the self-understandings of the political elite, documented from primary sources, Davison argues that these institutional differences are in fact not understood as anomalies by the political elite but are part of a coherent project of separation. Here we find the typical struggle between the analytical and hermeneutical schools of thought. In both cases, however, laiklik becomes exceptional, and "a new meaning" of secularism.

Comparative historical questions can offer an alternative route of analysis. After all, France also had institutionalized state-salaried clerics in the nineteenth century, which ended only when a slight majority in parliament passed the *Loi du 9 Décembre 1905*. The *Loi du 28 Mars 1882 sur l'enseignement primaire obligatoire*, which turned religion into an optional course given outside of school buildings, had to win over other proposals in the parliament on religion in the public school curriculum. Coming up with a periodization that allows one to locate moments where the same set of institutional questions are up for debate across the boundaries of Europe, across France and Turkey, is another way to dissolve the status of "anomaly" and replace it with comparative empirical puzzles. How did these laws pass the French parliament, and what were the losing options and their political arguments? How, in Turkey, did the institutional relations between state and religion become locked into the institution of state-salaried imams and religion courses on Sunni Islam in the public school curriculum? There is also another significant way of dissolving the status of anomaly.

The Anomalous Secular State and the Question of Modernity Inside and Outside the West

The anomalous secular state of the non-Western world has a long past in the academic literature embodied in long-standing conceptual distinctions such as "modernization from above," "modernization from below," "secularism from above," and "secularism from below." The first part of the dichotomy describes Western and the second part non-Western trajectories. For instance, Partha Chatterjee discusses the interference of the Indian state in the sphere of religion in the name of secularism under the heading "anomalies of the secular state" in India. Furthermore, he underscores that academic scholarship has dealt with these anomalies mostly by normalizing them through a "'new meaning of secularism' argument" whose culmination has been the position of "Indian exceptionalism."[34] Another example, Nikki R. Keddie's "Secularism and the State: Towards Clarity and Global Comparison," argues that the rising discussions on secularization are still nonpolitical and centered around social and economic change and do not pay sufficient attention to "changes in ideas, political movements or the state." Keddie's argument aligns this purely analytical and methodological point with areas of study: the reason for the excessive focus on social and economic factors in some discussions is that these discussions are "on Great Britain, with some attention to western Europe," and the "non-Christian and non-Western worlds are generally omitted from this debate," where secularization has "been more influenced by government action than by autonomous societal changes, and trends toward secularization have sometimes been dramatically reversed."[35] This may well be empirically true in many cases, but what is at stake here is the turning of these distinctions into epistemological lines where certain empirical realities are eliminated from view for good by suggesting analytical impossibilities. The distinction between the priority of society's role in the West and the state's role in the non-West, when turned into an epistemological line, discourages one from looking for and weighing the role of the state in the West and that of society in the non-West, not only historically speaking but in coterminous contemporary time frames of analysis as well.[36] Instead of reverting to such shorthand analytical eliminations, we can make an effort to train our eyes to see the state in the West and the society outside the West.

The key example for state secularism in Keddie's article is Turkey. In 2009 Turkey's ruling AKP initiated a series of outreach meetings called the National Unity and Brotherhood/Sisterhood Project (Milli Birlik ve Kardeşlik Projesi) as part of its Democratic Opening (Demokratik Açılım) campaign. One part of this project was an eight-month period of dialogue in the format of workshops between the government and societal organizations on what the government called "the *Alevi-Bektaşi* Question."[37] In chapter 6 I look at the role of society, as well as the state, in the building of institutions in Turkey. I lay out in detail, from the 1,796 pages of published minutes of these workshops and public statements in the media, positions that various societal and government actors have expressed on laiklik and democracy in Turkey.[38]

The focus on role of the state in secularization exclusively in the non-West and not in the West has long contributed to making the anomalies of the secular state look like an exclusively non-Western phenomenon. However, the past two decades of conspicuous interventions by the U.S. government and various European governments in the spheres of religion call attention to a focus on the state in the West. Federal funds in the United States have supported religion nationally and internationally, especially through the White House Office of Faith-Based and Neighborhood Partnerships (formerly the Office of Faith-Based and Community Initiatives), established by an executive order in 2001.[39] Saba Mahmood highlights a project of "training Islamic preachers, establishing Islamic schools" in certain countries headed by the Muslim Outreach Program of the White House National Security Council.[40] European states have engaged actively in the religious sphere in the past decade in the formation of Muslim Councils, or, for instance, when Germany granted the right to special education courses for Alevis under article 9 of the German Constitution. In 2003 the Commission de réflexion sur l'application du principe de laïcité dans la République presented its report to the French president; in 2004 a law banning *signes religieux ostensibles* in public elementary, middle, and high schools passed parliament; and in 2010 the French parliament passed a law banning the wearing of the burka in public spaces after the parliamentary commission passed a judgment on proper religious practice.[41] In chapter 4 I look at the role of the state, as well as society, in contemporary France in the building of institutions.

Defending Institutions from General Principles or Deep Convictions?

Lack of attention to arguments in defense of institutions as endogenous but distinct elements of the struggle over institutions has hampered a fuller description of the political field of secularism. For the sake of underscoring its relevance for refurbishing our analytical frameworks, I would like to demonstrate this point from what I find to be a serious misreading of Brian Barry's position on the headscarf question in the current political theoretical discussions on secularism. This misreading is one of many instances where the line between institutions and the arguments in their defense is lost.

In *Secularism and Freedom of Conscience*, Jocelyn Maclure and Charles Taylor distinguish "the moral principles grounding political secularism from the institutional arrangements that realize these principles." They call for a discussion on "the constitutive principles of secularism" and deriving anew from rethought principles the institutional and policy "options available to societies facing dilemmas associated with how to manage moral and religious diversity."[42] The distinction between *old* and *new* challenges to secularism is central to their argument, and this distinction also figures central in Taylor's numerous recent writings on the subject: the old challenge was the "separation of state and religious institutions," and the new challenge is to find "the (correct) response of the democratic state to diversity."[43] Maclure and Taylor define the main problématique of secularism as "moral autonomy" under conditions of "moral pluralism." The state has to guard "certain core principles, such as human dignity, basic human rights, and popular sovereignty," and cannot be neutral vis-à-vis these principles.[44] In Rawlsian terms, the "core principles" constitute a "general" moral conception but not a "comprehensive" secular philosophy.[45] Maclure and Taylor focus on the wearing of a headscarf as the key problématique in pushing forward the constitutive principles of a liberal-multicultural secularism. To provide equally for the moral autonomy of all under conditions of moral diversity, state neutrality is necessary, and to maintain its neutrality the state has to make "reasonable accommodations." But why could limited state neutrality—limited by core liberal principles—not provide the conditions for moral autonomy? Why is it that now in the name of reasonable accommodations, limited state neutrality has to be limited one more time? The answer is that, in its republican form (they explicitly refer to France and Turkey), "the secular state, in working toward marginalizing religion, adopts the atheist's and the agnostic's conception of the world and, consequently, does not treat with equal consideration for citizens who make a place for religion in their system of beliefs and values."[46] And in all its other forms, the "multiculturalist critique" that Taylor articulated in "The Politics of Recognition" still applies.[47]

For Maclure and Taylor, "One of the central arguments in favor of multiculturalism as a principle of political morality is that certain public norms applying to all citizens are not neutral or impartial from a cultural or religious point of view." As they continue to give concrete examples from Quebec, it becomes apparent that the nonneutrality of the state is often not only limited to legitimate general "core principles." "The cross on Mount Royal in Montreal," a reminder of the past rather than a religious identification on the part of public institutions, is one thing, but as they mention in disagreement, "prayers said at the beginning of sessions of a municipal council or the crucifix above the Speaker's chair in the Quebec National Assembly" can compromise the neutrality of the political space; "after all, the Quebec National Assembly is the assembly of all citizens of Quebec." It looks like what are being "reasonably accommodated" here are not only the practices of minorities but also the state's comprehensive doctrinal nonneutrality not limited to the "core principles."[48]

And which accommodations are reasonable? People's "'core' or 'meaning-giving' convictions and commitments" that do not violate the core principles and are necessary for the people's moral autonomy. Maclure and Taylor maintain that "reasonable accommodations" do not advantage religion over secularism because secularism is also a deep conviction, a way of life. One in-passing partner in dialogue in articulating the liberal multiculturalism position in the book is Brian Barry, who penned the most widely acknowledged liberal-egalitarian critique of multiculturalism. According to Maclure and Taylor, Barry's liberalism neglects that some rules can be "indirectly discriminatory toward members of certain religious groups," and "convictions of conscience" are "a particular type of subjective preference."[49]

The interesting point is that on the particular question of wearing headscarves in public or private schools, Barry, in *Culture and Equality*, never takes a position for a ban, as he has been mistakenly thought to do by other scholars. For instance, Cécile Laborde has absolutely mistaken Barry for an official French laïc: "So far, we might say, so liberal. For laïcité closely resembles the anti-multiculturalist, egalitarian liberalism recently defended by Brian Barry."[50] The defenders of official French laïcité were for a ban. Barry, if anything, found the reasoning from laïcité in defense of a ban in France unconvincing. But not only that: the argument of *Culture and Equality* mobilizes more *against* a headscarf ban. When Barry discusses the question of wearing headscarves in schools, he discusses it together with donning of religious symbols at work. And on the precise question of "the demands made by educational institutions or employers" he writes: "I suggest that we should draw a sharp distinction between cases in which what is being asked for is a waiver of the application of the criminal law and cases in which what is being asked for is relief from the demands made by educational institutions or employers, whether public or private. Cases of the second kind fall under a principle of non-discrimination."[51]

These two cases Barry, like Taylor, also considers under "indirect discrimination." He concludes:

> The examples considered [wearing a headscarf at work or at school] in this section have been ones in which the case against enforcing a rule that worked to the detriment of religious and cultural minorities was strong. On the one side was a denial of equal occupational or educational opportunity, and on the other side no interest that was worthy of protection. Wearing a headscarf to work or a turban to school threatened no danger to the public or to the individuals concerned, nor could it plausibly be said to interfere with the effective functioning of the business or the school.[52]

In other words, the real difference between Barry and Maclure and Taylor is not their position on the headscarf but rather how they argue for keeping students with a scarf in the classroom.[53] Maclure and Taylor argue from a completely opposite direction—from deeply embedded individual practices (this style of argumentation is also central to Will Kymlicka's defense of multiculturalism, although Kymlicka seems to separate religious groups from his understanding of a cultural group[54]). They reconceptualize, dissect, and divide preferences and qualify "convictions of conscience" as a special "type of subjective preference"; they are deep (keep the girls because they are special), as opposed to arguing from generality in the laws and practices of the state (remove the cross from the parliament house first and keep the girls because they do not disturb the working of general institutions). Such convergences on policy from different angles and the particular distinction between arguments from generality and deeply embedded individual practices are not only matters of political theoretical discussions but parts of concrete historical and contemporary struggles. It is impossible to fully describe the comparative trajectories and the political fields of secularism in France and Turkey without them.

Neither sociology nor ideas directly reach institutions. There is a "gap"—quite large, heterogeneous, layered, and differentiated—where the secular and the religious often encounter, pass by, converse with, deliberate with, negotiate with, bargain with, or test each other. This gap is the political field, the "nuts and bolts" of institution making. This is where institutions and political agency interact, political agency turning those ideas, sociology, past and comparative examples of institutions into arguments—which may express or constitute or provide the pretext for their actions—at moments where institutional change is up for debate. By explaining multiple institutional movements in France and Turkey, I demonstrate that the struggles over the institutional relations between state and religion at all these moments is mainly a struggle among actors pursuing three competing political ends in both countries: demobilizing religion, mobilizing religion, and state neutrality toward religion. I locate these ends not in the general ideologies or surface-level public statements political actors make nor in the institutions they prefer but rather in the precise *political arguments* they articulate in defense of one institutional option over others. Both ideologies and institutional preferences are poor predictors of political goals, which are shaped under specific contextual constraints and under conditions of what I call "institutional dualism,"[55] that is, the capacity of an institution for serving opposite ends, a radical case of what Thelen calls "institutional conversion."[56] In the following chapters I show that institutional outcomes in France and Turkey are the result of struggles among political actors with these three competing goals, and their power vis-à-vis one another, under conditions of institutional dualism and historical contextual constraints. Institutional relations of state and religion in Turkey are moving further in the direction of state–civil religion-ism (state mobilization of religion as the cement of society), whereas in France this tradition ended in 1905 but recently showed a resurgence.

CHAPTER III

The Institutional Politics of Laïcité in the French Third Republic

The *Loi du 28 Mars 1882 sur l'enseignement primaire obligatoire* did not include religious instruction in the public school curriculum but instead provided a free day during the week for those parents who wanted their children to receive religious instruction outside school buildings. The law was one among the many acts of the moderate republicans, Républicains opportunistes, who dominated the parliament in the 1880s.[1] Jules Ferry, known as the architect of education laws, served as minister of education and as prime minister between 1879 and 1885. The *Loi du 9 Décembre 1905 concernant la séparation des Églises et de l'État* passed parliament just after the Émile Combes government. The law ended the French state's Concordat with the Catholic Church under which Catholicism was recognized as the majority religion and the state paid the salaries of clerics.[2]

In both of these moments of institutional change, republicans who were defending the state's institutional religious neutrality won the day against political actors who expected the state to mobilize or demobilize religion. This was a harder parliamentary battle in 1905 than in 1882. This chapter documents the most contested aspects of the law of March 28, 1882, on free public obligatory education and the law of December 9, 1905, using the *Journal officiel de la République française,* Débats parlementaires, Chambre des députés, and other primary and secondary sources. I focus on what institutional preferences are defended with what arguments and for which political ends and document the nature of the political equilibrium behind the winning and losing institutional options. The latter is particularly important for the 1905 law, for it passed the chamber on July 3, 1905, by a mere 108-vote margin.[3] It would have taken only 55 more legislators to change sides for the law not to pass.

This chapter, together with the following chapters on contemporary France and Turkey, shows that an alternative common political field can be charted from a multilevel focus on political ends, arguments, and institutional preferences expressed in parliaments, constituent assemblies, and other public forums in both countries and at different time periods. The comparative trajectories of secularism across the two countries and through time, and the politics of these trajectories, can be mapped in nuance with overlaps and differences on this alternative political field.

Républicains Opportunistes, Laic Education Laws, and Optional Religious Instruction

The Third French Republic's *Loi du 28 Mars 1882* is historically one of the cornerstones of laïcité. During the Third Republic, the annual state budget share of the *budget des cultes* was more than that for public education until 1878 (53,643,995 to 53,640,714 francs in 1878) and quite close until 1883 (53,365,866 to 63,738,226 francs in 1881).[4] In 1883, the year after the law was instituted, the state budget for public education more than doubled over that of the cultes (52,951,306 to 133,817,451 francs).[5] The law had as its main target the March 15, 1850, law known as the Falloux law, which was responsible for the advance of Catholic education in France.[6] The bourgeoisie of the Second French Republic (1848–1852) found the church the best defender of social order.[7] According to Roger Saltau, with the events of 1848, the French bourgeoisie approached the Catholic Church to act as a bulwark against socialism, and the church, having in mind the possibility that anticlericalism could become powerful, accepted the alliance. This alliance is one of the fundamental elements of the rich analysis Karl Marx offers in *The 18th Brumaire of Louis Bonaparte*. Evelyn Martha Acomb, in her *French Laic Laws 1879–1889*, provides some numbers as to the effect of this law on education.[8] The Falloux law opened up teaching to all religious orders, and the number of unauthorized teaching religious orders rose from 45 in 1850 to 140 in 1878. In 1878, 16,478 primary schools were directed by authorized religious orders of nuns. Authorized orders of monks had 2,328 public and 768 private schools. In 1880, 2,197,775 students out of 4,949,591 were taught in these schools.

In 1850 authorized orders had property of 43 million francs, and in 1879 the amount reached 421 million francs. In 1879 unauthorized orders had 160 million, and Jesuits alone had 42 million worth of property. These are just some numbers; a more exhaustive account can surely be provided. Also, the Vatican marked the beginning of the Third Republic with two statements of Catholic mobilization: an encyclical in 1864 called the *Syllabus of Errors*, which condemned the fundamental premises of modern democratic society, particularly targeting rationalism, liberalism, pluralism, and socialism, and the first Vatican Council's reassertion of the papal Doctrine of Infallibility in 1870.

The question of optional religious instruction figured centrally among the general principles behind the entire March 28, 1882, law on obligatory primary education. The parliamentary commission set up to examine the proposal for a new education law, presided over by Paul Bert, submitted its report, *La loi de l'enseignement primaire (Proposition Barodet): Rapport présenté à la Chambre des députés*—known as the Bert Report—to the chamber on December 6, 1879. The cornerstones of the Bert Report were free, obligatory, and laic education. The report devoted seventeen of its thirty pages on the "General Principles of the Law" to explaining why religious instruction was not part of the required curriculum but optional.[9] This question was debated in the chamber on December 17, 19, 21, 22, and 24, 1880. Gathering these debates from the *Journal officiel de la République française* shows that the struggle was between monarchists (Union des Droites), who opposed the entire law; governing republicans of various shades who gathered together as Républicains opportunistes, wanting to exclude religious instruction from the curriculum and just provide a time slot during the week for those parents who wanted their children to receive religious instruction outside of school hours and grounds (some among these Républicains opportunistes showed a tendency toward state-civil religionism); and the left, who wanted to eliminate religious instruction from public school altogether.[10] The Républicains opportunistes dominated the parliament; therefore their plan passed. The adopted final version of the March 28 law states in its second article: "Public primary schools will allot one day per week, other than Sunday, in order to permit parents, if they desire, to have their children receive religious instruction, outside of school edifices. Religious instruction is optional in private schools." Before turning to the chamber discussion on the report and on article 2, I will briefly review the main parts of the Bert Report's argument for optional religious instruction.

Liberty of conscience and mutual respect and tolerance were the first reasons put forth in the Bert Report for not including religious instruction in the obligatory school curriculum. In its discussion of the proposed law, the report distinguished between moral and religious instruction, placed moral instruction together with civic instruction as part of the obligatory curriculum (article 3), and put religious instruction as optional and outside of school buildings and left it to the departments (French local administrative divisions) to regulate the hours (article 22).[11] What is quite striking for contemporary debates differentiating between old and new questions of laïcité—the old being how to handle the institutional separation between state and religions; the new, how to face the challenge of diversity—is that how to address a plural student body, religiously diverse as well as in other respects, was a central question for the republican architects of the law for obligatory public primary education. I quote at length from the report:

[The State] assures the father of the family that nothing will be taught which can undermine the liberty of conscience of his child. That is to say, "religious instruction" has to stop being a part of the program of our public schools, or, at least be given only to children whose parents would have made a special demand . . . if religious instruction has to be maintained as obligatory in public school. . . . It will be necessary, at the least, to have in each village within the reach of parents a school for each culte recognized by the State. This is the system that the law of 1850 [Falloux law] had seemed to adopt, but that it had skillfully restricted to *communes*[12] where the different cultes are publicly professed, which suppresses all guarantee for scattered protestants and Israelites. . . . We would oppose with energy the establishment of those separate schools for each culte; because that separation gives birth to and develops, in the early ages in the mind of the child, the idea of sect with hostile sentiments, passions which have formidable consequences for public peace. *It is good, necessary that the children of jews, christians, and free-thinkers encounter each other in the same benches and take the habit of mutual respect and tolerance.* (15, 16–17; italics mine)

The report found the principles of "liberty of conscience" and what it called "law of majorities" in conflict: "It is necessary above all that a religion does not invade this education in the name of the majority. Because, we are here in the domain of conscience, at the threshold of which the law of majorities stops" (17).

As for optional religious instruction, the report acknowledged a common argument of those demanding the primary school teacher to give religious instruction: "According to them [the critics], the priest, surcharged by his minister, could not suffice to give religious instruction; on the other hand, parents, being either ignorant or indifferent, cannot effectively come to his aid; he needs that the primary school teacher would do some part of his task: reading of the Gospel, recitation of catechism" (20–21).

The report argued against the primary school teacher giving such instruction:

> The primary school teacher has to be a laic, not having any official competence for teaching religious dogmas. . . . If religious education becomes a part of the curriculum, it may be only given by the various ministers of cultes. . . . [But actually the] representatives of the Catholic religion in Belgium just refused to accept such a system . . . that way each is master of his own home: one, the school, the other, the temple. . . . We would say that [public primary education] is laic as to content, and laic as to personnel. (18–20)

Other criticisms against the proposed law were also addressed. A law on obligatory public primary education would create "atheist schools" and "chas[e] God from school," therefore undermining liberty of conscience and eliminating moral instruction altogether from schools. The report found the "liberty of conscience" criticism paradoxical, pointing out history and the recent papal encyclical, *Syllabus of Errors*, as evidence, and stated that this criticism did not "really merit a response. What we chase from the school is intolerance" (20).

Among all the criticisms it countered, the report underlined the following argument as the "capital objection" to the proposed law: suppressing religious instruction is suppressing moral instruction. It remarked that "this pretention has been in all times that of all religions; but none has proclaimed it more loudly than the Catholic religion, who declares that outside of the minority it represents, there is nowhere and there has never been any morality on earth" (22).

In the *Journal officiel*, "neutrality," "diversity," and "law of majorities" emerge as the key ideas defining the political field of discussion in the chamber. Neutrality was the primary concept centering the discussion, and the main axis of debate was set between those political actors arguing from the premise of diversity in defense of institutional neutrality and those arguing from law of majorities against institutional neutrality. On December 17, 1880, a deputy named Arthur Chalamet (moderate left[13]) argued that optional religious instruction for public primary schools should be given by representatives of three cultes depending on the will of the parents.[14] In countering the argument of "atheist schools" and "chasing God," he posed the question more at the level of differentiation of spheres and asked whether the guardian of children's faith is the family or the state:

MR. CHALAMET. There it is, the true theory of the modern state. The State is incompetent in questions of religious or philosophical conscience. . . . Eh! Fine, I ask you, which one is the true guardian of the faith of children? Is it the State? Is it families? All the question of laïcité reduces itself to this simple question. . . . We do not want to chase God from the school; we do not want to make a school against God either; we just simply want to put back things in their normal state, that is to say, leave the school to the teachers and the church to the priests *("Very Good!" from left.—Interruptions from right.)*.
MR. DE LA BILIAIS [UNION DES DROITES]. And why did you remove the Christs from the schools of Paris then? (12427)

Chalamet spent a quite a bit of time discussing the Falloux law and contemporary catechism books, with special attention to their fostering of antipluralism and compromising liberty of conscience. He offered a particular reading of the French policy in Algeria at the time of the law. Referring to the government of that time, he stated:

MR. CHALAMET. This government issued a decree concerning the French Muslim schools in Algeria. It was on 14 July 1850. In the program, there is not a word on religious instruction [in the curriculum]; such that a government that came to make the 1850 law and that considered absolutely indispensable that the State establish itself as the guardian of religious faith of all the children of France, does not even say a word, does absolutely nothing for the religious faith of Arabs who became French and who were governed by French law. Why this difference? And to whose profit it is made? According to me, I do not hesitate to say it, it is to the benefit of

Arabs, and I confess that the French are right in being jealous: the government of the time respected the liberty of conscience of Arabs, while it had not respected the liberty of conscience of the French (*Murmurs to the right, "Very good! Very good!" to the left*). . . . You see, Sirs, the Government, which has had for origin the 2nd December, employed the Catholic religion as the government of the first empire had employed it; that is to say, like an instrument (*Protestations from various benches to right*). (12428–29)

Chalamet's was a typical statement of separation—"each one to his own home." The next speaker, Agénor Bardoux (Centre gauche), defended that moral instruction in school had to be based on religion. After having stated that he thought confessional religion should not be taught at schools by priests, rapidly going over the laicization movements in Europe with mention of Belgium and Holland (12432), he focused on England and then on Switzerland, which all removed sectarian religious education but included optional (with an opt-out option in the case of England) primary education, within school hours, in morals based on the belief in God and immortality of the soul and afterlife:

MR. BARDOUX. I come to the present project for law, after having well demonstrated to you that in all of Europe, all liberal nations had always thought that the school, to be able to be open to all the various (*divers*) cultes, was required to exclude only confessional religious education, but that it [the school] was required to take as a basis of morals the principles common to all religions, that is to say, the belief in God and afterlife. (12433)

Bardoux clearly put religious instruction as the basis of morals and as a bulwark against materialism, against, quoting from Jean Victor Duruy,[15] "the industry for developing an excess of taste for material well-being and for turning ideas exclusively toward their progress" (12433–34). Bardoux linked his insistence on the religious grounds of morals with the practical problems he found with institutional neutrality:

MR. BARDOUX. You will not be able to prevent the father of the family from thinking that neutrality is a negation; you will not be able to prevent that they demand from the primary school teacher at least an appearance of respect for God. . . . We want definitely that in the program of primary education, morality should be based on God and afterlife.

A MEMBER OF THE LEFT. On which God?

MR. BARDOUX. We believe that it is necessary for the Republic, necessary for morality in itself, necessary for the education of the populations which constitutes universal suffrage. We believe that it is necessary for liberty. . . . Whatever our political divergences are, wanting to try to raise the countryside people outside of faith in God and in afterlife, I say, it is impossible. (12434)

On December 19 Ferdinand Boyer (Union des Droites) rejected the project for a law entirely. For him, what drove the law on obligatory laic public education were the French Revolution and the Paris Commune. He quoted Alexis de Tocqueville and Pierre-Joseph Proudhon to underscore the antireligious character of the revolution. He pointed out that the Paris Commune asked for separation of church and state, and for the suppression of the *budget des cultes* on grounds that it was against liberty of conscience, because it imposed on citizens against their own faith. Boyer referred to the Bert Report and stressed that "we are faced not only with the obligation [of public instruction] and curriculum laicized, but laïcité complete, that is, of the personnel." He targeted the three cornerstones of the Bert Report:

MR. FERDINAND BOYER. For me, the obligation [in education] as well as [education] being free of charge is an injustice. . . . as for laïcité, complete or incomplete, it is not neutrality, neutrality is impossible in these matters, it is the exclusion from schools of the idea of God, the negation of God. The school will certainly be the school without God; it will soon be atheist school. . . . We are asked to accept a complete formula: free of charge, obligation, and laïcité. Separately, these principles are already bad, together, they constitute a real danger.[16]

Boyer concluded that the Bert Report "is both an antiliberal and antireligious work." In what he formulated as a "liberal" defense of the church, he pointed out that the church was here to educate the people before other institutions. He added:

MR. FERDINAND BOYER. I live in a mixed region, where we live in peace thanks to the respect of beliefs. This is the regime of liberty, each to his/her home. Catholics and protestants, we have our distinct temples, like our distinct cemeteries and our schools. . . . No one in the south of France has thought about making catholics enter the *consistoires*, and the protestants enter the *conseils de fabrique*.[17] For this old regime of mutual respect and support, you want to substitute a so-called neutrality, maintained by the exclusion of any religious idea. We have, it is true, in some villages, schools mixed from the religious point of view, consisting only of two or three catholics or two or three protestants. The number of these minorities does not permit the creation of two distinct schools; the dearest wish of those who want to respect all beliefs, the liberty of children, and that of fathers of families, that is the state or commune resources permit one day to create, everywhere where there will be two cultes, two confessional schools. . . . Paul Bert cited three letters from protestant pastors, a bit ardent, who complained of the mixed school and of catholic oppression in some villages. . . . I am surprised for that matter to see protestant pastors, if they are christians, preferring neutrality or laïcité of school to mixed schools. (12527)

Boyer's statement and many others from the members of the Union des Droites in the following pages did not underline metaphysical or practical difficulties of neutrality but rather were just statements against neutrality. Boyer simply wanted collective institutions to provide more religion. He and others from his group coined any solution short of "more-religion," where state institutions positively engaged in promoting religion, as antireligious. He referred to neutrality as a "disguised negation, at the expense of christian principles . . . be it catholic or protestant" (12527). Even if there is no religion of state, he argued, Catholicism is the religion of the majority. He mobilized the "law of majorities" argument, showing that the French population was 98 percent Catholic (of a total population of slightly more than thirty-six million at the time) (12528). Then he asked his primary question, which clearly exposed a homogenous, antipluralist vision of society as the ground of collective institutions:

MR. FERDINAND BOYER. Which is more to blame, the monarchy which, faced with a religion of the State, has forced a very weak minority of dissidents to follow the lessons of catholic primary schools, or the Republic, which wants to oblige 35,387,703 catholics, 580,757 protestants, and 49,439 israelites to put up with the lessons of the laic school or school without God, to please 81,951 free-thinkers? . . . One of our honorable colleagues, whose name I forget, has expressed exactly this thought [of a world upside down] in an intervention: "This is the oppression of the majority by the minority!" . . . Governments do not live in fiction, they are obliged to take account of facts, religious convictions of citizens, and their number. (12528)

Boyer continued his speech in the next session of parliament on December 21:

MR. FERDINAND BOYER. If I am permitted to borrow from Paul Bert the language he speaks well, the scientific language, I would say: Obligation is the vehicle with which one wants to penetrate the soul of people's children with the new poison that is called laïcité complete. There is only one [laïcité]. The matter is not, as you know, to distinguish the laïcité of the curriculum from that of the personnel.[18]

Finally, he explicitly stated that for him there was no solution short of obligatory Christian education; in other words, he was just against neutrality: "Let the authors of the bill find a way to give us an obligatory christian education; the discussion will end right there."[19] Against Boyer's criticisms of the Paris Commune, Paul Bert responded that there were Congregationists among the Commune.[20]

Jules Ferry also spoke. The big division among the governing Républicains opportunistes was "between the republican left of Grévy and Ferry and the Republican Union of Gambetta."[21] Ferry was a Gauche républicaine within the governing Républicains opportunistes and the architect of the education laws of June 16, 1881, and March 28, 1882, both known as the Ferry laws. On December 19, 1880, at the time of the discussion, he was the prime minister and the minister of public instruction and fine arts. Ferry started out by observing that the debate had focused on obligation, and he would like to focus on "the other principle contained in the bill, on the principle of laic or neutral school."[22]

MR. LE PRÉSIDENT DU CONSEIL [JULES FERRY]. No doubt, one will have to demonstrate to us how the principle of obligatory religious education can reconcile itself with liberty of conscience and how the neutrality of the school, which is the aspiration . . . the living reality in countries of many believers of the world, can constitute a threat or offense for religious conscience. I hope that this demonstration will be brought to this tribune.

MR. FREPPEL [UNION DES DROITES]. Perfectly! (12614)

Two main axes of conflict emerged in the parliamentary discussions over the education law: the possibility and the desirability of neutrality, and the possibility of decoupling religion and morality. For instance, Émile Keller (Union des Droites) did not find neutrality in religion to be an important principle to follow in building institutions:

MR. KELLER. The curriculum will successively become positivist, everywhere congregationist education will be suppressed. This positivism is decorated in the name of neutrality. I do not believe that, sirs, neutrality can be possible. . . . I do not believe in neutrality.
MR. LE RAPPORTEUR. That is why neutral schools are necessary. (12623)

A major opposition to the optional religious instruction in the proposed public education law was articulated with the indispensability of religion as the basis of morality. Keller opposed the decoupling of religion and morality, and in his remarks he also underlined some practical concerns:

MR. KELLER. If the soul is not immortal—I repeat it and I repeat it seriously—if the soul is not immortal, it is not worth to prescribe to ourselves the troubles and embarrassments of a morality. . . . If God did not exist, if there wasn't in God the principle and the sanction of morality, I would not permit myself the right to formulate a morality. . . . You [to left] laugh a lot about the credulity of christians who recognize the authority of the pope; I would find thousand times more ridiculous the one who recognizes our short-lived authority for making morality. . . . What will they think, the young girls exiting your primary schools and who will marry without having received any religious instruction, any moral education other than you will have given? You affirm them the indissolubility of the conjugal bond, while tomorrow you count on voting for divorce?
FROM SEVERAL BENCHES TO THE LEFT. No doubt! We will vote for it.
MR. KELLER. I come to property. . . . If marriage and property are not part of morality, I do not know anything. (12625)

At the end of the December 21 session, the chamber decided by 356 votes to 122 to pass to an article-by-article discussion of the law (12628). There were several amendments proposed as the discussion for each article began. The first amendment was by Bishop Charles-Émile Freppel, a member of Union des Droites, and it read: "Primary education consists of religious and moral education (art. 23, 1st of the law of March 15 1850)."[23] Freppel's amendment and speech deserves some attention for, first, in this speech he responded to Ferry's earlier challenge for a demonstration that neutrality was a threat to liberty of conscience. Second, Freppel remained a monarchist Catholic. He opposed Cardinal Lavigerie's famous toast at Algiers on November 12, 1890, asking French Catholics to give up their monarchist loyalties and rally for the republic.[24] He also opposed the papal encyclical on May 15, 1891, *Rerum Novarum*, which officially launched the Catholic mobilization for the support of the republic, known as the *Ralliement*.[25]

In his speech, Freppel explicitly differentiated two questions: obligatory education and the suppression of religious education in primary schools. He did not want banned from school "prayers, reading of the Gospel, study of the history of saints. . . . (*A member of the left: There will be nothing more left to do in the Church then!*) Diocesan catechism." Freppel argued from the "law of majorities":

MR. FREPPEL. [quoting Jean Victor Duruy] "There are in France 36 million Catholics against less than 2 million dissidents. . . . Laws cannot be made for the exceptions; it is sufficient that the minority is given guarantees for its liberty of conscience."[26]

He continued:

MR. FREPPEL. And, for my part, in my diocese I do not know any child whose parents did not do his/her first communion (*Very good! very good! from the right*).
FROM THE LEFT. It is their right!
MR. FREPPEL. All rights will be safeguarded: that of the majority by religious education; that of the minority by exemption and abstention. . . . No doubt, I know it well, there are logicians in excess who are going to pretend that the presence of a single dissident child is sufficient for depriving his fellow students from the benefits of religious instruction.
MR. BARODET. Your parish priests are there for giving it! (12677)

Freppel continued, asserting the necessity of the schoolteacher and the student to be from the same culte:

MR. FREPPEL. From the moment where, by your own admission, these are catholic schools, composed of catholic children, you do not have the right to place at their head a protestant or israelite or a free-thinker (*interruptions to the left*).... I add, sirs, that you would hurt the character of the primary school teacher [referring to Catholic teachers], because if this man has loyalty, honor, and fineness—and he has each of these—he will never consent to educate children belonging to a culte different from himself. (12677)

Freppel underlined that if the "law of majorities" is compromised by rights of minorities, then everybody would ask for something, including the socialists:

MR. FREPPEL. But sirs, reflect well on the consequence of a similar theory. If the presence of a single dissident child is sufficient for depriving all his fellow students from religious instruction, it is necessary to go resolutely till the end and accept all the consequences of the principle posed in this way; because the domain of conscience is quite immense. Once armed with this so-called right, any father of family will come to tell the primary school teacher: I don't want to hear that you speak of the spiritual spirit in front of my child; because I am materialist and you would hurt my liberty of conscience. Such others will tell her/him: I do not want that you taught to my child the legitimacy of individual property.... (*Murmurs to the left and center*), because I am collectivist, I am socialist from the school of Proudhon or Karl Marx, and for me individual property, is theft. (12677)

Finally he referred to the Bert Report and landed on "neutrality":

MR. FREPPEL. You want to reassure us by saying that in the school you conceive, there will be strict neutrality; that is, it will be spoken neither for nor against religion.... I only ask you if such neutrality can survive in any part. Will it be possible for an ordinary primary school teacher to cross out God from his teaching? And would he want it, what way to push aside a name that the child has on his lips and in his heart . . . that he mixes to all instinctively, that he finds everywhere, which appear to him in each page of lecture books? (12677)

Freppel came back again and again to "neutrality":

MR. FREPPEL. Allow me, sirs, to insist on this point, because it is the crux of the question. . . . It is thought that the silence of the primary school teacher on religion is equivalent on his part to an act of neutrality; this is a pure illusion. Don't talk about God to the child during seven years, while instructing him six hours per day, he will positively be misled that God does not exist. . . . Explain to the child the duties of man toward himself and his fellow man, and guard a profound silence on the duties of man toward God; it clearly implies to him that these duties do not exist. . . . Your neutral school will therefore only produce skeptics and indifferent people. . . . The primary school teacher will contain himself in a complete abstention with regard to religious matters! But, sirs, on this major point, abstention is impossible; because according to whether one believes or does not believe in the existence of God and in the immortality of the soul, human life and thought take another path altogether. In such case, and on the part of the primary school teacher, silence is equivalent to negation. (12678)

For Freppel, religion and morals were inseparable. He continued that "religion is not a study where an exercise is assigned in its place and hour; it is a faith, a law which should make itself felt constantly and everywhere." The "only just, the only rational, the only fair, the only french, the only legally based" solution, Freppel saw, was the protection of the religious character of the 70,000 Catholic schools of France, because the "neutral school . . . will become logically, inevitably, the atheist school, the school without God." Freppel's amendment for keeping religious education in primary schools was rejected by 324 votes to 139 (12679).

The next proposal for amendment was by Henri de Lacretelle (Union républicaine). The amendment read, "The general notions about the existence of God independent of all dogma, about the immortality of the soul, about the organic principles of republican government will be given to students of the two sexes starting at ten years old" (12683). As a republican, Lacretelle was an ardent defender of free and obligatory public education, and he had actually given a proposal for a public education law to the chamber as early as September 6, 1871.[27] Yet, along the lines of Bardoux quoted above, he was defending state-civil religionism. Lacretelle started his speech by pointing out that there were a considerable number of republican and spiritualist free-thinkers in France:

MR. HENRI DE LACRETELLE. I confess, sirs, I have been often tired of hearing the great word "God" pronounced exclusively by the right. God is not the personal property of [lists names] . . . God also belongs to us, it belongs to the Republic (*Laughs to the right*). (12683)

He explained:

MR. HENRI DE LACRETELLE. I arrive, sirs, to the more technical and more difficult part of my amendment. Mr. Paul Bert, in his admirable speech, seemed to be saying that I demanded that primary school teachers make long lectures to the children on the existence of God and on the immortality of the soul. That pretension would be ridiculous. I have had in no way that idea. I believed that it was moral, that it was necessary to put, like the seeds for the future, germs of those grand principles in the spirit of a child who should later on be a soldier and a citizen; I believed that we improve the moral physiognomy of the Republic in inserting the word "God" in a law which we make for the people. (12683)

Lacretelle continued with an explanation of his amendment in distinction to atheism. He explicitly stated that he mentioned "atheism" with sympathy but without believing in "convinced and persistent atheism" and underlined that "the supreme hour, for me, is not the hour of the priest, but that of God," presenting an anticlerical but religious line. However, from the perspective of republicans further to the left, Lacretelle's amendment violated the principle of neutrality. Jules Maigne (Extrême gauche), who in the chamber session two days later would vote for the rejected Barodet amendment eliminating any references in the law to religious education in public schools, started by pointing out that the argumentation of those who were against the law simply "consists here basically of saying that whoever is not for Catholic religious education in schools, is an atheist, a man who denies God and the immortality of the soul." "I am not an atheist," continued Maigne, "but then, why do I come to combat the amendment of Mr. Lacretelle? This is the question." Because, he said, the amendment "would compromise the essential character of this law; that is to say, the neutrality of the

[44] LAÏCITÉ IN THE FRENCH THIRD REPUBLIC

government in education, the complete liberty of conscience." And in his argument, not "violating conscience of others" figured centrally:

> I do not want that in the name of deism, one would make what has been made in the name of catholicism, and that, when the school receives the children of different cultes, when it receives the children of atheists, of materialists, like those of deists and catholics, the professors would take sides for one or other of those beliefs and would make violence to the conscience of the child. I want that it rests neutral, and leave the religious instruction of children to the family. (12684)

In the next session of the chamber, December 24, 1880, Jules Ferry took the floor in order to address one more time the question of the neutrality of the school from a confessional point of view:

> MR. LE PRÉSIDENT DU CONSEIL, MINISTRE DE L'INSTRUCTION PUBLIQUE [JULES FERRY]. The religious neutrality of the school, the secularization of the school, if you want to take a word more familiar to our political language, it is, to my eyes and to the eyes of the government, the consequence of the secularization of civil power and all social institutions, of the family for example, which constitutes the regime under which we have lived since 1789. . . . Our adversaries would like that the primary school teacher be, in certain cases, the catechism coach [*répétiteur*] [Freppel had demanded] . . . but in these conditions and if they do no aspire to anything else, if their views, if their intentions do not go further, is it necessary to declare religious education obligatory? . . . In the domain of full liberty, outside of official rules, outside of duties prescribed by regulations, outside of class hours . . . who can prevent from this side of the chamber (*the speaker points the left*) a congregationist primary school teacher from reciting the catechism to his students? Surely, nobody.[28]

"It is not at this point that we disagree," continued Ferry. Freppel wants "religious instruction to be part of the mandatory program" with "a reason which appears quite strong, because it bases itself on numbers: It is the arithmetic of majorities":

> MR. LE PRÉSIDENT DU CONSEIL [JULES FERRY]. It is always by the *argument of majorities* that all the conquests made by liberty of conscience in our country

have been demolished. . . . And we say there is no other argument:—but, in fact, isn't it that there are 35 million catholics, isn't it that the immense majority ask the priest to consecrate their union [to God], isn't it that the majority of protestants make consecration by the pastor of their culte? It is always the same argument [of majorities], but it is an argument of oppression and it is easiest to transform. Because the argument of the majority is like the religion of the majority, which resembles . . . the religion of the State.

MR. DE LA BASSETIÈRE (EXTRÊME DROITE). It is the religion of the minority which is today the religion of the State! (12791; italics mine)

Ferry pointed out that Freppel defended primary school teachers being religion coaches (*répétiteur*) by stating the "fact" that the majority of children are Catholic, and that these children were obliged to be Catholic by doctrine and education. He concluded:

MR. LE PRÉSIDENT DU CONSEIL [JULES FERRY]. With respect for the liberty of conscience of the primary school teacher, with respect of the great principle which demands that all [state] functions be accessible to all the French regardless of their religion; whereas your principle results in excluding the functions of education for all those who do not profess the catholic faith (*Very good! very good! to the left.*) . . . [quoting from François Guizot] It is said: "The State is atheist." Certainly no, the State is not atheist, but the State is laic and must stay laic for the benefit of all the liberties that we have conquered. The independence and the sovereignty of the State is the first principle of our public law. (12791–92)

Ferry continued:

MR. LE PRÉSIDENT DU CONSEIL [JULES FERRY]. The primary school should be neutral from the religious point of view. But, here, our adversaries pose and pose to us and particularly to the government this question: Which neutrality? What is it that is neutrality? There are two kinds of neutrality, or, if you want, two ways of understanding neutrality, that is to say: there is the confessional neutrality and philosophical neutrality. . . . There is only here, in this law, confessional neutrality.

MR. FREPPEL. I demand the floor. (12793)

Freppel intervened and remarked under protestations from the left and center that still the proposed public primary school is "school without God" and that "God has been left aside like a simple metaphysical hypothesis" (12797). He argued that the statement "we do not deny God, we do not affirm him, we are simply not occupied by him . . . is the proper formula of positivism applied to primary education." He said that the position expressed by the republicans, "we do not deny God, we just defend a school that neither speaks for or against God," and that "God only appears in the program of religious morality," is the formula for pushing through a positivist school, and that is the school without God. (*"Various benches from left and center exclaim. 'That is the laic school!'"*) Article 1 was adopted by a vote of 346 to 136 (12798).

The next set of amendments addressed the practicalities of neutrality. The Alexandre Ribot, Bardoux (Centre gauche), and Émile Beaussire (Centre gauche) amendment called for loosening the strict conditions under which religious leaders could teach on school grounds (12800). Bardoux criticized the proposed law for its antireligious and antagonistic character through the application of strict conditions on the use of school grounds for religious instruction outside school hours. He explained that "there isn't a free nation, Switzerland, Holland, England, America—I take, sirs, all the advanced countries in primary instruction—where the priest doesn't have access to school for giving religious teaching when it is the wish of fathers of families" (12801). Paul Bert contested that not allowing the priest to enter school grounds was necessarily antagonizing. He gave an example from Belgium that the bishops protested against the new education system and refused to enter school grounds (12802–3). Ribot criticized the image of the militant and ultramontane[29] Catholicism he found suggested in Bert's argument: "Besides militant catholicism, ultramontane, which can have excessive pretentions, there is in Belgium like in France, sirs, as Mr. Littré called it one day . . . 'catholicism according to universal suffrage' . . . a catholicism that does not associate itself with the ultramontane campaign . . . a catholicism that accepts the Republic, that accepts our institutions" (12803). This amendment was not taken into consideration (12805).

An amendment eliminating religious instruction altogether from public primary education (not allowing even optional instruction) was rejected (the Barodet and Bousquet amendment, rejected by 277 votes to 137) (12805–6). Jean Barodet and Victor Bousquet were both from the Union républicaine group, and about half of the votes in support of their amendment came from their group and the other half came from groups to their left in the chamber. Later in the 1880s a majority of the Union républicaine members moved to these more leftist groups. Barodet himself moved to the Radical-socialiste group in 1889. Jules Ferry, for instance, voted against this amendment (12807).

The final attempt in the opposite direction, toward what Baubérot calls *religion civile conciliatrice* (conciliatory civil religion),[30] was Jules Simon's proposed amendment to article 1 ("school teachers teach their students their duties toward God and toward the patrie" as part of the obligatory primary school curriculum, first adopted by the Senate on July 5, 1881), which was later rejected by the chamber.[31] According to Baubérot, conciliatory civil religion had simultaneous elements of "catholicization of the nation" and "nationalization of catholicism" and differed from Combiste civil religion, which was about "nationalizing catholicism without catholicizing the nation."[32] As Jean-Marie Mayeur and Madeleine Rebérioux underscore, "disagreement between the Chamber of Deputies and the Senate, where moderate republicans like Jules Simon joined the right in defending the teaching of religion and 'of duties to God and one's country,' resulted in the adjournment of the vote on the law, which was not passed until March 28, 1882."[33]

This snapshot view of the debate on the question of religious instruction in schools in the making of *Loi du 28 Mars 1882 sur l'enseignement primaire obligatoire* sufficiently and comparatively lays out the political ends, arguments, and institutional preferences of monarchist Catholics, republicans who wanted to put religion at the service of the nation as a cement of society, republicans who defended neutrality, and republicans who aimed to eliminate religion courses altogether from the public school.

Républicains Opportunistes and the Concordat

The republican left in parliament between 1879 and 1885 demanded institutional separation between churches and the state. Républicains opportunistes, on the other hand, had campaigned on separation in the 1869 elections at the end of the Second Empire,[34] but once in government after the establishment of the Third Republic, they defended the Concordat. Jules Simon, the first *ministre des cultes* of the Third Republic, had written in his book *La Liberté de conscience* (1857): "The church in the state is the abdication of religious faith; the state in the church is the absolute negation of all liberty;

the Concordat is faith completely debased and liberty proscribed."[35] In a pamphlet distributed to electors on his candidature for the elections of May 1869, approximately two years before the Third Republic, Jules Ferry defended separation: "France will not have Liberty as long as a State-clergy, a Church, or official Churches exist: the alliance of State and Church is good neither for the State nor for the Church."[36] Yet, after Opportunistes came to power, Jules Simon declared the *budget des cultes* a public service for citizens. In 1881 Jules Ferry declared in parliament on multiple occasions that he wanted the "anticlerical struggle, but never the antireligious struggle."[37] On May 29, 1881, during a discussion in the chamber, Ferry defended the Concordat for preventing the centralization of the power of the Catholic Church, and therefore the more doctrinally conservative the church got, according to him, the more reason there was for keeping the Concordat:

MR. LE PRÉSIDENT DU CONSEIL [JULES FERRY]. I listened to my honorable and very spiritual colleague Mr. Lockroy, making an allusion to this doctrinal revolution [*Syllabus of Errors* in 1864, Doctrine of Infallibility in 1870] in pulling together an argument against the Concordat: that would be, for him, an excellent reason for denouncing it. I have the opposite point of view: this is for me a decisive reason for conserving it, because the more the ecclesiastical power is concentrated, centralized, the more it takes the form of true *césarisme*. (*Applause from center.—Laughs from right.*)[38]

He continued:

MR. LE PRÉSIDENT DU CONSEIL [JULES FERRY]. . . . When our fathers of 1789 substituted a salaried Church for a property-owner Church, they have made an act of wisdom and foresight, and we would be guilty in their memory if we follow another politics (*Applause from left and center*). . . . When two grand powers, obliged to live side by side, like séculière power and ecclesiastic power, are bound by a contract, it is necessary that they respect it and they profit from each other, and that these two powers don't tear apart the contract with the strikes of a needle. I said this all the time, it is the fundamental word of this discussion, it is the point of view which is necessary not to lose even for an instance: your politics, in the relations of the Republic with the Church, have been very resolutely anticlerical, it has never been an antireligious politics. (*Excitement from right.—Applause from center.*)[39]

In the same session he also responded to his left critics who were pointing out that he defended separating the school from the church but not the ceasing of state salaries for clerics, that is, the abolishment of the Concordat:

MR. LE PRÉSIDENT DU CONSEIL [JULES FERRY]. He [Mr. Lockroy] said in his last speech: You see a strange situation! You have separated the school from the Church and you do not want to separate the Church from the State! He could have added: A strange spectacle, remarkable, a government of free-thinkers who defend the Concordat and the recruitment of seminarists! Sirs, no doubt, it is not in this situation that which pleases the amateurs of excessive logic, but if there is a contradiction in the state of our law, it is that this contradiction exists profoundly in the mental state and morality of the population which we represent. (*Very good, very good!*). I do not teach anything to anybody, you have the voters. (*Exclamations and laughs from right.*) You have the catholic voters, practicing, attached to their faith, to practices of their culte.

MR. LE VICOMTE DE BÉLIZAL [UNION DES DROITES]. And we are proud of their vote!

MR. LE PRÉSIDENT DU CONSEIL [JULES FERRY]. They are believers, they care that the position of priest is not unoccupied, and when by chance they are vacant, they write to us to replace the priest or the *desservant*. But they do not take advice neither from the desservant nor the priest in municipal elections, as well as in legislative elections. It is a contradiction; it is strange, it drives the right to despair (*Applause from center*) . . . but allow me to say that this is the characteristic trait of the french population at the present moment. . . . It is called [according to Mr. Littré] "catholicism according to universal suffrage."[40]

Régime Concordataire (1801–1905): The Order Replaced

The Concordat of 1801 was signed between Napoléon Bonaparte and Pope Pius VII. It was both a control of the Catholic Church by the French state and a legal privileging of Roman Catholicism in France. The first paragraph of the Concordat declares Catholicism the religion of the great majority of French citizens: "The Government of the Republic recognizes that the Catholic religion, Apostolic and Roman, is the religion of the great majority of French citizens."[41] The main text of the Concordat (without the organic articles) designates the following relation between the French state and the Vatican: the pope expects from the "incumbents of the French bishoprics that for the benefit of peace and unity . . . every kind of sacrifice, even that of their sees" (article 3). If they disobey, the head of the French state can make new appointments to those posts (article 4), and the head of the French state will also make the nominations for bishoprics that just become vacant (article 5). Bishops will pledge any allegiance to the French Republic before "assuming their function," which includes a promise that they will inform the government of any plots against the state (article 6). A prayer, "God save the Republic, God save the Consuls," will be "repeated at the end of divine office in all Catholic Churches in France" (article 8). Bishops' nominations for the parishes will be "limited to those persons agreeable to the government" (article 10). All "nonalienated churches" will be at the "disposition" of the bishops (articles 12, 13). The salaries of the clerics will be provided from the French state budget (article 14).[42] If the first council in the future is not a Catholic, the Concordat will be renegotiated (article 17).

The organic articles added unilaterally to the Concordat by Napoléon strengthened the control of the French state over the Catholic Church. The Concordat put religion in service of the crown by allowing the church to mobilize in France, but the organic articles went further. They were meant to strengthen the Gallican church and nationalize Catholicism.[43] This could also be seen as opposed to religious orders to keep the monopoly over the religious sphere. Reformed and Lutheran churches were given their own constitution in these organic articles. The articles of the Concordat attested to the control of religion by the state. In the words of Jean Baubérot, the organic articles "clearly showed that henceforth, 'the Church is in the State,' whereas 'the State is not in the Church.'"[44]

Two issue areas were central to the settlement of the Concordat: the appointments and salaries of bishops. The French state was to pay the salaries of bishops, justified as compensation for the church property confiscated in the 1789 Revolution. In turn, the state could nominate bishop candidates. Napoléon established an Administration des Cultes on October 7, 1801, and a Ministère des Cultes in 1804.[45] Its main task was to monitor and act as an intermediary between Rome and the French state especially on the two issues of nomination and salaries of religion personnel. As Maurice Larkin, historian of state-church relations in France, explains, "French Direction des Cultes maintained a list of suitable candidates which it based on the various recommendations it had received from civil servants, members of parliament and certain of the more Republican bishops."[46] Reformed and Lutheran clergy in April 1802 and Jewish rabbis in February 1831 also received state salaries, hence becoming civil officials.[47] In 1881 a decree included salaries for Muslim religious personnel of Algeria in the *budget des cultes* as well.[48]

Reconfiguration of Political Forces: Toward the 1902 Chamber of Separation

The elections of 1889 had clearly beckoned the end of the monarchists, and those of 1893 marked the emergence of the Socialistes. With the electoral defeat of the monarchists, Pope Leo XIII called on Catholics to attend to the working classes and rally to the republic in order to defend Catholicism from within rather than seeking a return to monarchy.[49] Cardinal Lavigerie's famous toast at Algiers, asking French Catholics to give up their monarchist loyalties, and the papal encyclical on May 15, 1891, *Rerum Novarum*, had launched the Ralliement.[50] *Rerum Novarum* was the founding official document of the Ralliement calling French Catholics to attend to the problems of the French working class.[51] After reviewing the poor conditions of the working class in its first three articles, *Rerum Novarum* engaged in a critique of socialism in articles 4 through 15. Article 4 states:

> To remedy these wrongs the socialists, working on the poor man's envy of the rich, are striving to do away with private property, and contend that individual possessions should become the common property of all, to be administered by the State or by municipal bodies. They hold that by thus transferring property from private individuals to the community, the present mischievous state of things will be set to rights, inasmuch as each citizen will then get his fair share of whatever there is to enjoy. But their contentions are so clearly powerless to end the controversy that were they carried into effect the working man himself would be among the first to suffer. They are, moreover, emphatically unjust, for they would rob the lawful possessor, distort the functions of the State, and create utter confusion in the community.[52]

The political Catholic movement emerging from the Ralliement, *Ralliés* as they were called, aimed to fill the void left by the monarchists in the chamber. The right wing of the Républicains opportunistes, who now called themselves Républicains progressistes, not having the sufficient majority to rule since 1885, were looking for a new right coalition against the Socialistes. For instance, Paul Deschanel, a Républicain progressiste in the 1902 chamber, called the right wing to form a party as early as the 1889 elections.[53] Jules Ferry, architect of the laic education laws of 1881 and 1882, was already with the Républicains progressiste group in the 1885 chamber. And they turned to the Ralliés for a coalition against the rising Socialistes.[54] This new realignment of interests was coined as the "New Spirit" of toleration after a speech Eugène Spuller, ministre des cultes, gave in 1892. Spuller called for a reconciliation of Catholicism and democracy:

> When the Republic had to struggle against a coalition of the old parties, when the Church constituted a link between those parties, I myself supported the policy the circumstances demanded. . . . Where religion is concerned the country is no longer in the position it was ten or fifteen years ago . . . I maintain that the Church itself had changed and is evolving in spite of its pretension to infallibility. I believe that now, instead of acting as a link between the various monarchist parties, we can see the Church hurriedly striving to lead democracy. . . . That is why . . . I think democracy should be animated by a new spirit. . . . In place of a mean, pettifogging, irritating struggle (*protests from the extreme left and applause from the center*), what is needed is a generous spirit of tolerance and an intellectual and moral reform." (*Signs of approval from the center and noises on the left.*)[55]

The Méline government (1896–1898), the longest-duration government of the 1890s, rested on this coalition between right Opportunistes and Ralliés.[56] We will see later that the "New Spirit" has many similarities with the turn the Turkish Republican People's Party took in 1947, emphasizing the need to embrace religion's social force rather than regime "threats." The decade of experiments toward a "New Spirit"[57] to form a conservative coalition between Républicain progressistes and Ralliés (the Méline and Ribot governments) came to an end when the Dreyfus Affair realigned French politics.[58] In 1901 and onward, two leaders of the Ralliés, Albert de Mun and Jacques Piou, tried to turn this political Catholic movement into a political party, Action libérale populaire (ALP), capable of challenging the post-Dreyfus block of Radicaux and Socialistes in Parliament.[59] The anticlerical governments of Pierre Waldeck-Rousseau (June 22, 1899–June 4, 1902), particularly the July 1, 1901, Law of Associations,[60] and of Émile Combes (June 7, 1902–January 24, 1905) took fundamental steps to create the context of the chamber debates on the *Loi du 9 Décembre 1905*, which began on February 10, 1905.

After the Ralliement, decentralized religious orders were a common enemy of the Catholic Church and the Républicains opportunistes. These orders threatened the centralization of power, a goal that the Vatican and moderate republicans shared, and were seen as a threat to the church hierarchy and centralizing ambitions of a unitary nation-state. Rather than religion or Catholicism as such, Ferry, in the 1880s, had often singled out the Jesuits as the main threat: "What we aim at are only the nonauthorized congregations, and among them, I am not afraid of saying it out loud, a congregation that is not only unauthorized, but that is also forbidden by our history, the Company of Jesus. Yes, it is from that congregation, Sirs, we want to take away the souls of French youth."[61]

The two most politically influential religious orders in France were the Jesuits and the Assumptionists. The former were powerful in the realm of education, while the latter had a strong role in the press via their newspaper, *La Croix*. *La Croix* was especially successful in shaping and diffusing an anti-Semitic message in rural France during the Dreyfus Affair.[62] Nancy Fitch's analysis of anti-Semitism in two French villages at the end of the nineteenth century underscores succinctly the power of *La Croix*. According to Fitch, in the context of a fin de siècle economic crisis, in two French villages that had no Jewish inhabitants, anti-Semitism rose in the one where Assumptionists were strongly organized and did not rise at all in the other village where Socialistes were organized. The Assumptionists were against the Ralliement and made attempts to undermine it.[63] Waldeck-Rousseau's Law of Associations of 1901 mainly targeted these two religious orders.[64]

Waldeck-Rousseau belonged to the Union républicaine between 1879 and 1889. In 1899 he took support from the left and became prime minister, consolidating a republican defense against militant nationalism and clericalism rising with the Dreyfus Affair. Waldeck-Rousseau, in the tradition of Jules Ferry, was in favor of maintaining the Concordat. However, his Law of Associations (1901) had a divisive effect on the parliament, and the elections of 1902 were mainly fought between those for and those against his law, between Catholic defense and republican defense.[65] On January 24, 1900, the court dissolved the Assumptionist order. Waldeck-Rousseau "also reproved Cardinal Richard, who had visited the Assumptionist fathers to express episcopal sympathy, and suspended the salaries of six bishops who had protested against the sentence of dissolution." He also asked the church to eliminate all the teachers from religious orders in their seminaries. Religious congregations were required to get approval from the Conseil d'État (State Council). His Law of Associations changed the task of authorizing religious orders from a decree to a legislative task and banned members of unauthorized religious orders from teaching.[66] According to article 13 of the law, religious communities, as opposed to nonreligious communities, could not be formed without legislative authorization.[67] The general purpose of the law was to regulate nonprofit organizations, as stated in its first article. It declared illegitimate all associations aiming to undermine "national territory and the republican form of government." Article 10 empowered the State Council to advance or withdraw the status "of public utility" in the case of all associations. Article 13 particularly addressed religious associations, empowering the State Council to decide on their establishment and the Council of Ministers in their dissolution.[68] Article 14 placed limitations on education by religious orders in order to reverse the effects of the Falloux law discussed above: "No one is allowed to run, either directly or by persons interposed, an educational establishment, of whatever order it is, or give an education, if it belongs to a nonauthorized religious congregation."[69]

Malcolm O. Partin provides numbers from the Ministère des Cultes on requests for legalization by religious congregations after the promulgation of the law, adding that these numbers are better treated as approximates: "64 men's congregations submitted requests for 2,009 establishments; 685 women's congregations requested approval for 11,003 establishments."[70]

Émile Combes was the chairman of the committee examining the bill on the Law of Associations under Waldeck-Rousseau's government and succeeded Waldeck-Rousseau as prime minister in June 7, 1902. Combes was much more radically anticlerical than Jules Ferry or Waldeck-Rousseau, and he used the institutions of the Concordat, Ministère des Cultes, and *budget des cultes* to drastically combat clerics. The suppression of clerical salaries could be used to punish antirepublican clerics. The Waldeck-Rousseau government used this economic threat for political ends from June 1899 to June 1902, but Combes did so to a much greater extent.[71] When the latter took office on June 7 there were already twenty-five salary suspensions: twenty-one from Waldeck-Rousseau's government and four dating from before 1899. From June to August 1902 Combes suspended the salaries of eighty-six lower-ranking clergy on grounds that these clerics had used their influence against republican candidates in the elections of April 1902. Another common ground for suspension was opposition by clerics to the closure of religious schools. According to a memorandum of the Ministère des Cultes in September 1903, eleven bishops had their salaries suspended, eight of them specifically at the request of Combes. By the end of 1903, 335 clerics had had their salaries suspended. Combes's total record for suspensions was 632, and Waldeck-Rousseau's was 150.[72] This was not a significant amount given that the French government paid the salaries of 43,000 clergy, but it still showed how the dependence of the church on the state via the Concordat provided anticlerical governments with the economic means to fight the clergy.[73]

When Combes was criticized for pushing policies to fight the religious orders he replied, "I took office solely for that purpose." His fight was supported by the Radical, Radical-socialiste, left ex-Opportuniste, and Socialiste groups in parliament. One of the legacies of Waldeck-Rousseau's government was that the demands for authorization from religious orders were to go to both chambers. However, Combes secured a ruling from the State Council that only the lower chamber could decide on the issue. Many applications of religious orders for state recognition were rejected. Bishops were advised to prohibit all services in the chapels of religious orders; most bishops protested and their salaries were suspended. A new law on July 7, 1904, forbade any teacher from the religious orders, authorized or unauthorized, to teach. In seven years, from 1904 to 1911, 1,843 religious order schools were closed, 272 cases were brought to court for not complying with the law, and 637 out of 1,429 people were found guilty. Their property was confiscated.[74]

Combes was much more radical than his predecessor Ferry, who had declared a more moderate stance on religion, that "attitudes of mind are more difficult to change then reasoned opinions." According to Adrien Dansette, Ferry "would have thought it mad to declare war on the religion professed by the majority of the population."[75] Combes thought otherwise. In December 1902, instead of suggesting nominations for bishoprics to the Catholic Church from which the church would choose—this was the practice established by the Concordat (articles 4 and 5)—Combes sent to the nuncio the final decisions on bishop appointments and recalled the French ambassador from the Vatican.[76] During the Combes administration (1902–1905), one out of three Catholic schools closed down. Clearly, none of the premiers of France since 1899 wanted separation.[77]

The Politics of the *Loi du 9 Décembre 1905*

The elections of 1902 determined the chamber that would debate the separation law. It is difficult to find two works that use an identical set of political group categories in discussing the composition of the 1902 chamber; therefore in figure 3.1 I have recharted it from the political group affiliations in the web archives of the French National Assembly.[78] Six political groups, in terms of number of seats, dominated the 588-member Assembly: Gauche radicales (87 seats), Radical-socialistes (94), Socialistes parlementaires (32), Union démocratique (50), Républicains progressistes (64), Action libérale populaire (52). The rest comprised a small number of monarchists and political fragments consisting of a synthesis of these major groups, seventy-three deputies who did not affiliate themselves (*non inscrit*), and twenty-nine for which there are no data available in the web archives.

On May 30, 1902, *Le Temps* and *L'Année Politique* announced the formation of Union démocratique, which declared "itself determined to continue

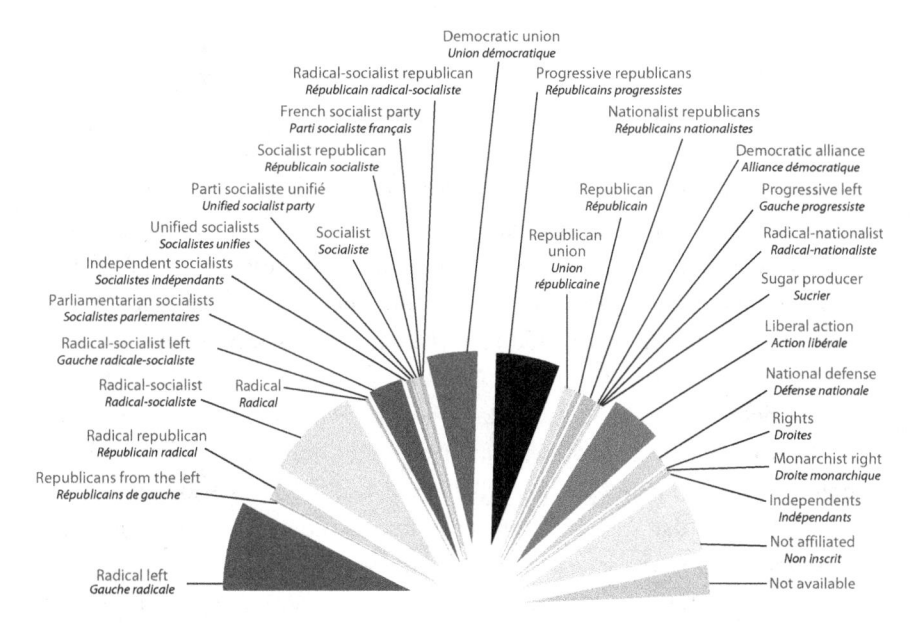

Figure 3.1 Distribution of Seats by Political Group in the Chamber of Deputies, 1902. (*Source*: My compilation from *Journal officiel*, July 3, 1905, 1258–64. Group memberships are taken from the website of the National Assembly of France.)

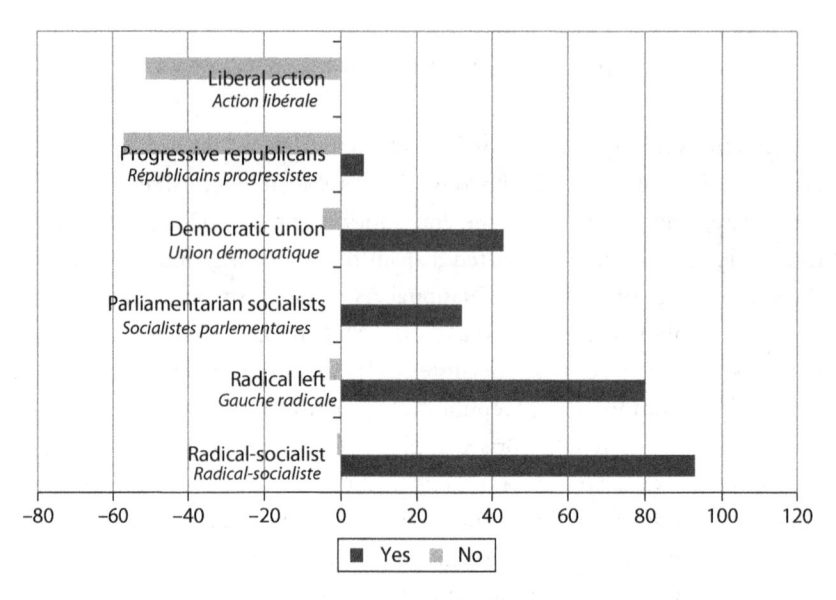

Figure 3.2 Distribution of Chamber of Deputies Vote on Separation Law across Six Major Political Groups, July 3, 1905.

the clearly democratic and anticlerical politics of Waldeck-Rousseau Ministry."[79] Union démocratique emerged from within the Républicain opportuniste group and positioned itself closer to the left of the chamber. Initially only the Socialistes and Radical-socialistes defended separation of churches and state.[80] Their position was fundamentally to take the religious question off the agenda. Radicals were in the beginning significantly divided on the issue, and the political calculation was multidimensional. The questions were, first, whether the church would be more dangerous separated than salaried and, second, if separation would provoke a reaction among the electorate. Union démocratique was also making similar calculations. A categorization of the vote on the Law of Separation in the chamber on July 3, 1905, by political groups (figure 3.2) shows that Radicals and Socialistes voted in block for the law and that Action libéral populaire was the largest group that voted as a block against the law. Two groups in the 1902 chamber had emerged from a split within the governing Républicains opportunistes of the 1880s: Union démocratique and Républicains progressistes. These were the two major groups whose vote was divided the most. Union démocratique cast forty-three votes for and five votes against the separation law; the Républicains progressistes, six votes for and fifty-seven against.

The opposition between Union démocratique and Républicains progressistes was central in the passing of the separation law, as Maurice Larkin correctly observed: "No separation bill could pass parliament without the support of at least fifty of them [Union démocratique]—and in 1902 this seemed most unlikely."[81] This in fact was the case, as attested to by the comparative sizes of the political groups, the 108-vote margin by which the law passed, and the shifting politics of the Opportunistes on religion. On June 1, 1904, Jean Jaurès, head of the Socialiste group in the chamber, wrote in his article in *l'Humanité*, "The Separation and the Union démocratique," that the Union démocratique was hesitant about the law.[82]

According to many historians and accounts of parliamentarians at the time, article 4 of the separation law was the critical discussion leading up to the final vote. The article addressed the terms of the transfer of the goods from the state to associations. It was precisely these terms and the question of which associations got to claim the property that became the central and most divisive subject of discussion in the chamber. The article was debated for three days, April 20–22, 1905, and the question posed in the chamber against the Briand Commission's version of it, which ignited and mainly determined the axis of the debate, was given together by Alexandre Ribot, Paul Deschanel, and Louis Barthou: two Républicains progressistes and a Union démocratique parliamentarian. In the final vote, Ribot voted against the law with the majority of Républicains progressistes, Barthou voted for the law with the majority of Union démocratique, and Deschanel voted for the law and in the next legislative elections (1906) changed his affiliation to Union démocratique. This attempt to bring together a republican coalition against the law ultimately failed, and the two groups cast their votes differently. What were the political concerns of each group, how did Union démocratique end up supporting the law, why were ALP and Républicains progressistes opposed to it, and how did the Socialistes parlementaires push for a majority for it?

The first article of the *Loi du 9 Décembre 1905* stated: "The Republic assures the liberty of conscience. It guarantees the free practice of faiths [*cultes*], under the only restrictions hereinafter enacted in the interest of public order."[83] The second article suppressed the *budget des cultes*, except for a state budget for chaplains in public establishments, including elementary, middle, and high schools:

> The Republic neither recognizes nor pays a salary to or subsidizes any faith. Consequently, as from January 1 which will follow the

promulgation of this law, all expenditures relating to the exercise of faiths will be removed from the budgets of the State, departments, and communes. However, those expenditures relating to services of chaplaincy and intended to ensure the free exercise of worship [culte] in public establishments, such as elementary schools, middle schools, high schools, hospices, asylums, and prisons, can be entered in the budgets.

Article 4 read:

Within a year from the date of the promulgation of the present law, the movable and immovable property of the menses,[84] fabriques, presbyteral councils, consistories, and other public religious [culte] establishments will, with all the charges and obligations with which they are constrained, and with their special purposes, be transferred by the legal representatives of those establishments to the associations, which, complying with the general rules of organization of the faith [culte] that they propose to ensure the practice, will have been legally formed according to the prescriptions of article 19 for the practice of that faith in the former districts of the said establishments.[85]

Multiple historians agree that the threshold for passing the law was in the debate over article 4. In *Church and State After the Dreyfus Affair*, Maurice Larkin underlines the significance of the debate that was a battle between those who insisted on recognizing religion in its particularities and those who approached religion as a general category:

> The proposed system of *associations cultuelles* reflected the legal principle that, after Separation, the State could recognize the Church only as a group of French citizens engaged in a certain activity. . . . For this reason the Separation bill made no mention of Pope or bishops, since it was not the law's business to give definitions of the Church. To have done so would have been to remove the right of French Catholics to change their concept of the Church.[86]

Jean-Marie Mayeur and Madeleine Rebérioux, in *The Third Republic from Its Origins to the Great War 1871–1914*, note that when the separation law was first drafted in the winter of 1904–05 and socialist Aristide Briand presented his report on the draft on March 21, 1905, one division among the republicans was clear: "Was the separation to be the last stage in the secularization of the republican state or a weapon in the struggle against the papacy, 'the last of the idols,' and for the triumph of 'emancipated reason'?"[87] The authors explain that the particular disagreement was on article 4 concerning religious associations. Those who saw the separation law as a new weapon for weakening Catholicism in France (followers of Émile Combes) advocated that in the regulation of religious organizations no direct or indirect reference be made to the Vatican. This was seen as a way of further breaking ecclesiastical hierarchy. "Indeed, there were those who looked forward to seeing discontented priests and groups of laity breaking with the hierarchy and insisting on having their own local church building, thus weakening the Church with schism and division—or, putting the case in more elevated terms, there would be scope for freedom of thought and the expression of lay opinion within the authoritarian shell of Catholicism."[88] The other republican camp saw the separation law just as a means to remove the religious question off the agenda and an opportunity to pursue questions they saw as more fundamental, such as those dealing with finances, political and social peace, and social reforms.[89] Aristide Briand was of the latter camp, and the majority of the parliament supported his compromise amendment to article 4 that all religious organization after the separation had to conform "to the rules of the general organization whose faith they propose to ensure the exercise of."[90]

As John McManners explains: "The law of separation would not be useful or improving if it was rejected by the Church and the country was left in a state of undeclared civil war. The difficulty lay in the *associations cultuelles*, and Briand worked to make them compatible with the current Catholic view of ecclesiastical government, not instruments of potential schism."[91] In *La séparation de l'Église et de l'Etat*, Jean-Marie Mayeur puts the disagreement over article 4 and its resolution as the turning point in the process toward separation:

> Since the Revolution, churches, dioceses, grand seminaries, presbyteries were the property of the State, of the department, of the commune. To whom in the new regime of cultes were these edifices restored . . . ? The entire bill rested on the constitution of *associations cultuelles* to whom the devolution of goods of the public establishments of cultes (estimated 400 millions francs) had to be made, and to whom the use of cultuel edifices would be granted. The initial text [of the bill] made

no mention of the organization of the Catholic Church. . . . The fear of catholics increased in the face of the undisguised hopes of a number of anticlericals to favor thanks to *associations cultuelles* the birth of schisms and sects.[92]

He continues his argument that it became necessary to give some guarantee to the Catholic Church that the liberty of religious associations would not override ecclesiastical hierarchy:

This expectation of schisms and reforms is grounded on the liberty of *associations cultuelles* vis-à-vis the [ecclesiastical] hiearchy. For making the regime of separation acceptable to catholics it was indispensable to give them guarantees. . . . Therefore, the Commission reconvened on 19 April with the agreement of minister of public instruction and cultes modified the first paragraph of original text of article 4 of the bill.[93]

The debate on article 4 is critical for charting the political field of institutional separation in the Third Republic. Even after the law passed, the pope's encyclicals against the separation law, *Vehementer Nos* (February 11, 1906) and *Gravissimo Officii* (August 10, 1906), had article 4 as their main target.[94] The debate over article 4 in the Chamber of Deputies took place on April 20, 21, and 22, 1905. I now turn to an analysis of commission reports, newspaper and journal articles, and chamber discussions in order to chart the political field of institutional separation from a multilevel focus on political ends, arguments, and institutional preferences.

Action Libérale Populaire and Separation

Although Albert de Mun, leader of the ALP, was a parliamentarian in the chamber of 1902–1906, neither he nor any other member of the ALP spoke in the chamber debates on article 4. However, Mun collected his articles that had been published in various journals and newspapers on the separation law into a volume entitled *Contre la séparation* (1905).[95] This volume is a rich source for delving into the reasons behind the ALP's block of "no" votes. In an article originally published in *Le Figaro*, "De la rupture à la séparation: Séance du 22 octobre 1904," Mun wrote:

Just after the [chamber] session of October 22, Mr. Jean Jaurès wrote in the [newspaper] *Humanité*, "So, by his eloquent intervention, Mr. Deschanel [Républicains progressistes] will have served and precipitated the grand work of the laïcité initiative, together with the republican government and the republican majority." Mr. Jaurès is right and Mr. Deschanel, no doubt, does not find him wrong . . . separation, offered by the same hands full of lovely promises, I do not want. Mr. Deschanel thinks that the Concordat of 1801 is "only expedient." Mr. Combes says "a buffer [*tampon*]." . . . Mr. Deschanel adds that the Concordat "cannot be the definitive regime of democracy in the twentieth century . . . religions organized within the service of the State, this is an idea of the past. The future, it is the neutrality of the State in matters of religion." The applause of the left has exploded at that moment and I am not surprised: all the theory of those who want to smash the christian tradition of France is contained in these words. *No! I do not believe at all in the neutral State in matters of religion*, that is to say, apparently, the State does not recognize any religious culte, does not profess any in the act of national life, and that this is necessarily the State of the future.[96]

Mun's criticism of Paul Deschanel is particularly important because Deschanel stood precisely on the boundary between the "yes" and the "no" vote. He belonged to the Républicains progressistes in the 1902–1906 chamber and to the Union démocratique in the 1906–1910 chamber, moving across the boundary of right and left Opportunistes, precisely where the vote on the separation law split. Deschanel finally did vote for the law.[97] Mun's remarks on neutrality are crucial not only for a better understanding of the ALP opposition but also as a vantage point from which to look at today's conceptualizations and skepticism about neutrality. Mun poses neutrality not as a "comprehensive" but a "practical-institutional doctrine" which he understands as no funds or any other kind of recognition for any religion, and he is just against such "neutrality."

In another article written for *Le Gaulois* two days after the chamber voted to open the discussion on the separation law in its February 10, 1905, session, Mun asserted: "In two words, I stay resolutely concordataire, as a catholic and as a French. Most certainly, the Concordat of 1801 does not realize, for me, the ideal relations of Church and State in a christian society. It would be too easy to criticize [the Concordat] from this point of view, and add all the protestations the Church brought up for a century on the organic articles."[98]

Mun's position, in short, was the following: the pope did not want the abolishment of the Concordat. Christianity had been uprooted in France over the past twenty-five years, and the Concordat at least "assured the legal existence of religious life in our country."[99] Maurice Larkin also argues that for Rome, the Concordat was a source of international recognition by its "eldest daughter," France, at a time when its international power was declining.[100] Across the border, Bismarck was proceeding with his *Kulturkampf*. In 1871 he had abolished the Catholic Bureau within the Kultusministerium (Prussian Ministère des Cultes). In 1875 Catholic religious orders and congregations were abolished, and religious guarantees were removed from the Prussian Constitution. At the end of the 1870s, when the *Kulturkampf* was waning, "more than half of Prussia's Catholic episcopate was either in exile or in prison."[101] Given these circumstances, official recognition of Catholicism by France as the religion of the majority of citizens was important for the Catholic Church. Mun's argument continued as follows: France is a Catholic nation, "brought up in the arms of the Catholic Church," and with the abolishment of the Concordat what is offered instead of a "grand public service" is with article 4 "to reduce the Church in our country to an ordinary enterprise, only an association formed between private individuals":

> I remember that it was twenty years or so, Mr. Yves Guyot [Extrême gauche], in a discussion of the *budget des cultes*, expressed this idea that he would treat religion like an industry, "*industrie cultuelle*," and subjugate it to the professional syndicates law.... Yet, here we are, and we have stepped further, because there are catholics who already accommodate themselves to this regime of "*l'association cultuelle*." This is the great danger, against which I believe it is urgent to react. Therefore the saying goes: "My God defend me from my friends, I take care of my enemies."[102]

Mun's position of liberty for religion sometimes gives way to the necessity of religion for statehood and governance. He spoke of religion as the "gendarme" of the soul of which all states should take heed, an analogy that we will see later in Turkey, uttered by certain Kemalists as well as certain political Islamists. Mun goes on: "In a country like ours penetrated to the marrow with Catholic education, the State cannot ignore the Church . . .

the Church remains a moral power that no government can ignore. One has to persecute her or negotiate with her."[103] And: "And for a start, can religion be in our country only a question of private order, to which public powers must be disinterested? No statesman will believe that; none will support that a moral power that, in all parts of the nation, has an effect on a multitude of souls, which penetrates into most families, which sits nearly in all homes, can be ignored by the government of the country."[104]

In *Le Figaro* on March 20, 1905, Mun wrote:

> I do not plead anymore for my faith, I said: I plead for France. Because the apostasy that we are proposed, it is not only a rupture with the Catholic Church, or not even the abandonment of the christian faith: it is a rupture with God. . . . The separation, he says [Mr. Buisson], it is the coronation of our work after the school, after the old people's home, after the asylum, after the courtroom without God, it is finally the State without God, that is to say, the public life, the civil life of the nation evades entirely all contact with God, all knowledge of divine law. . . . Neither the ones nor the others think that this is simply the formula of barbarism, that in a country where the divine law would have no action on men anymore, no influence in legislation, where human law would not be protected before conscience only by the gendarmes, would be close to return to the savage state.[105]

The theme of religion, statehood and governance figured central also in his *Le Gaulois* article cited above:

> "Everything would be simple," wrote le duc Albert de Broglie [Orléaniste] more than forty years ago, "if the church would be only an institution of prayer, the state an institution of government [police]." It is not the case. Between the two powers, contacts are inevitable. Napoléon knew it, and that is why he signed the Concordat.[106]

All ALP members voted against the separation law, but between opening the law for discussion in the chamber on February 10 and July 3, 1905, there were voices within the ALP who welcomed separation. I would like to flesh out some of the ALP members' defenses of separation because such disagreement on institutional preferences among political actors who share political affiliation and political ends is crucial for charting the political field of institutional separation, and this can be done by a focus on the precise arguments these political actors advanced. For instance, on February 11, 1905, the day after the discussion on the law opened, ALP parliamentarian Mr. l'abbé Gayraud said he welcomed a separation between church and state if certain conditions were met:

MR. GAYRAUD. There is, I say, only one man with whom one can deal for reaching an agreement with the Church of France, it is the pope who sits in Vatican. You want to make the separation between the State and Catholic Church,—be it. I demand: Is it in your interest, yes or no, that this separation be peaceful and would make the religious peace in this country, one respectful of liberty of conscience, one that does not trouble catholics neither in their beliefs nor in their religious practices? This is a preliminary question, if I may say. Fine, if you understand the interest that there is in making the separation a liberal and peaceful regime, I add—and you must understand me—that there is only one way very certain: it is dealing with the Holy See and conferring with him, ask him what conditions of separation would be acceptable for the Church. (*Exclamations on the left*.) I do not mean to say, sirs, that the pope will make the law in France. I am, from the point of view of French interests, as independent as anyone else before the Holy See. (*Applause on the right*.)[107]

Important elements of these ALP argumentations repeat in the arguments of the Républicains progressistes during the discussions on article 4. Gayraud clarified that France is ruled by French law, and he advocated a separation "acceptable for the religious conscience of catholics." As we will see later in this chapter, Républicains progressistes also take the pope and the institution of the Catholic Church as representative of Catholic conscience. In other words, there is no distinction between the institution and individual conscience. Gayraud received criticism in the chamber precisely for that by Albert Vazeille (Radical-socialiste), who distinguished Catholics from the Catholic Church and remarked, "It is the french catholics who have to be the judge of the conditions of separation. The pope has nothing to do with this question of domestic order" (275). Gayraud further remarked:

MR. GAYRAUD. I am not inclined to accept a separation that would not be one. Because, in my view, separation is not only the denunciation of the

Concordat, it is not only the refusal by the State of the engagements taken toward the Church in 1801, it is more and above all the liberty of the catholic conscience. If you propose us a separation which safeguards all the liberties and all the rights of catholic consciences.

MR. DAUZON. And the israelite and protestant consciences?

MR. GAYRAUD. All religious consciences.

MR. DAUZON. And atheists?

MR. GAYRAUD. Because it is about cultes, it cannot be a question of consciences which are not religious. If you want, I said, to submit to us a project of separation which takes account—I am not going to push the requirements a long way—of the declaration of the Central Council of Reformed Churches of France, I am content!

ON THE RIGHT. What do you think, Mr. Albert-Le-Roy?

MR. GAYRAUD. Grant us what the Protestants, what the Central Council of Reformed Churches of France demand: complete liberty of culte, the use or ownership of buildings necessary for the culte (*Interruptions from the far left.—Very good! very good! from the right*), ecclesiastical pensions equivalent to that of the Central Council of Reformed Churches of France. (275)

Gayraud continued:

MR. GAYRAUD. Here I address myself especially to our honorable colleague Mr. Ferdinand Buisson, president of the commission for the separation of the Churches and the State, who will be examining the project of the Government [submitted to the chamber February 9, 1905]. He no doubt knows especially the demands of the Reformed Churches of France. If the rapporteur of this commission presents a project that is inspired by their observations, which gives us satisfaction on all these points that I come to list, I am all ready to accept this separation and support it. I know, sirs, that a great part of the clergy of France suffers in their dignity from the situation which for thirty years has befallen the Church in this country. Yes, the clergy is suffering from this situation, I know it well. . . . It would be an error to believe that the clergy of France takes the concordatory convention as an ideal relation between Church and State. The Concordat has never been a way for establishing friendly relations between the two powers. . . . But for the new regime to constitute a real progress compared to the prior regime, it is necessary that it is inspired by the principles which you cherish. (*The speaker points to the left.*) I say that you particularly cherish, not that they would not be equally dear to me—but because I address myself to you. *These principles are confessional neutrality of the State and liberty of conscience and cultes.* It is there that you ground yourself for demanding the separation of Church and State. Eh! Fine, it is by virtue of these very principles that the formula of separation of Church and State should be: each to its home; the State to his, the Church to hers. (276; italics mine)

Mun wrote a critique of Gayraud's speech in the chamber the next day, on February 12, 1905, in *La Croix*, the Catholic newspaper:

> I couldn't have, without a profound emotion, heard Mr. l'abbé Gayraud declaring that he "would be content with a project of separation which takes account of the declaration of the Central Council of Reformed Churches of France." . . . But even besides any consideration of faith or doctrine, the position of the Catholic Church in France, from the national point of view alone, has nothing in common with that of Reformed Churches: it is her which has shaped our country; its history is deeply and intimately mixed to that of France, and an indestructible tradition of centuries of long labor, even among the nonbelievers, survives in the souls. The French nation cannot, without being hit at her heart, treat the Catholic Church like a simple association of the faithful.[108]

An axis of struggle already emerging from these discussions, which also had a central place in the chamber debate on article 4, was between, on the one hand, treating religion as a general category in law and likewise religious associations as any other associations, and, on the other hand, recognizing a particular religion, Catholicism as such, in law. This axis could sometimes pass through the ALP, as well as through the ex–Républicains opportunistes, pitting its right wing, Républicains progressistes, against its left wing, Union démocratique. This was one of the axes of struggle that marked the conflict between Socialistes and Républicains progressistes on article 4. Gayraud followed his call of February 11 for a liberal and a peaceful separation with a motion on procedure on March 21, 1905. The motion, rejected in the chamber on March 22, showed a procedural axis of conflict as well. The rejected motion read:

The Chamber, considering diplomatic loyalty and political honesty, not less than the interest of public order and religious peace, demand the denunciation of the Concordat . . . and the separation of Churches and State be amicable, decide to postpone all deliberations on the bill relating to this subject and invite the Government to convene an extra-parliamentary commission of ministers of diverse cultes, together with the heads of interested Churches, in order to prepare an agreement with these Churches on the conditions of the separation.[109]

The internal ALP debate discussed above shows a disagreement on institutional preferences but a shared reasoning by the disagreeing parties from the perspective of promoting a Catholic way of life as opposed to reasoning from institutional principles. Mun's position was that despite all the problems emerging from its organic articles, the institutions of the Concordat and the state *budget des cultes* were indispensable for maintaining Catholic life in France. While Gayraud's position was that "the clergy of France suffers in their dignity" and, in other respects, under the Concordat, therefore a "correctly" termed separation would be better for Catholic life in France. The Catholic separationist position that Gayraud expressed was actually shared by many intransigent Catholic bishops. For instance, the Aristide Briand Report on separation, *La séparation des Églises et de l'Etat: rapport fait au nom de la commission de la Chambre des députés*, submitted to the chamber on March 4, 1905, discusses the separatist movements led by ultramontanes within the clergy (e.g., Lamennais, Montalembert, Lacordaire). These clergy asked for the suppression of the Concordat for assuring a peaceful conscience and for the power to fight for Catholicism more independently. "Ultramontanes," detailed the report, "partisans of the predominance of the spiritual over the temporal, they claimed for the Church an absolute independence."[110] The journal *L'Avenir* (a Catholic journal founded in 1830) was defending this separatist position from within the clergy.[111] *L'Avenir* asserted that all religion needs is freedom, and its force is in the conscience of people and not in the support of governments. The debate in the *L'Avenir* was between clergy who argued that a government that respects liberties is fine, because the more the government takes part in the appointment of bishops, the higher the ecclesiastical budget (defense of the Concordat), and clergy who argued that they wanted neither protection nor privilege from the government; one had to decide and choose between God and the treasury; liberty of our conscience, culte, and hierarchy is primary. The report also cited an ultramontane,

Lamennais, calling on Catholics: if they want the prayers, they "need to pay."[112] The separationist clergy delineated by the commission report figures also in Larkin's *Church and State After the Dreyfus Affair,* Acomb's *The French Laic Laws 1879–1889,* and Dansette's *Religious History of Modern France.* Many events before the separation, such as the Aix Affair, had surfaced a preference for separation among some clergy.[113]

Mun's articles often made comparative references. In an article published in *Le Figaro* on March 20, 1905, "An Enterprise Without an Example in Europe," Mun referred to the separation law under deliberation in the French parliament as an exception in Europe, and as fundamentally a rupture with God, not only a rupture with the Catholic Church. After listing what he found as "more civilized" examples of institutional arrangements from other countries more welcoming of a public place for religion than France, he ended the article with an ironic and orientalist tone: "Will it be necessary, in conclusion, to cite to the French the example of the Turks?"[114]

In his article "An Enterprise Without an Example in America," published on March 23, 1905, in *Le Figaro*[115] and spread through many of his other newspaper articles, Mun contested the rampant references to the United States in the chamber in support of the Briand project for law. On February 12, 1905, he wrote in *Le Gaulois*:

Other countries are cited [in the chamber]: America is invoked! This is the decisive argument. Tocqueville wrote sixty years ago, "religion which for the Americans never directly mix with the government of society, should however be considered as the first of their political institutions"; and, yesterday, President Roosevelt said, "The future of our nation depends on the way we combine force with religion." Here it is! The mental state of American democracy. Is it ours?[116]

In another article published in the same newspaper on October 31, 1904, he wrote:

Our official atheism constitutes more and more an exception among peoples. The only nation of the world which is, at the present time, a great organized democracy, offers a totally opposite sight. Last year, the monument of William Shermann [sic] was inaugurated in Washington, one of the most famous generals of the United States Army during the war of secession. After the inspection, opened in front of President

Roosevelt, in the presence of the immense assembly, standing up . . . Doctor Stafford, catholic priest of the Saint-Patrick Church, started the ceremony by an admirable prayer, that here are the first words, "God, all powerful and eternal, Father of all nations, abase your regards on us, deign us blessings."[117]

In his article published in *Le Figaro* on March 23, 1905, he went on to comment:

I showed that in Europe, there was no example of the absolute secularization of the State. So, where will we find it? Is it in America? Among the States of the new world . . . take the United States, the classical land of liberty, the country which the french catholics who are in love with "separation" see in golden dreams. I say "golden dreams," because I believe that in all the good things reported to us about America there is a little bit of illusion, above all, more often an error of point of view. The Catholic Church is yet in formation; it will be necessary in order to pass a definitive judgment on its organization, to still wait for a long time. The burning question of nationalities which clash on this new land, that of immigration which throws in it many foreign elements, that of the blacks which is far from being decided, holds a prominent place, like in the country itself, in the history of the church. It is impossible to make an abstraction and speak of an american catholic movement. Our separatists perhaps forget very often. Without talking much of the other reasons drawn from history and from a variety of races, it is sufficient for my eyes to render vain all analogy between France and the United States.[118]

Mun criticized the argument that the Concordat will be replaced by liberty in his *Le Gaulois* article:

By liberty, it is said. Which liberty? . . . Let's not give in to the deception of words, to the façade of legislative articles. . . . What? These men who have destroyed our congregations, proscribed thousands of men and women, guilty of the only crime of applying the precepts of the Church; they have ruined christian education, expelled God and religion from all institutions, tracked like suspects all who remain faithful: they have accomplished this violence in the name of liberty, and we would believe in what they promise us! To tell the truth, that is to close the eyes to daylight....

The project submitted by Mr. Briand in the name of the Commission and that Mr. Combes has accepted as "an excellent base for discussion" offers the evident proof, especially under the title concerning the policing of cultes, which organizes in fact a putting in place the surveillance of the catholic clergy.[119]

Mun made a pass at right Républicains opportunistes who would at times defend putting religion as a cement of society at the service of the nation-state. Below is a reference to Jules Simon in the same article:

But, is it that, they tell me, that you have fear of the struggle which threatens your religion? Yes. Like Jules Simon said to the socialists of his times, "I have the honor of having fear!" I fear that in the disorganization of parishes under the surveillance of communal delegates, in the middle of inevitable violence which everywhere will put believers to the mercy of sectarians protected by power, I fear that the catholic culte would suffer a horrible trial. With all my forces, I would like to spare her [from this trial].[120]

In his "Le nouvel article 4" of April 25, 1905, in *La Croix*, Mun found the new article 4 insufficient and argued that as long as the civil tribunal was sovereign on the redistribution of church goods and property, the position of the Catholic Church was compromised. He spent quite a bit of time discussing the position on article 4 of Alexandre Ribot (Républicains progressistes) in the chamber, which he found closest to his own—and to ALP—among all the others:

Mr. Ribot posed the burning question, carefully eluded: between two associations, one led by a priest [*curé*] in communion with the bishop, and the other lead by some priest, who will the [civil] tribunal choose? Mr. Briand did not hesitate: It is necessary to recognize his loyalty. He declared that the view of the bishop will be prominent.... The following day, however, he [Mr. Briand] ... came up with a new redaction, adopted ... by the majority of the Commission which attributed the goods of the *fabrique* to associations established "complying with the general rules of organization of the culte."... Then started the battle of three days. Mr. Ribot steered it with an incomparable mastery annoying the adversaries with precise questions, closing all retreats.[121]

Mun sided with Ribot's struggle for having more precision in the law, which for others was a demand compromising the "generality" of law.[122]

Briand Report, March 4, 1905

In its opening remarks, the Briand Report distinguished the material and spiritual power of the Catholic Church, addressed the former, and presented the diversity in beliefs as the crucial reason for separation of churches and state:

> In presenting to you this report, our objective is to prove that the only solution possible for the domestic difficulties that result in France from the present concordataire regime is in a loyal and complete separation of Churches and State. We will juridically show that this regime is the only one which in France, a country where beliefs are diverse, keeps and safeguards the rights of each. . . . It is not . . . for satisfying political grudges, or for hate of Catholicism, that we demand the complete separation of Churches and State, but in order to institute the only regime where peace can be established between followers of *diverse beliefs*.[123]

After long historical accounts, the report summed up:

> However, in the absence of any new regulation, the principles of the 1801 Concordat and the organic articles constituted the base of the relations between the Vatican and the French Government. But the laic power remained incapable of respecting this Concordat, whose only reason of being was to enslave the Church; whereas the obligations of the State toward the clergy were enormous, the clergy remained free of any obligations. There is more; the clergy combatted the spirit that underpinned the Concordat by working toward ruining and replacing the civil authority. (96)

The next section was entitled "Campagne séparatiste" and discussed the separatist movements within the clergy led by ultramontanes like Lamennais, Montalembert, and Lacordaire (97). After a section on the *Syllabus of Errors* and the Doctrine of Infallibility, the report addressed the period 1870–1905. The analysis of this period started with the observation that at the beginning of the Third Republic the state *budget des cultes* was more than the state budget for public education. It also pointed out that the Falloux law had put bishops and archbishops in the High Council of Public Instruction and in the department Council of Public Instruction, who could name or dismiss primary school teachers (126–27). The report pointed out the Ferry laws, mentioned the Law of Associations of 1901 as a prelude to separation, and then underscored the "energy" of Combes (128). After analyzing the *budget des cultes* for Catholic, Protestant, and Jewish cultes, the report took a comparative angle and offered examples from legislation in other countries. It came up with a threefold categorization of countries: theocratic, half-laic, and laic. As we will see later, the exact categorization was also made by scholars and then mobilized in political discussions in Turkey as well.

> Several countries of Europe are still in the first phase, theocratic or quasi-theocratic, in which the State is, if not subordinated to the Church, at least closely united with her; it recognizes the predominance of one religion over all the others and admits that the social institutions conforms to the principles of that religion. Others, much more numerous in Europe, have achieved the second stage, that of half-laïcité; they proclaim and apply more or less completely the principles of liberty of conscience and liberty of cultes, but considering, nevertheless, certain specific [*déterminé*] religions as public institutions that they recognize, protect, and subsidize. Finally, in some European countries and above all in many large American Republics, the third stage of the evolution appears. The state is really neutral and laic, the equality and the independence of cultes are recognized; the Churches are separated from the State. (175–76)

The report went through the most crowded second category of *demi-laïcité* with a particular focus on Great Britain, Ireland, and Switzerland and took a comparative focus on European and American trajectories:

> The regime of separation of Churches and State, weakly and incompletely put into practice in Europe, is, on the contrary, widely adopted in the New World; Canada (where a law of 1854 has secularized certain

ecclesiastical goods and has taken from the Church all official character), the United States, Mexico don't know any other than the regime of separation. One can encounter it [the regime of separation] as well in the young Republic of Cuba, in three republics of Central America, and finally in the more important of the States of South America, United States of Brazil. (201–2)

The report paid particular attention to the United States and focused on its constitution and other legislation:

The principle of laïcité and of neutrality of the State is established in the federal constitution, which decides that no declaration of religious faith can be required as a condition of aptitude to obtain public functions and charges depending on the federal government (article 6) and which prohibits the Congress from making any law to the effect of "establishing" (that is to say recognize officially) a religion or prohibiting its free exercise (same article, amendment 1). These very principles, which at the beginning of the twentieth century were not yet applied in all the United States, are today uniformly declared and put in practice on all the territory of the Republic. Almost all the constitutions of the States declare that no one should be forced to contribute to expenditures of a Church or to yield to its offices; many prohibit any mark of preference with regard to a particular sect. The equality of diverse cultes is also as complete as their liberty. But the neutrality of the State does not include in America either hostility or indifference with regard to religions. It is from the incompetence of the laic power in religious matters and from a deep sentiment of equality that these legislations excluding all official religion stem from. The neutrality of the State is essentially a benevolent neutrality with regard to religions whose utility is very generally recognized. As Minghetti justly observed there is a juridical separation, but a true moral union between the State and Churches, and Mr. Bryce could go as far as saying that "christianity is in fact considered as being, if not the religion legally established, at least a national religion." "The founders of our government and the authors of our constitution have recognized that between the christian religion and a good government there is an intimate connection and that this religion is the most solid foundation of a healthy morality." (202–3)

Finally the report carried on an evaluation of various propositions made to the commission and offered its own proposal for a separation law with a discussion of each article. It presented the Combes proposal for a separation law in full and followed with a commentary. Article 24 of the Combes proposal stated that "Direction des Cultes will continue to function for assuring the execution of the present law." The Combes proposal ceased state salaries for clerics (article 1), suppressed the budget for cultes (article 1), and stipulated that religious buildings would go to associations (article 2) and the new associations could not organize above the departmental level (article 8). There was no explicit mention of freedom of conscience and cultes, except in the title of the largest third section—the proposed law had four sections and twenty-five articles in total—which consisted of ten articles (articles 11–20). This section was entitled "government [*police*] of cultes and guarantee of their free exercise"; however, the emphasis was on the "policing" rather than on "free exercise." The "policing" aspect looked like a clear continuance of the past two years of anticlerical campaigns.[124]

The Briand Report found the Combes proposal for the law in "flagrant disaccord" with the commission proposal. First, the Combes proposal gave much power to the state in settling the question of property and "as a result, had to perpetuate the interference of the State in the administration of ecclesiastical things. And therefore, the project of the government [Combes proposal] saw it necessary to conserve the direction des cultes [while] the Commission considers [the Direction des Cultes] from another point of view [and thinks that it] can be suppressed." The commission differentiated between two kinds of property: "those that have been constructed on State or commune land or purchased by means of subsidies; and those, on the contrary, that have been built on land given by the believers or purchased with their donations and generosity. The first was declared the property of the State or of communes; the second, property of the Churches." Second, the government proposal put stricter measures on settling the pensions of the last group of state-salaried clergy.[125] Third, limiting religious organizations to the level of the departments in France not only interfered in the internal organization of religions but also made it very difficult for Protestants and Jews who were spread through France in small numbers and could not adopt the departmental restrictions. Fourth, in the chapter on governance (*police*) of cultes, there were significantly arbitrary state measures against religious organizations.

Now I turn to the chamber discussions on article 4 and particularly the amendment "en se conformant aux règles d'organisation générale du culte dont elles se proposent d'assurer l'exercice [complying with the general rules of organization of the religion which they propose to ensure the practice]." I have already laid down the ALP position with its internal tensions, and I have started documenting the Socialiste block's position with the Briand Report in contradistinction to the Combes Project for Law. The chamber discussions will complete the charting of the political field by deepening the articulation of these positions, as well as by placing on the political field the Républican progressistes, Union démocratique, Radical-socialistes, and Gauche radicale.

Chamber Discussions on Article 4

The discussions on article 4 in the chamber started on April 20, 1905, with a question of clarification posed by Alexandre Ribot, leader of the Républicains progressistes,[126] Paul Deschanel, Républicains progressistes, and Louis Barthou, Union démocratique. Ribot, an anti-Combiste and even at times a critic of Ferry and Gambetta, had led three governments in the 1890s. The more conservative of the Républicains progressistes had supported the New Spirit of the Méline government, which called for friendlier relations between republicanism and Catholicism later in the same decade.[127] Ribot demanded an explanation on the new amendment to article 4 in the chamber on April 20, 1905:

MR. RIBOT. The first redaction submitted to the Chamber gave the [civil] tribunal a kind of undefined arbitrary power, without legal criterion, for choosing among associations which would present themselves in order to take over establishments which are no longer public. We [I, Mr. Barthou, Union démocratique, and Mr. Deschanel, Républicain progressistes] have directed a criticism against this article . . . we have declared that we did not want to interfere in the interior organization of each culte, that we were obliged to take as the internal organization of each culte, what each culte's authorized representatives design for themselves, take like a fact which we do not mean to guarantee, or impose, but like a fact we respect, because it is an expression of religious liberty. We said that this was an American doctrine and practice and that it should be, in a regime of loyal and sincere separation, the practice we were all obliged to join. . . . We said that, like in America, we are obliged to let the catholics themselves take care of tracing the rules of their organization, we added that we could not, either directly or in a roundabout way . . . impose upon them a different organization . . . without violating their liberty (*Very good! very good! center and right. Interruptions from extreme left*) . . . The catholic culte rests everywhere in the world on the authority of bishops (*Various movements*). . . . It is a fact. I do not assess or see myself as the judge of the hierarchy and organization of catholics. I do not have the pretention or the right . . . the authority of bishops does not exert itself only on questions of doctrine . . . but also on questions of temporal organization, in this sense like all associations, all the commissions of administrators of Church goods, goods destined for the culte must be subject to the authority of the bishop. . . . Such is the fact on which we are obliged to agree.

MR. LEVRAUD AND MANY OF HIS COLLEAGUES IN THE EXTREME LEFT. But no!

MR. RIBOT. If the commission thinks, indeed, that one cannot make the devolution of goods, and that one cannot hand over the churches only to those associations which will be in communion with bishops, submitted to episcopal authority and created by it, I demand from the rapporteur to give an explanation. . . . According to me, the redaction submitted to us is evidently preferable to the present, to the precedents. I simply demand from the rapporteur to tell us . . . what precise meaning he attaches to the formula adopted by the commission. (*Lively applause at the center and various benches.*)[128]

Aristide Briand's (Socialiste parlementaire) response came from a fundamental angle of how to settle the question of religion in law, which required a general frame rather than a particular mention of specific religions. According to Briand, statements treating France as a Catholic-majority country missed the diversity of religious establishments. Briand underscored that he and a majority of colleagues in the commission considered the original wording of article 4 sufficient:

MR. ARISTIDE BRIAND, RAPPORTEUR. I hurry to declare that there is nothing in this modification which would be in contradiction or simply in disaccord with the spirit in which article 4 has been conceived and drafted in its first text. . . . We would not want that someone, tomorrow, be able to accuse us to have set up a trap under the feet of the Church through one of the provisions of the law. . . . Our first duty, as legislators, at the moment where we are called to regulate the fate of these Churches [catholic—apostolic and roman, Israelite, and protestant] in the spirit of neutrality which we conceive the reform, is to abstain from doing anything detrimental to the free constitution of these churches. . . . The patrimony of the Catholic Church is the property of the religious collectivity constituted for assuring the exercise and upkeep of this culte. Or it is a specific [*déterminé*] culte . . .

MR. LE BARON AMÉDÉE REILLE [RÉPUBLICAINS PROGRESSISTES]. It is that.

MR. LE RAPPORTEUR. . . . which we know today by its particular organization and which we do not have the right to paralyze by an interpretation very strict and rigorous. . . . We record a state of things and we make the devolution of goods according to that record. . . . We are told: in granting this right of competition to the catholics, you are going to create disorder, you will give some kind of incentive to agitation and to schism.[129]

After stressing that this is not the interpretation he and many of his colleagues in the commission shared, he articulated an argument fundamentally based on the distinction between particular cases and general laws:

MR. LE RAPPORTEUR. We have not wanted to design the rules too strictly and too precisely for the judges, because we do not only have in mind the case of schism which has preoccupied especially the defenders of the Church. We thought that tomorrow the legislator will find himself in the presence of infinite cases, extremely varied, which will not only be based on a different interpretation of *cultuelle* organization but can be the result of local conditions, and we estimated, in one matter, that the judge is called upon in fact to deliver his verdict, that is to say, assess with good sense and fairness, the most dangerous would be to want to design for him the rules of application too rigorously for cases which can be very varied. (1607)

. . . Sirs, it would be childish to believe that the promulgation of the separation law will lead to a complete disruption of the ecclesiastic organization. It is the public establishment of culte, that is to say, an ecclesiastic organ that makes the transmission of goods; it is it, in reality, which is going to form the first association. It is more than probable, it is certain, that the associations will be composed, if not in totality, at least in their major part, of members which constitute, at the present time, the public establishments of culte. (1608)

According to Briand, more precision in the law would actually interfere in the internal matters of the Catholic religion:

MR. LE RAPPORTEUR. What will the Catholic Church do at the moment that it will constitute these associations? It will give them a formula, a statute, which will be uniform in entire France. You must expect that tomorrow, catholic associations constitute themselves for maintaining and practicing the catholic religion, apostolic and roman in accordance with rules and prescriptions of this Church. And these rules will be specified. In case of juridical trial, these statutes will be evidently the principal element of assessing for the tribunal. It was therefore useless, I maintain, to modify the text. If we have done so, it is only to clear the misunderstandings. But it is necessary to guard against pushing things too far. In demanding from us more precision again, one would risk leading an attack on the liberty of the catholic community [*collectivité*]. We want, we, that in a regime of separation this community [*communauté*] could evolve freely. And also, without separating itself from its general organization. (1608)

Briand clearly differentiated between institutions and individual rights, and between giving guarantees to the institution and interfering in its internal matters. For him, the *Républicains progressistes* were asking for interference in the church's domestic matters in favor of the hierarchy:

MR. LE RAPPORTEUR. If the community of fidels as a whole can, thanks to the liberties which we will leave to it, exercise a certain pressure on the ecclesiastical hierarchy . . . do we have to make an obstacle to that possibility? (*Very good! very good!*) (1608)

Briand underscored that the question of schism and its relation to separation of churches and state was much more complicated:

MR. LE RAPPORTEUR. On this point of view, do not be mistaken, the great danger for the Catholic Church is not in our articles 4 and 6 combined, it is in the gift that we give her in leaving to the Holy See the care of naming the bishops itself. There it is, the true danger of schism for the Catholic Church. (*Very good! very good! to the left.*) That is what could lead all the french catholics with their priests to formulate demands to Rome. But we do not have to, I repeat it, impose on the Catholic Church a new organization: we simply have to keep account of the state of current things, that we record, which to us is impossible to be unaware of, that will result from this organization. As for those of our colleagues who would like to talk us into narrower precisions one more time, I repeat to them that they [further precisions] will not be without danger. . . . In effect, a French bishop, at the present time, by the organization of the Concordat, borrows the stability of his post from the guarantee of the State. This guarantee he will lack tomorrow. It may occur that following the promulgation of the law, the pope having alone the right of nomination, fifteen, twenty, thirty bishops be sent from Rome for replacing the current concordatory bishops. Which direction would you have given to the judge in the presence of a conflict of this nature? You see clearly that it is impossible to inscribe in the law a precision of this nature. (*Various movements.*) (1608)

Ribot spoke after Briand, repeated the comparison with the United States and his and his friends' point of taking church as a fact "that we respect, because it is the expression of religious liberty," and still kept on the line of argument for more precision:

MR. RIBOT. The catholic culte, there are the priests in communion with the bishop and the believers communed with the priest, attached themselves to the bishop and after to the pope; it is this, the organization,—It will be necessary, I say, that the association, for obtaining this devolution and the use of the church, show in case of contestation, that she has in effect a priest, as Mr. rapporteur said, and I add after him, a priest in communion with his bishop. (*Vivid applause at the center and right.*) And if this priest is in communion with his bishop, he is also in communion with the pope; because it is the Catholic Church. . . . This is what we want not to guarantee, but respect in its liberty. I thank Mr. rapporteur for his explications. (1608)

Mr. Vazeille (Radical-socialiste) contested the positions of both Ribot and Briand on the particular question of the relation among individuals, religious institutions, and state institutions and also contested Ribot's reference to the United States:

MR. VAZEILLE. For me, I estimate that it is the catholic citizens, that it is the collectivity of catholic individuals grouped in association who have the right to this patrimony; it is not such and such bishop sent by Rome. . . . The example of America has been cited; I would not know that in America, it would be the catholic bishops who arrange absolutely the goods of the community! . . . I insist quickly on this point: you talk to us today of *cultuel* associations which will exist tomorrow; but, after the project of law you have proposed us, these associations can reduce themselves to seven persons who can in their communes constitute a small catholic aristocracy, closed clique who will have absolutely and indefinitely at their disposal the patrimony that you give them. There it is, therefore, what I do not want in virtue of the principles which govern the modern State: . . . all catholic citizens, all who will adhere to the status of catholic, would have the use of the catholic ecclesiastical patrimony; that is, if one day these citizens would come to a break with the catholic Church, this patrimony, locally constituted, in a certain sense communal, administered presently by the *fabriques*, . . . rest in the disposal of the local collectivity for determining the [religious] works. (1609)

Charles Dumont (Gauche radicale) asked Briand, as the spokesperson of the commission, who would judge the "en se conformant aux règles d'organisation générale du culte dont elles se proposent d'assurer l'exercice," and Briand answered that the "civil courts" would judge (1609). Then Dumont gave an example of a city where *conseil de fabrique*[130] consisted of *hobereaux* (petty aristocracy) and where the priests were democratic and republican. When the issue of education came up in the parliament, the priests refused to obey the *hobereaux* who asked the priests to resist, and the bishop sent a warning to priests calling them to obedience upon the complaint of the *conseil de fabrique* and protested against a law detrimental to the right of the church to educate children. The priests did not obey and the bishop retaliated (1609–10). Dumont asked how the civil tribunal would judge this situation. "The tribunal was free with the old text. I doubt that it will still be with the new" (1610).

Briand underlined that the priest would be like any other citizen in front of the justice system after the separation law and that, in other words, if the state was sovereign, then the criticism of the role of civil courts with respect to articles 4 and 6 applied to the whole logic of the separation law:

MR. LE RAPPORTEUR. The new competence attributed to the civil courts . . . it is said, to become the judges of orthodoxy and assess canonical rules, disturbs profoundly a lot of our colleagues. But this competence will not only result from article 4 and from article 6; it will be the very consequence of the separation law. (*Interruptions from various benches.*)

MR. JAURÈS. It is obvious.

MR. LE RAPPORTEUR. Do you want an example? Take a priest in the regime of separation. He has been dismissed by his bishops and deprived of his salaries. Like any other discharged employee, he will have the ability to formulate his complaints in front of the civil courts on the grounds of the rupture of his work contract if he believes to have the right to a compensation. . . . These things happen in other countries as well. . . . Tomorrow, for a french judge, the ecclesiastic pleading against his bishop will not be a priest coming under special jurisdiction for his case because of his concordatory office; he will be a pleader like any other, having right to the same justice. (*Exclamations in various benches.—Various movements.*) . . . The priest will have the right of asserting his interests even against a bishop in front of civil justice. I do not say that the judge will find him right all the time, but he will be obliged to offer him justice in cases where inevitably today he has to declare himself incompetent.

TO LEFT. Evidently! (1610)

Briand underlined that the civil courts did not have to say beforehand what criteria or elements they would base their judgment on in settling the conflict between the priest and the religious organization. Ribot repeated Dumont's question, stating that Briand missed the object of the question, and insisted on a clear answer as to what would happen if a priest split with the bishops: could he take church goods under another association or not?

Ribot turned the discussion to one of abuse of religion and responded that if the bishop was abusing power, canonical law was called to judge the situation, that one could not substitute canonical law with the civil tribunal:

MR. RIBOT. If the bishop abuses his power, there is a procedure established by canonical law. I accept perfectly if the civil authority leaves time to the priest to exhaust the degrees of canonical jurisdiction; but you do not have the idea, I think, of substituting the civil courts for ecclesiastical jurisdiction.

MR. LE RAPPORTEUR. But No! I did not say such a thing. (1610)

MR. RIBOT. Consequently, it will be necessary to wait for the ecclesiastical authority to pronounce [its verdict]. The day when ecclesiastical authority, the spiritual power will have decided that the priest is removed from the Catholic communion . . . that day . . . the goods have to rest with believers grouped around the new priest designated by the bishop (*Applause at the center and various benches.*) (1610).

MR. LE RAPPORTEUR. But, sirs, I have said nothing contrary to this interpretation (*Applause at the center, at the right and from various benches to the left.*) I simply wanted to show to my colleague, Mr. Dumont, that things do not happen all the time as in the example he gave. It will not suffice that a bishop strikes without reason a priest, or for a reason unrelated to the culte, for the association grouped around that priest to find itself by that fact deprived of all right of asserting its interests before our courts. And I say again that, in a certain measure, the civil court, among the assessments of facts which can determine the case, can consider ecclesiastical rules. (*Exclamations and noise at the center and right.*)

VARIOUS MEMBERS FROM RIGHT. This is inadmissible.

MR. LE RAPPORTEUR. Sirs, you accept that tomorrow, for the devolution of goods, the judge would keep track of the general organization of culte, and when the interpretation of these rules can turn against the bishop, to the benefit of the priest, you don't accept it anymore! (1610–11)

Briand concluded by pointing out that the law can judge against the bishop and for the priest. In other words, he underlined that the question is not the actual consequence but the procedure. The next comment came from Fernand de Ramel (Droites) and again addressed the same question of indeterminacy of outcomes and stated that there was too much leeway for interpretation. Barthou (Union démocratique) took the floor and stated that he was in agreement with the commission for substituting judiciary authority for administrative authority—State Council or prefects: "I stay loyal to this opinion, a supporter like Mr. le rapporteur [Briand], of a separation loyal and liberal, I prefer to refer to the authority which will raise less protestations and less suspicion." Barthou stated that, to him and his friends, it was not clear what will guide the civil courts, but that he "will vote for the new text in the interest of the grand reform to which the republican majority is attached (*Applause from various benches at the center, at the left and extreme left*)" (1611–12).

There were also criticisms from other angles. Hubbart (Radical-socialiste) started by stating that "the concession snatched from the commission in this moment appears to me excessive and contrary to liberty." He challenged Briand's statement that free thinkers would easily accept this amendment:

MR. HUBBART. What does the commission do in introducing in the law the rules for the general organization of culte, to serve the rule and to guide the judge? It created a presumption against liberty of the functioning of the *cultuelle* associations. . . . It prejudges, in introducing the dogma and the religion in the law, the decisions that the tribunal has to pronounce only in reference to a jurisdiction and to the laic and civil laws. (1612)

Jean Bepmale (Radical-socialiste) also stated that "by this disposition inserted in article 4 the commission officially and legally recognizes the catholic hierarchy (*Various movements*)," and "by this text, you put secular arms at the service of canonical jurisdiction, at the service of the bishop," "you reestablish the definitive supremacy of the roman hierarchy on all believers," and that the addition would create conflict between different associations over who represented the true religion. Bepmale and others also pointed out that this amendment contradicted the nonrecognition principle in the first article (1613). Dumont (Gauche radicale) also exclaimed that "the recognition of the internal and general organization of the catholic culte" was being introduced into the law, and Briand exclaimed, "That is inexact!" (1614).

Georges Leygues (Union démocratique) and his friends from Union démocratique and Gauche radicale presented an amendment that mobilized the prefects in bringing more determinacy to the devolution of ecclesiastical goods. Leygues took the floor and before getting to the details of the amendment expressed the general view of those who signed the amendment:

MR. GEORGES LEYGUES. I heard preceding orators say that if the separation of Churches and State has become inevitable, it is the fault of the government. I do not share this opinion. . . . The separation is incontestably the end of the laic evolution. . . . But it is necessary to accomplish this work without offending the consciences, without troubling the traditional habits that are respectable and which at times are as strong as beliefs. Yet, our country has in its past fifteen centuries of catholicism, and out of thirty-eight million inhabitants there are around thirty-seven million catholics. (*Various movements to the left.*) . . . The Church and State will be separated. But, you sense well that even separated, they won't be able to ignore each other. The Catholic Church occupies in our country too big and too strong a position to be held a negligible quantity. . . . The inhabitants of these [rural] communes demand three things: to keep their church and priest . . . after the separation, not to pay more than they currently pay for the culte.... Finally they want that the edifices of culte by no means become a charge for the communal budget.

MR. LEVRAUD [RADICAL-SOCIALISTE]. They don't have much religion!

MR. GEORGES LEYGUES. They say: "Pay the minister of culte more, if you want but surveil him." And we respond to them: "The priest will no longer be surveilled, but it is you who will pay him!"[131]

Leygues set the problem as a reconciliation of expectations of the rural communities and the proposals for law. He pointed out that rural communities lack basic needs and therefore would not be able to pay for the church, the churches would close, rich communes would dominate poor communes in offering church services, and conditions would emerge for the flourishing of the old congregations. Another result of the proposed law, Leygues underlined, is that it touches the lower clergy more than the upper clergy. Yet another danger he addressed was the creation of *associations cultuelles*. Leygues found such pluralism a risk to public order, because it raised many questions such as how the associations would function, who would lead them, and how they would gather members. When the state lets go control of clerical appointments, members of ancient congregations and strangers (non-French) could move into clerical posts. Leygues insisted that the separation would open the way for Catholic mobilization and allow them "to constitute a true State within the State." He remarked:

MR. GEORGES LEYGUES. You demand from us to suppress the Concordat, because it does not offer sufficient guarantees. Yes, I want this like you do. But you replace it by a regime which from the republican point of view, from the point of view of the laic State, from the point of view of the independence of the lower clergy, and from the point of view of the authority of the princes of the Church, would be a hundred times more dangerous than the present regime.

MR. RIBOT. Then, keep the Concordat.... You are, Mr. Leygues, a little bit of a lukewarm separatist.

MR. GEORGES LEYGUES. Mr. Ribot, I am a separatist. (1628)

Leygues listed the contributions of his amendment. The state administrators would designate the new associations that would become the new owner of the ecclesiastical goods. The commission proposal would suppress the *budget des cultes* without any benefits to the taxpayer, the Leygues amendment would return to "each commune under tax relief the whole sum that the state paid in that commune for the exercise of the culte" (1629).

Jean Jaurès responded to Leygues's speech and the amendment, suggesting that it looked like a friendly critique of separation, but it was actually a defense of the Concordat:

MR. JAURÈS. You have, however, ignored, Mister Leygues, a part of the traits which at the present time, constitutes the features of the republican peasant of France. He is not as incapable of movement in the mind, of intellectual experience and of political education which you seem to imagine. (*Applause extreme left and left.*) He has beliefs ten times *séculaire*, he has practices ten times *séculaire*, but he also has, for several centuries, the experience of the support the organized Church has lent to the forces of conservation and reaction against him. . . . He has, especially since the Revolution, the experience of the permanent effort of the Church in the commune which he knows well, as well as in the State, which he guesses, for making obstacles to the institutions of liberty, Republic and democracy. (1629–30)

Jaurès underlined that if *associations cultuelles* were not formed by liberty but by administrative and governmental acts as the Leygues amendment asked for, a "State Church" would be the result: "you suppressed the Concordat between the pope and the emperor only to establish the Concordat between *les marguilliers*[132] and the advisors of the prefectures (*Applause and laughs from extreme left and various benches*)" (1630). Jaurès continued, pointing out that the amendment suggested for article 4 did not change its "original and essential sense,"

MR. JAURÈS. And that is why in the law, instead of simply speaking of associations, you speak of *associations cultuelles*; that is why you preoccupy yourself with the conditions in which now the exercise of culte will continue. But which culte? It is not of any culte. (*Very good! very good! From extreme left and various benches center and right.*) It is for the associations which are going to create themselves in all liberty by the devolution of patrimonies, without putting their roots in the past, it is the possibility of unlimited new cultes diversified to infinity. But for the cultes opportunely which a regime of transaction is instituted, it is almost a naivety, it is a truism to say that of existing cultes, defined by their very existence and by the conditions of their existence . . .

Therefore, sirs, by the mere fact that instead of planting your new regime on virgin soil, you plant it on earth where the roots of old cultes subsist and by the mere fact that you keep account in your law of the transition of *cultuelle* existences organized today, you take account evidently of the very existence of these organizations. If it is so, and if the new text brought by the commission had no other effect in specifying, in making appear in plain light that which was the sense at least implied, and in my point of view, already very clear in the project of the commission, than that of clearing in the mind of catholic representatives and in the mind of the catholic country itself those erroneous mistrusts . . .

MR. HUBBARD. That is it! Make their separation, to them, till the end!

MR. JAURÈS. I told you that according to me, the addition of the commission does not modify the essential and profound meaning of the project that you would accept. (1637–38)

Jaurès addressed the criticism that giving a say to the civil tribunal would be "to enter in the dogma and discipline of each Church, and it will be canonical right that would serve as a rule of functioning for the civil justice, for laic justice!" And some critics have remarked that "it will be a return to the Middle Ages!" Here Jaurès turned to a comparison with the United States and a claim to the modern:

MR. JAURÈS. It will be the most modern practice since it will be the natural practice of countries which have realized the great modern reform, that is to say, the separation of Churches and State. If there is one country which cannot be suspect of retreating through its roots back to the Middle Ages . . . it is called the United States. (*Very good! very good!*) Eh fine! Under which form has the United States constituted, regulated the functioning of *cultuelle* associations for all cultes? . . . Civil justice. (*Applause to the left and center.*) (1638)

Jaurès underlined that nobody has a right to bother the liberty of small clergy, laic Catholics who might want to set their own route:

MR. JAURÈS. You forget, some of our colleagues, haunted by the surviving phantom of the Concordat, forget precisely the inevitable and natural effects that in all loyalty, without artificial intervention on our part, the regime of separation is going to produce. Today, the vast Church of outside, the vast Church of believers, have no way to appeal against the catholic hierarchy, against episcopal authority; the Church can live today with the Concordat [concordatairement] without the believers grouped around her—and there is the same incredible paradox in the Concordat that the Church could survive today artificially with the *budget des cultes* even apart from believers. (1639)

Jaurès went over the incomes of churches independent of the *budget des cultes* and made the point that they had quite a bit of income in addition to the *budget des cultes*. Jaurès pointed out that the Concordat created a church independent of its believers and that in the new regime, the church had to depend on its believers more. This dependence on the public was generally *the* check on regime's actions:

MR. JAURÈS. It is there, sirs, that is the break; it is there that the guarantee lies, not the deceitful, oblique, hypocritical guarantee but a fundamental guarantee, stemming from the very conditions of existence of our nation and from the very functioning of the new regime of liberty we are going to institute. (1639)

Jaurès argued that if priests come forth who want to modernize and democratize Catholicism, for instance, "make a critique of the traditional exegesis," a priest who is not schismatic but the bishop wants to oppose for intellectual reasons and for reasons of political order, and a priest, who is held in respect by his *associations cultuelles*, the hierarchy will not be able to interfere with them. "And if—it is that, republicans, the guarantee of the judgment of civil courts that you appear to fear—if the bishop wants to deprive one of these *associations cultuelles* under the pretext that by their attachment to a priest who displeases a bishop, that association moves outside the catholic organization, then the bishop will be obliged to provide evidence." He continued: "And at that moment, I hear well! There are republicans who tell me: Here is the danger; civil law is going to sanction the rigor of the bishop. Yes, sirs; but through how many difficulties and obstacles!" He counts all the events and procedures that would have to pass by for a civil court to act against a bishop (1640).

A member of Gauche radicale who had not signed but supported the amendment, Joseph Noulens, then took the floor. He addressed what he found to be the two vantage points of the discussion: that of public utility and that of the interest of the collectivity of believers. He defended a legal constraint of public utility on the use of the ecclesiastical goods that passed to *associations cultuelles*. And he continued:

MR. NOULENS. We are told: . . . by granting the status of public utility to these associations, you maintain, between them and the State a bond which is incompatible with the separation of Churches and State. We can for a start respond . . . that there are number of associations which have nothing common with the State and which yet obtain each day the status of public utility . . . societies of artists, writers, gymnastics. . . . However, if the associations [*cultuelles*] which will be formed after the application of the law on the designation of the representatives of public establishments lose the character of public utility, the day when these associations, demeaned or having died, it will be necessary to allocate these [ecclesiastical] goods to a new association, we then consider that the decree issued by the State Council . . . will intervene to confer the character of public utility to these associations. We come back then to the application of the principles of our public law and the article 10 [article putting a limit of public utility on associations] of the 1901 law for the recognition of the character of public utility for the association. (*Very good! very good! on various benches to left.*) (1643)

Noulens stressed in conclusion that "every time the associations will want to make alienations [of goods], a prefectoral order will be required" (1643). Then he continued on the second issue of the interest of the collectivity of believers: civil courts were given a right that they should not have. They would be often left in a situation to judge between competing claims, and such power of judgment "can only belong to a discretionary power, that is to say to the government" (1644). Noulens related his point on discretionary power to the amendment:

MR. NOULENS. We conferred this [power of] attribution [of new rights to an association] to the Government, yet framing this exercise of discretionary power with guarantees, in particular making the State Council intervene. . . . In depositing this amendment . . . we believed that the State could not be disinterested in the surveillance and control of goods which still belongs to public establishment of culte and besides, in respect of religious convictions of the population which we represent, we have been worried about the conservation of patrimony which belongs foremost to the collectivity of believers and which, in case of the disappearance of the *association cultuelles*, should return to the communal collectivity. This is what has been our preoccupation which, while giving the full liberty of culte to persons, subjects the goods to surveillance. (1644)

Briand took the floor. He pointed out that the specification in the amendment for the dissolution of cultes put as a criterion of "sufficient guarantees of the continuation of the same culte" and "grave irregularities and disorders" (1645). He underlined that in order to judge these you also needed a court. An administrative tribunal, which would issue from delegating the power to the government rather than the courts, was totally imprecise and an oxymoron. This amendment would put us, Briand argued, back to a new Concordat, because it was unstable and would just keep growing fast until it stabilized in a new concordatory regime:

MR. LE RAPPORTEUR. If some among you, who really fear the usage the Church can make of this liberty; if they believe firmly that she will become too formidable that the very existence of the Republic can be compromised, then I say to them: your duty is not to vote for separation. (*Lively applause from a large number of benches.*) . . . For us republicans, the separation, it is the disappearance of the official religion, it is the Republic returned to the sentiment of its dignity and to the respect of its fundamental principles. They command it to take again its liberty, but they do not demand that it be with a gesture of persecution. It is necessary that the separation marks also for the Church a moment of liberty wider and more complete. (1645)

Briand counted all institutional elements as constitutive of the moment of separation and emphasized that all other considerations are of secondary importance:

MR. LE RAPPORTEUR. For me the separation is, all in all, in the denunciation of the Concordat, the suppression of the *budget des cultes*, the disappearance of the official character that is invested today in the Church and its ministers, and which constitutes the best of their prestige and force. Such are the preoccupations which must especially direct you at the time of the vote. . . . The republican country has common sense; it also has fairness; it will not demand from you to make a law of persecution or cunning against the Church. The free thinkers do not desire that either. (*Applause to extreme left*.) What they simply want is that you snatch from the Church the official shield behind which she can shelter against the efforts of free thinkers; what they only have the right to demand is that the State put them face to face with the Church for fighting with equal arms . . . for being able to oppose finally in a fair combat the force of reason to brutalities of dogma (1646).

Joseph Caillaux (Union démocratique) took the floor, defended the amendment, and criticized the commission's version of article 4 for benefiting the Catholic Church. He gave the example of a liberal priest (Loisy) whose book has been banned by the papacy. In these cases the priests would lose the right to claim ecclesiastical property if the rule of conforming to the general rule of culte was imposed and a minority in that region who was in agreement with the bishop would inherit the goods instead of the community of believers. He criticized the commission for individualizing collective goods (1647–48).

Jean-Baptiste Bienvenu-Martin, minister of public instruction and liberal arts and cultes, took the floor. He stressed that the government was in agreement with the commission proposal on article 4. He found the amendment neither complete nor liberal; "they [the defenders of this amendment] accept it [separation] not to separate from the majority which prepares itself to vote, but they try to retain as much as they can from the concordataire regime." Charles Bos (Radical-socialiste) responded to Bienvenu-Martin's criticism that the amendment of Union démocratique and the radical left was trying to preserve as much as possible from the Concordat: "It would suffice that the Union démocratique would not vote in order that the law would hit the ground! Therefore, you cannot say that!" (1649). And on the question of the role of civil courts as opposed to administration, the minister remarked:

MR. LE MINISTER [BIENVENU-MARTIN]. When a lawsuit is raised in the civil court and that its solution implicates that it is an administrative question, the court sends back this prejudicial question before the administrative judge who settles it; the civil judge decides afterward. Why in such a case, the administrative judge must decide before the civil judge? Because it [such a case] finds itself in the presence of two powers; each in the limit of its jurisdiction has a capacity for saying its word in the affair. When the separation is pronounced, there will be for deciding on the disagreement between *associations cultuelles* only one competent authority, there will only be one judge: the civil court. (1650).

Ribot repeated his point that "it has to be in agreement with the bishop because in our country the bishop is the authorized representative of the catholic culte" (1650), and if the civil tribunal was not going to follow this rule, then he would not vote for the law or advocate that his friends vote for it.

On the final day of discussion, April 22, 1905, Leygues evaluated the responses in the previous meeting of Minister Bienvenu-Martin and expressed that he understood both the minister and Briand, as the head of the commission, saying that the view of the bishop was *not the sole but one of the elements* of judgment for the civil court. Leygues and his friends pulled back the amendment, and Leygues underlined that this was the difference—*not the sole but one of the elements*—that marked the line between left and right in the chamber.[133] In the rest of the session many amendments were evaluated. Maurice Allard (Socialiste parlementaire) pointed out that the problem seen in the new version of article 4 was already there in the first text and started precisely in the limitation of the devolution of goods only to *associations cultuelles*, and this limitation was the first door opened for making the authority of the bishop part of the discussion. Allard defended that the goods should be liquidated to any association. His amendment was refused by a vote of 123 to 453 (1662). The next amendment, the Levraud amendment, asked for all the goods to go to the state. Léonce Levraud (Radical-socialiste) argued that this was the only way of the state not taking a positive role in giving direction to religion, that riches were not necessary for religion, and the amount of property in question was significant. The Levraud amendment was rejected by a vote of 102 to 472 (1662–64).

Briand pointed out that the commission was always being asked to clarify its position, and it had; he asked Eugène Réveillaud (Gauche radicale), who had criticized the new article 4 for making ecclesiastical law penetrate state law, to clarify how he thought the attribution should be done, particularly in case of competing claims. Réveillaud answered:

MR. RÉVEILLAUD. My response is easy. . . . I consider—it is according to me a question of fairness—that the goods belonging to the collectivity of believers should in good justice be divided between the two competing associations, if they are two, in proportion to the number of believers [*fidèles*] belonging to each. (*Exclamations to center and extreme left.*)

MR. JAURÈS. Believers of what?
MR. EUGÈNE RÉVEILLAUD. I repeat, you yourself have expected that contestations over goods can emerge, since you have made the courts judges of these disputes. (1670)

The session closed with two separate amendments suggesting the suppression of the new addition to Article 4, both voted together and rejected by 200 to 374 votes. And finally Article 4 was adopted by 509 to 44 votes (1681).[134]

This close look at the two major constitutive moments of the current French institutions of laïcité in the Third French Republic displays "neutrality," "diversity," the "law of majorities," the relation between "religion" and "morality," "generality" of laws, and religion as a "general" or "particular" category as the key concepts and distinctions for mapping part of the political field of struggle over institutions. The distinct routes of arguments created by political actors from this set of concepts challenge some of the common conceptual relations and distinctions erected in the contemporary literature on secularism and religion, but, more significantly, they do not necessarily display an isomorphic relation with institutional preferences, therefore posing a challenge to the current hermeneutical turns in the literature attributing a sovereignty to "ideas" in accounting for institutional outcomes as well.

The current questions on secularism and religion are dominated by an analytical distinction between secularism as neutrality versus the challenges of diversity. The Third Republic discussions clearly show that diversity was a premise presented in defense of institutional neutrality. Furthermore, the current critiques of neutrality often directly state or suggest its ontological failure for grounding state institutions; however, the firmest critics of neutrality in the Third Republic, the political Catholics and monarchists, in fact, conceptualize neutrality in a similar way as the republican proponents of neutrality, although they simply do not institutionally endorse it. The most common axis of struggle emerging from the deliberations is between the premise of diversity and the law of majorities, religion as a general category and as designation of particular faiths, or general institutions as ends in themselves and as means to particular ways of life.

Concepts, distinctions, and the precise arguments built with them are part of the political field, at least because the political ends of actors are better located in these arguments rather than in general ideologies they advocate or surface-level public statements they make, or institutions they prefer. This is especially true if their arguments are collected from various primary sources on concrete issues. However, political ends gathered from precise political arguments are only *part* of the political field because they do not always have an isomorphic relation with institutional preferences. Three political ends stand out in the making of the *Loi du 28 Mars 1882 sur l'enseignement primaire obligatoire* and *Loi du 9 Décembre 1905 concernant la séparation des Églises et de l'État*: demobilizing religion, mobilizing religion, and state neutrality toward religion.

During the chamber deliberations of the *Loi du 28 Mars 1882*, those who were pursuing the political end of mobilizing religion were the monarchists and a small number of the governing republicans (Républicains opportunistes). The monarchists wanted to mobilize Catholicism at the regime level in all spheres of life, stressing the law of majorities, while some of the Républicains opportunistes conceptualized religion as a general category abstracting from particular faiths and wanted to mobilize it not at the regime but at the policy level as a supplementary cement of society in order to maintain an obedient youth, especially in the face of socialism. During the chamber deliberations of the *Loi du 9 Décembre 1905*, Action libérale populaire was for mobilizing the Catholic faith; however, there were at times internal debates on whether institutional separation or maintaining the Concordat would serve that end. Républicains progressistes, the largest political group who voted against the separation law, shared with ALP the position that the Catholic Church is *the* representative of the conscience of Catholic individuals. They were not mobilizing the Catholic faith as directly as ALP leader Mun, who explicitly dismissed institutional neutrality, argued from the "law of majorities," and took religion as the "gendarme of the soul"; however, like the ALP, Républicains progressistes were not supporting a distinction between religious institution and individual conscience. They were not arguing against institutional neutrality, but they were not arguing from it either. Worried about the demobilization of the Catholic Church, they were pushing for a precise reference to Catholicism in the law. All these groups were partaking in what I have termed state-civil religionism. Those who were pursuing the political end of demobilizing religion were among the Opportunistes and the groups to the left of the Opportunistes in the chamber in the 1880s, and among the Radical-socialistes and Gauche radicale in 1905. Again, there was no isomorphic relation between this political end and institutional preferences. In the 1880s some in the left of the chamber found abolishment of the Concordat as serving this end, while many Opportunistes called for separation before the coming of the Third Republic in 1871. In the 1880s they saw the Concordat as demobilizing religion and worried that institutional separation would empower the Catholic Church. During the chamber deliberations of *Loi du 9 Décembre 1905*, a majority among the Radical-socialistes and Gauche radicale defended the distinction between religious institution and individual conscience and saw the reflection of this distinction in the law as the key for a separation that would demobilize the Catholic Church. Union démocratique was the key group expressing this doubt whether institutional separation would empower the church. The unsuccessful Union démocratique and Gauche radicale proposal for an amendment (Leygues amendment) to make sure that separation disempowered the Catholic Church shared with the Républicains progressistes the call for *precision* in the law. While the former were asking for such precision to disempower the church, the latter were asking for it not to disempower the church; both positions, from the perspective of the Socialistes parlementaires who successfully gathered a majority for the law, were calling for a recognition of the Catholic Church in the law, violating neutrality and generality.

Both the Socialistes parlementaires in 1905 as well as the Opportunistes and the left defending the 1882 education law were not defending their institutional preferences for or against the political ends of demobilizing or mobilizing religion but instead were speaking from the principles of neutrality and diversity. In other words, comparatively speaking, they treated institutions as ends in themselves. Especially in 1905, it was only through such a position of liberal institutionalism, law as defining general and neutral institutions of society and embodying uncertainty vis-à-vis concrete political outcomes of conflicts emerging under the general institutional framework defined by law, that they were able to push toward the gathering of a majority for the 1905 separation law.

The reality of this political field itself points out the insufficiency of sociological and ideational accounts of institutional separation in the Third Republic. Furthermore, during the deliberation in 1905, the various interpretations of the case of the United States of America were a significant element of the battleground and gave this ground a comparative dimension. I will explore the significance of this comparative dimension for the theoretical discussions on multiple modernities in the conclusion.

CHAPTER IV

The Politics of *Laïcité Positive* and Diversity in Contemporary France

A scarved girl losing the right to her high school diploma just a year to graduation, teachers going on strike against her, school officials considering the advice of a mosque on the controversy, the political right against the scarved girl in school but for building mosques, Muslim organizations, and Muslim high schools; the political left against her but for teaching religious facts as "culture," as "heritage" in public schools; a Turkish civil society organization in France for a ban on scarves in schools; bishops and rabbis defending the girl, while Al-Azhar University, Le Conseil Français du Culte Musulman (CFCM), and Union des Organisations Islamiques de France (UOIF) approve a ban; classroom presence of a scarved girl and the appearance of her scarf on her national identity card photo (*Carte nationale d'identité*, CNI) treated as the same matter; girls expelled along with the scarf and the photo; a "scientific" commission replacing public discussion; national law for case-by-case decisions (*affaire d'espèce*); ministries and high councils instead of school councils; democratic European states that faced fascism and the Catholic Church unable to face a scarved girl; and a small group of leftists standing in her defense against this farce with the weight of laïcité's history on their side stigmatized as "Islamist" and "multiculturalist." What are we to make of this public discussion, which for a topic of a general matter chooses a particular dress, "a scarf"? Jean-Jacques Rousseau said that the "general will discusses general matters"; here, the particular takes over the general. Yet the question remains: can the "scarved girl" bear the weight of all the politics of

[97]

religion, laïcité, and institutional change in France or in Europe at large? Is it that whatever happened, happened because institutions responded to the scarved girl, "the new state of diversity," "the new challenge"?

What I call the "triple movement"[1]—a legal ban on the scarf in schools, the rise in public Muslim infrastructure (the establishment of Muslim high schools and the CFCM), and a general push for religion infrastructure in public space (e.g., mobilizing the Catholic Church, calling for the teaching of religious facts in public schools)—suggests a much more complicated picture when challenging the common academic evaluations of the law of March 15, 2004, banning religious symbols as a reassertion of laïcité, reviewed in chapter 2. This chapter argues that in fact laïcité in contemporary France is moving away from the laïcité of the Third Republic in fundamental respects.

Laïcité Positive and the Mobilization of the Catholic Church

In France the "new meaning" theoretical approach, addressed in chapter 2, declared itself as a political movement par excellence because, of all people, it was the former president of the republic, Nicolas Sarkozy, who developed and pushed a "new meaning" of laïcité. In his book *La République, les religions, l'espérance* (2004), when discussing his preference for a change in *Loi du 9 Décembre 1905 concernant la séparation des Églises et de l'État*, Sarkozy, then minister of interior, argued that a certain kind of laïcité, namely, a *laïcité positive*, would defend state support for building religion infrastructure such as places of worship and religious schools: "I believe in *laïcité positive*, this is to say a laïcité which guarantees the right to live one's religion like a fundamental personal right. Laïcité isn't the enemy of religions. Quite to the contrary. Laïcité, it is the guarantee for each to be able to believe and live his/her faith."[2] In his speeches in the Lateran, Vatican, on December 20, 2007, and in Riyad, Kingdom of Saudi Arabia, on January 14, 2008, the content of Sarkozy's *laïcité positive* found expression in clearer words.[3] The Lateran speech made his effort in forging consent for the CFCM in 2003 look like a pretext for opening the way for Catholicism to be recognized as the moral bond of society.[4] "Positive laïcité" resonated the most with Catholic organizations. This was acknowledged on the French government's website, which declared France a laboratory for Vatican politics: "The organization in Paris, at the Pope's initiative, in March 2011, of a dialogue with nonbelievers in the 'Parvis des Gentils' (Court of the Gentiles) highlights our country's test role, perceived as particularly secular, as part of the new evangelization of Western Europe that Benedict XVI wants to launch."[5]

President Sarkozy's speech at the Lateran suggested some new questions on a current formulation of secularism and religion as a matter of reasonable accommodation to the new challenges or as a way to cope with the new state of diversity. However, behind the façade of references to diversity and acclaim for a new meaning of laïcité, there seemed to be nothing new in Sarkozy's speech, just the old game of the social mobilization of religion at large, in the spirit of the 1850 Falloux law.[6] In his speech he claimed that Christianity is at the roots of arts, culture, history, hopes, and morality in France. He alluded to the "Muslim question" in claiming that "France has changed a lot. The French citizens are from many more diverse convictions than before. Therefore, laïcité affirms itself as a necessity and I would dare say, a chance." Sarkozy continued with the "christian roots of France," how that religious heritage is a "cement of national identity," and he even went as far as to include nineteenth-century *régime concordataire* talk when he stated that "the catholic religion is our majority religion." He complained that theology diplomas do not get the respect that they should. Sarkozy did everything but explicitly say, "I am the Catholic president of a Catholic nation," although he conveyed as much. He framed the problematique as finding a way to combine the "christian roots of France" and laïcité, and his way was *laïcité positive*:

> It is why I wish the advent of a *laïcité positive*, that is to say, a laïcité which, while attending to the liberty of thought, to that of to believe and not to believe, does not consider religions as a danger, but rather as an asset. That is not to modify the great equilibrium of the law of 1905. The French do not wish for it, and the religions do not demand it. It is on the other hand to seek dialogue with great religions of France and to have for a principle the easing of the daily life of great spiritual currents rather than trying to complicate it for them.

In his Lateran speech, he articulated a theme that was already in his book *La République, les religions, l'espérance* on the relation between morality, religion, hope, poverty, and governance:

> But a man who believes is a man who hopes. And the interest of the Republic is that there would be a lot of men and women who hope.

The gradual disaffection of rural parishes, the spiritually deserted suburbs, the disappearance of patronage, the penury of priests, have not rendered the French very happy. It is a fact. And then I also want to say that, if a human morality independent of religious morality incontestably exists, the Republic has interest that a moral reflection inspired by religious convictions also exists.

In a speech at the Elysée Palace on September 12, 2008, Pope Benedict, who had arguably coined the term *laïcité positive* even before President Sarkozy, also expressed appreciation for this new meaning of laïcité:

> You yourself, Mr. President, have used the fine expression "*laïcité positive*" to characterize this more open understanding. At this moment in history when cultures continue to cross paths more frequently, I am firmly convinced that a new reflection on the true meaning and importance of laïcité is now necessary. In fact, it is fundamental, on the one hand, to insist on the distinction between the political realm and that of religion in order to preserve both the religious freedom of citizens and the responsibility of the State towards them; and, on the other hand, to become more aware of the irreplaceable role of religion for the formation of consciences and the contribution which it can bring to—among other things—the creation of a basic ethical consensus in society.[7]

Sarkozy's Riyad speech in 2008 continued and deepened some of the points from his 2004 book and the 2007 Lateran speech. He underlined that "it is not religious sentiment that is dangerous" but "its utilization for regressive political ends in the service of a new barbarism," and that he did "not know a country whose heritage, whose culture, whose civilization does not have religious roots." He went on to say he did "not know a culture, or civilization where morality besides incorporating various philosophical influences, does not have the slightest touch of a religious origin." Sarkozy kept a civilizational angle with emphasis on dialogue: "The West has gathered the greek heritage thanks to the muslim civilization." He slowly narrowed down on the strength of religion: "It is perhaps in the religious that what is universal in civilizations is the strongest," and "it is religions that taught us first the principles of universal morality and universal human dignity, universal value of liberty and responsibility, honesty and rightfulness." Then he turned to diversity: "A civilized politics, is a politics of diversity. . . . It is a value that I wanted respected in France in creating Council of the Muslim Faith [*culte*]. It is the value that has inspired me when I want to facilitate the construction of mosques in France. . . . Diversity is a civilizing [*civilisatrice*] necessity."[8]

These speeches and Sarkozy's book could have been seen just as election politics to get the Muslim vote or a matter of international relations diplomacy, which in one sense they definitely were. Yet what I called the state-led "triple movement" suggests a much more complicated picture in challenging the common academic evaluations of the March 15, 2004, law banning religious symbols as a reassertion of laïcité. Immediately after Sarkozy's speeches in the Lateran and Riyad, Jean Baubérot, a well-known professor of history and sociology of laïcité, responded with a book, *La laïcité expliquée à M. Sarkozy . . . et à ceux qui écrivent ses discours.*[9] In it and in his other writings, Baubérot points out that a process counter to that which resulted in the separation law of 1905 is underway under claims of French exceptionalism;[10] laïcité is turning into a matter of identity and way of life rather than a principle that is articulated at the level of general institutions of society:

> Laïcité has become a consensual representation of national identity. . . . And while in 1905 Briand demanded that France join countries where "*the State is really laic*" (he cited a good dozen), in 1989 a new theme appeared, "*laïcité as a French exception*" which "*foreigners would not be able to understand*"! In fact, whereas all the "old French"—including those in Alsace-Moselle, where the founding laws of French laïcité (the Ferry laws on public school, the law of separation) are not applied—are considered laic in essence, the "new French" (the descendants of immigrants) would have to prove that they are. Some of them indeed . . . would become the alibis for advocating a new type of *laïcité intégrale*, since it would apply only to a part of the population. At the same moment, the president of the Republic, in the name of a "*laïcité positive*," wants "*to valorize the essentially christian roots*" of France. That means, under the cover of patrimonialization, putting back a certain religious dimension in French political identity. We therefore find ourselves in a dialectic opposite to that of 1905.[11]

This move of laïcité from the institutional level to the level of identity also finds an articulation at the level of narration. Narratives of the politics behind the law of March 15, 2004, which simultaneously claim this moment as a reassertion of laïcité, "new challenges," and a "new state of diversity," assume an empirically ungrounded distinction between laic French people in favor of the law and Muslim immigrants against the law. Most of the "immigrants" in question are actually French citizens; therefore this distinction cannot be one of legal citizenship. Also, the political coalitions for and against the March 15 law cut across the laic French versus Muslim French distinction. In fact, the politics of laïcité and religion that the March 15 law is submerged in are visible only by gathering together the moments swept under binary distinctions, such as laic people for the law and religious people against the law, French citizens for the law and Muslim immigrants against the law. These sweeping binaries lose even further credibility when the other two layers of the three-layered movement are put in place and laid out, and the state-led infrastructural politics of laïcité, religion, and diversity (or multiculturalism, for Sarkozy uses "diversity," "culture," and sometimes "civilization" interchangeably) become visible.

The Stasi Report and the Law of March 15, 2004

When the law against wearing religious symbols in French public schools was passed on March 3, 2004, proponents argued that it was continuous with the French tradition, simply the application of the principle of laïcité under current conditions. Such a defense was central to the report submitted to President Jacques Chirac on December 11, 2003, by La Commission de réflexion sur l'application du principe de laïcité dans la République—also known as the Stasi Report after the head of the commission, Bernard Stasi. On February 10, 2004, the National Assembly of France voted for legislation to regulate the wearing of religious symbols in public schools by a super majority of 494 to 36 votes. On March 3, 2004, a law changing the education code was adopted and the following article was added: "Art. L. 141-5-1. In public elementary schools, middle schools and high schools, the donning of signs or dresses by which the students ostensibly [*ostensiblement*] manifest a religious belonging is banned. The school regulation reminds that a dialogue with the student precedes the start of a disciplinary procedure."[12]

The law was prepared on the recommendation of the Stasi Commission. The commission consisted of Bernard Stasi (president); Rémy Schwartz (rapporteur); Mohammed Arkoun, Jean Baubérot, Jacqueline Costa-Lascoux, Régis Debray, Gilles Kepel, Henri Pena-Ruiz, René Rémond, Alain Touraine, and Patrick Weil (all university faculty members); Hanifa Cherifi (mediator at the Ministry of National Education); Ghislaine Hudson (lycée headmaster); Marceau Long (honorary vice president of the Council of State); Maurice Quenet (rector of the Paris Academy), Michel Delebarre (Socialist Party, representative of the North); Nelly Olin (UMP, party senator of Val-d'Oise); Nicole Guedj (lawyer, general secretary of the UMP responsible for human rights); Gaye Petek (president of Elele, an association for the integration of Turkish immigrants in France); and Raymond Soubie (president of Altédia Consultants).

The report's comparative perspective on France was limited to a brief discussion on certain decisions and judgments of the European Court of Human Rights, and Turkey figured as the major reference point. This brief review underscored that "the approach of the Court rests on a recognition of the traditions of each country, without seeking to impose a uniform model of the relations between Church and State."[13] The report cited a total of six European Court decisions in order to use "national tradition" as the significant comparative variable: the case of Cha'are Shalom ve Tsedek against France (2000), Dahlab against Switzerland (2001), Refah Party and others against Turkey (2003), Kalaç against Turkey (1997), Karaduman against Turkey (1993), and Valsamis against Greece (1995). Yet these cases differ not only in context but even more so in subject matter. The topics involved ranged from individual behavior to civil society organizations and political parties: an organization's ritual slaughter, a Muslim primary school teacher wearing a headscarf in the classroom, political party activity, the religious belief and practice of a military officer, identity photos and university diplomas, and religious practice and school rules. In fact, the variation in "national tradition" was quite limited, since three out of the six court cases cited were from Turkey, and in all the three cases, the European court had ruled in favor of the Turkish state. Such comparative references to Turkey in the report (making way for the March 15, 2004, law) were also matched here and there in the media and academic works, and these comparative references sometimes reached back as far as the Ottoman Empire, making analogies with the empire's Millet system.[14] Such references are theoretically significant for they mark a reversed path of "traveling" vis-à-vis the "modernities," "alternative modernities," and "multiple modernities" literature reviewed in chapter 2, which focus on traveling out of Europe only. Therefore, viewed together with the comparative references to the West, Europe, or particularly France, in Turkey in the following chapters, they make it possible to talk of "mutually interacting modernities." This matter will be discussed in the concluding chapter.

After setting a comparative context bound by national traditions, the Stasi Report began with an observation of a change in circumstances, heading in the direction of the "new challenges" and "the new state of diversity" approach. The report stated: "In comparison to the context of 1905, French society has changed: the hold of the Catholic Church [on society] is no longer perceived as a threat." Rather, France was facing a new state of diversity: "In the last couple of decades new religions developed. Islam, resulting principally from populations originated from Maghreb, Africa, and the Middle East, is represented [in France] by the largest community of the European Union, the Orthodox faith is also present, Buddhism as well. Thus, France today is the most diversified among the European countries." Therefore the ends of laïcité had to change: "Our political philosophy was founded on the defense of the unity of the social body. This concern with uniformity dominated over any expression of difference that was perceived as a threat. . . . Laïcité today is facing the challenge of forging unity while respecting the diversity of society."[15]

The report posed its main problem as finding an equilibrium between two principles of laïcité, "neutrality of the State" and "protection of liberty of conscience," which the report underlined could in practice sometimes run into conflict (22–31). The report put the neutrality of the state as the first condition of laïcité. It listed two parts of neutrality: First, neutrality is equality before the law without distinction. Second, the state administration has to practically assure neutrality. For instance, public employees cannot express religion or its symbols, and the second article of the 1905 law prohibits state finances to any religious organization. The report commented that, "very generally, our law has foreseen adjustments permitting the conciliation of the State's neutrality with religious practice" (23). It called such adjustments "reasonable accommodations" and gave as examples the final part of article 2 of the 1905 law ("However, those expenditures relating to services of chaplaincy and intended to ensure the free exercise of worship [*culte*] in public establishments, such as elementary schools, middle schools, high schools, hospices, asylums and prisons, can be entered in the budgets"), and also the Ferry law of March 28, 1882, which gives a day other than Sunday in laic schools for allowing students to go for religious education. According to the report, these were "reasonable accommodations," "tempering the exigencies of absolute neutrality," "in order to preserve respect for religious conscience in the framework of laic education" (23). The tension arose from the fact that "like all public liberties, the manifestation of liberty of conscience can be limited in cases of threat to public order" (25). After giving examples from court judgments and State Council decisions, it underlined that the boundary between public order and freedom has been dealt with case by case. It gave examples of this tension in military prisons and hospitals and then focused on this tension in the domain of education:

> Within school boundaries . . . in a partially closed milieu, students, taken in charge for a long time, must learn and live together, in a situation where they are still fragile, subject to exterior influences and pressures. The functioning of the school must permit them to acquire the intellectual tools intended to assure in the long term their critical independence. Reserving a place for the expression of religious and spiritual convictions is therefore not obvious. The existence of confessional education under associational contract with the State permits entirely the affirming of religious liberty with the taking into account of the proper character of a religion. . . . In this framework, it is evident that no juridical disposition opposes the creation of muslim schools. (28)

Then the report evaluated the decision of the State Council in 1989 that found that students wearing headscarves in schools did not violate the law. The decision stated:

> In school establishments, the wearing by students of signs through which they manifest their belonging to a religion is not, as such, incompatible with the principle of laïcité, as far as it constitutes the exercise of the freedom of expression and the manifestation of religious belief, but this freedom should not authorize students to display signs of religious belonging which, by their nature, by the conditions in which they would be worn individually or collectively, or by their *ostentatoire* character or claim [*revendicatif*], would constitute an act of pressure, of provocation, of *proselytism*, or of propaganda, would infringe upon the dignity or liberty of students or other members of the education community, would endanger their health and security, would disturb the flow of activities of teaching and the educational role of the teachers, eventually would trouble the order in the establishment or the normal functioning of public service.[16]

The Stasi Report highlighted from the council's decision its emphasis on public education for all, except in cases of "acts of pressure, provocation, proselytism, or propaganda . . . behaviors damaging to the dignity, pluralism, or freedom of students or to all members of the education community, as well as those compromising their health and their security . . . all that gets in the way of the activity of education" (29–30). The report underlines that the State Council did not find the donning of religious symbols as fitting any of these cases; unless it took "an ostentatious [*ostentatoire*] or protest [*revendicatif*] nature," it could be judged case by case. The report observed that the State Council distinguished between "the neutrality of the program and the teacher" and "the liberty of conscience of students." It continued with some practical difficulties of judging case by case, such as "in practice, it has been impossible for the heads of establishments to trace the boundary between illicit ostentatoire and licit non-ostentatoire signs" (31).

What Charles Taylor has called "the independent ethic"[17] version of secularism—keeping public space free of religious organization and ethics—historically speaking can be most strongly associated with the French experience. Yet, some sections of the Stasi Report—e.g., sections 4.3.1 and 4.3.3—embody suggestions that direct away from an "independent ethic" version of secularism. Section 4.3.1 was entitled "Teaching of Religious Fact at School" and read as follows:

> The teaching of religions, other than in concordatory departments, must not be proposed within the confines of laic public service of education. On the other hand, numerous reasons stand in favor of a reasoned approach to religions as facts of civilizations, as has been developed by Rector Joutard as early as in 1989 and very recently by philosopher Régis Debray. A better mutual understanding of different cultures and traditions of religious thought is today essential. The education programs have been revised in recent years in order to better integrate the study of religious fact in the teaching of French and history about which the commission is pleased. It [the commission] does not believe in the hypothesis of a new course per se but advocates for the development of a transversal approach to religious phenomena, notably by means of new interdisciplinary pedagogy. The occasion of affirming an *active laïcité*, developing the reasoned knowledge and critical approach to texts, should be seized.[18]

Section 4.3.3, "Implementation of Existing Texts Concerning Chaplaincies," reads as follows:

> The commission regrets that in fact not all religions benefit from the advantages that are conferred to them by law in matters of chaplains. It has already been mentioned that there is a lack of muslim chaplains in many public services such as hospitals or prisons. There are no general chaplains in the army, and at times muslim military officers are attended by rabbis. The commission proposes that a general muslim chaplain be established in the same conditions as the general chaplains of other religions.[19]

Various headscarf affairs preceded the commission, convened in the summer of 2003; two of them more widely popularized, the first in 1989 and one in 1994. In September 1989 three students—two Moroccans and one Tunisian—were expelled from their public school in the commune of Creil because they were wearing headscarves in the classroom. The headmaster, Ernest Chernière, defended the dismissal on the grounds of laïcité. In 1994 Minister of Education François Bayrou issued a circular to schools declaring that "ostentatious" signs of religious belief are proselytism, and many students were dismissed thereafter. Much has been written on these affairs so I will not go into a descriptive account of the events but rather will highlight a few points.[20] First, a division among public intellectuals presented itself as early as 1989, seen in the contrast between two public letters, one published in *Le Nouvel Observateur* on October 27, 1989, and the other in *Politis* on November 9–15, 1989. Each group of signatories had one person who later became a member of the Stasi Commission: Régis Debray in the pro-exclusion letter, "Teachers Do Not Give In!," and Alain Touraine in the anti-exclusion letter, "For an Open Laïcité." The pro-exclusion letter called the affair "the Munich of the Republican school" and includes some parts striking contrasts with the Third Republic's Bert Report:

> An exclusion is only discriminatory when it aims at him or her who has respected the rules in force in an establishment. When it touches the student who has infringed on the rules in force, it is disciplinary. The present confusion between discipline and discrimination ruins discipline. . . . To negotiate, like you [Minister of National Education

Lionel Jospin] do . . . is called one thing: to give in. Such a "diplomacy" only encourages the very persons it intends to cajole—and if they demand tomorrow that their children be spared from the study of the Rushdies (Spinoza, Voltaire, Baudelaire, Rimbaud . . .) which encumber our education, how refuse them? By exclusion? . . . The right to difference that is so dear to you is only a liberty if it includes the right of being different from difference. It is not, Mr. Minister, by bringing together in the same place a catholic child, a muslim child, a jewish child that the laic school is constructed. The school endeavors to set up a space where authority is founded on reason and experience: that is accessible to all. For this reason, and because it addresses itself to all, the school does not admit any distinctive signs marking deliberately and a priori the belonging of those it welcomes. It cannot admit any exemption to its program or schedule either. . . . You say, "Welcome all children." Yes. But, that has never meant to bring to school, with them, the religion of their parents. . . . Instead of offering to this young girl a space of liberty, you imply to her that there is no difference between school and the house of her father. In authorizing de facto the Islamic foulard, symbol of the submission of women, you give a blank check to fathers and brothers, that is to say to the hardest patriarchy of the world. . . . In a single phrase, you have disarmed those thousands of young muslim women who fight here and there for their dignity and their liberty. Their most certain ally against the authoritarianism of fathers was the republican and laic school.[21]

The article was followed in the same issue of the *Le Nouvel Observateur* by a cautious "Muslim voice" entitled "Do Not Leave the Floor to Fanatics!"[22] The signatories began by stating that they are "intellectuals originating from a land of Islam, we do not pretend to speak in the name of a community crossed by multiple currents, but in our own name" and called on Muslims to speak for themselves and not let fanatics speak for them:

The question of the veil poses itself less as a religious problem than as a social and political one today: that of the status of women of islamic faith in a laic society. We are convinced that French society will only open itself without reluctance to the populations of islamic tradition if its fundamental achievements are not put in question. Laïcité is one of these achievements. It is a weapon given to the adversaries of ghettos, a means offered to those who want to tear themselves [*à celles et à ceux*, emphasis on both genders] from the weight of traditions which violate young consciences.

The anti-exclusion letter was published approximately two weeks later in *Politis*. I quote extensively:[23]

> Will laic universalism serve as a pretext for exclusion? Will those who evoke today "the Munich of the Republican school" trigger the Vichy of integration of immigrants? To exclude the adolescent girls in foulard from French schools, it is indeed leading to a dramatic dead end in matters of integration. The duty of resemblance. This is where the exigencies of pure and hard laicists lead. A brutal (black?) conception of integration. Yet, in recent years, the forces of antiracism had in this domain groped delicately—the problem is complex—around the question of the identity of France and its diversity. It is passed from "right to *difference*" to "*right to resemblance whatever our differences are*." Then to "*right to indifference*." . . . Now the debate around the foulard brings an unheard-of conception: "*The right of being different from difference.*" Bravo! . . .
>
> Laic universalism is an undeniable achievement of two centuries of French history. Yet it should be noted that muslims, the second religion of France, don't have right to the advantages of the 1905 law. There aren't subsidies for private islamic schools, as there are by the tens of millions of francs for catholics, protestants and jews. The laic contract between state and religions does not exist with the muslims. . . .
>
> In fact, two conceptions of laïcité confront each other. That of a school which would fear differences above all: laïcité of the gray blouse which supports neither the foulard nor the kippah nor the crucifix. And that of a more open, a laic and obligatory school above and in respect of all particularisms. A conquering laïcité which would offer each the objective conditions for individual choice at each one's own pace. . . .
>
> The exclusion opens the way for fundamentalism [*intégrisme*]. And also for the National Front.[24]

In the first letter there was an emphasis on disobeying the rules of the public school, the public school as a place of liberty and an institution countering family socialization. According to the letter, not being strict on this matter enabled the brothers' and father's dominance over the scarfed girl. In the second letter there was an emphasis on segregation, the lack of Muslim private schools, the right to education, and exclusion as a cause of fundamentalism rather than vice versa. What was even more significant for mapping out the politics of laïcité, religion, and diversity, of which the headscarf affairs were only the tip of the iceberg with high costs for many young people, were the shifts in positions from 1989 to 2003 (e.g., Touraine changed his position to defending the law) and the composite position of pro-exclusion and pro-teaching of religious facts in public schools. This composite position was represented, for instance, by Régis Debray, who wrote a report to the Minister of National Education in 2002, *The Teaching of Religious Fact in the Laic School*,[25] which was later cited in the Stasi Report, and around which the National Ministry of Education organized a conference in 2002.

On October 7, 2003, Minister of Interior Nicolas Sarkozy spoke in front of the Stasi Commission.[26] He remarked on the first and second articles of the *Loi du 9 Décembre 1905 concernant la séparation des Églises et de l'État*: "The Republic guarantees the free exercise of cultes under limitations of public order" and "the Republic does not recognize any culte." He maintained that he is against a reading of the former as "absolute right to difference in the name of liberty" which he associated with communitarianism and a reading of the latter as "laïcité made of passivity and of ignorance of religious facts." He started by laying out his *laïcité positive*: "I call, to the contrary, for a positive vision. Laïcité in my view, is the recognition of the need that man feels for hoping and therefore, for believing, without ever attempting to orient his step toward such and such religion, as well as the right not to believe." As minister of cultes, "it would be a mistake on my part not to share the great moments of religious life, and to refuse to enter a church, a temple, a synagogue or a mosque." As minister, his role was not "to ignore, to forbid, or to privilege." He understood "neutrality with regard to religions" as the "liberty to choose and exercise his/her culte," "all with the same rights and duties."

> One must not fear to assert that men, ever since they are aware of their particular destiny, feel the need for a spiritual aspiration. This aspiration is not contradictory with the republican temporal ideal. In this way, in the French countryside of yesterday, for accompanying the work of the primary school teacher, there was a parish priest. The Church

fulfilled a civic function. This work of moral and civic formation which was made in the past; today, who makes it in the suburbs where very often there is no longer either a pastor, parish priest, imam, or rabbi? . . . This conviction is the heart of my determination to give Muslims the right to live their religion.

Then Sarkozy elaborated further on neutrality and "what it is for the State and more particularly at school." For the state, it is simply that "the Republic recognizes all citizens without distinguishing according to their religion, skin color or their origins," and it requires that state employees do not "display their religious convictions"; yet the school calender, for example, could be modified to also include religious holidays other than those of Christianity. Sarkozy underlined, however, that it is not up to religions to decide "the content of laïcité," or "the questions of the wearing of the scarf at school and by state employees and the question of gender mixing at municipal pools," and he also gave the example of photos on national identity cards, which had been a matter of public discussion earlier in the year. In his speech on April 19, 2003, at the annual meeting of the Union des Organisations Islamiques de France, he had spoken against photos of women in headscarves on national identity cards.[27] On the other hand, he stated that "neutrality is not passivity . . . as soon as a state recognizes a religion, its first duty is to ensure that it has exactly the same rights as other religions, not more and not less." However, Sarkozy stated, "I have my reservations on the principle of a new law on laïcité, which doesn't prevent being opposed to the wearing of religious symbols at schools." "The manifestation of religious convictions at school is not acceptable if, in reality, it seeks to affirm the superiority of a religion, or of a practice, over another, or to affirm a rejection of fundamental republican values." However,

> I am convinced that a law will be experienced as a humiliation which will lead to a radicalization of the ones and the others. Law must not be seen as a weapon of combat. Its objective is, to the contrary, to create the rules of a calm common life. To be clear, the law must not be used for compelling a religion. . . . This law would not be immediately useful. . . . [The situation] can be managed by way of a regulation [*réglementaire*] or a circular [*circulaire*] so that all headmasters have precise directions offering them satisfactory juridical security.

In sum, Sarkozy argued for some kind of control on the scarf but through lower-level legislation than a national law, because a national law would radicalize Muslim communities and endanger the more reconciliatory politics he was pursuing with some of them. It would also endanger his reconciliatory politics toward religion more generally. On the one hand, in defense of his push to establish a representative body—the French Council of the Muslim Faith (CFCM)—and for more religion infrastructure for Muslims, he emphasized that "muslim believers do not have sufficient mosques for practicing their religion. There is still an islam of cellars and garages . . . muslim space in cemeteries is rare. There aren't muslim chaplains in schools. There isn't an institute for the training of imams in France," and when there is inequality of this kind, the state has to engage to guarantee equality among religions. Yet, on the other hand, Sarkozy did not confine the question to Islam but addressed religion in general. He defended the introduction of religious facts into the school curriculum:

> I notice with regret that in the name of the neutrality of the State, we have totally ignored teaching the history of religions at school, and this has deprived entire generations of the knowledge of one of the major sources of western culture and has exaggerated sociological readings regarding religious facts. Tolerance is the principle victim of this reluctance, because it is from ignorance that racism and a turning in on oneself are born.

The causal link between teaching religious facts and an increase in tolerance and decrease in racism is far from obvious, but this is not the most striking part of Sarkozy's position. His position clearly pushed religion at the institutional level while circumscribing it at the behavioral level (no scarf but you can have more mosques and study religious facts). This position could not simply be subsumed under a claim of "new challenges–new state of diversity" from below. When a journalist posed a question on the decline of religious practice in France and noted that only 15 percent of Muslims were regularly practicing, Sarkozy responded by diverting the question of religion and religious organization from a matter of "culte" (faith) to a matter of "culture":

> Religion is not simply a *cultuel* [of religious faith] phenomenon. It is also an element of cultural identity. . . . Religion does not only have a

spiritual dimension. It also has a cultural dimension. . . . Saying "muslims of France" does not exclude atheist and agnostic muslims; on the contrary, it gives a name to a component of french society the integration of which we have to organize so that a temptation to withdraw [from society] and a communitarian temptation which are already strongly present are avoided.[28]

Here was yet another clear example of politics of "new meanings," where Sarkozy differentiated *religion as such* from *religion as culture*, in order to maintain that his defense of an increase in religion infrastructure was not dependent on a sociological fact of religious practice. Sarkozy's position was not unique at all, as the next section shows—this "no scarf, read history of religion" position actually even cut across the left and right in France. Luc Ferry, UMP minister of youth, national education and research, and Xavier Darcos, minister responsible for school curriculum, both spoke in front of the Stasi Commission against a law but for the teaching of religious facts in the school curriculum. Ferry underlined that under the current law, education personnel cannot wear religious symbols, and a student who refused a part of the required program or a course could be expelled. He listed some problems with making a law against wearing religious symbols in schools: First, it risked a contradiction with French law that did not prohibit religious belonging or its expression, as well as the European treaties France has ratified. Second, if in the name of laicization France keeps producing "martyrs," this will inevitably lead to an increase in Koranic schools. And finally, getting into the regulation of dress will produce all kinds of strategies of getting around the law that will have to be dealt with. Ferry wished for two things: a law of orientation (*loi d'orientation*) communicating to students that expressing religious belonging in a school setting with various groups of different youngsters and the teacher can contribute to a priori categorization of one another. And he explicitly stated that he was in favor of Régis Debray's proposition of the "teaching of history of religions," which he found to have not only a cultural function but also an ethical and political function.

It is not possible to say that Sarkozy kept to the position he expressed in front of the commission, for his correspondence with selected national and international leaders in Muslim communities about his plans to establish the CFCM preceded the shifts in the position of these leaders. After Sarkozy's meeting with Mohamed Sayyed Tantaoui of Al-Azhar in late December 2003, Tantaoui declared that he supported a French law against the scarf, and Sarkozy was quoted in *Le Monde* saying, "He knows what I do in France for the muslim community, for integration in general. Many reproached me for the creation of the Conseil français du culte musulman, but it opens the doors in all these countries. Me, I continue imperturbably my path of finding the interlocutors with whom one can construct something."[29]

There were initially three vetoes in the Stasi Commission to the ban on religious symbols: sociologist Alain Touraine—one of the signatories of the public letter "For an Open *Laïcité*" in defense of the scarved girls' right to education in 1989; sociologist Jean Baubérot; and high school headmaster Ghislaine Hudson.[30] Finally, Baubérot maintained the only veto in the commission on the part of the report suggesting a ban on "ostensible" religious symbols, which for him clearly targeted the Muslim headscarf. Touraine explained his change in position in an article on published January 7, 2004, in *Libération*:

And I, who has constantly in the past defended the young scarved women, I want to clarify why in signing the report of the Stasi Commission, I have kept the same ideas. . . . For taking a position in a concrete situation, it is necessary to add that we are confronted with the rise of a radical islamism which attacks what I have defined as the nucleus of modernity [equality of men and women] and which seems to me to be entirely distant from the projects of many of the scarved women. As it would be impossible to convince the French that in authorizing the scarf and the kippa, one prepares to fight against fundamentalism [*intégrismes*], it has been necessary to act in the opposite way and ban at school ostensible symbols of religious or political belonging. . . . My hypothesis is that the law can stop the islamist movement which wants to undermine the school and hospital organizations.[31]

Touraine concluded by underlining that the priority is to save the young women from the double domination they are subjected to: fundamentalist Muslims and French racists. This could be possible if Muslims and non-Muslims took initiative together for the women, for reaching the double goal of "saving the spirit of citizenship from the dangers of communitarianism and at the same time recognizing liberty of conscience." Baubérot grounded his objection to a scarf ban on laïcité.[32] He pointed out in his article in

Libération that the ban on ostentatious religious symbols, for him obviously an allusion to the Muslim headscarf, was discouraging Muslim girls from going to public schools and encouraging them to seek an alternative in private schooling. Therefore for him the law—paradoxically defended in the name of laïcité—was undermining the public education system, which historically and theoretically is the main constitutive institution of laïcité.

Baubérot correctly pointed out that the undercutting of public education had in fact started with the *Loi Debré* in 1959. At the beginning of the Fourth Republic, the Catholic Church was seen as complicit in the Vichy regime. Marshal Pétain had reintroduced catechism in the public schools, religious orders were granted permission to teach in 1940, and in October 1941 Pétain had granted state aid to religious schools. These policies were abandoned with the Fourth Republic. Yet the issue of state funding to religious schools remained on the agenda. Conservative governments of the 1950s were successful in introducing legislation to provide funds for Catholic education despite the opposition of socialists and radical republicans. Given these strong tendencies against the separation law of 1905, Prime Minister Michel Debré introduced the Debré law as a compromise on December 31, 1959.[33]

The Debré law introduced state funding of private education, 90 percent of which was Catholic. The law allowed for two kinds of contracts between the state and private schools: a simple contract and an associational contract. The former provided state salaries and insurance, while the latter also offered funds for maintenance of school buildings and equipment.[34] In return for financial aid, the state had control over staff appointments and school curriculum. The law required Catholic schools "to offer exactly the same curriculum as public schools and to accept pupils without selecting them for the religious or other beliefs of their parents."[35] Moreover, according to the law, the French state dealt with individual Catholic schools rather than with the Catholic Church in settling the issue, and according to Beattie, "the assumption was that those schools would sink or swim in competition with public schools, and the mechanism for survival would be parental choice."[36]

Given the already existing divergence from the laïcité of the 1905 law with the 1959 Debré law, Baubérot's position was that a ban on headscarved women in the public schools in the name of protecting the public sphere from "religious fundamentalism" was an incoherent and therefore stillborn project, since the girls who refused to remove their headscarves would now go to "private" schools, which are not exactly "nonpublic" spaces because the

Debré law had undermined the distinction between public and private in the French education system.

Baubérot was not the only critic of the law. A petition launched by Étienne Balibar, Saïd Bouamama, François Gaspard, Catherine Lévy, and Pierre Tévanian entitled "Yes to the Secular School, No to Exclusionary Laws" gathered significant support against the law.[37] Tévanian argued in his book *Le voile médiatique. Un faux débat: "L'affaire du foulard islamique"* (The media veil. A false debate: "The Islamic headscarf affair") how the media played a major role in the making of the affair.[38] Balibar discussed in his article "Dissonances within *Laïcité*"[39] how the public education system was positioned right in between the public and the private, and it was in this intermediary space where the public became the public, first of all by participating and interacting in the same space. I quote at length from the text of this petition to underscore one more time how the law of March 15, 2004, was not a reassertion of laïcité but a struggle within it, where the weight of history was behind the position opposing the ban. The petition admitted that there may be many diverse realities but in any case "exclusion is the worst of solutions, and the law aimed at a very "strict," narrow, definition of laïcité. The petitioners explained:

> We are not "supporters of the veil"; we are simply supporters of a laic school that works toward the emancipation of all, and not toward exclusion. Because laïcité, as defined by the laws of 1881, 1882, and 1886, is an obligation that concerns school premises, school programs, and education personnel, and not the students. . . . It is not legitimate to increase the demands on the young in formation, who come to school precisely for learning, forming and transforming themselves—especially if these demands have no necessity from the point of view of the functioning of the school. Several of us encounter or have encountered these veiled students in school establishments, and we testify that not in any moment has their presence prevented the teachers from teaching, or the students from studying. We do not forget the equality of sexes, just the contrary. But whether the headscarf is an object of choice or is imposed, one cannot consider the veiled young women as guilty, and in any case it is not her who should "pay." In all cases, it is in welcoming to the laic school that one can help her in emancipating herself, in providing her the means of autonomy, and it is in dismissing her that one condemns her to oppression.

The petition also found the law as part of an emerging, more general, movement—"the colonization of all the space of social life with a punitive logic"—and "it will only be felt by all of the students as a brutal and discriminatory measure, serving to redouble all the injustices they already suffer in their district, the young of popular milieus, especially those that stem from postcolonial immigration." The petition also criticized the turning of the "veiled girl" into a scapegoat by relating her to, for example, "sexist or racist insults and inscriptions" and insisted that such insults be sanctioned, "but the sanction should apply to those who are the authors, and not to those girls who are most of the time respectful and studious." The petition concluded by calling the headscarf discussions a false debate, and one that hides the many problems facing the education system such as overloaded classrooms, a shortage of personnel, and insufficiency of support for students failing or having difficulty in classes. This false debate also takes the focus away from attention on common institutions, the education system in this case, and a real discussion of its real problems, to a focus instead on identity matters:

> We refuse the fantasies and amalgams and the locking up in a false debate which encourages all divisions and all confrontations of identity (between "France" and "immigrants," between "the Republic" and "Islam," or again between various confessions), while the main problems are socioeconomic and political: liberalization of the economy, mass unemployment, precarity of salaried employees, extension of social control and of security logics, permanence of racist discriminations and of the social inequality between men and women.

Another striking aspect of the opposition was that almost all major religious organizations made public statements against a law while, as the next section discusses, the CFCM shifted its position from opposing to supporting the law. The chief rabbi of France, the Reformed Church of France, the archbishop of Paris, and the president of the Bishop's Conference of France all took public positions against a law.[40] *La Croix* published a joint letter by Christian leaders against a law on December 9, 2003. The final headscarf incident expelling students before the passage of a national law concerned the Levy sisters at Henri-Wallon High School in Aubervilliers in 2003, with five teachers writing a letter to *Libération* arguing that the expulsion was sad but necessary and that they are against a national law because it would promote communalism. Thirty-four out of the thirty-six students in the girls' class voted for a strike, a tactic that would continue after the promulgation of the law as well. On March 11, 2004, *Le Monde* reported teachers going on strike against a scarved student in another high school.[41]

Forging of CFCM and Establishing Muslim High Schools

Appearing alongside the Stasi Report and the law passed against religious symbols on March 15, 2004, were other significant developments in France. The first private Muslim high school, Lycée Averroès, was established under state contract, and the CFCM was founded in the summer of 2003. These were institutional developments opening up alternative paths for Muslims to become "part" of French society. The UMP, and particularly Nicolas Sarkozy as minister of interior and later as president of the republic, played a major role in these moments of institutional change; however, these new institutions had been in the making at least since January 28, 2000, when the socialist interior minister Jean-Pierre Chevènement met with various Muslim organizations. The document adopted at this meeting, "Principes et fondements juridiques régissant les rapports entre les pouvoirs publics et le culte musulman en France" (Principles and legal basis governing the relations between public powers and the Muslim faith in France), included plans for Muslim high schools and a centralized organization for Muslims in France. Sarkozy put this organization into effect during his time as minister of the interior. In his book *La République, les religions, l'espérance*, he defends the CFCM by explaining that religion in general is the cement of society, and that being a Muslim is not only a matter of faith but, more important, a matter of cultural identity. Through these institutions, cultural identity was brought into French public space by the very hands of the state. While veiled students were excluded from the constitutive institution of laïcité, the public education system, Muslims in general could be included in French society via these identity-specific institutions. However, a quick look at the internal dynamics of the CFCM suggests that this institution empowered men over women.

One member of the Stasi Commission, Patrick Weil, director of research at Centre National de la Recherche Scientifique (CNRS), acknowledged that the Stasi Report encouraged Muslim girls to attend private schools. In an article he wrote for the web forum *Open Democracy* on March 25, 2004, Weil commented:

> I admit that the law passed by French parliament has one unfortunate consequence: the right of Muslim girls who freely want to wear the scarf in public schools, without pressuring anyone else, is denied. What will happen to them if, after the period of dialogue established by the law, they do not want to remove their scarf? It is most likely that they will be offered the opportunity to attend private religious schools—probably Catholic, Protestant or Jewish (there are only three Muslim schools in France). These schools, if they are under state contract (as 95% are), have an obligation to accept applications from pupils of other faiths. More Muslim schools under state contract (which entails authority over the curriculum) will develop in future.[42]

The first of these Muslim schools, Averroès High School, was established in September 2003 in Lille, in northern France. The decision of French education authorities to establish the school was concurrent with the decision to form the Stasi Commission—both were decided in early July 2003. The school received 150,000 euros in private donations.[43] It had approximately fifteen students in the 2003–04 academic year and forty-five in the 2004–05 academic year. At the annual meeting of the Union of French Islamic Organizations in March 2005, the most radically inclined Muslim organization among those that constitute the CFCM, there were approximately a dozen projects seeking to build private schools for Muslims.[44] The Fethullah Gülen community, a Turkish-origin religious community whose leader is now based in Pennsylvania in the United States, also established a school after the March 15, 2004, law was passed.

Les filles voilées parlent (Headscarved girls speak), published in 2008, gave the headscarved students a voice and particularly focused on the application of the law. Many students lost their right to education and faced discrimination; few turned to the newly established private schools because either they lacked the necessary financial resources or there was no Muslim private school in their vicinity. The accounts of the students show that the law of March 15, 2004, created distrust in the French system and radicalized those students who decided not to take off their headscarves. There were discrepancies from school to school in the application of the law. While some students replaced their headscarves with bandanas to continue at school, this option was not afforded other students whose school headmasters adopted a stricter application of the law. Students in those schools were dismissed by disciplinary action. Many others, foreseeing the pressures and difficulties they would face, simply quit school and turned to the option of preparing for the *baccalauréat* from outside with the help of civil society organizations—e.g., Union of Lyon Muslim Sisters—or the National Center for Distance Learning (CNED).[45]

Now let's turn our focus to the CFCM. With the document emerging in January 28, 2000, from the meeting of socialist minister of the interior (and hence the minister of cultes as well) Jean-Pierre Chevènement with Muslim organizations, the participating Muslim organizations declared their general commitment to articles 10 and 11 of the French Declaration of Human Rights, to the first article of the constitution, and to the 1905 Law of Separation between churches and state and vowed that they would "respect the public order and preserve the neutrality of the Republic" and oppose all discrimination based on gender, religion, ethnic appearance, or customs. The document strictly specified the field of activity of the organizations following article 4 of the Law of Separation as matters of religious faith and addressed issues of mosques, chaplains, and private Muslim schooling, which did not yet exist in France. The first elections for the CFCM were held on April 13, 2003, and there have been a total of four elections since: the second in June 2005, the third in June 2008, and the fourth in 2011. When Nicolas Sarkozy became interior minister in 2002, he reclaimed this project and succeeded in forging together the organization despite disagreement among different Muslim groups. This involved the significant compromise imposed by Sarkozy that the institution would be presided over by Dalil Boubakeur, the rector of the Grand Mosque of Paris, whose faction never won a majority of seats at election.

However, the role Sarkozy had in mind for CFCM went beyond practical matters of religious faith. Sarkozy wrapped the council in his Tocquevillean project of religion as a political institution. In *Democracy in America*, Alexis de Tocqueville gives a significant place to religion in the workings of democracy. "Religion," he writes, "which never intervenes directly in the government of American society, should therefore be considered as the first of their political institutions, for although it did not give them the taste for liberty, it singularly facilitates their use thereof."[46]

Sarkozy's book *La République, les religions, l'espérance*, published one year before the presidential elections, started with the following epigraph from Tocqueville:

> It is not to such as they that I speak, but there are others [in France] who look forward to a republican form of government as a permanent and tranquil state and as the required aim to which ideas and mores are constantly steering modern societies. Such men sincerely wish to prepare mankind for liberty. When such as these attack religious beliefs, they obey the dictates of their passions, not their interests. Despotism may be able to do without faith, but freedom cannot. Religion is much more needed in the republic they advocate than in the monarchy they attack, and in democratic republics most of all.[47]

Sarkozy truncated the quotation just before Tocqueville's striking conclusion. The next sentences in *Democracy in America* read: "How could society escape destruction if when political ties are relaxed, moral ties are not tightened? And what can be done with a people master of itself if it is not subject to God?" Tocqueville clearly expresses the substitution of moral ties for political ties, and the necessity of subjection to God, in his own term, in order "to educate democracy."[48] Sarkozy did buy into Tocqueville's conclusion and placed the CFCM into his politics of pushing more religion into public space. In his book he set the role of religion as follows: "Everywhere in France, and much more in the suburbs where despair is concentrated, it is much more preferable that the young can have hope spiritually rather than having in their minds as the only 'religion,' violence, drugs and money." And he continued in his Tocquevillean line of presenting religion as contributing to liberty: "This hope is capable of offering, in the collective dynamic of a society, a vision of mobilization for the common good and a keen sense of life. I am convinced that religious spirit and religious practice can contribute to appeasing and regulating a society of liberty."[49]

Yet where Tocqueville attributed the significant role he finds played by religion in America to the separation of church and state,[50] Sarkozy pursues the same goal by political interventions in the organization of religion and in the hope of changing the institutional separation of churches and state in France.[51] For instance, for Sarkozy it was not important that religious practice in France in general and among Muslims in particular may have been on the decline. Even if it were the case, he still defended additional religion infrastructure, if not on "religious practice" grounds, on "cultural" grounds, and all that he articulated with a discourse against communitarianism.[52]

In practice CFCM has been stuck between being a representative institution for the regulation of the life of Muslims in France and a corporatist mechanism in the hands of the government. Here it is crucial to recall the literature on corporatism. Although this literature mainly addresses the organization of economic forces, Ruth Berins Collier and David Collier remind us that there is no reason for it not to be extended to the phenomenon of interest representation in general. They review the literature on corporatism and offer the following definition: "One may define a system of state-group relations as corporative to the degree that there is (1) state structuring of groups that produces a system of officially sanctioned, non-competitive, compulsory interest associations; (2) state subsidy of these groups; and (3) state-imposed constraints on demand making, leadership, and internal governance."[53]

The relation between the CFCM and the French state satisfies all three conditions: (1) The CFCM was initiated as an officially sanctioned single interlocutor of the state. It is not compulsory but is noncompetitive. (2) Recent offers of state land at low rent for the building of a mosque in Marseille qualify as a state subsidy, and Sarkozy had plans to change the law of 1905 so that the state could provide subsidies to religions, especially to the "late-coming" religion Islam. (3) One state-imposed constraint on the CFCM was on leadership; although lacking a majority of votes, Sarkozy imposed Dalil Boubakeur, rector of the Grand Mosque of Paris, as the president of the council.

Since its founding the CFCM has not accomplished much with respect to the daily lives of Muslims, but it has been quite active in backing up state politics. Dounia Bouzar, the only woman representative in the CFCM, quit the council in 2005 on precisely those grounds. When asked why she quit the Muslim Council, Bouzar responded: "Because I served as an alibi, giving the French general public the impression that there was room for muslims born in France. But in reality, it was better to call it 'CFCM from above' which takes decisions with the minister of interior serving various political interests."[54]

Since its founding, the CFCM has only accomplished nominating chaplains for hospitals, military, and prisons, a goal also set forth by the original Chevènement agreement and also by the Stasi Report. The council's time has been occupied more with providing legitimacy to the state. In October 2003 CFCM declared, two months before the Stasi Commission made its report public, that it was against a ban on the headscarf and demanded to be a party to the debates on laïcité:

> The wearing of the headscarf is a religious prescription. In conformity with the fundamental texts of the republic, in particular [the texts] on liberty of conscience, religious liberty, and individual liberties, the French Muslim Council (CFCM) demands with force the application of the principle of laïcité and the advice of the State Council in 1989. The French Muslim Council regrets the decisions taken against the wearing of the "headscarf." The last event of the exclusion of two young girls from the Henri-Wallon High School in Aubervilliers is a setback from conducting dialogue. The French Muslim Council is persuaded all the more that all the means of conciliations were not exhausted. The Administrative Council regrets that the French Muslim Council was not included in the national debate on laïcité and the presence of religious symbols at school raised by the Stasi Commission, the informative mission of National Assembly and the State Council. The French Muslim Council intends to be at the disposal of public powers in order to contribute to these debates and to provide all necessary light for the enrichment of these ongoing reflections.[55]

Yet in the CFCM's open letter to President Chirac after the Stasi Report had been made public, the issue of the scarf was addressed with less force. Soon after, *Le Monde* reported the council president, Dalil Boubakeur, declaring that "the law of the state is our law,"[56] affirming the Stasi Report, and right before a large demonstration against a law on the headscarf in January 2004, he discouraged any demonstration against the law.[57]

Teaching Religion "as Fact" or "as Culture" but Not "as Faith"

The first report on teaching religious facts was commissioned by the socialist minister of national education, Lionel Jospin, in 1988.[58] The second report, "Teaching of Religious Fact in Laic Schools," written by public intellectual Régis Debray—a member of the Stasi Commission who supported the law for a ban—and published in 2002, was commissioned by socialist minister of education Jack Lang during Jospin's prime ministry and the presidency of Jacques Chirac, who won the presidency in the elections of 1995 and 2002. The report defended "a reasoned approach to religions as facts of civilization," an approach that would also endorse a quest "through the universality of the sacred with its prohibitions and permissions" of "unifying [*fédératrices*] values" in order to direct "civic education" and "to temper the explosion of reference points like the unprecedented diversity of religious belonging we confront."[59] It began by explaining that "the goal is not to put 'God in school' but rather to prolong the human itinerary characterized by multiple paths, as far as its *cumulative continuity*—that one can also call *culture*—that distinguishes our animal-species from others, less fortunate. Religious traditions and future of Humanities are embarked on the same boat" (5; italics in original). It is noteworthy to highlight the distinctions here between "God in school"—an obvious reference to the Third Republic discussions—"religious facts," and "culture," which recalls also Sarkozy's distinction between religion "as such" and "as culture." The religion versus culture distinction was also mobilized by the writers of the Turkish military coup constitution in 1982 for including an article that required a course in primary and secondary education on morality, religion, and ethics without provoking a major debate on laiklik. After being criticized for constitutionalizing the "teaching of religion," they sought to make compatible their self-claimed laic position and the teaching of a course on morality, religion, and ethics by reverting to a distinction between religion "as such" and "as culture" and claiming the course to be "as culture." Recently the same distinction was mobilized by Turkey's governing party, AKP, with the help of lawyers to defend the introduction of a new optional course on religion in addition to the already existing required one. They argued that the old course was not "religion" but only "culture"; therefore the principles of neutrality and equality could not be discussed and met through this course but only through a new one on religion "as such."

The Debray Report continued to carve out a nonreligious space for religion: "the teaching *of the* religious *is not* religious teaching" (9; italics in original). Instead of a teaching that "presupposes the incomparable authority, above all others, of the revealed word," it suggested the possibility of "a descriptive approach, factual and notional of religions in the present, in their plurality from the Far East to the Occident without trying to privilege one over the other" (10). The report put this as a kind of current and historical necessity:

Cultures, languages, religions, identities, heritage mobilize demonstrators by the millions in the street, much more today than yesterday. . . . The symbolic universe as such—in which can be equally listed for various reasons law, morality, art history and myth—for which the School, especially through philosophical teaching, has to broaden reflexive and critical intelligence. How to recount the irreversible adventure of civilizations without taking into account the trails left by great religions? The effort is all the more needed when economic paradigms, new technologies, and references to enterprise and to management impose themselves or propose themselves today to students . . . as the only and the final horizon. (11)

The report sought a middle way between "devitalizing" and "mystifying" religions—something like religions in context—by probing the relation between religion and knowledge:

The point of view of faith and the point of view of knowledge do not make a zero-sum game. The latter begins by making a division . . . between the religious as an *object of culture* (entering in the remit of public instruction, which has an obligation to examine the contribution of different religions to the symbolic institution of humanity) and the religious as an object of culte (demanding a personal voluntariness in the frame of private associations). (13)

The report considered this middle path for secondary education, but rather than pushing it as a specific discipline and course, which the report argued would render it "a decorative place . . . like the music course" (17), said it should become a part of all relevant courses, such as history of art, history of science, liberal arts, and humanities. And here came the punch line: this was not in contradiction with laïcité because "laïcité is not a spiritual option among others, it is that which makes their coexistence possible, because that which is common by right to all men should take precedence over what separates them by fact. The faculty of accessing to the globality of human experience, inherent to all individuals endowed with reason, entails the path of making the fight against religious illiteracy and the study of systems of existing beliefs. Thus one cannot separate the principle of laïcité and the study of the religious" (19). The report underlined that the contemporary and historical understanding of laïcité is constituted by dichotomies such as reason versus faith, which were the backbone of the idea of science as "to shed light on the obscure." It called for going beyond a "certain naive scientism . . . infantile malady of science in advance," because the context had changed and religion was no longer the threat it used to be in the nineteenth century (20–21). Then it turn to laïcité and Islam:

> If laïcité is inseparable from a democratic aim of truth, to surpass prejudices . . . to relax the identitarian noose . . . in a society more exposed than ever to fragmentation of collective personalities, it is to contribute to defuse various fundamentalisms that have in common this intellectual dissuasion: one needs to be from a culture to be able to speak about it. It is precisely in this sense, without excluding other confessions of faith that one can move forward: laïcité is a chance for Islam in France, and Islam of France is a chance for laïcité. (21)

This is, for Debray, a way of going beyond the exceptionalism of France in Europe, an exceptionalism that, he states, France shares with Turkey. And this is neither *laïcité plurielle* nor *laïcité ouverte* but rather *laïcité d'intelligence* as opposed to *laïcité d'incompétence* (21).

On August 8, 2002, a UMP senator posed a written question to the UMP minister of youth, national education, and research, Luc Ferry, asking him to clarify what he planned to do with the Debray Report, particularly given that it talked of a shifting from *laïcité d'incompétence* to *laïcité d'intelligence*. The minister answered on January 23, 2003:

> In accordance with its mission, the public school must give to all the reasoned knowledge and cultural references without which free and autonomous citizens cannot exercise their judgment. The understanding of our contemporary societies and our daily environment renders indispensable the knowledge of religious fact in its social and cultural inscription, in its multiple dimensions, temporal and spatial, literary, artistic and philosophical. As the minister delegated to school teaching has called it in the opening of the interdisciplinary national seminar on "the teaching of religious fact" organized by the Directorate of School Teaching (DESCO), November 5–7, 2002, the politics of the ministry rests on the refusal to create a specific teaching concerning religions. The Debray Report on "The Teaching of Religious Fact in Laic Schools" presented March 14, 2002, which situates itself in

continuation of a reflection that started within the school in 1980–1990 (report of Rector Joutard), shows that the journey of students in the cycles of secondary education—college and lycée—allows them to tackle the study of religious fact in light of the different disciplines taught. The mechanisms like that of the itineraries of discoveries, in college, or that of supervised personal works, in lycée, permit today the implementation of a transverse and multidisciplinary approach as part of the existing teachings and programs, drawing from these materials and sensitive facts proper to each of the disciplines (texts, works of art, maps, etc.) and in establishing a clear distinction between the registers of knowledge and of belief. The approach accomplished by historians and geographers can be extended to literary figures, philosophers, and even professors of artistic teaching or of languages. The creation of the European Institute in Sciences of Religions and a national seminar on "teaching of religious fact" are examples of efforts undertaken so that the professors of primary and secondary education can benefit from the reflection of the best specialists during the course of their initial and continuing training. With a distance to all partisan positions, a comprehensive and critical study of religious facts and of systems of beliefs, in respect of liberty and equality, must rest itself on the highest values of the republican school: in this, laïcité is both a principle and a method.[60]

The French National Ministry of Education colloquium mentioned in Minister Ferry's response took place on November 5–7, 2002, and centered the discussion around the Debray Report. President Jacques Chirac sent a written message for the opening of the conference, which read:

In the world today, tolerance and laïcité cannot be found on more solid grounds than knowledge and respect of the other, because it is turning in on oneself and the ignorance that nourishes prejudices and communitarianisms [*communautarismes*]. Strengthening the knowledge of religions, improving the teaching of religious facts in all the concerned subjects at college and lycée, following its manifestations in history, in the arts, in the culture of each, all that will strengthen the spirit of tolerance among our young fellow citizens, giving them the better means to respect the beliefs and cultures of others. That is why I am delighted by the start-off that constitutes this national interdisciplinary seminar and I welcome the founding of the European Institute for the Sciences of Religions [Institut européen des sciences des religions], which will bring together our best specialists.

After reading President Chirac's message, the minister responsible for school teaching, Xavier Darcos, followed with his own opening speech, which included the following excerpts:

> While up to the present, the problems that religious teaching can pose were principally presented in a historical and geographical perspective, from now on they must concern more the professors of literature, the philosophers, the professors of artistic and modern languages. This multidisciplinary dimension is essential because it can in particular allow a more transversal approach to religious fact, through interdisciplinary mechanisms put in place at colleges and lycées. . . . Philippe Joutard's report on the teaching of history in 1989 clearly showed evidence for the cultural deficit born out of ignorance of facts pertaining to the religious. If this deficit is not remedied, it will lead to a growing loss of the codes of recognition which will risk finally to affect whole sections of knowledge. . . . In sum, these purposes appear to me to be able to gather around three great axes. First, teaching religious fact comes down to recognizing the specific language which allows for naming and decoding the signs. Understanding, in short, one of the ways of expressing the world. Next, teaching religious fact allows the youth to gain access to innumerable masterpieces of humanity's heritage. Finally, teaching religious fact consists of rendering the students capable of understanding the role that the religious plays in the contemporary world. . . . It goes without saying that our approach is totally laic, as the president of the Republic forcefully stated. Teaching religious fact, it is not—is it necessary to underline?—interfering with the conscience of each. It is not, to retake an expression of Régis Debray, "to put back God in school." The approach appropriated is descriptive and comprehensive, but remains critical and reasoned. Teaching the religious fact means, as for all teaching, that it bases itself on the fundamental values of the republican school.

What is crucial to note and often goes unnoticed by eyes fixed on the "scarved girl" is that one political position in France brought together and defended both the teaching of religious facts and a law banning the "scarf" or against the wearing of the scarf but also against the means of national law on this matter.[61] For instance, Minister Darcos addressed the March 15, 2004, law on public television station France 2 on January 20, 2004, and was clearly against the wearing of the scarf, although his testimony in front of the Stasi Commission did not approve making a national law. The France 2 interview focused on violence in schools and the question of religious symbols (without any explicit reason why these two subjects were addressed together). After discussing the question of violence, the interviewer asked the minister if he thought "there is a radicalization that one can fear in the school around that [religious symbols]" and if he had a message to French youth. The minister was now clearly for a law:

> We make everything to guarantee the liberty of conscience for the right to practice religion, and in particular the muslim religion. We are not the enemy of consciences and we are not the enemy of religious practices. Simply, when one is at school, to begin with, one does not present oneself as belonging to such and such current of thought or religious current. And especially, one does not come with a sign which, at the same time, demonstrates the belonging to a religion and especially implies the discrimination of the woman.[62]

Régis Debray himself was a member of the Stasi Commission, which recommended the law on the scarf with the exceptional veto of Jean Baubérot, and in the 1989 headscarf affair he was a signatory to the petition against the "scarved girl." Although Debray strove, during the conference of November 5–7, 2002, to qualify what he meant by "fact," a collection of essays published in 2003 that particularly focused on the Debray initiative showed clearly that different religious leaders and intellectuals understood and expected different things from the "teaching of religious facts." *L'enseignement des religions à l'école laïque* included essays by a previous great rabbi of France, the director of the laboratory of the philosophy of religion at the Catholic Institute of Paris, the rector of the great mosque of Paris, and Philippe Joutard, who had written the 1989 report. A brief review of their statements on the Debray initiative shows that each translated "the teaching of religious facts" significantly differently from the "factual" focus the Debray Report wanted to keep, simply because religion as a subject itself implies different things to different people, and sometimes radically so. Taking note of the variety of understandings and divergences and translations the "teaching of religious facts" goes through in these comments suggests that the Debray Report opened the Pandora's box.[63]

Previously great rabbi of France and currently UNESCO chair of Knowledge Exchange Between Religions, René-Samuel Sirat started his essay by quoting from the Talmud and from Genesis to underscore the importance of education in religion. With frequent references to the need to study and practice the "word of God," and of religion as a force against a culture of consumption and violence, he acknowledged the Debray Report, underlined the richness of the Islamic tradition and how the youth of the suburbs have "a right to know the fundamental values of their religion," and cited the Koran to underscore that there is no compulsion in religion in Islam. Then he delved into the subject of who would teach. By that point the "teaching of religious facts" had already become the "teaching of religions" and was treated as a separate course, which should be taught by those who have an "empathy for the subject" to all students, be they a believer or nonbeliever, and "ethics must become the first preoccupation in rank." Sirat concluded that "this teaching will be without any doubt the base of school programs during the course of the next decade."[64]

Philippe Capelle, philosopher at the Catholic Institute of Paris, who had also been in charge of coordinating the Catholic chaplains in public education in the northern region of France, also made multiple references to the Debray Report in the same book. Capelle started out with the "law of majorities" argument bolstered by some public surveys in 2002 that suggested that the majority of the French public thought of religion taught in schools as a good thing.[65] He then elaborated on scientific, political, pedagogical, and institutional reasons in defense of teaching religions in school. It was not possible to fully convey France's literary, artistic, pictorial, architectural, musical, and philosophical patrimony by erasing the religious memory, he said. In elaborating the political reason, he quoted from President Chirac's opening message to the conference hosted by the French National Ministry of Education on November 5–7, 2002, that "tolerance and laïcité cannot find more solid ground than knowledge and respect of the other" and "ignorance nourishes prejudices and communitarianism." Capelle's own conclusion was that "fractures in knowledge" lead to "socio-ethnic, political, and religious" fractures, and the state had to address the issue and could not leave the teaching to nonstate actors. Not as a separate course but diffused into the already existing courses, it would serve the pedagogical purpose of clarifying the boundaries between science and religion and open up various approaches to religions, as historical facts, as particular beliefs, and so forth. In a friendly critique of the Debray Report, which had swept aside religious institutions of higher education in its initiative, Capelle called on Catholic institutions of higher education especially, for they had a history of dealing with the boundary of science, religion, and laïcité.

Dalil Boubakeur, rector of the Great Mosque of Paris and the first president of the CFCM, claimed that although "religion has its place in the evaluation of today's world," its basic elements were absent in present French laic education. He claimed to speak "in the name of French Islam." He clarified that it was not a question of modifying the Ferry laws, but "there isn't a dichotomy in the life of individuals, there isn't laic on one side and religious on the other." He emphasized that the teaching of religion would ignite philosophical reflection:

> Our generation has taken up the philosophy course after having completely been deprived during our adolescence of moral or spiritual pursuits. Students who have not during their adolescence reflected, for good or bad, on the role of parents, on the place of the elderly, on solidarity, etc., arrive resourceless in front of the concepts of moral philosophy. . . . The young are lost because they don't see to what [these concepts of moral philosophy] correspond to in their lives. . . . In my view, the teaching of religions, in the most elevated sense of this term, would provoke a personal experience of reflection on religious values.

With frequent references to God throughout the text, and emphases on "the teaching of religious facts" not only as a descriptive teaching but also including a focus on spiritual and transcendental experience, Boubakeur concluded with the religious as a source of morality, love of the other, and tolerance.[66]

Rector Philippe Joutard, who in 1989 had written the report on teaching religious facts diffused into existing courses in the school curriculum rather than as a separate course, underlined a "factual" approach and stressed that laïcité does not mean ignorance and lack of culture. Not only was the teaching of religious fact necessary for understanding one's past and heritage, but also in the twenty-first century religion had become a "powerful factor of identity and acculturation." He referred to all the people who had been pushing for the teaching of religious fact in schools: Régis Debray, Jack Lang,

Luc Ferry, Xavier Darcos, Jacques Chirac. He said that not as a separate discipline but as part of all the relevant courses, literature, arts, history, geography, liberal arts, and so on, such teaching would aim at both "respect for diversities and respect for universal values."[67]

A module on "the philosophy of laïcité and instruction about religion," as recommended by the Debray Report, has since been introduced in teachers' training colleges, ten hours per year,[68] signaling the advance of a state project for the teaching of "religious facts."

This chapter has documented the multiple movements and struggles over laïcité around the March 2004 law banning the wearing of religious symbols in French public schools. This exclusionary movement in one public sphere was accompanied by an inclusionary movement in other public spheres, the creation of the CFCM and Muslim private schools, the question of the teaching of religious facts in schools, and Sarkozy's call to the Catholic Church, which is arguably a restructuring of the public sphere toward communitarianism but happened precisely under the opposite claim of "anticommunitarianism."

All this could be made visible starting with a hermeneutical approach, paying close attention to the self-articulation of various actors but not stopping there, and with an analytical commitment, weaving these self-articulations together in context. Such an approach goes beyond a simple interpretive approach focused on difference in meaning, particularly those claiming nationally shared meanings and meanings as some kind of simple determining forces, addressed in the introduction and in chapter 2. For it assesses the difference and changes in meaning in relation to one another and in context, sometimes uncovering multilayered yet clear political directions simply packed in "new meanings." For example, *laïcité positive* is obviously a door for more religion in public space. I will return to this methodological discussion in the concluding chapter.

Laïcité was not reasserted in France through the debates and institutional changes around the 2004 law. To the contrary, its trajectory was reversed, and it turned away from the general institutional level it occupied in the Third Republic toward the level of identity. While the premise of diversity at the societal level had finally grounded laïcité as neutrality at the institutional level in the Third Republic, in contemporary France the decline of laïcité to the level of identity opened the way for diversity at the institutional level, through the CFCM, religious high schools, and the teaching of religious facts. It was the civil religionists who cashed in on this retrieval of laïcité from the general institutional level. Sarkozy's politics are a good example. His political end was not only "to reasonably accommodate Islam"; this was a subset of a more general goal of mobilizing religion as the cement of society, and on that he agreed with the dominantly male Muslim elite, if not with the scarved students who lost their right to public education. He was committed to this goal and therefore redefined laïcité as *laïcité positive*, not the other way around. There is nothing new about *laïcité positive*; it is just the old game of state-civil religionism that I presented examples of from the Third Republic in the previous chapter.

Rather than an exclusive focus on the headscarf ban, as is common in current academic discussions of laïcité, this chapter put the ban in the context of significant coterminous institutional movements. The exclusive focus on the headscarf affair for studying laïcité has ended up deducing the competing ideas of laïcité from the preferences on the ban only, thereby eliminating from view a certain kind of opposition to the ban. This was not in the name of accommodating "diversity" but in the name of laïcité as a general institutional principle. The exclusive focus on the headscarf for mapping the politics of laïcité also hid from view how defenders of teaching religious facts in school, a demand in drastic contrast to the Third Republic institutions, emerged both from the groups in favor (scarved girls out, "religious facts" in!) and opposed to the ban. And abstractions such as *religion as such versus religion as culture, as ethics, as heritage, as fact*, which were frequently mobilized on the question of new courses at school and on Sarkozy's challenge to the 1905 law while forging the CFCM, or in his remarks at the Lateran, are reminiscent of the civil-religionists during the parliamentary discussions on the law of March 28, 1882, such as Lacretelle and Bardoux, who both tried to abstract a general notion of religion from confessional religion. For the former, "it was necessary to put, like the seeds for the future, germs of those grand principles in the spirit of a child who should later on be a soldier and a citizen; I believed that we improve the moral physiognomy of the Republic in inserting the word 'God' in a law which we make for the people," and for the latter, in order to fight "the industry for developing an excess of taste for material well-being and for turning ideas exclusively toward their progress."[69] As we will see in the following chapters, such abstractions are not peculiar to France. Kemalist laicists in Turkey as well have relied on such abstractions while defending civil religionism at the institutional level. Virtually all these abstractions in the final analysis can be traced to an old distinction between "utility of religion" as opposed to "its truth."[70] Such abstractions normalizing mobilization of religion at the institutional level have, in the end, opened the path for religion *as such*, and this dynamic can be seen in how religious leaders picked this entry point in France. We will see later, in its Kemalist laicist versions, how it opened the path of further mobilizing religion *as such* by the AKP in Turkey.

CHAPTER V

The Institutional Politics of Laiklik in Kemalist Turkey

How did the institutional relations in Turkey between state and religion get locked in on state-salaried imams administered by the state's Directorate of Religious Affairs (DRA) and on religion courses on Sunni Islam in the public school curriculum? In Third Republic France, the struggle between anticlericalism and state-civil religionism was resolved by aiming at liberal institutionalism—law as defining general and neutral institutions of society and these institutions embodying uncertainty vis-à-vis concrete political outcomes of conflicts taking place under them. State-civil religionism rested on the idea of a majority religion and the utility of religion. Political Catholics advanced the most explicitly utilitarian arguments on religion. In Turkey, however, most moments of institutional change were directly top down, and even when they were not, they excluded through different mechanisms those actors, such as minorities and the left, who could potentially produce these liberal arguments.

The struggle in Turkey has remained encapsulated between anticlericalism and state-civil religionism, the former also frequently joining the ranks of the latter. State-salaried imams and religion courses have been used like levers to mobilize as well as demobilize religion. After the coup d'état in 1980, the Kemalist military constitutionalized compulsory Sunni religion courses in the public school curriculum and redefined the constitutional role of state-salaried imams as serving national solidarity. The portion of the literature that takes Kemalist laicism as anticlerical qualifies this moment either as a mere contradiction or as some kind of necessity emerging from the different nature of Islam for reaching laicism in a Muslim society. However, the constituent assembly debates in the making of the military constitution of 1982 show that the military's institutional preferences came from an explicit interest in mobilizing religion (as the cement of society) against leftist movements and had nothing to do with the "threat of Islam." As some Third French Republicans were trying to abstract a general notion from religion in order to "improve the moral physiognomy of the republic,"[1] or against "an excess of taste for material well-being,"[2] the Kemalist Turkish military officers were, in the words of one of them, "giving a course in the *culture* of religion, not a course on religion,"[3] on utilitarian grounds against the left. As one member in the Constituent Assembly put it: "Instead of . . . Lenin, Mao, and Castro, let's teach the Turkish child his/her religion in a real sense and under the license of the state within the principles of Atatürk."[4] The military reinterpreted some examples from Europe and pushed the distinction between religion as such and religion as culture in order to normalize this anomaly. Of the people who applauded the military for such an act, most were religious leaders, and one of them is reported to have remarked that military "revolutionaries [*İhtilalciler*] did what republican governments could not do."[5] The coup cleared the ground of leftist movements and handed society over to Islamist movements to mobilize. The 1982 moment was a landmark in the history of the republic for its authoritarian means but definitely not for its institutional politics of religion.

The first major shift in the politics of state-salaried imams and religion courses happened with the transition to a multiparty system in 1945 in the context of the emerging Cold War. The official records of the Turkish parliament provide no evidence as to the origins of the idea of state-salaried imams administered by the Directorate of Religious Affairs (established in 1924). We do not know, for instance, whether the directorate was modeled after the Direction des Cultes that existed before the separation in the Third French Republic. This chapter documents from the records of the Turkish parliament (Türkiye Büyük Millet Meclisi Tutanak Dergisi) and other primary sources that in establishing this institution, Turkey's founding Republican People's Party (CHP) shared the same political ends as the French Républicains opportunistes discussed in chapter 3. The union of education laws in Turkey in 1924 would separate education from religion, and the DRA would make sure that religion did not mobilize to the political level and become a regime threat. In the words of Mustafa Kemal Atatürk, it aimed to "liberate the religion of Islam, within which we have been living peacefully and happily with devotion, from the customary ways in which it has become a means of politics [*vasıta-i siyaset*] (*Bravo, applause*)."[6]

The lack of a counterpart like the Catholic Church in Turkey did not radically change the paradigm of separation. Républicains opportunistes in France were guarding against the Catholic Church and religious orders while the Kemalist laicists were only guarding against religious orders (*tarikat*). But in both cases state-salaried imams/clerics prevented alternative claims on the sphere of religion with the potential to countermobilize a movement at the regime level and at the same time maintain the majority religion as the cement of society. At that point, it was anticlerical and opportunistically not antireligious. At the dawn of Turkey's transition to a multiparty system in 1945, a widely shared perception among the CHP—similar to the perception among republicans in the French Third Republic after the fall of the monarchists in the elections of 1889—was that the regime was consolidated. And from this critical juncture common to France and Turkey, France institutionally separated religion and the state while the CHP turned toward the DRA and religion courses in the public school curriculum to mobilize Sunni Islam, first against socialism along the exact antisocialist line some Républicains opportunistes pushed in the 1890s when they renamed themselves Républicains progressistes, and second against the rising liberal conservative Democrat Party, in order to preempt the DP's challenge to the CHP's past anticlericalism.[7] The paradigm of separation had changed. As one CHP member put it in the 1947 party convention, "Today, the Kemalist Revolution [that] we have embraced as a nation has resolved problems once and for all. Dear friends, since superstition has been understood and the revolution embraced, I believe that to instruct our children in the fundamentals of religion in primary schools . . . has many moral benefits."[8] As another remarked in the December 24, 1946, session of the parliament, "Consciences and hearts are like *patries*. If they are left vacant, they will be occupied by the enemy. We are not afraid of these new religions [socialism], but we are afraid of our own religion. . . . Religion has an otherworldly [*uhrevi*] side, and also a practical [*tasarrufi*] side."[9]

In contrast to the Third French Republic debate, the shared antisocialism of the CHP and DP encapsulated the terms of the debate over the institution of state-salaried imams and religion courses in the public school curriculum to one premised on the "law of majorities" rather than on "diversity." The utilitarian politics of religion were not specific to the CHP of that time.

The first parliamentary discussion in 1951 on the future of state-salaried imams during the DP government shows that what framed the debate over separating or keeping the institution was a question of which option would provide a stronger religion to fight communism. The position of "separation for more religion" was also present in the French Third Republic but as just a few dissident political Catholic voices. The DP increased the state budget for state-salaried imams even further and moved the optional religion courses from outside class hours to within class hours and changed the terms from opt-in to opt-out. These institutional changes were hotly debated among teachers and DP ministers at the annual National Education Congress in 1953, where many examples from European cases were laid on the table. This discussion focused more on institutional principles; however, it was still framed by the idea of a Sunni Muslim majority country disregarding non-Muslims and non-Sunni Muslims. It also exposed further vicissitudes of making liberalism compatible with even *optional* religion courses during class hours, such as utilitarian approaches to religion being able to penetrate liberal principles with less than visible, minute institutional adjustments.

In another critical juncture, during the development of the military constitution of 1961, which drew the institution of state-salaried imams into the constitution, there were a few non-Muslim, non-Sunni Muslim, and liberal republicans in the Constituent Assembly. Although they were not able to change the outcome, they ignited the most important discussions, supported by some minority petitions to the Constituent Assembly. And at all these moments, various political actors were trying to situate disparate institutional politics of religion and secularism within what they understood European secularism to be.

The Kemalist Republican People's Party: Républicains Opportuniste or Combistes?

Authoritarianism in the single-party era (1923–1945) against all political or societal opposition has been significantly documented.[10] It is clear from parliamentary discussions at critical moments that the Republican People's Party's institutional choices on religion were the result of their political goal to preempt religion from becoming a focal point of countermobilization to the republican regime. In a speech he gave in January 1923, Mustafa Kemal stated that "our religion is the most reasonable and most natural religion, and it is precisely for this reason that it has been the last religion. In order for a religion to be natural, it should conform to reason, technology, science, and logic. Our religion is totally compatible with these."[11] In his famous *Speech* delivered to the Turkish nation over three days in October 1927, Mustafa Kemal explained why a constitutional amendment on October 29, 1923, declaring the founding of the Turkish Republic also included an article (article 2)[12] declaring Islam as the state religion:

> After the founding of the Republic, while the new Constitution was being made, with the purpose of not providing an opportunity for those who are inclined to interpret the phrase "laic government" as antireligious [*dinsizlik*] and take advantage of such an interpretation, it has been allowed that a meaningless phrase [declaration of a state religion] be added to article 2 of the constitution. . . . The Nation should remove these unnecessary phrases from the Constitution at the first opportunity![13]

On March 1, 1924, two days before the March 3, 1924, laws passed parliament and abolished the caliphate, created a public education system, and established the Directorate of Religious Affairs, Mustafa Kemal remarked that the aim was to "liberate" Islam from becoming a "means of politics" (*vasıta-i siyaset*):

> Honorable members! The principle of keeping the army separate from the general life of the country is a point which the Republic always regards as fundamental. (*Applause.*) In the path which has been followed thus far; armies of the Republic, as the trustworthy and strong guards of the motherland, have kept a venerable and powerful place. Along the same lines, we see the reality that it is indispensable to liberate the religion of Islam, within which we have been living peacefully and happily with devotion, from the customary ways in which it has been a means of politics. (*Bravo, applause.*)[14]

On March 3, during the parliamentary discussions on the abolishment of the caliphate, the minister of justice remarked:

> ADLIYE VEKILI SEYID B. In Islam, unlike christianity, there is no spirituality [*ruhaniyet*]; in other words there is no spiritual Government [*Hükümeti*

ruhaniye]. . . . The Nation says . . . I do not need a representative [vekil]. I will manage my own affairs with the most beneficial form of Government, that is the Republic, and the procedure of consultation [meşveret]. In that case, who can say what? Nobody can say anything. Because the right belongs to the nation. (*Applause.*) Kuran-ı Kerim as well points out to its permission with clarity. It says that muslims manage their own affairs among themselves with consultation. (*Applause.*) . . . All the civilized world has been advancing on the route of progress with giant steps. Are we going to be left behind? . . . How odd! if we muslims . . . were left behind when the Religion of Islam is so noble and so progressive. (*Laughs and applause.*)[15]

State religion was removed from the constitution on April 9, 1928, by a vote of 264 to 51.[16] In the foreign press this removal was depicted as the abolition of religion in Turkey.[17] The proposal was signed by İsmet Paşa, the man who became the second president of the Turkish Republic after the death of Mustafa Kemal, and 120 other members. The constitutional change was presented as another step toward the laic state;[18] however, it was followed immediately by a cautious preemptive argument on how laiklik was not being antireligious (*dinsizlik*):

The principle of the separation of religion and state should not imply the advocacy of irreligion [*dinsizlik*] by the state or by the government. The separation of affairs of Religion and State is the guarantee for the prevention of religions from being tools in the hands of those who govern the state. The Turkish Revolution [*İnkılap*[19]], in light of the experience and knowledge it has acquired from the contemporary science of law and from history, by removing the article which mixes the affairs of religion with that of the world and which is inclined to cause various difficulties, and by providing the Constitution [*Teşkilatı Esasiye*] by a clear and sincere text, will have given the Turkish Republic in a pure form its real shape. In this manner, religion, which undertakes the spiritual [*manevi*] happiness of mankind, by obtaining its exalted place in the conscience, will have become a sacred means of contact between God and the individual [*fert*]. There are those who find this sacred contact in Mosques or Churches, Synagogue or just in their conscience. The State and its laws are the protector of those all.[20]

Halide Edib Adıvar, a well-known republican novelist, commented on the removal of state religion from the constitution in her article in the *Yale Review*, pointing out that institutional separation in Turkey was still incomplete as long as the Directorate of Religious Affairs was a state institution:

> No secular state can logically have an established state religion. The removal of this clause [on state religion] from the Turkish constitution was therefore in true and necessary accord with the nature of the new Turkish state at its last stage of secularization. "Render therefore unto Caesar the things that are Caesar's, and unto God the things that are God's." The Turks have at last rendered up the things that are Caesar's or the state's. On the other hand, Caesar, or the state still keeps things that belong to God. Unless the Directorate of Religious Affairs is made free, unless it ceases to be controlled by the office of the Prime Minister as it is now controlled, it will always be a governmental instrument. In this respect, the Muslim community in Turkey is to-day less privileged and less independent than are the Christian Patriarchates . . . there is danger in it of the use of religion for political ends. Now that the state has rid itself entirely of religious control, it should, in turn, leave Islam alone. . . . The fundamental meaning of the long and very interesting phase of secularization is that the Turkish psychology separates this world from the next. To take religion out of the political state, but to keep the state in religious affairs, is one of the last phases which must be corrected.[21]

On February 5, 1937, the term *laik* was put in the constitution, religious orders (*tarikat*) were removed from the protection of article 75 on the freedom of conscience,[22] and the freedom of philosophical opinion was now listed before freedom of religion. The minister of the interior explained in the parliament as follows:

> DA. V. ŞÜKRÜ KAYA. We do not interfere at all with the freedom of conscience of the individual and the religion she/he wishes to follow. Everyone has freedom of conscience. The freedom we want, what we mean by laiklik [laicness] is to provide that religion is not influential and effective in the affairs of the country. For us this is the frame and boundary of *laikçilik* [laicism]. . . . We say that religions stay in the conscience and places of worship, and not interfere in material life or affairs of the world. We are not mixing them and we will not mix them. (*Bravo, applause.*) . . . One

other evil thing which the Turks have inherited is to be devoted to some kinds of religious orders [*tarikat*]. To our knowledge, the only true path and *tarikat* for the Turk is nationalism grounded on positive science. . . . For this reason, if here and there in the hearts of our citizens has there been any bounds left to these wrong paths, we want to eliminate for good these bounds and keep them away from these religious orders with the decision of the Grand National Assembly. (*Bravo.*)[23]

There were few critics within the party on the state budget for imams; such criticism was always met with silence, and there was no engagement in discussion. One such view was expressed by Hakkı Kılıçoğlu:

HAKKI KILIÇOĞLU. Yet, I contend that there is an institution that is particularly in contradiction with the second article. The Directorate of Religious Affairs. (*Some others laugh.*) I am not against this institution. I am not the enemy of religions or religious persons. But after leaving all religious matters to the conscience of the individual, I contend that, especially given the new second article of our constitution, this institution cannot have a place in the state budget.

Kılıçoğlu highlighted the contradiction between the two moves in the constitution: on the one hand, a move to privatize religion, and on the other hand, a move to make religion public by establishing a state-funded Directorate of Religious Affairs. "Maybe," he remarked, "there is a formula which can reconcile these two forms." Then he added, "I am not aware of this formula. . . . Yes we have places of worship, there are personnel who take care of these places. I am not saying that we don't take care of these places. But statutes on these can be included directly as a separate section of the law on waqfs."[24]

The Union of Education Law (Tevhid-i Tedrisat Kanunu) closed down religious schools (*medrese*) and established a unified national education system. The 1924 law placed one hour of religious instruction per week in the third, fourth, and fifth grades of primary schools, but the same year religious instruction in secondary schools was reduced from a compulsory three hours to one hour per week. In 1928 compulsory religious education in secondary schools was completely eliminated.[25] In 1930 primary school religious instruction was reduced to an optional half hour in the fifth grade, and in 1931 it was completely eliminated. Twenty-nine İmam Hatip four-year secondary schools (schools for the education of Muslim clerics) were established in 1924 in place of the *medrese*s in order to bring up imams and preachers loyal to the Republic.[26] The number of İmam Hatip schools declined steadily from 1924 until 1930 because of a lack of students, and in the 1929–30 academic year they were all closed. The Faculty of Theology at Istanbul University was closed in 1933, after a report by a European scholar documented the small number of registered students.

Jean Baubérot, in a brief piece, finds Kemalism closest to Combisme among the republican currents of the Third Republic. Both placed the state in control of religion rather than institutional separation, both combatted religious orders, and both led or inspired movements that put the republic at the level of faith.[27] The Turkish Language Association's dictionary in 1945 had under the entry "religion" as an example for "religion as principle" the sentence, "The Turk's religion is Kemalism."[28] The question of which Third Republic republican movements Kemalist laicism resembles the most is not an easy one. One cannot ignore the fact that these movements in the Third Republic were competing in elections and therefore had to calculate for winning votes and winning majorities in a diverse chamber, while this was not the case for the Kemalists, single-party regime. Both Opportunistes and Combistes were against religious orders. Opposing Assumptionists and Jesuits, groups that would at times get into conflict with the Vatican as well, was at the top of their anticlerical agenda. This was also the case for Kemalism: the banning of religious orders in 1925 and their removal from the protection of the constitutional article on freedom of conscience in 1937 are cases in point.

The main difference between the Opportunistes and Combistes was how they approached the institution of state-salaried clerics before separation and at the moment of separation in 1905. As documented in chapter 3, a "salaried church as opposed to a propertied" church was a guarantee against regime threats from monarchical movements for the Opportunistes in the 1880s under the constraint of elections; that is, they were calculating a loss of votes from a possible reaction from their voters to the cessation of state salaries for clerics. However, one part of the Opportunistes was also fighting against the Republican left. For instance, Jules Ferry did not allow a discussion on the practices of Catholicism in France and in 1883 in a letter to his wife stated, "We have reduced the clergy and religious orders to submission. . . . We can now pursue a moderate policy."[29] This wing of the Opportunistes renamed themselves as Républicains progressistes in the 1902 chamber, opposing the suppression of state salaries for clerics, not on grounds of a regime threat but, to the contrary, for maintaining religion as the cement of society. In other words, there was not only a contextual change—regime threat from monarchists had pretty much disappeared with the 1889 elections—but also a change in political ends. Combistes, on the other hand, mobilized state salaries for clerics to depower the Catholic ecclesiastical hierarchy in France quite radically, by laying off clerics they considered antirepublican; however, once they were convinced that the regime threat was gone toward the end of the Dreyfus Affair, they finally opted for separation.

Here the lack of a state-independent ecclesiastical hierarchy in Turkey makes the comparison difficult, for the question of how the Kemalist CHP would react to such an organization remains a counterfactual. However, the snapshots above from parliamentary discussions do show that the CHP also saw state-salaried imams as a guarantee against regime threats, with frequent statements that document that they did not want to look antireligious, similar to Jules Ferry's famous statement, "We are anticlerical but not antireligious." Recep Peker, general secretary of the CHP, at a conference at Istanbul University to introduce the party program in 1931, remarked; "Today, in Turkey religious view is a matter of individual conscience which belongs to each citizen," however, "laiklik never means being without religion or to want to be without religion. In Turkey, everyone's practice of worship, by each as he/she wants, is under the protection of the constitution. A citizen who considers him/herself religious can simultaneously keep his beliefs and sincerely be laique."[30]

With this preliminary comparative sketch, a critical question to push the comparison further is: what direction did Kemalist CHP's laicism take once the party saw the republican regime as consolidated? That critical juncture came in 1946.

Kemalist Republican People's Party's New Spirit with the Transition to a Multiparty System: Républicains Progressistes?

The major opposition to the Republican People's Party was the Democrat Party, founded on January 7, 1946. It was a conservative liberal party of big landowners, and its founders were former CHP members who had disagreed with the party mainly on the question of land reform. Among the new parties formed with the transition to a multiparty system were also socialist parties. Although the socialists did not have much presence on the political scene, their mere existence was sufficient to influence CHP policies in the international atmosphere of the Cold War. At the time the CHP and DP were accusing each other of being soft on the left, and on December 16, 1946, the Turkish Socialist Party and Turkish Socialist Workers and Peasants Party were shut down by martial law.[31] In the parliamentary elections of July 21, 1946, the DP gained 66 seats (as opposed to CHP's 395). The election's validity, however, has been widely contested; therefore the 66 seats do not necessarily represent the exact support for the DP at the time.[32] In the next elections, on May 14, 1950, the DP received 52.7 percent of the vote and 408 seats in the parliament (CHP, 39.4 percent and 69 seats; Nation Party, 4.6 percent and 1 seat).[33] Article 14 of its 1951 party program stated:

> Our party understands laiklik as the complete detachment of the state in politics from religion, and that no religious creed is influential in the ordering and application of law and refuses the misinterpretation of laiklik as antireligiousness. It takes religious freedom, like other freedoms, as among the sacred rights of humanity. It is necessary that a program is prepared by experts on the question of religious education and institutions for the education of clerics [*din adamı*]. Faculty of theology in the university and institutions similar in scientific regards should be autonomous [*muhtar*] as other similar institutions of the National Education Ministry. The use of religion as a political tool, as a propaganda tool for disrupting love and solidarity among citizens, or for igniting feelings of fanaticism as opposed to free thought [*serbest tefekkür*] must not be tolerated.[34]

The period from 1946 until 1950 saw a return to religion by the CHP. In 1947 the CHP provided funding for the hajj to Mecca, and in 1949 it included optional religion courses for fourth- and fifth-grade primary school students to be administered on Saturdays. Parents had to petition for their children to attend the class.[35] The CHP also reopened the İmam Hatip schools.[36] In 1947 it almost doubled the budget of the Directorate of Religious Affairs, from 0.15 percent in 1946 to 0.24 percent of the state budget (see figure 5.1). The parliamentary discussions of December 24, 1946, on the national education budget already had some clues as to the nature of this return to religion.[37] This discussion portrays an internal CHP debate only, for the DP parliamentarians were not present in the parliament at the time.

They had boycotted budget discussions by leaving the parliament a week earlier and had still not returned.[38] In this session of the parliament, Muhittin Baha Pars (CHP) complained about the decline in the moral conditions of the country, pointing out three examples: an editor protesting against moralist children's books, a case of rape, and a free public talk in the liberal Beyoğlu district of Istanbul, all of which for him epitomized self-indulgence preempting national consciousness, and that new "leftist religions" had emerged. I return to a speech quoted from earlier:

MUHITTIN BAHA PARS. Consciences and hearts are like *patries*. If they are left vacant, they will be occupied by the enemy. We are not afraid of these new religions, but we are afraid of our own religion. . . . Religion has an otherworldly [*uhrevî*] side, and also a utility [*tasarrufî*] side. I will not talk about that side [the other worldly side]. Nobody has the right to interfere between God and the subject. . . . But religions have moral sides. Every child, every young person should know this closely. . . . Friends, wisdom [*hikmet*] starts with the fear of God. . . . I am not saying that [religion] is the only way of improving public morality. . . . We do not want to destroy what Atatürk started, we want to support it. If Atatürk were alive, he would also do the same. . . . I think this matter should be discussed in this budget.[39]

Another CHP parliamentarian pointed out that public opinion wanted to see a "more virtuous, soft-spirited, abstemious, appreciative" youth and complained that all moral instruction had been removed from primary school and after (431). Hamdullah Suphi Tanrıöver remarked as follows and with comparative references:

HAMDULLAH SUPHI TANRIÖVER. Great love and great faith have created great periods in the history of nations. When defeat starts in the spirits, faith collapses, if a faith of similar strength does not replace the collapsed faith . . . disaster has started. Two faiths can be given to the Turkish youth. There is also a third faith, the Turkish public refuses it, it is a social and political faith. We see that one in other countries, like Communism. In this country, one can find a few fools who would defend this one as a principle of education. But the conscience of the Turkish Nation has removed it from its horizons. Another faith . . . is religion. And there is also a new faith: our nationhood. . . . I consult our Minister of National

Education to say something clear on nationhood to the child he takes from the hands of the Turkish mother and father and brings to the State school. (437–38)

He gave examples of the resilience of religion in Russia and underlined that in Turkey as well religion had to be put in place as a source of morality. Then he turned to France:

HAMDULLAH SUPHI TANRIÖVER. The French revolution was the site of many antireligious activities. Churches were seized. These churches, except two of them, were returned to religion and in the year 1913, during my visit to Paris, I saw the French public worshipping in Notre Dame Church. . . . During the Combes government, France separated religion from the State, but it was allowed that all institutions belonging to religion are kept alive by the public. . . . There are seminaries, in other words, *medrese*s in Paris. The French public satisfies its religion needs by its own organization. (439)

Next he turned back to the question of communism:

HAMDULLAH SUPHI TANRIÖVER. They have reached a level that worries us and this Government . . . courts, police, gendarme, punishments are not sufficient panaceas [for these currents]. We have to reinforce the spiritual make of the Turkish public against these illnesses. For that the opportunity has to be provided so that the Turkish nation can benefit from its great spiritual sources, religion and nationhood. (440)

Prime Minister Recep Peker responded to these remarks as follows:

BAŞBAKAN RECEP PEKER. In Turkey, religion, as it is not the case in many places, has ceased to be a danger to society, it is no longer a tool to worldly simple calculations and it has been put in its divine and celestial place. . . . I insist and believe it that nowhere in the world as in Turkey—including the laic States which have just been presented as examples . . . do citizens not face any reprimand [*muatebe*] in front of the law or the State for their faith and worship. (*Bravo*.) To the contrary, in all places of worship, the prayer and the worship of the citizen is under the protection of the State.

> Our State does not only allow freedom of conscience, it defends it as the most important work of the revolution [*inkılap*]. (444–45)

He continued with how religion has been abused for self-interest:

> BAŞBAKAN RECEP PEKER. Dear friends; those people who abuse a religious view point, put the relation between conscience and God outside its limits and inflict the material world with its effect, are people who poison society. (*Bravo.*) Today here, the necessity of relying on certain ideal and spiritual wealths for protecting society from some malevolent social influences and doctrines was mentioned. Yes fundamentally, I appreciate it, but the one and only means for the protection against the mentioned poison is the feeling of the nation. (*Bravo, applause.*) To insist that a . . . devout muslim will not turn communist, or that religion in general provides a resistance to communism, is in contradiction with the realities of the day. . . . I am a muslim, my nation is Turkish, my political doctrine is Kemalist . . . in other words I am laic. (*Bravo, strong applause.*) With these attributes, no ideas or movement upsetting religion can emerge from me. But, for the tranquility of the *patrie*, I would fear giving way to religious propaganda. . . . Dear friends, the morality of the modern person has to be a morality that looks like the examples in the advanced scientific and human thoughts of today's new world. . . . I have to say that the claim that there cannot be a consistent morality not based on religion . . . is just not true. . . . The real inner [*manevi*] force that will protect us against the dangerous currents we would like to avoid is the understanding of nationhood. I don't think it is pertinent to present the case as if we are in pain from a lack of religiosity and our society is suffering in this regard. . . . I think that it is not beneficial or pertinent to discuss such deep and great matters in the narrow frame of a budget discussion. (*Applause.*) (445–46)

On September 28, 1947, the newspaper *Cumhuriyet* reported on an ex-military officer and DP parliamentarian arguing publicly that there was no morality without religion and discrediting the CHP's attempt of what he called "trying to win broken hearts by putting optional religion courses in public schools."[40] The question of religion infrastructure was a major item in CHP's Seventh Party Congress on November 17, 1947, and a general push for state funds into building religion infrastructure was clearly visible. One member remarked as follows:

ŞÜKRÜ NAYMAN. Friends, you all know that, today, we have two institutions under the Prime Ministry. . . . One of these is the Directorate of Religious Endowments, the other one is the Directorate of Religious Affairs. But the Directorate of Religious Affairs is almost nonexistent. The Directorate of Religious Endowments is not in a condition to be able to care for and make live religious institutions. Friends, imams and hatips are hungry and destitute. (*Voices: Allah Allah.*) Yes, with thirty liras of wages can an imam or hatip be raised? It's not the right moment for muttering Allah. This amount of money cannot feed religious ideas, religious thought in the country. Only by staying under these conditions does religion become a propaganda tool. The men of religion we need cannot be raised.[41]

The question of state funds for religion infrastructure was mainly addressed in the congress during the discussion of article 15 of the CHP party program, on laiklik. The article read:

> Our Party regards the main factor of success in the improvement and progress of our nation, that all laws in the state administration, regulations, and procedures be made and applied according to contemporary civilization, according to the principals and forms derived from sciences and according to the necessities of this world, and that religious ideas are kept separate from affairs of the state and this world and from politics. Religion is a matter of conscience and therefore it is exempt from any kind of intervention. No citizen can be interfered with for worships and ceremonies not banned by law. (448)

During discussions on the laiklik article, investing in religion infrastructure was defended from various angles, but all concluded with its compatibility with laiklik. One CHP member, Vehbi Dayıbaş, differentiated between laiklik as a *regime question* and as *state policy* and argued that since the issue of laiklik as a regime question had been resolved, there could only be an advantage in a state policy of instituting courses on religion in primary schools:

VEHBI DAYIBAŞ. Today, the Kemalist revolution we have embraced as a nation has resolved problems once and for all. Dear friends, since superstition has been understood and the revolution embraced, I believe that to instruct our children in the fundamentals of religion in primary schools via a course program to be arranged by the Ministry of

National Education is not harmful, and to the contrary it has many moral benefits.... Most respected friends, those who go to churches and attend ceremonies there read something about their own religion. What will our children read during worship? We want our children to be instructed on this issue. (448)

Instead of leaving instruction in religion to private education, argued Dayıbaş, this could be dealt with in public schools via optional courses. A different angle was to point out that Mustafa Kemal was against religious orders but not religion. The second speaker, Abdulkadir Güney, advocated a course on religion in primary schools and a department of theology in universities. He maintained that a nation that studied its religion attained permanence and that instruction in religion did not contradict the six arrows of Kemalism.[42] All immoralities and social calamities, he argued, resulted from a lack of attention to religion:

ABDÜLKADIR GÜNEY. I do not want to question our six arrows, but I want the meaning and understanding of these arrows to provide for the spiritual and temporal happiness of the nation and country by having them materialize in practice. Most respected friends, Eternal Chief Atatürk wanted to eliminate religious orders for he saw in these orders activities contrary to religion, morals, and humanity under the pretext of religion, and he thought this [elimination of religious orders] possible by including laiklik among the six arrows and he was successful in all this; but all this ... does not mean that we should ignore the development of our religion. (449)

Another argument was to present the place of non-Muslim organizations under the Lausanne Treaty as a privilege and argue that Muslims were being discriminated against in their own country. The third speaker, Sinan Tekelioğlu, an ex-military officer with a law degree, acknowledged the plurality in Turkish society and pointed out what he saw as one of the most serious contradictions of Turkish laiklik: non-Muslims have more freedom in their religious affairs than the Muslim majority in Turkey.

SINAN TEKELIOĞLU. Dear friends, what is laiklik according to the science of law? Let me convey this according to my studies; laic does not mean being without a religion. Laic means, as it is stated in our party program, and as it is everywhere in the world, to separate the affairs of religion, the affairs of the world, and the affairs of politics, and to give no privileges . . . to any of the religions in this country. Now we can evaluate the program prepared by our party: the first aspect of our definition is in place; but there is also a second aspect of the definition; this is missing: to give no privilege to any of the religions in the country. Yet this kind of an affirmation has not been included in the program. Friends, according to the Constitution in hand, all persons present in Turkey are Turks regardless of their religion and race. Even a child born to foreign parents is a Turk until he becomes 18 years of age. This child can choose the nationality he/she wishes when he/she becomes 18 years of age. Friends, in our country, according to its structure, I wonder if laiklik is present in its full meaning? We look; affairs of religion, world, and politics have been separated, but the second aspect is not present, why is it not present? There is a Directorate of Religious Affairs, we pay the salaries of the officials [Muslim clerics] in its cadre. On the other hand there are Turkish christians and Turkish jews. But these do not have representatives or members in the Directorate of Religious Affairs. That means, we have given the administration of their pious foundations to them and placed the "Directorate of Religious Affairs" at the head of the religious community belonging to the religion of Islam. . . . But we have left its hands tied. . . . Whereas christian and jewish Turkish religious communities have established schools for themselves, have trained priests, rabbis, and grave diggers. But the Turks who constitute 8/10 of this country . . . do not even have someone to bury their dead. We never want our State to part with the principle of laiklik. To part with the principle of laiklik is to go backward. We do not accept traditional religious fundamentalism [irtica]. . . . I want the State to treat Turkish religious persons at the same level as it treats other religious people. . . . I want the Directorate of Religious Affairs, with all its cadre, to be removed from the State cadre and placed above the directorate of religious endowments [Vakıflar İdaresi], which has all the money our ancestors have endowed for managing this religion [Islam]. . . . Let the General Directorate of Religious Affairs with this money from the directorate of religious endowments establish schools and train modern and civilized hodjas, grave diggers, and imams who can preach to us. (450–51)

Sinan Tekelioğlu also highlighted comparisons with the United States and United Kingdom to underscore that religiosity is also a part of Western modernity; taking care of its religion infrastructure and advocating religion as a source of morality would take the Turkish nation more toward the level of contemporary civilization, because all civilized nations take care of their religions:

SINAN TEKELIOĞLU. Friends, right now I am addressing the Turkish Nation as well as the whole world, by doing this Turks will not have taken a step back, they will never have traced back a step they had already taken forward; to the contrary, they will have reached the level of modern nations. Friends, if we look at modern nations, we will see how they give importance to religion. Remember how Churchill and Roosevelt were praying on the ship, friends; nations without a religion cannot survive, certainly one day comes and they become extinct. History has proved this. Friends; today, in our country, gambling has inceased, alcohol consumption has increased, moral values are on the wane. In the country of a nation without a religion there is no fear left, for the nation to continue living, it has to fear something. For the continuity of its existence, an idea is necessary. No obedience to mothers, fathers, elders remains, no one respects each other if, when one is asked, what is God?, he/she does not know what God is. (*Noise and strong applause.*) (450–51)

Şükrü Nayman, again underlined religion as a source of morality for combatting materialism, alluding to communism, and also offered comparative statements on Europe and the United States:

ŞÜKRÜ NAYMAN. Friends, our Party, with this article that is the object of debate, by keeping the affairs of religion separate from affairs of State and politics and granting a complete freedom of concience to the citizens, does not qualify as satisfying today's needs. Today the Turkish Nation and Turkish youth are in need of spiritual [*manevi*] nourishment. In nations deprived of spiritual nourishment, and who only worship material things, the prevention of immorality has never been possible. In these cases humanity and society have fallen into mischief; history proves this and provides the most grand evidence. Friends, one who only worships material things, and a human being deprived of spiritual existence, before all other things, does not think of anything but to only spend his/her days with pleasure.

But if you look at [his/her] conscience, his/her mask falls and his/her terrifying state is revealed. Humanity has to embrace the spiritual ties of religion at all levels; as an individual, as a community, as a nation. Okay, how will the individual embrace these spiritual ties and from where will he/she provide for this need of his/hers? Friends, Let me speak frankly; we will find the means of satisfying this need only, and only in the laws of morality approved by the religion of Islam. (*Applause.*) These laws of morality will take this nation to the right path; today, those immoralities we complain of everywhere and all the time will be prevented. Most respected friends; to infuse human beings with spiritual nourishment is only possible through religion. To train the spirit is not possible outside religion. Because religion is a force that curbs tyrannical feelings and bad inclinations in human beings, society and individual are absolutely in need of religion. Friends; after having accepted that embracing spiritual ties is a necessity, I would like to say one thing briefly: as we can see, after the end of the war, radio stations in the United States and in Europe are incessantly broadcasting religious conferences, churches are full. On the other hand, we accept it as a novelty and are proud to do bridge and poker parties, men and women mixed, and set tables with alcoholic drinks, as opposed to setting iftar tables. (*Voices: there is no such thing.*) . . . Most respected friends; if we want to serve laiklik in its true sense and think as real revolutionaries [*inkılapçı*], we have to accept that the time has come and even passed that we help the development of religious education in the Turkish homeland. . . . We removed the ideals of religion, but what did we replace them with? We accept that 80 percent of our population is illiterate. Were we able to vaccinate them with love of *patrie* and nation? Who can defend that? In that case, we cannot demolish spiritual wealth, we have to offer religious education in schools. (451–52)

Hamdullah Suphi Tanrıöver listed many examples from Europe to underscore the point that laiklik and provision for the religious needs and services of the nation are compatible. Tanrıöver repeated the examples from Russia and France he had iterated in the December 24, 1946, parliamentary debate. The former, in his view, was a case of the impossibility of eliminating religion and religiosity; the latter, of how separation of religion and state does not interfere in religious practices. He added the examples of Switzerland, Belgium, Germany, and the United States, all laic states in which freedom of religion is freedom to build and maintain infrastructures, how some universities used to be seminaries, how all these countries have missionary organizations operating even in Turkey (455). "If similarly in our history, *medreses* were reformed, we could have been proud for having nine-century-old universities . . . but instead, we shut down *Medreses* and imam hatip schools."

HAMDULLAH SUPHI TANRIÖVER. Dear friends, today we have forty thousand villages, I imagine one small mosque [*Mescit*] in each. . . . I bring in front of my eyes towns and cities, at least ten thousand mosques. . . . Friends, do we need imams and hatips to serve in these *Mescit*s and Mosques or not? (*Voices: Yes, we do.*) . . . There is no need to panic, our [Kemalist] revolution cannot be destroyed. . . . Dear friends, I want to come to a point: the Turkish revolution's religious prosecution, under the influence of bitter experiences of the past periods, belonging to generations who suffer from men who speak in the name of religion, we closed these institutions. We did this as a temporary precaution; it cannot be permanent. Because, on the planet, there is no such laic State.

Dear friends . . . in Bosnia, Yugoslavians have referred some men to court . . . then to prison . . . *müftüs*[43] and imams. . . . Dear friends; because Communism diffuses like a religion, everywhere it follows clerics. In that case, if we do not open İmam Hatip schools, teach at our Istanbul University, History of Islam and history of Islamic Philosophy as matters of science like in all world universities . . . and open a higher education institution for religion, I wonder, where these poor minorities will get the men they need to defend themselves. Not only for our country, but also for the needs of the minorities we left outside we have to think about these institutions. (457–59)

Cemil Sait Barlas challenged Tanrıöver's comparative examples and his position on the use of state funds:

CEMIL SAIT BARLAS. Friends; I am a man whose nine-year-old daughter gets private religion courses at home. I believe that a religion course is a fundamental element of Turkishness and Turkish culture. . . . But my understanding of laiklik is not like Hamdullah Suphi Tanrıöver's at all. In fact, nowhere in the world is laiklik the way he understands it. The Turk's essence is neither religion nor faith. . . . The Turk's last bastion is in the noble blood in his veins. (*Applause.*) Hamdullah Suphi Tanrıöver, the information you have provided is totally wrong. . . . When does the State give money to the church in America, would you tell me? The Catholic universities in Belgium, don't they receive the money from the Pope? How much money has the German State given to Heildelberg University? . . . I defend religious reform, but this we cannot do, a man trained as a soldier cannot do a religious reform, Luther was a priest. . . . Hamdullah Suphi Tanrıöver, are you a priest or a *hodja* that you will carry on a religious reform? (459)

Barlas defended keeping to the original understanding of laiklik and not mixing it with anticommunism. He argued that in Europe laiklik had started with antireligious movements—for example, Bismarck against the Catholic Church and the French state against the Jesuits—and that in comparison Turkish laiklik has also been antireligious. He remarked that "religion should stay as a private matter between the subject and God" (460) and expressed his surprise at what he found was a change in position of somebody who had once carried flags in the country, like Hamdullah Suphi Tanrıöver.

Behçet Kemal Çağlar warned against plans for short-term gain in the transition to a multiparty system:

BEHÇET KEMAL ÇAĞLAR. Friends, what the real believer . . . regards best for his/her religion and faith is that . . . they are not casually made a tool of world affairs and political games. . . . Hamdullah Suphi Tanrıöver who would recount the deadly harms of zealotry better than anyone else, but with hyperbolic language bordering on irreligion [*dinsizlik*], is . . . from the Türk Ocakları [a nationalist organization founded in 1912]. We used to repeat the words of the Türk Ocakları orators with a smile of tolerance, "every minaret is a gravestone and underneath lies a village of islam," as a radical attack on religious conservatism. Then he was inclined to irreligion. Now, as an atonement of conscience, he redeems himself by inclining toward religious conservatism. We are rather in the middle of these two positions and take as a principle the separation of politics and religion. . . . Do we have to rely on examples taken from various parts of Europe? Why does the Turkish nation always turn to absolutely following [Europe] as a necessity? Today, even Europe is in the making, trying out new ways of becoming in a broad sense. The Church has reactionary politics, novelty is also novelty in the West, and conservatism (*irtica*) is also conservatism in the West. Respectful Tanrıöver, who remarked that religion is unifying, does he forget that Hitler was also praying to . . . God, King George as well. Their subjects destroyed each other, they were from the same religion. . . . religious sect fought in Anatolia. . . . We are Kemalists to our marrow. According to our principles, religion is separate from the State and politics. The State does not interfere in religion. . . . Who prevents the building of mosques? Let the believers build their Mosques instead of expecting it from the State. . . . [Anybody] who would teach religion in a town should meet the same ease and [bureaucratic] formalities as somebody who would open a knitting course. . . . If this is what is demanded, this is reasonable. (462–64)

Despite these internal conflicts, the CHP ended up channeling more state support to religious insfrastructure. The Kemalist motto of the 1920s, "Our laiklik is not antireligious," had become less of a pragmatic political statement with the primary purpose of containing Islam and had turned more to an advocacy of a civil religion tradition. On February 19, 1948, in a party meeting the CHP decided to put optional religion courses back in the fourth and fifth grades of primary school on school grounds after class hours (on Saturday afternoons) on the condition that parents would have to ask for their children to attend. The creation of the course books was given to the DRA under the condition that they would go through the approval of the Ministry of National Education. The ministry would choose the instructors of the religion course from among primary school teachers and, if necessary, from among local figures who were known to have the qualities necessary for instructing these courses; and the village institutes[44] would start giving religion courses to their first year students so that they could become instructors in primary schools. Primary school graduates under the age of sixteen could also attend these courses.[45] In November 1950 the religion course were added into the mandatory primary school curriculum by a Democrat Party government decree after consulting a commission of experts, and the terms of the optional course were changed from opt-in to opt-out.[46] Now parents had to petition if they *did not* want their children to attend the course. The Democrat Party also continued the trend of investing in the DRA that the CHP had started late 1940s (see figure 5.1). The question of optional religion courses in the public school curriculum was the central matter for discussion with comparisons to European cases in the National Education Congress of 1953. Now I turn to the records of this congress.

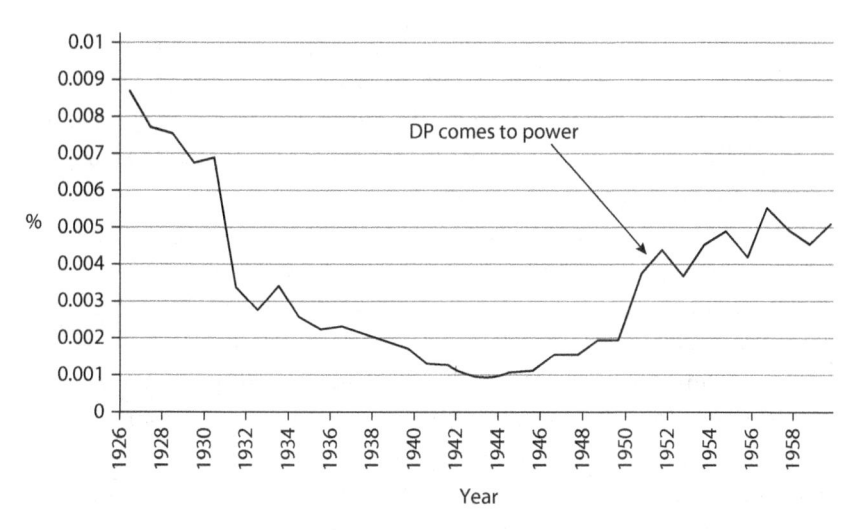

Figure 5.1 DRA Budget Spent as Percentage of Total State Budget, 1926–1959. (*Source*: Calculated from *Turkish Statistical Yearbook*.)

The Debate over Optional Religion Courses in the National Education Congress of 1953

It is one of the forgotten moments in Turkey's history that a university professor of law, Bülent Nuri Esen, opened a court case in 1950 against the teaching of an optional course on religion in primary schools.[47] The State Council decided against the applicant on the grounds that the appplicant's claim that religion courses in public primary schools were contrary to the constutional principle of laiklik was invalid. The decision published in the *Journal for State Council Decisions* in 1953 underscored that both the plaintiff and the defendant most of the time discussed laiklik and presented examples from Western law, theory, and practice. The decision continued with a claim on the importance of particular historical, social, and political causes in order to understand the meaning of the principle of laiklik and stated that the debates in the Turkish Grand National Assembly at the moment of the constitutionalization of the principle of laiklik in 1937 conveyed the correct meaning of laiklik; that is, "even the continuing presence of the DRA within the state budget has not been found contrary to the principle of laiklik," and parliamentary debates on the (re)establishment of the faculty of theology had cast

LAIKLIK IN KEMALIST TURKEY [157]

further light on the concept of laiklik, "a concept shaped by the inspiration of science and law, common to the world of civilization, and filtered by catastrophes and pains of our national history in order to carry a national meaning."[48] The February 5–14, 1953, National Education Congress meeting became the stage for a long and rich discussion on this question of optional religion courses in primary schools. Bülent Nuri Esen was also a participant in the congress,[49] while the decision of the State Council was still pending.

In the congress, Esen claimed that an optional religion and ethics course was against laiklik, and that Turkey had signed the 1948 Universal Declaration on Human Rights, which guarantees freedom of belief and religion; therefore religion was a matter of private and not state education. The DP Minister of National Education responded by pointing out that even the United Kingdom's Education Act of 1944 had stronger provisions for religion. The religion and ethics course in question was optional; therefore it was not against freedom of religion. The course was just a response to popular demand and needs, and if citizens had demanded to receive religion courses from the state as opposed to religious organizations, not having the course would present an initiative to religious organizations. Indeed, the minister continued, the United Kingdom's Education Act put collective prayer in the beginning of the day in all (county and voluntary) schools (part 2, 25[1]), and religious instruction was given in all schools (25[2]). Parents could demand to have their children opt out from collective prayer or religious instruction or both (25[4]) in order to take another kind of religious instruction or no instruction.[50]

Esen responded to the argument from a "social need" perspective (an argument very similar to the "law of majorities" argument in the French Third Republic) by refocusing the question on institutions. According to him, the question was not whether society wanted or needed religion; this was a social reality. The question was whether the state would engage in religious affairs. He also pointed out that the course had been instated by a decree without prior discussion by the National Education Congress. He stated that laiklik was Westernization, and "meeting this demand of citizens is not democracy.... Democracy has the same formula everywhere. One of its fundamental principles is that the state has to be laik." He continued: "The real question is whether we can demand from the teachers [state employees] this task or not.... The teacher is somebody whose religious belief is not known, we cannot ask him/her to teach a certain religious belief.... If s/he does, the student loses freedom of conscience.... this kind of instruction can only be given by a cleric [*din adamı*]," and state principles of laiklik in education and impartiality (*bitaraf*) are violated (386–87).

A village teacher remarked that villagers sent their children to ignorant local religion teachers (*hoca*) for learning Islam because the school did not offer a course on religion, and that in some cases this also became a question of school attendance. He told the story of a student with poor school attendance because he was instead receiving local religious instruction. He inquired with the teacher and realized that the religion course was not being taught properly. He then convened with the villagers and their children and read them the book on religion assigned by the state, and they found it detailed enough and sent their children back to school (388).

The discussion split those who did not want religion in state schools, those who wanted it and wanted the class teacher to give it, and those who wanted it but did not want the class teacher to give it. The latter position required a change in the curriculum of teachers' schools as well. One other axis of debate was the question of whether the optional terms of the courses would be opt-in or opt-out (391).

The legal advisor of the Ministry of National Education was also a participant in the congress and stated the position of the Democrat Party government. He emphasized both the belief and practice aspects of freedom of conscience, that the religion course in question was not required but optional, and that it simply provided an opportunity for the citizen to practice his/her right to freedom of conscience and religion freely and securely; an argument reminiscent of Nicolas Sarkozy's *laïcité positive*. There was no forcing of wills, and therefore there was no violation of freedom of conscience. He remarked: "If we had required children to take a religion course without asking their parents for their opinion and vote, then one could rightly put forth the argument for the violation of freedom of conscience" (393). He continued to clarify that laiklik was a principle of social politics and not a legal principle, and therefore it was up to the parliament to define its meaning and practices according to the social conditions and needs of the country. Therefore,

> although in laic states such as France, Switzerland, and even Belgium the church with all its organization stays outside state cadres and budget, laic and republican religious affairs personnel, organizations, and institutions in Turkey are just state offices covered under the state budget. And this situation is not seen contrary to laiklik in Turkey. . . . It is necessary to see this as natural. Because the state is not an abstract

thing outside life and reality. . . . As far as religion is concerned, its role in the national community is beyond the need of explanation. Therefore it is impossible for the state to be indifferent to religion. For this reason, today no civilized country, except communist . . . derives the meaning of antireligious from laiklik. (394–95)

The legal advisor for the ministry turned to the question of Western laiklik and made a counter claim on the West as an answer to Esen. He stated that in principle laiklik meant the separation of religious and state affairs and that state and religion were impartial (*bitaraf*) against each other, and the state did not have a connection with any religious creed or principles. He explained that the state made laws, did not ground itself on religion, and attempted to respond to (religious) needs. Anything beyond this definition, according to him, was political fanaticism, as one could see in the antireligious position of states behind the iron curtain (395). However, one should not forget that the legal advisor's position was on optional Sunni Islam courses only and therefore de facto fell outside the limits of an application of the principle of institutional neutrality. He dismissed fanaticism both in the name of religion and in the name of laiklik. "Laiklik is to separate the life of the state and place of worship, and to put in between a harmonious border most fit to national interests. This border cannot be hard and stiff. Like all moderate politics, according to the necessities of national life, it is natural that this [border] also has to be soft and permissive. . . . Therefore in the laik countries of the West, the school has not taken a position against religion" and leaves it to the choice of the parents (396). He continued by saying that optional religion courses provide for the constitutional principle of equality, particularly with non-Muslims (article 69, Civil Code article 266), for the exercise of a right depends on the presence of the infrastructural possibility, and the legal advisor pushed the same argument as Sarkozy's *laïcité positive*:

> Article 266 of the Civil Code says "decision for the children's religious instruction belongs to the parents." But how will the father and mother use this right given to them by law? A right is beneficial only if it is used. The use of a right is dependent on practical means. The existence of a right is meaningless if it cannot be used because of a lack of practical means. Therefore when the law grants a right to the citizen, at the same time it orders the government and the administration to provide for the means of the free exercise of this right. Indeed, for a

certain period after institutions educating religion *hoca*s have been closed and religion courses in schools have been removed, muslim citizens, who represent the great majority of the country, 98 percent, have no means to provide for the religious education of their children. . . . In return, in the school of our non-muslim citizens, all along, religious education and courses are offered, and these citizens' institutions for the education of clerics have not been discontinued. (396–97)

The legal advisor compared the government position and Esen's position:

In fact, there is no fundamental difference between my and Professor Bülent Nuri Esen's definitions of laiklik. Yet the difference is in the understanding of this definition, in other words, in its practice. And again, within the principles I have articulated, it is not contrary to laiklik to offer a religion course in primary schools. For example, if the curriculum at schools were made according to religious views or discussions, or students admitted or not admitted according to their position on religion, then it would be contrary to laiklik. (397)

The legal advisor to the Ministry of National Education was grounding the arguments on article 18 of the 1948 Universal Declaration of Human Rights: "Everyone has the right to freedom of thought, conscience and religion; this right includes freedom to change his religion or belief, and freedom, either alone or in community with others and in public or private, to manifest his religion or belief in teaching, practice, worship and observance."

Other speakers also pointed out that many European countries that have signed this declaration offer religion courses in public schools. But the difference lies in the question of whether the state will provide the necessary infrastructure for the freedom. During the congress, European examples were presented in detail. The legal consultant to the Education Ministry went on to list examples from Europe. He covered Italy, Belgium, Sweden, Norway, Spain, Switzerland, the United Kingdom, and Germany. He pointed out the presence of religion courses in each country's state schools ranging from only in primary school to primary and middle school to all three, including high school and with an opt-out option. He concluded that if Esen was right, then these countries were theocratic and not laic (398–99). He left the case of France to last and spent relatively more time on it because he claimed

Esen seemed to be basing his argument mostly on this country. In France, he explained, state schools offer no courses on religion, but the state makes all the necessary arrangements for those students whose parents want to have religious education for their children outside of state schools, and Thursdays are an official holiday for that reason. On top of that, in France there is a huge religious education infrastructure competing in all respects with state schools, and the republicans' struggle is to take students from church schools (400–401). In France the church is outside the state and strong; in Turkey there is no independently strong religious infrastructure.

Finally the legal consultant explained why the optional religion course started as opt-in but then was turned to opt-out:

> In the 1949–1950 school year the number of students in fourth and fifth grades in primary schools was 414,477, and those who did not attend religion courses were in total 5,799 students, 2,797 muslims, and 3,002 non-muslims. . . . In the 1950–1951 school year, number of students in fourth and fifth grades in primary schools was 418,953, and those who did not attend religion courses were in total 3,035: 1,437 muslims and 1,598 non-muslims. . . . As you see, dear friends, although no one has been forced to take this course, the number of students who attend is close to 100 percent. And let me add, with particular concern, among the students who take the course there are also children of non-muslim citizens. . . . Don't these numbers show clearly why initially a written statement was demanded from those who want to take the course, but later a written statement was demanded only from those who do not want to take the course? Instead of receiving close to half a million papers, we now receive less than 5,000 papers. (408)

An associate professor of psychology who also offered psychology courses in a theology department and was a member of the program commission that initially discussed the matter of a religion course gave a new direction to the discussion away from the comparative institutional debate and toward the purpose and possible results of giving a religion course. The state had decided to offer an optional religion course, now the question was what was the purpose and potential effect? To use religion in order "to assimilate the young generations to the context they live in, to bring him/her up with values filtered through national history and make her/him a beneficial part [*uzuv*, literally an organic extension such as an arm or a leg] of our society" (411). Beneficial meant, he explained, "right, obedient, honest, moral," and if this perspective on religion were accepted,

> there is no contradiction between the goal religion aims at within the school curriculum, and worldly curriculum aimed at within schools. I see no difference between the good man accepted by religion and accepted by the world. Especially in the case of islam, the last and best of all religions, I do not expect a quarrel with worldly matters. . . . The Program Commission also invited me. . . . There were long discussions on the matter. Our friends fully dealt with the matter and how to reach the goal in the shortest way? Yet there was a quarrel on whether it shall be optional or required, and we left without reaching a decision. But the matter is not on the question of optional or required. It is rather directly on the position of religion within the frame of the public program so that it only serves this purpose [of turning the youth into "right, obedient, honest, moral" parts of society], and this is precisely the gist of the proposal of the program commission. In fact, we said there [during the commission meeting]: Let us not quarrel here, this is a matter of expertise, let pedagogues, psychologists and clerics contribute. Let these experts go over especially the fifth-grade books. . . . In this decision we are in full accord in the commission. (412–13)

The professor continued reflecting on his teaching "psychology, pedagogy, and partly philosophy" in the "faculty of theology." He pointed out that some contest the teaching of these course in a faculty of theology; "yet religion, in its essence, is an institution which always supports duties, services, and goals in the world." He then referred to Europe:

> European scientists point out that there is no contradiction between the natural sciences [*ilim*]—physics and biology—and abrahamic sciences; and that, in the most important issues, such as the proof of God [*uluhiyet*], biology and physics will also be of service. Clerics who teach biology, physics, mathematics in European universities prove this point. That is to say, our function is to save religious education from the hands of those who . . . are simple, ignorant, and abusive, and hand it over to the hands of the Turkish teacher. (413)

Another participant remarked that these religion courses "will also bring to faith those half-Muslims who claim that they do not lose Muslimness by not going to mosques" (422), and the director of education of one city stated that they would ask the Ministry of National Education to open these new religion courses in schools to all citizens (424). The director of a Greek (*rum*) lycée stated that religion is a worldwide phenomenon and that all children around the age of ten demand religious knowledge. Given the lack of literacy in Turkey, this service had to be given by the state schools, and he shared his own positive experience in the *rum* lycée (425–26). A director of a Jewish lycée also gave support.

A member of the commission for the review of democratic principles grounding education and instruction in the fourth National Education Congress (August 22–31, 1949) pointed out that the courses were optional for the students, but their teaching was required for the teacher (428–33). Another participant pointed out that the constitution guaranteed not only religious freedom but freedom of philosophical view and belief, and that the latter encompassed the former, and therefore the rights of the teacher were violated. He cited the British Education Act of 1944, articles 29–31, where the teacher was protected in public and private schools. He also pointed out that it was not that easy to carve out the moral aspects of religion from its other aspects. And he underlined that the curriculum emphasized application, so if this came up in the case of religion courses, there could also be demands for building places of worship in schools. The minister of education intervened at this point and remarked, "Of course not" (433).

By the time of the closing remarks, Esen had already left the congress. The closing remarks were by Peyami Safa, a prominent novelist and a Turkish representative to UNESCO, who concluded the discussion with a long speech that in sum stressed that the lesson from Europe was that religion and science went hand in hand (435–37). UNESCO meetings had concluded that teaching religion at schools was a must for general morals and education of the mind; teachers who did not want to teach religion should resign for not following the state program. Finally he listed the pedagogical moves that the program commission made in content, considering the age of the students.

This debate took place in the context of a court case, and the DP, with its lawyers, presented liberal arguments and mobilized European examples. However, the debate over the terms of optional religion courses revealed further vicissitudes of making liberalism compatible with even *optional* religion courses. Utilitarian approaches to religion were able to penetrate liberal principles with less than visible minute institutional adjustments such as shifting the participation in the course from opt-in to opt-out. Moreover, the post–World War II turn of CHP and the DP away from a perception of European modernity as an integrated whole vis-à-vis the relation between state and religions (as was the case for the early CHP) and their rediscovery of Europe as consisting of varieties of institutional arrangements between state and religions exposing Europe as religious as well as a secular space are critical for current discussions on comparative modernities and the question of the *traveling* of European modernity. I will return to this point in the conclusion of this chapter and later in the concluding chapter. However, all this debate was taking place under the premise of the "law of majorities," in the words of the lawyer, "Muslim citizens, who represent the great majority of the country, 98 percent," the very premise that was also shared in the internal debates within the CHP at the dawn of the transition to a multiparty system and before; therefore the arguments were far away from neutrality or equality in state institutions. Furthermore, the organic political goal of raising "good citizens" through religion, which did not take center stage but was still pronounced in the background of the legal discussions in the congress, was an ongoing fundamental theme in the first multiparty parliamentary discussion on the future of the DRA.

The Question of a Separated DRA: The February 22, 1951, DRA Budget Discussion

On June 17, 1950, a DP parliamentarian, Feyzi Boztepe, put an oral question to the DP government. The text of his question, fully quoted in the newspaper *Milliyet*, demanded that according to laiklik, the DRA had to be separate (*müstakil*) and autonomous (*muhtar*), and it, not the Ministry of National Education, had to arrange for religious education. However, Boztepe asked that the state budget for the DRA continue, for, he maintained, it is the duty of the laic and democratic state to economically protect theologians and the personnel who work under them, especially, in the context of twentieth-century risks that humanity would lose its faith and belief in the face of modern progress. He argued that loving life and humanity and being able to commit to higher ideals would be possible only through belief, and therefore we need to care for the morality of our children. However, he continued, it was against laiklik if the Ministry of National Education organized religious education; therefore a separated and autonomous but state-funded DRA had to do it:

> When the borders of laiklik are determined in this way, in other words, the interference [*müdahale*] of religion in state affairs or the reverse, the tutelage of the state over religion, is eliminated, the institution [*müessese*] of religion finds the opportunity to develop separately in a mild-moderate environment, and it continues to do freely its spiritual [*manevi*] duty in social life. In its application, the percentage of responsibility falling on the government is large. It has to take the necessary . . . precautions according to law and order, in order to supervise [*murakabe*] against possible fundamentalist [*irticai*] inclinations, and be attentive to the defense of reforms [*inkılap*] which belong to the whole nation. . . . I kindly request from the Democrat government that has to come to power with the will of the nation to answer orally what it thinks on this extremely important matter.[51]

The government never directly answered this question, or at least I have not been able to recover such an answer in the records of the Turkish Grand National Assembly or newspapers of the time. The government expressed its position on the questions and issues Boztepe had raised during the DRA's budget discussions on February 22, 1951, where the question of autonomy (*muhtariyet*) for the DRA took up the major part of the budget discussion.[52]

More than twenty Democrat Party members, including Prime Minister Adnan Menderes, one CHP member, the only Nation Party parliamentarian, and one independent parliamentarian who used to be a CHP member took the floor. The independent parliamentarian was the first to speak, and he argued that state funds for a religion are antidemocratic and against laiklik:

> SINAN TEKELIOĞLU. Laiklik means separating world affairs from other-world affairs, in other words to separate religion completely from politics, and to separate politics from religion. The second principle of laiklik is not to privilege any religion in the country. Now by taking the DRA within the State budget are we following this principle of laiklik, or not? If we are going to follow this principle of laiklik, there are two other religions besides Islam in this country: Christianity and Judaism. Therefore it would

be necessary to treat these religions the same and offer them a State budget. At the same time, it would be necessary to take the waqfs in their possession and give them to the Directorate of Religious Endowments. Currently, is a religion privileged? Yes . . . I defended this position ten years ago in the CHP congress; I even gave a proposal, but it was rejected. . . . It can never be correct to discuss the Budget of the DRA as part of the State budget in the Grand National Assembly. . . . Let's attach the DRA to religious endowments as it is for other religions and leave it free. If necessary the State can keep surveillance [*murakabe*].[53]

A DP parliamentarian pointed out that "the protector of our inner being [*manevi varlığımız*], the DRA, had been neglected and its personnel insulted [by CHP governments] until May 14 [May 14, 1950, elections]," and "freedom of conscience, and particularly that of Muslims, had been violated despite the constitution" (427); therefore it is necessary to be "grateful . . . for the increase in the budget" (428). But the ideal would be "to connect the waqfs built for sustaining religious institutions to the DRA and to let this autonomous institution in line with article 14 of the Democrat Party program," and all this is also necessary for fighting "the enormous enemy . . . red ideology [communism]":

> AHMET GÜRKAN. Dear friends; look at America, the nations of the new world turn to religion for fighting communism. In 1938 northern European countries, Finland, Sweden, and Norway, come together . . . and decide that the religion of Islam is an institution to fight communism. . . . In America, from 1935 to 1945, the number of churches has increased from 199,000 to 253,000. . . . And about religious fundamentalism. . . . Revolutions [*inkılaplar*] made in our country are under the protection of our laws, and we can never, as parliamentarians, allow for religious fundamentalism. (*Bravo, applause.*) . . . Friends, we all accepted the religious courses system introduced by the Ministry of National Education. . . . I wish that religion courses would also be given in primary schools that do not have the fourth and fifth grades. (428–29)

Some DP members found the budget increase insufficient and demanded a higher budget either to increase the wages for religious and administrative personnel of the DRA or increase the total number of personnel and religious publications, or to build infrastructure for the education of the religion personnel so that they would be equipped to prevent religious orders (*tarikats*) from mobilizing and to eliminate the opposition between modern civilization and religion (428, 429, 435, 436, 444). There were also various references to Europe and the United States defending more state investment in religion infrastructure. One DP member added examples from Germany and the United States on "required" religion courses in primary and secondary schools. There were also multiple references to Churchill and Roosevelt, who "prayed in the church when the Second World War was starting" (442, 445), a comparative reference that was also stated in the CHP congress of 1947 discussed earlier. There were also more general statements on how the entire world was turning to religion against communism, particularly the rise of Christian democracy against communism in many European countries, and how Professor (Arnold Joseph) Toynbee had presented Islam as the way to fight communism when he gave a conference in Turkey in 1948 (445).[54] One DP parliamentarian, Burhanettin Onat, stressed that "if communism is lightning, then the lightning rod is religion; if it is a poison, then its antidote is religion; if it is a microbe, then its serum and vaccine is religion" (446). Another DP speaker, Yeredoğ Kişioğlu, stated that Turks are the leaders of Islam: "It is us, Turks who with our flag . . . we put on each continent made islam reach an exalted position." He added, "After the acceptance of muslimness [*müslümanlık*], what constitutes the moral and inner life of society is faith in God, Koran, and the sayings of the Prophet," and he underlined that religion has to be protected from communism (430–31). There were frequent critiques of CHP policies. A DP member divided the CHP into two, with 98 percent belonging to the category who give laiklik the meaning of antireligiousness (455). One member gave the example of the critique Hamdullah Suphi Tanrıöver received from the CHP for arguing that the CHP should invest more in religion infrastructure (438). The DP member just quoted on the Turkish leadership in Islam advanced a critique of the CHP and underscored the impossibility of complete institutional separation:

YEREDOĞ KIŞIOĞLU. It is this party [CHP] who understood the principle of laiklik in the constitution as antireligiousness [*dinsizlik*] and caused the neglect and misery of religion, whereas the principle of laiklik is about letting religion walk and flow in its own sphere. . . .

How will we separate? . . . Since under today's conditions, we cannot dismiss the institution [*müessese*] of religion—its principles, organization, and budget—and let it go even after having created its institutions, this separation has to be in the form of an institution whose budget is managed and provided by the State ... who chooses its own head ... an autonomous institution. (431–32)

Another DP member pointed out the necessity of having the DRA appoint well-educated imams for fighting discrimination/racism within Islam, for example, against Alevis (434). Some wanted to have the DRA provide assistance for national education's religion course (436), and some even wanted the DRA to completely handle these courses. Feyzi Boztepe, who had given the oral question on June 17, 1950, also took the floor. He built his argument for an autonomous but state-funded DRA on the premise of the "law of majorities" and on ethnographical claims (436). The law of majorities and ethnographical authority were mobilized on multiple occasions (see also 442, 447, 448) and were two forms of argumentation also common in the French Third Republic chamber deliberations documented in chapter 3. Boztepe claimed that villagers loved their religion and that "we are Turkish and Muslim," suggesting CHP's antireligiousness, and called for "reinforcement" of the "institution of religion" without suppressing the state budget. He read his stated question from June 17, with confidence that it had the government's approval (438–39). One DP member reported villagers remarking, "Protect our religion, we do not want anything else" (442).

What ignited the interference of Prime Minister Menderes in the discussion was a comment by Osman Bölükbaşı, the only member of the Nation Party (NP) in the parliament. Bölükbaşı had been a DP member but later found the DP critique of the CHP insufficient and became part of a group that split to found the NP. The NP was dissolved in 1954, at which time Bölükbaşı founded the Republican Nation Party, which later turned into the Republican Peasant Nation Party (CKMP), to whose party program Ali Fuad Başgil had contributed, and which ultimately became the far-right National Action Party (MHP). Bölükbaşı made the following statement:

OSMAN BÖLÜKBAŞI. There are often claims that this political party or that political party has turned religion into a tool of politics. It is highly possible that within political parties, members who have not digested the party programs, running after daily interests, might have acted as such. There is only one way to prevent such actions. It is to deal with the question of freedom of conscience and religion in its entirety, not piecemeal, and once and for all. . . . In order to have full and complete freedom of religion in this country, in our opinion, religion has to be regarded as a matter of religious community [*cemaat*] and separated completely from State influence. While insisting that freedom of religion exists in this country, we see that as State employees, the DRA administers religion. And there is a State budget for this administration. This is not compatible with laiklik. . . . Islam's religious community must have the right to administer its own religious affairs. . . . If there is a worry that such an institution can become a means of religious fundamentalism, one can say, the government has the right to check all institutions to see if they are working according to their set goals. . . . Now . . . does the government see religion as an affair of religious community or a State affair? (440)

Prime Minister Menderes responded mainly to Bölükbaşı and to some other questions:

BAŞBAKAN ADNAN MENDERES. First of all . . . the amount of money spent on religious affairs is not limited to the official budget. . . . So many mosques built and maintained in the country, many imams, *hocas* working in villages are all possible with the opportunities provided for by citizens. Our citizens are free to donate, have mosques built, get a *hoca*, do their religious practices, and worship according to their creeds. . . . In fact, Osman Bölükbaşı has not expressed how the establishment of an organization of religious community or the presence of the DRA within the state organization is related to freedom of religion. Therefore I have no answer to give him. Bölükbaşı said that: Let us resolve the matter by giving freedom of religion in full and once and for all, rather than piecemeal. Does he contend that to resolve this matter in full and once and for all is to establish an organization of religious community? If we consider that the fundamental part [*unsuru asli*] of the country is Turk and Muslim, it is not appropriate to talk about an organization of religious community, and we are of the opinion that it is not against laiklik to have a state budget [for religious affairs]. (441)

Religion as the only source of morality was repeated multiple times by many DP parliamentarians. Such statements were common: "A nation or individual without a religion has no morality . . . man without a religion [*dinsiz*] is a coward, a man with a religion is brave. . . . The Turkish and

Muslim Nation which has reached its National Sovereignty and relies on his God is above all" (448). More radical statements were made at times, such as that all national calamities happened because of irreligion, nations without religion could not survive, and it is scandalous that the increasing number of cinema halls even surpassed the number of mosques in some localities (449). Another DP member pointed out that "if tight relation between religious affairs and State services are considered, we would agree that this important service [religious service] has to be maintained in its public character as a State service for some time longer, rather than handing it over to random hands" (450):

NECDET AÇANAL. Religions preach morality, therefore they are related to instruction and teaching of proper behavior. From this perspective, they are related to the services of the Ministry of National Education. Religions dispatch police that are only visible to religious persons, to places where the police cannot enter or see; therefore they are of help to the Ministry of Interior. Religions put penalties for crimes which the penal code cannot punish and promise rewards to those who do things beneficial to society; therefore they are helpful to the Ministry of Justice. (450)

The sole CHP speaker, Hamdi Şarlan, reminded the parliament that the religion course and other advancements in religion infrastructure were also initiated from within the CHP and said that he appreciated the DP government's increase in the budget of the DRA. He also alluded to some earlier remarks by DP parliamentarians against particularly the CHP and remarked that under freedom of conscience in modern law, "no one could refer to another as irreligious [*dinsiz*]" (451).

Ali Fuad Başgil's Support for the Religion Course and the Question of Separation for More Religion

One public intellectual who supported the moving of the religion course from after school hours into the school curriculum (with an opt-out option) was Ali Fuad Başgil, military officer in the First World War, educated in France, PhD in law from the University of Paris, CHP intellectual in the 1930s, and professor of constitutional law at Istanbul University. How he articulated this support and made it compatible with his critique of the CHP's laiklik and his defense of "separation" exposed a certain position also defended in the budget discussions of 1951 and later by the CKMP in the writing of the military constitution in 1961. I call this position, which was also present in Third Republic France and expressed most explicitly by certain political Catholics, "separation if and only if it contributes to religious life."

It is crucial to situate Başgil as a public intelectual in context for an assessment of his support for the religion course as well as for a critical description of the Turkish political scene. A brief look at his career as an organic public intellectual belies his common portrayal as simply a conservative liberal, and his trajectory also calls into question the dichtomy between Kemalist laicism and political Islamism often taken for granted as an accurate description of the Turkish political scene. Başgil was an organic CHP intellectual and wrote in praise of the party's statism and pragmatism in the 1930s. In 1935 he even repeated Benito Mussolini (without citing him) in qualifying the statism CHP should aim at, that is, "always within the state, nothing against the state, nothing outside the state. . . . Here is the formula of statism today," and he often used organic analogies for describing society, such as "a beehive."[55] Later Başgil became a fervent supporter of the Democrat Party. He contrasted the relation between state and religion in the Ottoman Empire and in Turkey, called the former a state under the religion system and the latter a religion under the state system, and defended the third option of separation of religion and state.[56] Başgil participated in the Fourth National Education Congress, August 22–31, 1949, and was a member of the commission for the review of democratic principles grounding education and instruction; the commission's report had a totally moralistic understanding of the workings of democracy.[57] He was prolific as a public intellectual in the 1950s.[58] He had been a part of the group of legal experts and scholars who convened at the demand of Osman Bölükbaşı for the first time on October 21, 1960, to revise the party program of the CKMP, which later turned into today's nationalist right National Action Party (MHP).[59] In January 1961 he was charged with violating the law issued on December 12, 1960, banning criticism of the Constituent Assembly when his article criticizing it was published both before and after the law in question was promulgated, and he was imprisoned.[60] He did not participate in the writing of the 1961 constitution, although he was cited during the debates in the Constituent Assembly. He was a Senate member after the transition to democracy in the aftermath of the May 27, 1960, military takeover and actually a DP-supported presidential candidate, but he was talked out of candidacy by the military junta.[61] Başgil has also been mentioned quite often as a thinker inspiring the current government AKP.

While he was in prison in February 1961, Başgil received a letter from Ligue Française de l'Enseignement. The letter asked him whether the statement of the Turkey correspondent to *Le Monde* that Başgil was at the forefront of the antilaic movement in Turkey was correct. Başgil responded as follows:

> That I am against laiklik is maliciously false slander by my opponents who have not read my works. I am not against laiklik. I am against Godlessness (*Allahsızlık*). You, my French friends, know very well the difference between these two expressions. Because France, in its history and now, has lived and is still living both of them. I am convinced that as much as laiklik is necessary for a civilized country, Godlessness is as harmful and dangerous. I was educated in France. I learned from your big philosophers, such as Alain, Blondel, Chevalier, and your big statesmen, such as Edgar Quinet, that a Godless society will not have tranquility and rest. If my struggle against this big danger facing my country is a crime, then the real criminal is the one who taught me this: that is, France.[62]

Başgil argued for an independent Directorate of Religious Affairs in various works and newspaper articles. He proposed a law on the Directorate of Religious Affairs consisting of fifty-five articles in early 1950s. The first paragraph of article 1 of his proposed law states: "The Directorate of Religious Affairs is an institution with scientific, administrative, and financial independence and its institutional structure is as described in this law" (295). The head of the directorate is elected by secret ballot by an independent Council of Religious Affairs consisting of Islamic scholars (297). Article 2 strictly prevents anybody working for the DRA or in affiliated organizations and institutions from "entering political parties," "engaging in politics," or "interfering in the affairs of the government" (295). The state budget is suppressed (article 20), the directorate of waqfs merges with all its income into the DRA (article 4), salaries, and pensions of DRA personnel enter the discretion of the DRA bound by employment law (articles 5 and 6). The third article articulated the financial sources of the directorate:

> The Directorate of Religious Affairs makes and approves its own income and expenditure budget by the means described in this law.

The income of the Directorate of Religious Affairs comes from religious waqfs in place since old times, and newly made religious facilities, donations, and monetary assistance. The expenditures of the Directorate of Religious Affairs are wages, construction and maintenance of buildings, copyright and translation, costs of religious services such as instruction and education. (295–96)

The reasons Başgil gave for a separated Directorate of Religious Affairs are scattered among his many works, and these reasons decouple many of the associations taken for granted in the study of religion and politics not only in Turkey but also in other contexts. Başgil clearly wanted to see religion more present as part of the Turkish social fabric, and this was a lesson he had learned from Europe, particularly Switzerland, where he had spent many years. In his memoirs, *Yakın Maziden Hatıra Kırıntıları* (Remains of memoirs from the recent past), he wrote:

> In Western countries, there are institutions and organizations in order to control [*dizginlemek*] unruly youth. At the top of this list is the church organization. This is such an institution that, unyielding and without getting tired, is on duty. In Switzerland, children are taken to church almost every day by their mothers until school age. After they start school, children are taken to church to pray and listen to the preacher twice a week under the guidance of their teachers. A kid who grows up like this from an early age on, even if he/she is tempted at a later age, the feeling of God he/she has received is always a controlling element.[63]

Institutional separation of state and religion for Başgil was a means to give religion the social role he so vividly described in the passage above for controlling youth. This relation that Başgil sought between the institutional and the social world was most apparent in his great appreciation for the Catholic Church for various reasons, one being its resilience to communism:

> Here dear reader, the Catholic castle [referring to the church], which communism could not demolish in Europe, has been established in this way. This is the Catholic front . . . which Fascism and the armies of Hitler could not penetrate and therefore had to reconcile with. Today,

among the big religions, in terms of its worship places, organization, and personnel, the most impoverished one is, regrettably, the religion of Islam. We are not going to delve into the historical and sociological causes of this impoverishment here. Let it suffice to underline two fundamental causes. The most important one of them is that religion in the world of Islam has not parted with state control and declared its freedom from politics. According to us, the worship organization of Islam will continue to be impoverished as long as it is under the control of politics and serving politicians. Today, the only way for the worship organization of Islam to be set free from this condition and servitude is to achieve autonomy, even freedom, and in this way to part with politics and politicians. Today, the second fundamental reason for the impoverished state of the worship organization and personnel of Islam has to be sought in the constitution of the religion of Islam itself. The constitution of the religion of Islam is different from that of Christianity in an important respect: while Christianity is built upon the organization of spirituality [ruhanilik] and religious offices, in Islam there is no spirituality or religious office. In Islam, a sufficiently knowledgeable and experienced Muslim can lead the religious service.... Without doubt, this lack [of structure of religion personnel and offices] is a superior characteristic. In this way, Islam has attained the status of the most liberal among religions, and its followers have not been subject to the rule of Clerical class as has been the case in Christianity at different degrees during history. But, on the other hand, the experience of the past two centuries has shown that the lack of worship organization and religious office has created a lack of direction and proved to be a shortcoming.[64]

Başgil's synthesis of institutional separation, religion as a social bond, and the European experience sometimes bordered on Orientalism. In 1962 when he was in Geneva he wrote in his memoirs: "Everything [in Geneva] is as I have left it six months ago. Everbody is working, smiling and living in welfare/comfort. Boredom of life and life pains is a punishment God has given to Eastern nations."[65] However, Başgil, who had committed to free religion from the influence of the state in the 1950s, welcomed state interference when it came to the question of the religion course in primary schools in 1948 and 1950 and defended the 1950 version of the religion course as part of the school curriculum in the two articles he wrote for the newspaper *Zafer*. The first article started out with a contrast between the 1948 and 1950 versions of religion courses and critiqued the former:

> Two years ago, religion courses were put in schools. But, in our schools where even music and physical education are obligatory [*mecburi*]—I guess it is in order to ridicule religion—these courses have been made optional [*ihtiyari*]. Naturally, it did not work. And parents rightfully mobilized. In the face of insistence from a majority of parents, today's government, which is founded on national will rather than the heel of the boot, thought the issue through. Finally, with a decision of the Ministry of National Education, these courses were made obligatory.[66]

It is important to note here that Başgil, is referring as "obligatory" to the inclusion of religion courses in the public school curriculum with an opt-out option as opposed to the 1948 arrangement of having them outside school hours with an opt-in option. He responded to a critique of these courses that posited on the grounds of the freedom of conscience article in the constitution that in a diverse context of Turkish citizens consisting not only of Muslims but also of "Jews, Christians, Alevis, and Atheists [*Allahsızlar*]," the taxes of all cannot be used for the teaching of a certain religion in schools:

> As [the state] cannot inculcate [*telkin etmek*] in favor of a certain religion without the consent of parents, it also cannot, under a veil of laiklik, inculcate irreligion. Because, let's repeat, the religious education of the child depends on the will of parents, and it is their natural as well as legal right as stated in article 266 [of the civil law]. Let's pay attention, according to law in democracy, the law that gives a right, puts the state on duty for making possible, and if needed providing for, the actual and secure use of this right. . . . Therefore, making such an education de facto possible—I am not saying provide for—and to help parents on this issue is the duty of the state . . . let alone being against laiklik, it is the state's debt. Has the state paid its debt? For those who have not forgotten the insults and difficulties deemed proper for this country's muslim public for the past twenty or so years, it is not possible to give a positive answer to this question. . . . While Greek, Armenian, and Jewish citizens, in their own schools and institutions, could make their children benefit from the blessings of religious

education, on this side, a handful of self-interested persons who seized state powers have become an annoyance for our Muslim public and have deprived them from this blessing for years at all costs. . . .

This is a necessity [*zaruret*] until an autonomous religious organization is established and private institutions which give religious instruction and education give their fruits. Necessities permit the forbidden [*memnu*].

Past de-infrastructuring and state interference became a justification for further state interference. Başgil continued the subject in a second article a week later in the same newspaper. Here he also took a comparative angle, addressed for the first time the question of opt-out, which was the main mechanism still keeping the new institution relatively liberal, and also answered the question of the state building infrastructure with the taxes of all going for a certain religion:

If like the Greeks, Armenians, and Jewish, [Muslims] also had their religious waqfs . . . an autonomous religious organization was at their disposal . . . if old religious education institutions demolished twenty-five years ago, had been replaced by modern . . . institutions and had given their fruits, and if the lack of religious education which nibbles away the essence of the current generation and spiritual depression were not reigning, I would never have defended obligatory religion courses in the laic school. Because, first of all, I am not convinced that the laic school can properly give a religious education. I am for saving religion from being a political commodity immediately and once and for all. Unfortunately, in the name of personal grudge and ambition, not only history but the future has been carelessly sacrificed, and for no reason a dark interregnum which today we only see in Soviet Russia has been created in the country. Under these conditions, the government cannot tell muslim parents: my schools are laic, exercise the right which the civil code gives you with your own means and opportunities as do non-muslim citizens.[67]

Başgil took a comparative angle:

Laiklik takes a meaning and is applied according to the historical trajectory and national necessities of each country. Laic Switzerland's laic constitution begins in capitalized letters with "In the name of God." Swiss citizens do not even think of finding this against laiklik. . . . I just read in the newspapers the other day, the laic king of the United Kingdom, George VI, in his speech for the opening of the new parliament building, ended with a prayer, "Let God always bless this building and those who work in it." Did we forget the "God is with us" engravings on the German soldiers' bayonets and officers' swords? . . . As I think further and understand better with time that hostility for religion in our country and those who created spiritual depression, in this regard, are influenced by Moscow rather than western civilization of rule of law. . . . If required religion courses are a first step to get out of this dead end, what happiness for our muslim people . . .

Will this requirement be against the freedom of conscience of parents? . . . If we require religion courses for all children registered at school, without distinguishing religion and sect, and without asking her/his parents, yes. But, if we apply the requirement only to those children whose parents desire, no.

Başgil explained that this is how it works in many Western countries, and after the will of the parents is recorded, "at a certain time during the week, they send the children to the religion institutions to which they belong. In fact, religion courses are not given in school and by schoolteachers. In these countries this is not necessary. Because Catholic and Protestant places of worship are so well organized for these services that they make state schools envious."

He concluded by explaining how he would like these courses to be established in Turkey. The parents would be asked at the beginning of the school year. The children of those who do not want a course in religion would play in the schoolyard or have a discussion session under the supervision of a teacher. Those parents who wanted the course would then be asked if they simply want their child to attend or if they wish their child to take graded exams. He expressed that he was against schoolteachers giving these courses unless "there is a necessity" because this was against laiklik and there weren't many schoolteachers capable of giving the course; "these courses would be beneficial only if given by believers." Therefore, he continued, "as much as possible salaried teachers can be provided from among religious intellectuals, teachers (retired or working), state employees, military officers, lawyers, doctors. I even predict that among these persons there will be some who will do this sacred task without wages." He ended by responding to the critique that these courses and the budget of the DRA were from the taxes of all citizens, among whom were not only Muslims but also "non-muslims and Atheists." His response was the "law of majorities," that taxes were given as citizens, and not as Muslim, non-Muslim, or atheist citizens, and the budget was spent on public matters and, from the point of view of the majority, religion courses were a public matter.

Addressing Başgil's defense of religion course in public schools is significant because his proposed law for a separated DRA has been taken as one of the earliest well-articulated expressions of institutional separation in Turkey; however, a simultaneous close analysis of the reasons he advanced for his proposed law and for the religion course attest that his position was not a principled defense of separation but rather what I call "institutional separation if and only if it contributes to a more religious society." This position not only was present in some of the parliamentary discussions already covered but also had a continued presence at other moments, as we will see later.

The DP period ended with a military coup on May 27, 1960. The next critical juncture on laiklik came in the writing of the military constitution of 1961. This constitution turned the DRA into a constitutional institution and declared religious education and instruction to be optional. During the Constituent Assemby debates what ignited and drove the deliberation on laiklik was a proposal by the Professors' Commission drafting the constitution explicitly challenging the premise of the law of majorities. The Constituent Assembly writing the constitution was made up of an upper chamber of military officers, the National Union Committee, and a lower chamber consisting predominantly of CHP members and supporters, and the CKMP.

The Institutional Politics of Laiklik in the Writing of the 1961 Constitution

During my interview on October 29, 2009, with Vakur Versan, one of the ten professors who wrote the first draft of the Turkish constitution of 1961, he recalled a conflict in the Professors' Commission:

> The constitution was finished. We made it. Outside, an army major is waiting. He will take it to Ankara. Muammer Aksoy hesitated for a

moment. I tell you historical matters that nobody knows, it is very correct that you record them. Sıddık Sami turned to Muammer and said, "Muammer what happened? Something worries you." Indeed, we have agreed and finished, we will give it to the army major, he will take it to Ankara, and there it will be approved and become the constitution. "Yes, I have, professor," he said, "in the second article we say that Turkey is a laic state, and after, when we come to the section on the administration, we put in the constitution the Directorate of Religious Affairs, an institution that has nothing to do with laiklik and engages in religious affairs."[68]

This conversation took place in 1961, during the final session of the Professors' Commission, between the head of the commission, Sıddık Sami Onar, and a member, Muammer Aksoy. Onar's book, *İdare Hukukunun Umumi Esasları* (Public foundations of administrative law), first published in 1952, defined laiklik as the institutional separation of religion and state and strictly pointed out that religious services are not public services and the existence of the DRA cannot be reconciled with the principle of laiklik; therefore its presence is better explained by political principles and regarded as a temporary "policing [*zabıta*] precaution necessitated by the particular time and context of the revolution [*inkılap*]."[69]

From the position of an academic observer of the contradictions of laiklik in 1952, in 1961 Onar had turned into one of the subjects who instituted such contradictions in practice. To Aksoy's critical remarks cited above, he responded reaffirming what he saw as the still continuing particularities of the Turkish context:

Muammer, we discussed all these and reached this point, since you still have a concern, let's go over it. Now, you are right, there are articles in contradiction with the statement of laiklik in article 2, but these emerge from the *necessities* [*zaruret*] of Turkey. . . . Even if today religious affairs are under the control of the state, we still cannot prevent reactionism [*gericilik*]. And if we leave it [religion] free, it will altogether act against laiklik. In Turkey, in this society, it is still necessary to keep it under state control.[70]

In fact, the Professors' Commission's draft of article 12 (later article 19) on freedom of religion also had a paragraph on religious education (later removed), which has been widely ignored in the literature. The paragraph read: "The State, with the condition of compliance with the essentials of the constitution, establishes public services and the necessary organization which will provide for the religious needs or religious education and instruction of the majority of the people *or if necessary for those belonging to a minority religion or sect.*"[71]

The reference to minorities in this paragraph completely contradicted the original (1920s and 1930s) and the continuing "Sunni Muslim" and antiminority biases of the state position on laiklik. Figure 5.2 presents a flowchart of the writing of the 1961 constitution. In the records of the Constituent Assembly debates, the article on religious freedom is among the top three most debated articles.[72] The other two are article 2 on the attributes of the republic, which also triggered a debate on laiklik, and article 38 on the nationalization of property. The debates in the lower chamber of civilian representatives show that it was precisely the paragraph in article 12 cited above that ignited the longest discussion on laiklik. In a long speech in the lower chamber, Professor Hıfzı Veldet Velidedeoğlu argued in support of the paragraph that impartial institutional support to religions is the "real" laiklik and combined this institutional view with sociological observations:

The day when, although it is known that somebody is sunni, alevi, christian, or jewish or even atheist, nobody bothers that somebody; the day when those who go to mosque regularly are not belittled and in Ramadan, especially in small towns, restaurants are open and those who enter them are not frowned upon, there will not be the remains of an issue of being religious or not religious in this country. In other words, laiklik is not only the freedom of one religion, it is the freedom to belong to any religion or sect or freedom to not belong to any religion.[73]

In his memoirs, Velidedeoğlu recounts that a CHP member approached him in private and criticized this speech in the lower chamber. The CHP member requested that the statement be removed from the records because he believed that it might be interpreted as antireligious by the people who already, in his opinion, equated the Constituent Assembly with the CHP and CHP with an antireligious position, and Velidedeoğlu adds that he disregarded that criticism.[74]

Another argument in the Constituent Assembly, exceptional in context of the main themes in parliamentary and other discussions on laiklik covered

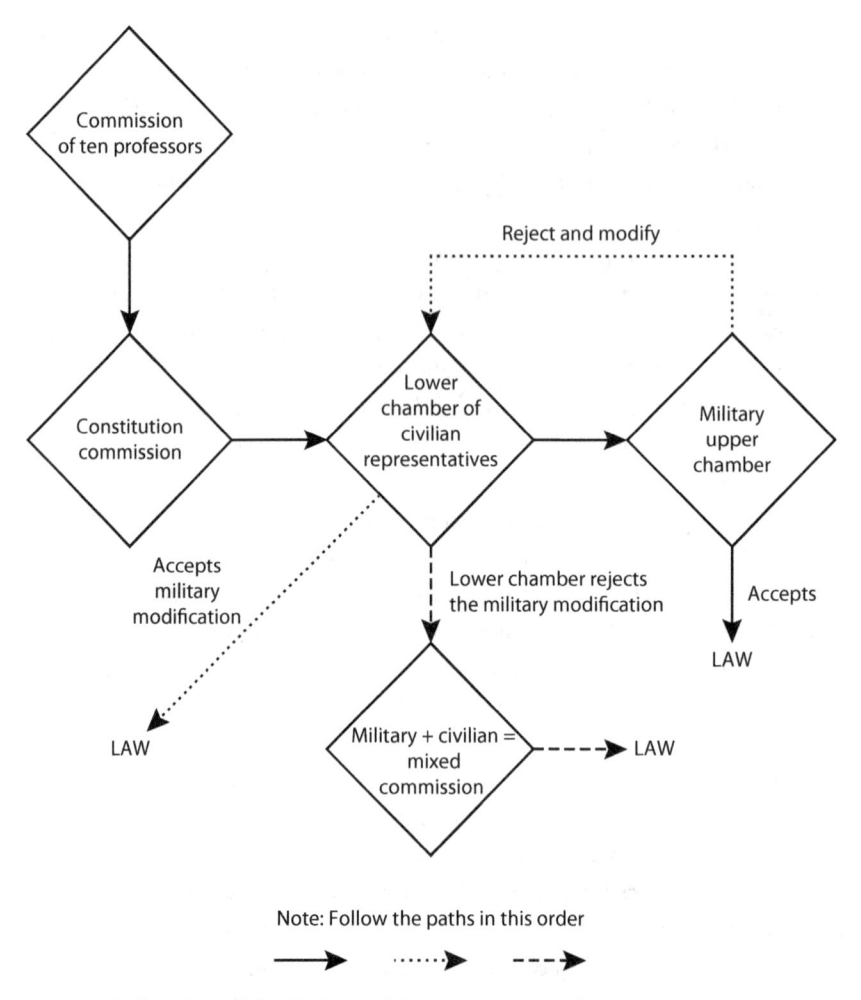

Figure 5.2 Flowchart of the Writing of the Constitution of 1961.

in this chapter so far, was the defense of laiklik as nondiscrimination. It was put forth in defense of the Alevis,[75] Armenians, and Greeks. Non-Sunni and non-Muslim minorites are often factored out in debates over institutions of laiklik, and their study constitutes a separate field. This empirical factoring out feeds the unquestioned references to Turkey as a Muslim-majority country and as a Muslim nation in the comparative and also often in the Turkey-specific academic literature and contributes to the reduction of the debate on the struggle over laiklik in Turkey to the dichotomy of

Kemalists versus Islamists. Even state documents, such as the ones analyzed here, if examined closely bespeak the presence of these minorities. In the lower chamber, Arslan Bora, the CHP representative from Tunceli, Hermine Kalüstyan, and Kaludi Laskaris defended Alevi, Armenian, Greek minorities, respectively. An article in the newspaper *Dünya* reported on July 26, 1960, "A Bizarre Application to the Constitutional Commission: 'Alevi Group' applied to the Constitutional Commission to have Alevilik recognized by the State,"[76] and *Cumhuriyet* reported that a group of Alevis "asked for state recognition of their sects."[77] In my reading, the titles of these news articles mispresent the demands of the Alevi group as they are listed in *Dünya* on July 26, 1960. The demands articulated fit much better under difference-blind liberal demands on state institutions rather than group-specific demands for the recognition of difference.[78] Let me mention the four most relevant demands here: (1) to separate the DRA from the state administration, an institution that only defends the Hanafi denomination and looks down on other believers, but to spare funds for it from the state budget; (2) to give the right to convene and conduct religious ceremonies to the Alevi Bektaşi Muslims; (3) to stop the broadcasting of Koran readings on the radio, for even if these broadcasts may have started with good intentions, they end up being exploited by those who would like to see religion as a tool of politics; and (4) removal of religion courses from state-funded schools.[79] Arslan Bora maintained a position of nondiscrimination and negative liberties rather than group recognition in his speech in the lower chamber on the religious freedom article.[80] "Although we are a laic state," he stated, "until now the Alevi group has been prevented from practicing its religious beliefs and worship . . . under prevailing [antidemocratic] laws [their] religious gatherings have been only possible in secrecy."[81] Later, during the discussions of the article on the DRA, he linked his conceptualization of laiklik as nondiscrimination to institutions:

> Dear friends, in fact, since the affairs of the State and religion are separate, the DRA has no place in the constitution. Yet the DRA has today again taken its place in the constitution. But still, I would like to express . . . that the answer of the Constitution Commission to my question [here he is referring to the assurance that the commission gave on nondiscrimination during an earlier discussion] has made me and an [Alevi] group of ten million grateful. I salute you all and hope that

the answer of the Constitutional Commission will reflect in the organization of the DRA and the understanding of religious affairs.[82]

Hermine Kalüstyan had entered the lower chamber from the president's quota, and after about two months as a member of the lower chamber, on February 19, 1961, she joined the CHP.[83] Educated in mathematics in Paris, she taught math at Galatasaray High School and was the headmaster of Esseyan Girls High School. With differences in nuance, Kalüstyan's defense of the Armenian minority also fell within a call for nondiscrimination. During the debate on the religious freedom article she made the following speech:

> Paragraph 2 [of the article on religious freedom] provides for freedom of worship. If religious freedom is granted only to individuals, it is possible to deduce the conclusion that the individual carry on the religious worship by himself/herself. Maybe the religion of islam is open to such an interpretation. Yet in christianity this is not possible at all. The individual can pray alone. But the individual cannot conduct mass or *sacrament*.... There are close to a thousand armenian citizens in Ankara. They do not have a church.... They have applied for the establishment of a church. The answer they got was, "If there used to be a church in Ankara in the past, you could have practiced your religious ceremonies. You cannot build a new church."[84]

Upon this analysis, Kalüstyan proposed the addition of the following sentences to paragraph 2: "Religious groups conduct these religious services and ceremonies in places of worhip and by the appropriate religion personnel."[85] These voices were left in the margins as far as the constitutional outcome was concerned. The understanding of military officers' racism in the passage below is worth noting:

> Even if we give up nationalism, will they give up racism? Let me give you an example: in the lower chamber when a representative from the *Rum* [Istanbulite Greek] race was asked "Are you Turkish?" he/she responded, "I am Turkish citizen from the *Rum* race." When he got a response, "Don't dwell on it, are you Turkish or not?," he has responded again, "I am a Turkish citizen from the *Rum* race" but has not said, "I am Turkish."[86]

The brief episode between the two law professors, Aksoy and Onar, was at the beginning of the writing of the 1961 constitution, and a huge speech by a changed Aksoy in the lower chamber, as the spokesperson of the Constitution Commission (see figure 5.2), was at the end. Aksoy had totally given up his position in opposition. What he saw as contradictions in his earlier talk with Onar were now necessities:

> When we take into consideration the circumstances in our country, we have witnessed individuals who want to give very general and dangerous meanings to laiklik, such as "State under the control of religion." . . . Obviously laiklik does not mean being without a religion. However, if the concept of laiklik in the West, where a different social and political development and different conditions exist, is accepted 100 percent in our country, the result will not be positive but completely negative. Separation of religion and State is sufficient for laiklik in the West to reach its end. But for us it never serves the end. If religion, even when it is organized, is left outside the control of the State, because of particularities of this country that I will express in a short while, it can become a political force, and it has done so from time to time. Finally, in a country where the principle of general elections has been accepted but the level of literacy and education is very low, it is possible to take advantage of a momentary carelessness of the people and reach the goal of a "theocratic state." In other words, in the final analysis freedom of conscience and the principle of laiklik can end altogether. It is exactly with this idea that some individuals . . . some so-called ulema . . . have come forth with the motto the complete separation of religion and State, and under the guise of Western-appearing "allegedly complete laiklik" have in reality wanted "to place the State under the complete control of religion."[87]

The excerpt above from Aksoy's speech in 1961 is one instance in the Constituent Assembly where laiklik is explicitly and vividly reconceptualized as the state control of religion. A whole array of conceptualizations were put forth that fell defeated to that in Aksoy's speech in one of the longest discussions in the Constituent Assembly. There were thirty-one speakers in total, and twenty-seven of them spoke long enough to offer a conceptualization in detail. Table 5.1 presents the array of conceptualizations and the number of speakers in each category.

TABLE 5.1
Conceptualizations of Laiklik in the 1961 Constituent Assembly Debates on Article 2, Article 19 (12 in First Draft), and Temporary Article 2

Comparative perspective		Non-Western (NW), 5	
		Western (W), 3	
Sociological (So)		Privatization of religion (PR) or differentiation of spheres (DS), 6	
		Utility of religion (UR), 2	
		Nondiscrimination (ND), 2	
		Impartial state support (ISS), 2	
Institutional	Separation, but the Turkish Context necessitates state involvement in order to ... (SB)	Be at least egalitarian, if not laic, 1	
		Put religion under the state, 2	
		Help to ensure religious freedoms, 1	
		Control religious content and practice, 7	
		Police (zabıta) (P), 1	
	Separation (S), 5		

Note: The major categories are not mutually exclusive, but the subcategories are. In other words, sometimes a speaker did offer an institutional and a sociological conceptualization and simultaneously put Turkey in comparative perspective, but no speaker, for instance, tried to simultaneously conceptualize laiklik as separation and impartial state support.

The discussions in the lower chamber cannot be treated as the main determinant of the resulting constitutional institutions, because, as diagrammed in figure 5.2, the military had the upper hand in writing the constitution and the lower chamber was dominated by the CHP in numbers. Although officially there were 74 seats in total reserved in the Constituent Assembly for two political parties, the CHP and the CKMP, the newspaper *Milliyet* reported that 142 out of the 272 total seats were held by CHP supporters.[88] In his memoirs, Velidedeoğlu reports 225 CHP supporters.[89] Kadircan Kaflı, a member of the CKMP and a newspaper columnist, reported 220.[90] Yet the discussions offer an opportunity to study the relation among conceptualizations of laiklik, proposed institutional arrangements, and political ends.

Table 5.2 maps the different conceptualizations in table 5.1 onto the proposed state role vis-à-vis building religious infrastructure (education in religion, maintenance of mosques, training and paying clerics, etc.) in general. In a close reading of these debates one cannot miss that the struggle over religious infrastructure is much more at the center than the liberal question of the limits of state power over religious action and speech. Sixteen of the thirty-one speakers who did not necessarily agree otherwise explicitly established a relation between religious freedom and infrastructure. The question of infrastructure emerged in the debates from an emphasis on the dual aspect of religious freedom: the expression of ideas, on the one hand, and practice, on the other. The common argument voiced repeatedly in the lower chamber in defense of a focus on infrastructure was that religion was not only a matter of faith (*iman*) but also a matter of practice (*amel*), and practice needed infrastructure.[91] This again recalls to mind Sarkozy's *laïcité positive*, the views of some AKP parliamentarians, and the conceptualization of laiklik in the 2012 Turkish constitutional court decision defending AKP's new education law. This struggle over infrastructure in the writing of the constitution of 1961 posed an important challenge to the liberal paradigm on state and religion relations, which focuses only on the limits of state power over religious expression and treats the question of infrastructure as exogenous.[92] The institutional proposal of "State Builds Infrastructure for the Majority" (see table 5.2) was the institutional arrangement that was defended from within the greatest number of different conceptualizations of laiklik. Below I examine the multiple routes converging on this institutional proposal.

TABLE 5.2
Mapping Conceptualizations onto Institutional Propositions

State builds some aspect of religious infrastructure for majority and minorities (SBIMM)	State builds some aspect of religious infrastructure for majority (SBIM)	State-induced centralized independent religious infrastructure (SICIRI)	Religious groups build their own infrastructure (RGBI)
(Impartial state support) [2] (Separation, but) (anti–Western) [3]	(Separation) (anti–Western) [1] (Separation) (Western) [1] (Utility of religion) [1]	(Separation) [1]	(Separation) (Western) [1] (Separation) [1] (Nondiscrimination) [2]

Note: "(Separation) (Western) [1]" means one speaker conceptualized laiklik as Western and as separation.

Multiple Routes to "State Builds Infrastructure for the Majority"

Defending Religious Freedom and More: The Limits of Separationism under Infrastructural Constraints

The five speakers who conceived laiklik as separation were from the CKMP. Conceptualizing laiklik as separation was one of the two points common to all five speakers. The other point common to all five was that they all agreed that religious freedom requires guarantees against government coercion, and three of them linked this explicitly to the past where the republican elite had pursued antireligious policies. The last common point was that the five speakers clearly shared the goal of increasing the space for religion and found the emphasis on regime threat exaggerated.[93] None of the five speakers addressed nonmajority religions; two of them explicitly declared Turkey a Muslim-majority country, and three defended a limit on speech critical of religion; therefore the observation of Tarhanlı that "the conservatives [in the 1961 Constituent Assembly lower chamber] have defended classical Western laiklik where state and religion affairs are strictly separated"[94] does not present the full picture. Only two speakers, either through silence on the state's role or as an expression of worries on state involvement, implicitly seemed inclined toward religious communities managing their own affairs. The other three explicitly welcomed a state role in some aspects of religious affairs. None of the five established strong links between the conceptualization of laiklik as separation and "the West" beyond the few explicit references to it as the "worldwide meaning" or "scientific meaning."[95] One of them, Kadircan Kaflı, actually had an explicit nationalist-religious anti-European line along with his conceptualization of laiklik as separation.

The general stance of the CKMP was stated by the head of the party, Osman Bölükbaşı, on October 12, 1960, while the constitution was still being drafted by the Professors' Commission, in a lead article entitled " '27 May' and the Order We Expect" in the newspaper *Kudret*. The newspaper's general position was succinctly captured in its motto written right under its title in the front page: "We defend real democracy and politics based on morality." In the article Bölükbaşı explained that, "to render the order we expect permanent and fruitful, an appropriate moderate [*vasat*] and spiritual ground has to be made ready before anything else. In order to prepare this ground, morals and right examples [*ibret*] have to be placed at the foundation of this order."[96] A member of the CKMP in the lower chamber, Kadircan Kaflı, in an article in the newspaper *Tercüman* on June 1, 1961, took this emphasis on morality one step further by putting morality even before the constitution: "The real foundation of democracy is morality, but other sources are also needed, [and] the first of these other sources is a perfect constitution."[97] And in a newspaper article on the question of religious reform that he wrote on May 8, 1961, Kaflı argued that any state-led reform of religion is against laiklik as separation.[98] Yet Kaflı was one of the three speakers who welcomed a state role in some aspects of religious life, and the one point common only to these three speakers among the group of five was the emphasis on the importance of infrastructure for religious freedom. The argument was that because religion was not only a matter of faith (*iman*) but more so a matter of practice (*amel*), religious freedom required sufficient infrastructure for citizens to practice.

Sadettin Tokbey, one of the five defending laiklik as separation and supporting an institutional proposal of a state-induced separation, made the clearest statement on the matter. "Freedom of conscience is a circuitous phrase,"[99] he said. He differentiated between belief and practice and stated that "it is our duty to provide the facilities for practice for those who feel the need for practicing [religion]." He placed the emphasis on infrastructure when he stated that "to be able to use all these rights we need organization."[100] These CKMP members argued that this was especially the case given how the infrastructure for Islam had been weakened by past Republican policies. The state had to take an active role in rebuilding that infrastructure. In the rest of the argument there were two positions. Two of the speakers defended the DRA as is. The other, Tokbey, wanted to see it separated from the state but retained a role for the state during the transition period to separation. The common point of these speakers was that the focus should be on institutionalism under infrastructural constraints only and away from the regime threat on which CHP members based their arguments.

Defending the Regime against "Unlimited" Religious Freedom:
Stitching Up Institutionalism and Modernist Sociology with
Historicism, Culturalism, and Expertise

All speakers in the Constituent Assembly who offered a sociological conceptualization of laiklik were either from or sympathizers with the CHP. A state role in regulating religious institutions was justified by an argument of sociological necessity, and the interplay of expertise, culturalism, and historicism in this justification was crucial.[101] The head of the Constitution Commission (see figure 5.2), a member of CHP, offered a sociological conceptualization of laiklik: "Laiklik, as far as its historical trajectory [*tarihi seyri*] is concerned, is not only the separation of religion and the state. It is the separation of religion and science, religion and art, religion and law, and religion and economics."[102]

The widening of the question of separation from an institutional focus to a sociological terrain and bringing in "historicism" allowed institutions to be turned from an "end" to a "means" to reach a certain sociological condition. The speaker quoted above topped this sociological move with more contextual specifics. First, there had not been religious reform in Turkey, and second, as a result of the low level of education in the country, Islam had been intertwined with ignorance. He concluded by commenting on infrastructure to argue against any claim of contradictions of the Turkish state's involvement in religious affairs and for the compatibility of laiklik with the DRA:

> Since there are no clerical classes [*ruhban sınıfları*] in Turkey, obviously a few persons gathering together cannot be allowed to establish a religious organization. This is impossible. In addition, the persons who are given the duty to provide religion services are not spiritual [*ruhani*] persons. They are civil servants. In other words, they have neither holiness nor greatness. From this perspective, if we accept the Directorate of Religious Affairs as an administrative institution, then the [principle of laiklik in the] Constitution is not violated.[103]

In a nutshell, the argument by the head of the Constitution Commission was that if the state did not build and maintain the infrastructure others would, and in the Turkish context of an intertwined low level of education and religiosity such decentralized formation of religion infrastructure outside the state would be a regime threat and, if materialized, would interrupt the historical trajectory of laiklik.

This historicist argument in defense of state involvement in religious affairs was given a new twist by the role of a European scholar in the closure of the Faculty of Theology in Istanbul University in 1933. Kadircan Kaflı from the CKMP underlined the closure as an example of the CHP's antireligious policies. A CHP member responded by arguing that the closure of the Faculty of Theology was not a result of a Republican antireligious policy but rather just the result of historical development (*tarihi tekamül*), which Emin Soysal from the CHP defended with the European expert's report on the state of Istanbul University:[104]

> Atatürk did not close the Istanbul Faculty of Theology.... Then, in order to reform *Darülfünun* [Istanbul University], an expert with the name Professor Malsh was brought in from Europe. If you read the report this person submitted, you will understand.... Professor Malsh says in the report he submitted to the state: "I cannot have a say in the direction the religious institution of a nation will take, but this is the situation: it [the Faculty] has four students and approximately forty professors."... That is to say, on its own, as the result of a historical development this institution has been closed.[105]

On other occasions, historicism sometimes was preceded by outright denial of the contradiction the DRA as an institution posed for "separation." In this regard, Professor Bahri Savcı's position that he rearticulated through the writing of the constitution was quite interesting. He was one of the ten professors who drafted the 1961 constitution, and later he entered the lower chamber as an independent from the professional group quota for universities. In a written statement he had attached to the Professors' Commission Report, he strictly opposed religion courses in public education, and part of his argument relied on a claim of "Turkish difference," articulated more as culturalism than as historicism:

> One possible argument for the defense of religious education in public schools is that religious education by the state can help in fighting against reactionism [*gericilik*]. This argument is wrong. The only way of fighting backwardness is to realize positive science education.... The characteristic of the religion of Islam is to infiltrate the life of the State. The religion of Islam will enter through the gateway opened by this paragraph of article 12 [the paragraph that started the discussion, quoted above] and will aim at first controlling "the State" and then the whole society.[106]

However, in his speech on laiklik in the lower chamber, Savcı adjusted his position. He ended with an outright denial of the contradiction between a state-funded DRA and laiklik and followed with contextual necessities. He disqualified this state-funded institution as a public service and made accommodating remarks on religious education:

> And finally, laiklik is the following: religion is not a public service. . . . This is scientifically true. In this respect, our constitution as a whole and in its article 19 is completely laic. Yet a question will remain in the minds of the speakers who took the floor here . . . : if laiklik is that, then what is the place of and reason for the Directorate of Religious Affairs? The constitution mentions education in religion. What does that mean? Aren't these in contradiction with laiklik? In my judgment the answer to these questions is "no." Both education in religion and the Directorate of Religious Affairs are simple ways of policing [zabıta]. Because the Directorate of Religious Affairs is not the organization of a State religion or the organization of a religion within the political organization. . . . In any case, there is no state religion in existence. . . . Because our constitution . . . does not take religion to be a public service, the Directorate of Religious Affairs is not an institution established for this purpose. The Directorate of Religious Affairs is only for gathering the disordered religious affairs in society, centralizing and canalizing them. In other words, this is not the instituting of a public service but the providing of an order. . . . In addition, article 19 mentions education in religion. . . . But this education in religion, because the State does not have a religion, this education is not the indoctrination of a State religion. And because there is no religious organization in the State, this is not an education teaching the principles of this organization. For in our laic society, material [beşerî] needs are satisfied by material means.[107]

Toward the end of his speech, Savcı turns toward particular arguments about Islam to articulate the "Turkish difference" in between culturalism and historicism:

> This is the situation: the Religion of Islam is overtaken by superstition. And there is an illogical and unreasonable system of religious education. Now, it is not contrary to laiklik to show religion in its pure principles to the children of those who ask for it in order to save the religion of islam from superstition and the *à la turca* [oriental] system

of education. The education in religion in article 19 is not about conveying a state religion or to arrange all of our political, social, and economic life according to religion, but only to teach properly to the children of those who ask for it the pure principles of religion saved from superstition. Along with this situation, if we also remember the rules of no religion in the State organization and taking religion out of the State organization, what we have is a simple policing [*zabıta*] by the State for the sake of ordering a disordered field.[108]

Soon after came the "Turkey is different from the West" speech by Muammer Aksoy sealing off the discussions in the chamber cited in length above.

Utilizing Religion: Building Religion Infrastructure for Governance

During the deliberations on article 12, a utilitarian approach to religion[109] was articulated by two speakers as a conceptualization of laiklik. A military academy teacher who entered the lower chamber from the National Union Committee quota started his speech by stating that laiklik means that religion stays under the protection (*himaye*) of the state, but his articulation went way beyond that:

> The only institution spread all over the country . . . and which can gather citizens under a roof is the institution of religion. . . . If we can benefit from this institution properly, I believe that it will play a huge role in our national development. Because our national development does not only depend on material. For sure, it is set that development does not happen only with building factories. In parallel, there is the necessity to rise morally. . . . The principle of laiklik is still understood by the public as if it is a principle bringing irreligion.[110]

In line with his conceptualizaton of laiklik, the military academy teacher proposed turning optional courses on religion and morality that existed at the time into required courses and adding a new paragragh to the article on religious freedom that defines religion as an institution supportive to national education, a proposal that explicitly violates the differentiation of spheres (1358).

Another member of the lower chamber, who also was from the National Union Committee quota, articulated a utilitarian approach to religion as well. He underlined the problem as ignorance (*cehalet*) and articulated a utilitarian approach, with a focus on the moment of subjugation of a citizen:

> Why shouldn't we raise valuable clerics? It would be a big mistake to leave the religious education of this country in the hands of the ignorant. As you all know human beings have desire and need to believe in a higher being. This is unstoppable. The inner commands [*manevi hüküm*] of religion are laws of morality. Human beings do not encounter the police and gendarme at all times and places. That the fear of God is sovereign in hearts and souls is to be desired. The only reason for the drastic difference between advanced Western countries and the situation at home is that they have culture and we have ignorance. This cannot be denied. If we do not attempt to eliminate this ignorance and raise valuable clerics, it is not possible for the cause of laiklik to be resolved in a reasonable and firm way. (1446-47)

He proposed that the following paragraph be added to the article on religious freedom: "To give education and instruction in religion for the purpose of fighting religious ignorance is permitted under state inspection [*murakebe*], subject to the condition that individual freedom of conscience is not violated." One comparison he pursued was with France:

> In 1905 while in Paris for my education there was a grave incident in the French parliament. One of the Rightist Clerical Party members, Sgvetov, slapped War Minister Andri in the parliament. This event had a great impact on me. I wanted to learn the reason. Citizens and some Frenchmen I knew told me that there was a lot of tension between the two parties because the right-wing parliamentarians were convinced that the left-wing radical party wanted to interfere in the affairs of the church and religion. Furthermore, according to the right-wing party the radical government was collecting information on military officers who continued attending church and Sunday sermons. Just like it was here during the time of Sultan Hamid. . . . But then in France there wasn't a laic rule. But not so long after, the separation of church from the state was decided and put into practice. And France pronounced

itself an officially laic state. . . . Right after the decision taken by the Combes Cabinet, in France laicization came about. The year was 1905 or 1906. . . . Except [for] some demonstration[s] there was no upheaval. There was still a clerical party in the parliament. The party had a newspaper called *La Croix*. The French adapted to this new situation right away. This is the most significant point. The French obeyed the new law. They have religion schools, faculties educating men of religion, in other words they have higher education in religion. . . . This is the other important point. (1445)

Another comparison was with the United States: "What did I see in America? In Washington in some streets I saw street signs "To Church." I saw a priest pray in the American parliament before each session. Despite all these, in America nowhere is religion made into a tool of politics" (1446). He concluded that "the only reason for the drastic difference between advanced Western countries and the situation at home is that they have culture and we have ignorance" (1447).

The Institutional Politics of Laiklik in the Writing of the Constitution of 1982

From 1970 until the military takeover on September 12, 1980, Turkey had thirteen governments. During this period, the average life of a government was 9.2 months. The news reported armed conflict or bombings every day in the late 1970s, and as the decade was coming to an end reporting of individual violent events was replaced by headlines on bombings and armed conflicts in the plural.[111] To get the exact arrest and death toll of a military regime is quite difficult. For instance, Eric Zürcher reports 11,500 arrested in the first six weeks of the military coup in 1980 and 30,000 by the end of that year; 122,600 a year after the coup.[112] This much is well emphasized in standard accounts of the 1980 coup. What is much less emphasized and is overshadowed by the "anarchy and terror" account is that with Süleyman Demirel's minority government's January 24, 1980, decisions of devaluation and a reduced state role in the economy (all measures formulated by the prime minister's secretary Turgut Özal, who later founded the Motherland Party and won the first postcoup elections), strikes spread to all sectors.[113] The government's strategy of postponing strikes was proving ineffective and collective bargaining attempts were failing. By September 6, 2010, 53,350 workers were on strike after not being offered collective bargaining.[114] On September 7, 1980, the newspaper *Milliyet* reported that attempts at collective bargaining in the textile industry had failed and strikes were expected to expand.[115] By September 10, Demirel's minority government (November 12, 1979—September 12, 1980) had already declared sixty-nine strikes illegal since the beginning of the year, more than twice the number in all of 1979. On September 10, 1980, *Milliyet* reported that 80,000 additional workers were ready to strike.[116] On September 11, one day before the coup, the strike in the glass sector had completed its hundredth day.[117] The September 6 Konya demonstration of Necmettin Erbakan's National Salvation Party and the armed conflicts and bombings that are often highlighted as the main reason for the coup and facilitate the justification of the coup as maintaining "order and laiklik," overlook the level of strike activism that preceded the coup. Indeed, the first deed of the National Security Council when it took over on September 12, 1980, was to dismantle the political parties and the second deed was to dismantle two syndicates, the Confederation of Revolutionary Workers' Syndicates (DİSK) and Confederation of Nationalist Workers' Syndicates (MİSK). The third task was to dismantle almost all associational life.[118] The total number of syndicates dispersed in the first week of the military regime by the National Security Council was 703 (471 of them were independent).[119] This frontal attack on syndicates is exactly the same dynamic as in the Latin American coups.[120] The state-prone TÜRK-İŞ syndicates were the only ones reopened.[121] On November 6 the Work Ministry was rewriting the law on collective bargaining strikes and lockouts for a single syndicate.[122] The solution to the problem of collective bargaining came on November 23; it would be solved by a method of "exemplary contracts" (*emsal sözleşme*).[123] In other words, rather than bargaining with workers' representatives, the Work Ministry would decide on the current terms of work through an evaluation of past examples of collective bargaining documents, allowing only TÜRK-İŞ to partake in this decision process.[124] Most coups in Latin America struck left-wing governments and left Christian democrats in place; the Turkish trajectory looks exactly the same. Neither the shorter time of the military in power in comparison to Latin American coups[125] nor the media cover-ups could hide the level of military violence, particularly in Diyarbakır Prison no. 5, and in the sporadic right-wing attacks such as the ones in Çorum, Fatsa, and the Massacre of Maraş.[126] However, it is striking that the only news reported in *Milliyet* on the coup and Diyarbakır between September 1980 and September 1983 is coverage of a couple of activists in the Britain who suggested that there were deaths in the Turkish prison, while the *Financial Times* reported hunger strikes in prison on June 4, 1982.[127]

Significant religious communities were less touched by the coup, partly because they shared the anticommunism of the Kemalist military officers. After the September 12, 1980, coup, one leader of the Nur community, a denomination within Islam, came out publicly supporting the military regime and even wrote a letter to the head of the National Security Council (MGK) asking for more space in society for religion.[128] The largest wing of the Nur community was a group called Yeni Asya. The group had supported all those political parties who stood against past military coups.[129] However, a front-page article entitled "The Voice of Our Military," published in the newspaper *Yeni Asya* on February 10, 1971, and written by the lawyer of Said Nursi, founder of the Nur community, was explicitly in favor of the military regime calling on the military against the left.[130]

Fethullah Gülen, one current religious leader emerging from within the Nur community, had then split from the Yeni Asya group; however, some of his mosque sermons and lead articles in his group's journal, *Sızıntı*, widely accepted to have been written by him under a pseudonym, shared the same promilitary line. *Sızıntı* published two endorsements of the military, one right before the coup in June 1979 and the other right after, and as late as 1995 Gülen still had not criticized the military government of 1980–1983.[131] In the June 1979 piece entitled "Soldier," the soldier was depicted as the forerunner of "civilization" and "prosperity" "with its conquests and the following culture raids."[132] Starting with praises of the "military profession" as "of high esteem both at the level of God and the level of the people" the article ended with a section on "born soldier nations" alluding to the Turkish nation. In his piece right after the coup he continued to praised the military takeover and concluded, "Salute one more time to the soldier who came to our help fast where our hope was exhausted."[133]

Gülen had dispersed a nationwide boycott of the High Islam Institutes with his fatwa "there is no boycott in Islam" in 1977, and in some of his sermons before the coup he had asked, "Has the Prophet ever marched or chanted slogans?" In a sermon in 1980 he called on the public to turn in "anarchists and terrorists" to the state; if not they would be responsible to God: "Let the secret service hear, let the police hear, let the military hear, let the prime minister hear, let the president hear. If these traitors shooting at the police and the military do not receive the necessary punishment in court, neither the state nor the nation will remain."[134]

Gülen's biographer underscores that for Gülen, "despite having the disadvantage of destroying the democratic system," the coup eliminated the possibility of communism, which he saw as a higher danger. On the required religion courses put in the military constitution of 1982, his biographer reports him saying that military "revolutionaries [İhtilalciler] did what republican governments could not do."[135] A graphic representation of a military and Gülen movement agreement on antileftism was a drawing in the May 1989 issue of the journal Sızıntı of a young man sitting on a chair in a cell with hands and feet tied, head tilted to the side, clearly semiconscious or unconscious, and an interrogation light hanging over him; he had obviously gone through torture. Toward the top it read: "What if it is also closed to the beyond . . . ?"; toward the bottom it read: "This life which ends here with separation in pain and migration to foreign lands, could have at least been open to the beyond! What if it is not." Ruşen Çakır notes that here Sızıntı questions the conscience of the tortured and has nothing to say on the torturer.[136] This cartoon is a commentary on the communists' rejection of the spirit and of religious morality, tracing the torture to this rejection and endorsing the assessment that communism is a threat and that the military's response is the proper way to deal with that threat.

The Military Pushes for "Religious Morality," and the Emergence of Islamist Civil Society

The coup itself was an enabling factor for the rise of political Islam both by eliminating the organizational structure of its potential rivals from the left and by directly promoting religious morality as a characteristic of the "good" citizen and the solution to the precoup "crisis." The reorganization of civil society by military violence was followed by military policies establishing Sunni Islam as the cement of society. This opened new paths for religious communities after the coup in the economy, the state, and civil society.[137] Three concrete military acts of religio-cultural policy were the First National Culture Meeting, convened in October 1982;[138] articles 24 and 136 of the 1982 constitution ratified by referendum on November 7, 1982; and the opening of a preacher and prayer leader school (İmam Hatip high school) in Tunceli in 1985.

The officially stated reason for the opening of the İmam Hatip high school was anarchy, terror, and the ethnic makeup of the region.[139] However, this promotion of religious infrastructure was in fact part of the larger military project of investing in national culture, with Sunni Islam as its major element. General Kenan Evren opened the first National Culture Meeting on October 23, 1982 with the statement, "Civilization is international, culture is national." He offered a conceptualization of culture "as a combination of developments in a society's spiritual, aesthetic, inner, social, and intellectual planes . . . most appropriate for the goals for which the Culture Meeting has convened."[140] This practice of putting Sunni imams in Alevi villages was not only a military regime policy; it existed before the coup and was continued by the military regime.[141] It was part of the origins of the Turkish Republic and is still the case today, as discussions in parliament on a new law for the Directorate of Religious Affairs in July 2010 attest.

Mobilizing religion as the "cement of society" was expressed most vividly in articles 24 and 136 of the 1982 constitution. Article 136 reads: "As an agency of the general administration, the Directorate of Religious Affairs fulfills the duties indicated in its special law in compliance with the principle of laicism, and remaining outside of all political opinion and thinking, and having as its goal national solidarity and integrity." Article 24, paragraph 4, turned the optional religion and ethics courses in primary and secondary education to compulsory: "Education and instruction in religion and ethics shall be conducted under state supervision and control. Instruction in religious culture and moral education shall be compulsory in the curricula of primary and secondary schools."

The debates in the Constituent Assembly for the 1982 constitution were full of formulations that the socioeconomic crisis of the 1970s was a moral crisis that could be solved with religious education. The constitution was drafted by a Constitution Commission, discussed and a first text finalized by the Consultative Assembly, evaluated and necessary changes made by the National Security Council, and ratified by a referendum. Some statements from the Consultative Assembly working on the draft constitution before it was sent for approval to the military were: "Economic crises can be overcome in a short time by taking measures; however, moral crises are not like this. Many nations have been erased from history as a consequence of moral breakdown." "Instead of . . . Lenin, Mao, and Castro let's teach the Turkish child his/her religion in a real sense and under the license of the state within the principles of Atatürk." "There is no minority in the Turkey of Atatürk, there is [only the] citizen."[142]

The debates in the Consultative Assembly and the National Security Council present important clues to the politics of the 1982 constitution; however, the procedures set for writing the constitution were in the final analysis window dressing. General Kenan Evren relates in his memoirs some of the events that had taken place behind the façade of the openly stated procedures:

> We had diagnosed many malfunctionings emanating from the [1961] constitution and we had ordered the General Secretariat of the National Security Council to prepare a constitution draft that would remedy these malfunctionings. The general secretary was taking the matter close to heart and various experts were working on the task. Even before the Consultative Assembly had started working toward a constitution [draft], a constitution draft was almost ready at the General Secretariat. Because we had plenty of time ahead of us, we did not address the matter of the constitution. Anyhow, it would not be appropriate for us to start working on the constitution draft we had prepared before the preparation of a constitution [draft] by the Consultative Assembly. Only when the sessions of the Consultative Assembly had started and articles were being ratified by them, their ratified articles were coming to us, and in order to save time, we were holding our meetings over these articles unofficially.[143]

Article 24, paragraph 3, was drafted by the Constitution Commission as "Education and instruction in religion and ethics shall be conducted under state supervision and control. Education and instruction in religion is a matter of the will of individuals; in the case of minors it depends on the will of their lawful representatives." It was changed by the Consultative Assembly to "Education and instruction in religion and ethics is compulsory in primary and middle schools, and it is conducted under the supervision of the state. *The attendance of those individuals, who do not belong to the religion of Islam, to the courses on religion is voluntary*" and finalized by the National Security Council as "Education and instruction in religion and ethics shall be conducted under state supervision and control. Instruction in religious culture and moral education shall be compulsory in the curricula of primary and secondary schools.

Other religious education and instruction shall be subject to the individual's own desire, and in the case of minors, to the request of their legal representatives."

Two members of the Constitution Commission had already found the draft of article 24 insufficient. These two members maintained that instead of stipulating optional religious instruction in public schools, article 24 should have made religious instruction compulsory. One of them was İhsan Göksel, who was also a member of the National Security Council.[144] A civilian member of the Constitution Commission also expressed as his main concern with the initial draft of article 24, the absence of compulsory religious instruction in public schools. Tevfik Fikret Alpaslan argued that "education in religion and morals should be mandatory in primary and secondary levels of instruction," because "a citizen who possesses knowledge of religion and morals is always beneficial for the country."[145]

At the August 21, 1982, meeting of the Consultative Assembly, owing to an excessive number of proposals (fifteen) on article 24, the head of the Constitution Commission, Professor Orhan Aldıkaçtı, suggested that this article be rewritten by the commission in light of these proposals before being submitted to discussion in the assembly. When the article was brought for discussion, two modifications were noticeable in the paragraph on education. The assertion of the state supervision of religious education was made more explicit by the addition of the phrase "Religious and moral education and instruction is mandatory in primary and middle schools" with an explanation for the condition of "minorities," meaning non-Muslims: "The attendance of individuals, who are not members of the religion of Islam, to religion courses depends on their will; minorities are protected under laws specific to them."[146]

With this new formulation, members of the assembly who felt their proposals were accommodated withdrew them; yet there were still some remaining objections. The first proposal discussed in the assembly was signed by seventy-four members and was in favor of the paragraph asserting state involvement in religious education. On behalf of the signers, Nurettin Ayanoğlu thanked the commission for including the paragraph and explained, "Atatürk has said that 'the nation will learn its religion in school.'" He continued, "religious education and instruction, which will be conducted without state school and state supervision and control, will by time develop in the direction of the views of some religious orders [*tarikats*] and religious sects [*mezhep*]; and this condition will definitely damage national unity and togetherness [*milli birlik ve beraberlik*]" (272). He identified the cause for the increase in secret religious teaching contrary to regulations as the insufficient instruction in Islam in state schools. In other words, teaching Islam in state schools would eliminate private forms of teaching religion, such as by religious orders (272, 278). All this was necessary to prevent religion from becoming a means of politics (281–83).

Ayanoğlu continued, on behalf of all who signed the proposal in favor of compulsory education, and asked for further clarity on the article as drafted by the Constitution Commission. He pointed out that a clear distinction had to be made between legitimate and illegitimate involvements in the sphere of religion. He defended the part of the proposal that advocated specifying the main textual sources of religion. According to Ayanoğlu, "activities with the intention to teach religion from its main sources" should be legitimate while "propaganda-like" teachings and activities that aim to ground the fundamental order of the state on religious principles should be considered a criminal offense (272).

The addition in article 24 of the phrase qualifying the textual sources for teaching Islam was rejected, but Ayanoğlu had voiced one of the main tasks that religious education was put to: to solve the problem of societal fragmentation. This position had wide support in the Consultative Assembly. The typical argument rested on a conception of religion as national culture; religion had to be mobilized in order to protect national culture against societal fragmentation (274). Religion, on the one hand, was the cure against excessive pluralism, and on the other hand it was an alternative to a leftist political agenda (300, 302); therefore it was institutionalized to be a part of the content of social morality and national culture.

The Republican offense was not only against decentralized and radical forms of religion. It was a more general attack on minorities (295, 304–6). As noted in chapter 3, the French republicans at the end of the nineteenth century did not attack minorities as such but only as radical religious sects. The definition of religious teaching as national culture summarized above was to serve the end of a more homogeneous and therefore more governable population at the expense of excluding a constitutional acknowledgment of minorities in Turkey. Fevzi Uyguner, for instance, argued against the use of the term "minority" in the draft of article 24: "There is nothing called a minority in Turkey," he asserted, "anyone who is related to the Turkish State by ties of citizenship is Turkish" (275).

There were some alternative voices in the assembly as well. For instance, Kamer Genç agreed with the others on the social necessity of religion but argued that rather than public teaching of religion with compulsory courses in state schools, he opted for instruction in the private sphere, within the family (276). Public instruction in religion, he argued, was in contradiction with the laiklik of Mustafa Kemal Atatürk, which, according to Kamer Genç, meant separation of the affairs of religion and state. He more explicitly pointed out that at times religious teaching could contradict positive science (299) or the civil code, a situation that would undermine the legitimacy of the state. Contrary to the collective report of the Constitution Commission and members of the Consultative Assembly who supported this report, Kamer Genç saw the separation doctrine as incompatible with teaching of religion in state schools. Asım İğneciler criticized Kamer Genç for misunderstanding *Müslümanlık* (Muslimness):

> In Islam, in the Kuran-ı Kerim, in hadis[147] as we understand it, there are no religious sects. Therefore, here we did not come to implant the seeds of religious sects. If laiklik, as articulated today, had been against the principles [the six arrows underlying Kemalist ideology] of Atatürk, then religious education and mosques would not have been so highly valued by Atatürk and in the times just after him. (277)

After questions to the Constitution Commission, the head of the commission, Orhan Aldıkaçtı, introduced İhsan Göksel Paşa, a member of the National Security Council as well as a member of the Constitution Commission, to speak on behalf of the commission. Göksel pointed out that Islam is a unifying religion, and that religious sects had been formed as a result of the flourishing of multiple interpretations after the death of Muhammed. He advocated a peaceful cohabitation of the spiritual forces of nationalism and religion:

> Laiklik never means being without a religion [*dinsizlik*]. Laiklik means that affairs of religion are not mixed into affairs of state and into politics. Religious instruction and education is never against laiklik. We will learn our religion in its real aspects so that those ill-intentioned men of religion who would like to shake our loyalty to the principle of laiklik cannot fool our nation and cannot guide us to paths outside Islam [*Müslümanlık*]. If we make an art course, a handcrafts course, a music course required in the curriculum and not teach our nation our religion, which is among the greatest spiritual powers, then we can see that

the attempt to stay erect just by nationalism is like a man who has lost a leg and is attempting to walk.

Religion will be taught, but its practice will not be enforced. If its practice is enforced, then that is against laiklik. (280)

The National Security Council

The deliberations in the National Security Council over the constitution draft of the Consultative Assembly started on October 18, 1982.[148] A constitutional commission formed from within the council had already revised the draft. The head of this commission, Judge and Major General Muzaffer Başkaynak, defined the role of the military at this historical juncture in his introductory speech:

> To save the State, which has found itself on the verge and even within a civil war, the Turkish Armed Forces, who always believe in democracy, had come face to face with its unchangeable duty; the September 12, 1980, takeover is an expression of this duty. The Turkish Armed Forces, who have taken over the government of the nation temporarily, in order to return the government to its rightful owner, to correct its malfunctioning democracy and its constitution open to all kinds of deviant [çarpık] thought, interpretation and application, according to the principles and necessities of democracy, have had the constitution redrafted by the Consultative Assembly, which it [Turkish Armed Forces] has brought into being in the name of the Turkish Nation by the National Security Council. (335)

At the National Security Council meeting convened on October 18, 1982, there was almost no debate on the first twenty-three articles of the constitution. These articles were simply read, voted on, and ratified (335–39). The first speaker was on article 24. The president of the council explained what the new required religion courses meant:

> We are giving a course in the culture of religion, not a course on religion; in other words, we are going to teach the children necessary matters within history of religion and rules of our religion. When we say "course on religion," it does not mean to read the *Kuran'ı*

Kerim from cover to cover. No, not that. [Just that] the child has a culture of religion when she/he graduates from primary and middle school. (340)

Admiral Nejat Tümer asked the commission about foreign schools:

These foreign schools, especially *Rum* schools, have an education on religion they conduct at their own institutions. Besides, we have our French, German, Italian schools; in these places both Turks and foreigners study. Since this obligation is in our Constitution, does it also require the teaching of a course on religion in these schools, or are they exempt? (341)

General Başkaynak responded:

In our international agreements, in the Lausanne Treaty, there are statutes that stipulate that foreigners will be given cultural education in accord with their own religions at their schools in Turkey and these [rights] are reserved; the Turkish State does not interfere in this. In these schools where foreigners study, their own religion courses are taught, but Turkish student do not attend these courses. I guess, from this point on, besides these courses and cultural training the foreigners have on religion, those Turkish or belonging to the religion of Islam will at the same time study the culture of Islam. (341)

The president of the council, four-star general Kenan Evren, remarked with an example from the West to justify the teaching of a religion course on Islam in those schools where there was religious diversity:

When I was in Brussels, a child of an acquaintance was in second grade. At school, they were taking the Muslim children out during that [religion] session, and taught the principles of Christianity to the rest of the children, they don't take Muslims; but those who want can attend. They also have it, they give culture of religion. (341)

Admiral Nejat Tümer backed this example from Brussels with his experience in Naples: "The same practice exists in Naples as well" (341). The president affirmed: "Of course there is, it is not possible to make a nation religionless. If these children do not receive culture of religion at school or if their families do not give it . . . from where will it be given?" (341–42).

This chapter, like the previous chapters on France, has paid close attention to the articulation of various actors and has woven these self-articulations together in context at key moments of struggle over the institutions of laiklik in Turkey. In contrast to France, the political field at these moments remained encapsulated in a "law of majorities" and "utility of religion" framework oscillating between the political ends of mobilizing and demobilizing religion, between anticlericalism and state-civil religionism, and their different forms and combinations, except in the case of a few minority voices. The institution of state-salaried imams and religion courses could precisely be used like a lever to have state institutions mobilize or demobilize religion. This is crucial for a better assessment of Kemalist laicism in comparative perspective as well as vis-à-vis its challengers in Turkish politics. Among the Third Republic France republicanisms, Kemalist laicism in its origins fell closest to Républicains opportunistes who, in the words of Jules Ferry, were "anticlerical but not antireligious," a statement very similar to the widely repeated Kemalist motto "*Kemalizm dinsizlik değildir*" (Kemalism is not irreligious). With the transition to a multiparty system, the Kemalist CHP moved closer to the Républicains progressistes: its institutional politics of religion approached more state-civil religionism.

This chapter documented many crucial moments where the institutional preferences of the Kemalist CHP, intellectuals, or the military came from an explicit pursuit of the political end of mobilizing religion (as the cement of society) against left movements and had nothing to do with the common perception that the "threat of Islam" requires a strategy of containment. The deeper the Kemalist military laid religion into state institutions, the more they had to abstract from it, again a process also visible in Third Republic France. In 1980 Turkey's military abstracted religion *as culture* from religion *as such* in order to normalize the anomaly of a "laic" military constitutionalizing compulsory religion courses. Even at the few moments when institutional separation was seriously evaluated as an alternative, it was done so again on the premises of "law of majorities" and "utility of religion" and for the sake of mobilizing religion. The liberal arguments for institutions that ultimately resolved the struggle between anticlericalism and state-civil religionism in the French Third Republic could not reach the sphere of institution making in Turkey and remained limited to a few marginalized voices that ignited discussion but never could bear on the institutional outcome.

Comparative references to Europe in general, the United States, and European cases, France in particular, were a significant part of the discussions laid out in this chapter. The rampant presence of such references is theoretically significant in itself and can be taken as a part of the micro politics of modernization outside the "West." These comparative references display competing interpretations not only through time but also across political groups who are pursuing different ends. For instance, both the late 1940s CHP and the 1980 military claimed to directly follow Europe but rediscovered Europe as religious space in advocating religion courses in public schools, grounding themselves on distinctions such as regime versus policy, and religion as such versus as culture. While in the writing of the 1961 constitution the struggle was between those who found religion under threat and those who found the regime under threat, the latter defending a sociological and the former an institutional understanding of "the West." Those who found religion under threat dominated the whole episode and asserted a difference in sociological state between Europe and Turkey in order to defend institutions they found to be non-European.[149]

This contrast between a sociological and an institutional reading of Europe resembles the sociological and institutional readings of the United States in the Third French Republic, respectively defended by opponents and proponents of the 1905 separation law, documented in chapter 3. Such variety and shifts in referencing "Europe" in Turkey pose a challenge at multiple levels to the existing discussions on comparative modernities and secularisms, especially when evaluated together with the variety of comparative references to the "United States" and other European countries in the Third French Republic (chapter 3) and to "Turkey" in contemporary France (chapter 4). I will discuss this theoretical and methodological challenge in the conclusion.

CHAPTER VI

The Sincere Government (*Samimi Hükümet*), the Institutional Politics of Religion, and Diversity in Contemporary Turkey

The Justice and Development Party (AKP) won five consecutive parliamentary elections in 2002, 2007, 2011, and 2015. In 2002 it won 34.28 percent of the vote and 363 of 550 seats in parliament; in 2007, 46.58 percent of the vote and 341 seats; in 2011, 49.9 percent and 327 seats; in June 2015, 40.9 percent and 258 seats; and in November 2015, 49.5 percent and 317 seats. In the 2002 and 2007 parliaments the party had more seats than the 330 votes (three-fifths majority) required for approving a constitutional change, and in the 2002 parliament it was only 2 votes short of the 367 votes (two-thirds majority) required to overturn a presidential veto on a proposal for a constitutional change. In 2008 the head prosecutor of the republic indicted the AKP for violating laiklik. The Constitutional Court decided not to close the party but cut its public funding in half and issued it a warning.

The European and Turkish press, academics, and public intellectuals have taken as evidence for the consolidation of democracy in Turkey the electoral success of the AKP without subsequent military intervention, the pro–European Union position the party took in its first two terms in government in contrast to previous parties of political Islam, its participation in the Alliance of Civilizations Project,[1] the lack of references to Shari'a law in speeches by party members, the Democratic Opening: National Unity and Brotherhood/Sisterhood Project it launched in 2009, and its willingness and actual initiative for writing a new constitution to replace the military constitution of 1982. Religiously violent speech and the goal of a multi-juridical legal system had constituted the evidence supporting the ban of the Welfare Party by the Turkish Constitutional Court and the later approval of this ban by the European Court of Human Rights.[2] Moreover, the AKP era has been taken as an example of how strict secularism and consolidation of democracy are not complementary projects. In the current world context, where it is quite popular to associate Islam with violence, the AKP has been taken as the model of "Muslim democracy." For example, José Casanova writes:

> The AKP are using their electoral victory to advance legal and cultural Europeanization in order to meet the conditions to join the European Union. The notion that once they are accepted, they will reveal their true intentions and impose an authoritarian Islamic state seems to me preposterous. Yavuz offers a much more plausible argument, buttressed by convincing sociological empirical evidence of the transformation of the AKP from an Islamist to a Muslim Democratic party, that is akin to earlier transformations of the dubiously democratic Catholic parties of the 1930s into the Christian Democratic parties of the late 1940s and 1950s, the very ones which sponsored the project of the EEC.[3]

The exclusive focus on the headscarf question in mapping the political field of struggle over laiklik has long made the AKP look like a liberal alternative to the Kemalist establishment. In 2013 the headscarf ban was removed in all state institutions, including for state employees and students starting in fifth grade (age ten). This, however, was not the only change. The already required course on religion in Turkish public schools has now been supplemented by two optional courses: one on reading the Koran and the other on the life of the Prophet. Additionally, the DRA has been restructured to enhance the hierarchies among imams, and in all these restructurings minorities have been totally ignored. What happened? Has the AKP changed? I show that the roots of the recent institutional restructurings by the AKP have been present in parliamentary records and other primary sources since it first came to power in 2002. The AKP always worked out its institutional politics of the relation between state and religion from the premise that Turkey is a Sunni Muslim majority country. What has changed, however, is that the party's defense of institutions on the relation between state and religion relies less and less on arguments from within laicism. In this chapter I document this from parliamentary records and other primary sources on the party's politics around state-salaried imams from the time it took office in 2002 until it restructured the DRA in 2010; its Democratic Opening: National Unity and Brotherhood/Sisterhood Project, the party's project for writing a new constitution that finally failed in 2013, and the reintroduction of the new optional religion courses in the public school curriculum in 2012. The chapter particularly focuses on one aspect of the Democratic Opening Project, the Alevi Workshops, to assess the AKP's politics of religious diversity. I offer a close textual analysis of the approximately two thousand pages of state records on the seven workshops that took place between June 2009 and January 2010. Despite their anomalies and varieties, all Kemalists more or less took laicism as the battlefield. The parliamentary discussions show that AKP parliamentarians argue more and more from the point of view of religion as an end in itself or as a means to some particular political goal; laicism is losing its place as the framer of the political field of discussion. The AKP pushes state-civil religionism further by deepening and layering existing Kemalist laicist institutions and by appropriating a politics of diversity that further deepens religion as the cement of society. Some of the AKP arguments for the institutional changes in question approach those of political Catholics in Third Republic France; that is, they are no longer arguments from secularism.

AKP Politics of the DRA as Early as 2005

Prime Minister Recep Tayyip Erdoğan summarized the AKP's position on laiklik on December 12, 2005, six days before the parliamentary discussion on the budget of the DRA for 2006: "Religion is the cement of society,"[4] he said, advocating religion as a moral tie. On December 18, during the parliamentary discussions on a proposal to give Alevis representation in the DRA and a proposal to strengthen the existing structure of the DRA, particularly against Christian missionaries, the AKP took a clear position to strengthen Sunni Islam against minorities and missionaries. First, the CHP spokesperson argued during the parliamentary session of December 18 that the DRA should also recognize Alevis and have Alevi representatives as part of its institutional structure, and that a state budget should be provided for the group: "The [Alevis] have to be represented within the Directorate of Religious Affairs, and *cemevi*s [Alevi places of worship] have to be given a legal status. . . . These people are paying taxes to the state, but with these taxes we are supporting a single sect [Sunni]."[5]

In his response, the AKP spokesperson dismissed the CHP spokesperson's demand for representation for Alevis within the DRA by reiterating, perhaps ironically, the exact Kemalist laicist argument in defense of the DRA:

> Mr. President and esteemed parliamentarians, the fundamental goals of the Directorate of Religious Affairs are to enlighten society on matters of religion, to provide people with solid [religious] knowledge based on the fundamental sources of religion by a method that does not disregard modern life . . . and to maintain fidelity to religion and to the state, love and unity of the nation, positive values of the contemporary world, and societal agreement. . . . The Directorate of Religious Affairs is an institution that represents all Muslims by being equidistant on the basis of citizenship and not discriminating on the basis of sect, understanding, or religious practice. . . . Islam is a universal religion. . . . Dear friends, because I know our Alevi brothers . . . in all their aspects, I see them as Muslim brothers of mine. Because we have accepted . . . Ali as most respectable, we do not have the slightest doubt that . . . those who follow on the path of Hz. Ali . . . are Muslims. . . . Our Republican People's Party spokesperson mentioned here that Alevis are not represented in the Directorate of Religious Affairs and that *cemevleri* [Alevi places of worship] are not recognized as mosques, as places of worship. . . . Dear friends, in fact, because the Directorate of Religious Affairs represents all Muslims, our mosques are not the places of worship . . . of any one particular sect. They are the common places of worship of all Muslims.[6]

The references to the content of the religion of Islam as universal and compatible with modernity by the AKP are reminiscent of the statements from the early days of the republic by Mustafa Kemal and his supporters on the compatibility of Islam and modernity (see chapter 5). This similarity between the strictly antipluralist early republican ideology and the AKP position casts doubt on the commonly noted dichotomy between Kemalist laicism and political Islam that dominates the study of Turkish politics. It disqualifies the current politics of Islam in Turkey as a strictly new moment and calls for closer attention to detail without haphazardly enforcing or collapsing the opposition between Kemalist laicism and political Islam. While it is widely acknowledged that the DRA has always privileged a Sunni version of Islam, close attention to the defense of the DRA by the AKP and comparing it with the various Kemalist republican defenses of the DRA documented in chapter 5 expose significant convergences and divergences. For a start, AKP's defense of the DRA as an institution above religious sects is reminiscent of a strategy, also present among early and late Kemalist Republicans, of using the DRA for building a homogeneous society in religious moral terms. The AKP spokesperson quoted above explains the purpose of the DRA with exactly the same words of the Kemalist military 1982 constitution; that is, to "maintain fidelity to religion and to the state, love and unity of the nation."

During the December 18, 2005, parliamentary session on the budget for the DRA, the AKP spokesperson pointed out that Christian missionary activities posed an imminent danger to Islam in Turkey and around the world. This was in part due to the large number of staff vacancies in the DRA. He noted that some mosques were not even allocated personnel:

> Dear friends, you all know that in recent years in Turkey, as in all over the world, Christian missionaries have worked very intensely. At a time when the world promotes basic rights and freedoms, we need to provide the conditions for those from any belief to freely communicate their beliefs. Yet the . . . competition is working to the disadvantage of Muslims, as evidenced by intense propaganda of missionaries in Muslim countries and the financial support of the Union of Churches. Dialogue between religions and the elimination of conflict among them is applaudable, yet the competition among religions will last as long as the world exists. Competition can develop only under equal conditions and opportunities. Muslims must undertake more innovative activities. I believe that it is much more beneficial in the long run that these activities be within the standards of science and justice. Therefore the number of expert cadres of the High Council of Religious Affairs of the Directorate of Religious Affairs must be increased. We need to conduct research on Abrahamic religions under the directorship of the Directorate of Religious Affairs with the cooperation of a few well-staffed Faculties of Theology.[7]

This statement opens yet another angle on the contemporary dialogue and alliance of civilizations visions that dominate world politics. Visions of tolerance and mutual understanding may be the façade of competition among religious missionaries. The analogy between capitalism and religion has continued relevance: all capitalists, despite their explicit commitments to free competition, deep inside strive for monopoly, and likewise all religions, despite their explicit commitments to toleration, deep inside would like all to convert to their side.

The above discussions in parliament were one snapshot of AKP politics regarding the DRA as early as 2005.[8] The possibility of "autonomy"[9] sometimes voiced by AKP parliamentarians before and after their electoral victory in 2002 had been dropped completely from the agenda. These statements of "autonomy" have led many to think that the AKP would follow the separationist line of Ali Fuad Başgil, the conservative scholar whose writings were examined in chapter 5, forgetting that Başgil himself had diverged from "separation" when he had seen it as a pragmatic necessity. The AKP has continuously increased the DRA's share of the state budget (figure 6.1), to a level that now has surpassed the peak share that the Welfare Party (RP)—the party of radical Islam—had allocated to the institution in 1997.[10]

By 2007 the AKP had increased the DRA's budget to surpass the budgets of thirty-seven other state institutions.[11] In 2007 the DRA received more state funds than the Social Services and Child Protection Institution, the Ministry of Interior, the Ministry of Foreign Affairs, the Ministry of Transportation, the Ministry of Industry and Commerce, the Ministry of Energy and Natural Resources, the Ministry of Culture and Tourism, the Ministry

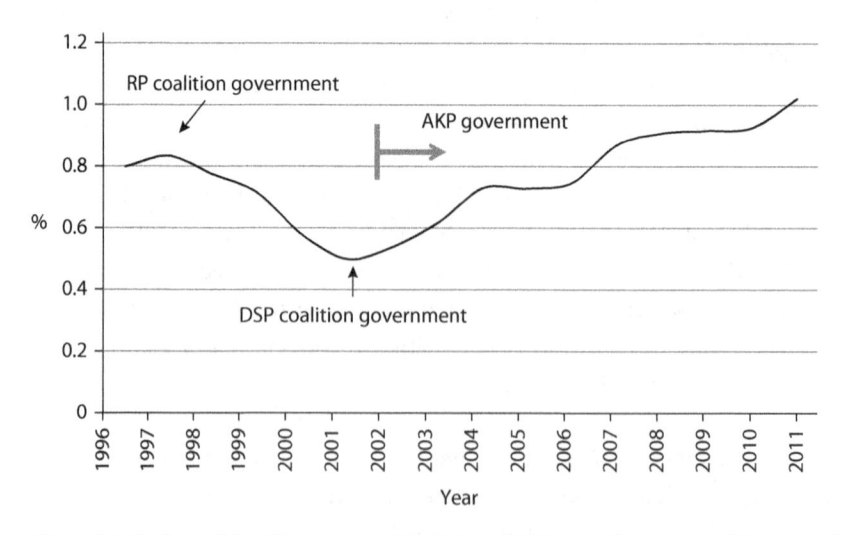

Figure 6.1 Budget of the Directorate of Religious Affairs as a Percentage of the Actual State Budget Spent. (*Source*: Calculated from *Turkish Statistical Yearbook*.)

of Forests and the Environment, and the Ministry of Public Works and Settlement. With the fifteen thousand new staff the AKP secured for the institution in March 2007, the DRA now enjoys the largest administration it has ever had since the founding of the Republic, even larger than when the Welfare Party was in government in 1997.

The December 18, 2005, session of parliament also had rich comparative remarks made on European countries and Turkey, underscoring one more time how comparison itself is a significant part of the comparative politics of secularism and modernity, and particularly important for addressing the question of *traveling*. For instance, an AKP member made the following comparison with Europe:

> This organization [DRA], which is providing religious services on five continents of the world through its international representatives, does not only serve the Turks in those countries but also serves all people who would like to learn about Islam. On October 3, 2005, we entered the starting period of the negotiations with the European Union. The strongest and most organized institutions of Europe are still churches and religious endowments. The financial and spiritual power of these institutions is nearly stronger than the states' budgets, and their spiritual authority and influence are stronger than those of heads of states. Although they are laic, according to the constitutions of strong European Union countries Germany, France, Italy, and England, laws contrary to Christian dogma cannot be proposed. . . . In order for our country to endure against Christian institutions with strong and rooted organizations, we have to evaluate and strengthen these three basic institutions to the best of our ability: . . . Ministry of Culture[,] . . . Ministry of Education[, and] . . . Directorate of Religious Affairs.[12]

These references to the persistent role of religion in Europe, despite the fact that sometimes they are inaccurate, have to be taken seriously. On the one hand, they are simple political rhetoric. In fact, references from within political Islam in Turkey to the diversity of relations between the state and religion in European countries started before the AKP.[13] In a proposal in 1994, the Welfare Party of Necmettin Erbakan demanded a constitutional amendment specifically calling for the elimination of the term *laik* from article 2 of the Turkish Constitution. The party had often called Europe a "Christian Club," but in its 1994 proposal it diverged from its anti-Western stance in the 1970s[14] and engaged in a comparative analysis of European constitutions. The proposal used French exceptionalism—that it is the only European country with the term *laïque* in its constitution—to argue for a constitutional amendment in Turkey. It also cited the fact that Norway, Greece, Denmark, and England have constitutionally established churches and emphasized that every individual has a right to religious instruction in Germany. In other words, a party of "radical political Islam" that had been banned by the Turkish Constitutional Court, and whose dissolution was sanctioned by the European Court of Human Rights, once used and bequeathed a strategy of "turning to the West" in political arguments.

On the other hand, such references have a different significance in light of religion's persisting role in Europe and the current state-led restructuring of state-religion relations under way in many European countries.[15] Examples include the discussion on France explored previously, the Shari'a courts established in the United Kingdom, and others. Such ongoing restructurings of European public spaces would give birth to interesting hypotheses putting Turkey and European countries on the same political field and calling for an approach to religion as a solution at large rather than a problem. The Alliance of Civilizations meeting in Istanbul on November 12–13, 2006, was quite revealing in this respect. The press release issued after the meeting was titled "Politics, Not Religion, at the Heart of the Growing Muslim-West Divide, New Report Argues." The title led one to believe that there was a shift from a religiously based understanding of the problems of the world order to a political understanding.[16] But the report cites religion among its guiding principles for a solution: "Religion is an increasingly important dimension of many societies and a significant source of values for individuals. It can play a critical role in promoting an appreciation of other cultures, religions, and ways of life to help build harmony among them."[17]

A statement by Mehmet Aydın, minister responsible for religious affairs, ended the December 18, 2005, session of the parliament on the DRA budget. The minister dismissed the immediate question of Alevi representation and turned as a solution to the possibility of a new law to restructure the DRA.[18] Here we have in 2005 the CHP, the heir of Kemalism, defending the diversification of the DRA by giving representation to Alevis, and the AKP defending the status quo. If we turn to parliamentary debates at the other two crucial moments (see figure 6.1) of the discussions on the DRA budget during the coalition government led by the Welfare Party in 1997 and during the coalition government of the Democratic Left Party (Republican Left,

DSP in figure 6.1) in 2001, we see variations in arguments but also overarching similarities across governments in defending the DRA. During the parliamentary discussion of December 13, 2000, on the 2001 budget of the DRA, the spokesperson for the Democratic Left Party introduced the party's position on the DRA as follows:

> Religion is at the heart of the people and not in the monopoly of politics. Islam is the common belief of our society. Islam is a religion grounded on love. If today our mosques are open and we can easily hear the call to prayer and can pray freely, we should not forget that it is thanks to the Great Leader Mustafa Kemal Atatürk and the laic and democratic republican state that he established. Therefore, in all the regions [of Turkey], particularly in the eastern and southeastern regions, it is crucial to organize conferences, in cooperation with universities, in religious and national institutions. . . . Especially in the East and the Southeast, we should not leave mosques empty [without an imam] and [should] appoint religious personnel with a high education. Recent history shows us how these vacant mosques are put to use by enemies of [our] religion and nation. Great duties fall upon the Directorate of Religious Affairs to straighten these unfavorable conditions.[19]

The spokesperson continued with an argument that the Turkish translation of the Koran has to be distributed more widely in Turkey so that people can learn the true religion and be protected against abuses of religion. Only in this way is it possible "to save in a truthful and scientific way our society and particularly our youth [from ignorance]. . . . For this program to be successful, important duties fall on the Directorate of Religious Affairs and the Ministry of National Education."[20] Virtue Party, the party of radical political Islam founded by the members of the Welfare Party after the latter was banned by the Constitutional Court in 1999, was in parliament at the time as well, and its spokesperson also underlined that the DRA was understaffed and that some mosques in Turkey did not have religious personnel. He stressed that religion is the cement of society:

> Some values are common to all society. . . . Religion is the first of these common values, most probably the most important one. . . . In other words, it is the common element of each one of us in this parliament. No one can claim exclusive property over religion. If she or he does,

harmony will be disrupted in the management and the ruling of society.... The Directorate of Religious Affairs has to view society from this perspective.[21]

The Virtue Party spokesperson concluded by stating that if the Directorate of Religious Affairs is weak, then "illegal religious activities will flourish." The spokesperson for the National Action Party—the party of the radical nationalist right—repeated the same theme by stating that "all nations have religion as the core of their culture." He continued, "The budget allocated for the Directorate of Religious Affairs is not sufficient to deliver its services in an effective and productive way.... It [the DRA] has to be restructured according to current service needs by issuing a law for its reorganization."

The December 12, 1996, parliamentary discussions on the directorate's 1997 budget during the coalition government led by the Welfare Party was not very different with regard to the positions on the DRA's role, except for the Democratic Left Party's insistence on the distribution of the Turkish translation of the Koran, and the position of the Welfare Party. The spokesperson of the Welfare Party amplified the party's stance on religious moralism and defended a state-funded autonomous DRA for the sake of a more religious society, a position the reader will recall from chapter 5:

Imagine that the seventy million are a faithless crowd. I guess all of you would agree that there would be no tranquility and order left. Therefore, instead of opposing religion, the most rational path is to make peace with religion, to love it and to purify it from falsehoods.... Therefore, it is self-evident that the Directorate of Religious Affairs has to be a part of the state administration and a state budget be allocated for it.... A law for its organization has to be issued right away. With this law, the Directorate of Religious Affairs has to be removed from the slippery influence of politics.... In short, the Directorate has to be made autonomous.... *Cemevi* is not an alternative to mosques, it is a place of gathering and conversation.... The Directorate of Religious Affairs serves all Muslims equally in Turkey; it is not under the rule of any religious sect or order; it embraces and guides all of them.... One of the fundamental duties of the state is to make the necessary arrangements for individuals to learn, live, and spread their basic rights. Therefore, it is a pedagogical, psychological, and sociological necessity that religious education and instruction in our schools start at a very early age. . . . Today, if we look at Europe and the United States and observe the bad habits we all reject such as alcohol, gambling, prostitution, and their consequences such as murder, divorce, and deadly disease such as AIDS, we realize how much of a blessing our Holy Religion Islam and the family structure built upon it is. . . . The Directorate is also effective at fighting terrorism, divisive political currents, and all kinds of harmful currents of ideas. . . . The budget of the Directorate we are discussing has been increased 25% compared to last year. . . . This is marvelous. . . . Due to the very important duties we expect from the Directorate, we need to increase it [its budget] more.[22]

The AKP and the Kemalist Military Establishment Take Steps toward Each Other

The first matter the AKP had to deliberate and decide in parliament each time they took office in 2002 and in 2007 was the question of a military operation across the Iraqi border. In both the 2002 and 2007 parliaments, the party had more than a simple majority; therefore, the decision was in its hands. In 2002 the parliamentary decision was against the operation, and in 2007 it was for the operation. The context of war started playing a role in the presidential elections on April 27, 2007, and the parliamentary elections on July 22, 2007. General Chief of Staff Yaşar Büyükanıt spoke on April 12 before the presidential elections and signaled the military's preferences to the government: the military wanted to enter northern Iraq, but the operation should be ordered by parliament, and the military wanted a president loyal to the republic, not in appearance but in essence.[23]

From April 14 to May 13 Republican demonstrations in five cities—Ankara, Istanbul, Manisa, Çanakkale, and Izmir—were organized by the Union of National Civil Society Organizations against the candidacy of Abdullah Gül (AKP) for the presidency. On the night of the first round of presidential elections, April 27, at 11:10 p.m., the General Chief of Staff Headquarters issued a warning about religious threats to laiklik on its website, popularized in the media as the e-coup (electronic coup).[24] The military document referred to the presidential elections and stated that the military would take action if necessary.[25] The tension between the AKP and the military was alleviated after a secret meeting between General Chief of Staff Büyükanıt and Prime Minister Erdoğan.

Abdullah Gül was the only candidate in the presidential elections. In the first round of voting on April 27, the attendance in parliament was less than 367, so Gül could not receive the required two-thirds majority of 367 (the AKP held 365 seats). The constitution stated that a simple majority in the third round would elect the president if no candidate received a two-thirds majority in the first two rounds; thus the procedural path suggested a high chance that the AKP would elect its preferred candidate.

Just after the first round, the opposition party in parliament, CHP, appealed to the Constitutional Court for an annulment of the first round of presidential elections on the grounds that the constitution specified not only a two-thirds majority in parliament for election to the presidency but also a two-thirds majority presence in parliament to be able to hold presidential elections.

For the first time in the history of Turkey, the Constitutional Court interpreted the two-thirds majority mentioned in article 102 as the requirement of convening, and on May 1, 2007, the court annulled the first round of elections. With this decision it became impossible for the parliament to hold an election because the AKP now needed the participation of at least two parliamentarians from the opposition parties in order to reach the 367 seats required and the opposition in parliament refused. If the parliament was unable to elect a president, the constitution required parliamentary elections. The election was rescheduled for July instead of its normal time in November. In the meantime, the AKP took advantage of the lower requirement for constitutional change (while two-thirds is required for electing a president, three-fifths is required for a constitutional change in parliament unless there is a presidential veto, which can be overturned by a two-thirds majority) and started pushing for a change toward presidentialism in the constitution. On August 28, 2007, Abdullah Gül became the final president to be elected by the parliament, after three rounds of voting. A referendum held on October 21, 2007, changed article 102 to have the president be elected by popular vote.

When the vice general chief of staff accompanied Prime Minister Erdoğan on his visit to the United States on November 5, 2007, the coalition that had been forming between the military and the AKP since April 2007 became blatantly public concerning the Kurdish question. After the visit, President

Gül declared in the media, "From this point on not diplomats but soldiers will speak."[26] From a position of opposing the military on the question of a cross-border operation in 2002, the AKP and Gül converged on the military position in favor of an operation in 2007. During the military operation across the Iraqi border in December 2007, Erdoğan stated, "single nation, single *patrie*, single flag, and single state,"[27] an exact reiteration of the military's position. Ten years earlier, on June 1, 1997, in the midst of the "postmodern coup" against the Welfare Party coalition government, the secretary of the National Security Council, the institution through which the military would dictate its preferences to the government, described the features of the laic state in almost the exact words Erdoğan used a decade later: "Everyone should know that the fundamental features of the modern and laic state founded by Atatürk will not change and will not be changed. These features are *single patrie, single nation, single state, single language, and single flag*."[28]

Concomitant with the military operation was the censorship of the media on coverage of the Southeast, and Turkey's head prosecutor launched a Constitutional Court case against the Democratic Society Party (a Kurdish political party) in parliament, charging them with having members who had not yet completely broken their ties with the Kurdistan Workers' Party (PKK).

The opposition between the AKP and the two last bastions of the Kemalist establishment—the military and the Constitutional Court—which for a decade was the main axis of Turkish politics, seemed no longer to be there. First, the mass arrests that started after a gunman shot a judge in 2006 (known as the Danıştay affair) continued with trials (known as Ergenekon trials) first against coup-prone factions in the military but later also against the civil democratic opposition, and the reappointment of high-ranking military officers following the Ergenekon trials started a restructuring of the military institution. Additionally, the judiciary was restructured in the 2010 constitutional referendum. The Turkish military probably had never been so committed to public silence on politics but simultaneously at war or war prone (the 2007 operation in Iraq in support of American troops, the on-and-off continuous war with the PKK, the current question of Syria), nor the judiciary so producing consistently progovernment outcomes. On the fiftieth anniversary of the Turkish Constitutional Court in 2011, the president of the court even made a public statement against separation of powers, that "the Constitutional Court is not a place to trip and make fall those who represent the will of the people."[29]

Democratic Opening: The National Unity and Brotherhood/Sisterhood Project

In 2010 AKP initiated a series of outreach meetings officially called Demokratik Açılım Süreci: Milli Birlik ve Kardeşlik Projesi [Democratic Opening Process: National Unity and Brotherhood/Sisterhood Project].[30] The Alevi Workshops were a practical pilot of the Democratic Opening Project. Reha Çamuroğlu, the AKP parliamentarian who was the prime minister's first consultant on the workshops, in an interview he gave to me on January 16, 2016, traced the origins of the idea to the 2007 elections. Çamuroğlu was invited to the Prime Ministry in May 2007 and right after was included in the party list for the July elections precisely to design a project on the Alevi question. He was convinced that "the party was trying to expand the front (*cephe*) in an attempt to resist after the April 2007 electronic coup,"[31] and he was assured in the May meeting that he would be supported and given the opportunity to take initiative. Seeing nothing materializing on the pre-election conversation and receiving no response to his demands for an appointment with the prime minister, Çamuroğlu finally resigned from all the parliamentary commissions in October. Only upon his resignation did he receive an impromptu meeting with the prime minister, where he was able to propose the ideas of organizing a breaking-of-fast meal with some Alevi representatives for the month of Muharrem, the fasting month for Alevis, and for workshops, and Prime Minister Erdoğan appointed him as his consultant.[32] In June 2008 Çamuroğlu decided to resign from this position.

The workshops were documented in detail. The minutes of the seven consecutive workshops from June 2009 to January 2010 total 1,796 pages, with a final government report of 202 pages.[33] The AKP government sitting at the table with Alevi associations was a critical moment for revisiting the questions of secularism and democracy in Turkey. As the workshops proceeded, critical evaluation in the media increased in proportion;[34] however, at their start, the workshops were celebrated by media and policy reports as the first time any Turkish government had sat at the table with Alevis, and they clearly impressed more than the AKP electorate.[35] An in-depth analysis of the *political field* opened by this dialogue project with civil society associations shows that what the government called "democratization" was in fact an attempt to enhance its hegemony by translating demands against itself to policy for itself and thereby expand the sphere of the state vis-à-vis civil society. Parts of civil society resisted—reducing the credibility of the government efforts—and other parts cooperated, augmenting its legitimacy.

In the published records, a foreword by Prime Minister Erdoğan presented the workshops as beneficial for listening directly to the "problems of Alevi citizens" and declared the workshops a "milestone in looking over and even reconstituting our state's historical memory related to our Alevi citizens."[36] Laiklik was the main issue of debate in these workshops, and the demands of various Alevi organizations, historically and prior to the government's "democratic opening," have almost all been related to institutions of laiklik. In the first workshop Alevi organizations agreed on five demands:[37] (1) legal status for *cemevis*; (2) an end to the politics of building mosques and appointing Sunni imams in Alevi villages; (3) the turning of Madımak Hotel into a museum (of shame);[38] (4) no *required* religion courses in public schools, and the inclusion in any such courses of Alevilik content (Constitution article 24); and (5) the return of the Hacı-Bektaş Dergahı and other Alevi places that were taken away from them with the coming of the republican regime in 1925. Although there was agreement among Alevi organizations that the DRA violated the principle of equal citizenship because it put the taxes of all citizens into sustaining Sunni Islam, there was no agreed-on solution. Some organizations demanded the abolishment of the DRA, while others called for its egalitarian reform by putting Alevi Dedes on state salaries as well and opening of Dedelik schools under faculties of theology.[39]

During the workshop period, a government proposal to reorganize the DRA was also being prepared in parliament. Some AKP parliamentarians in 2003, right after the party came to power for the first time, had defended autonomy for the DRA vis-à-vis the state.[40] However, following the workshops, more policy and institutional changes materialized against the demands of Alevi associations. The constitutional referendum in September 2010, right after the workshops, kept article 24 in place. The new law for the DRA, passed in July 2010, worked against Alevi demands. The workshops' moderator was promoted to the head of strategic planning section of the DRA. Two new optional courses on religion—one on reading the Koran and the other on the life of the Prophet—were added to the public school curriculum in March 2012 (see timeline in figure 6.2). The government turned the Madımak Hotel into a science and culture center under protests from local Alevi associations, who reminded the government that they preferred a "Museum of Shame." In February 2013 Prime Minister Erdoğan reiterated the Kemalist statist position on Alevilik. "It is not a *religion*," commented Erdoğan

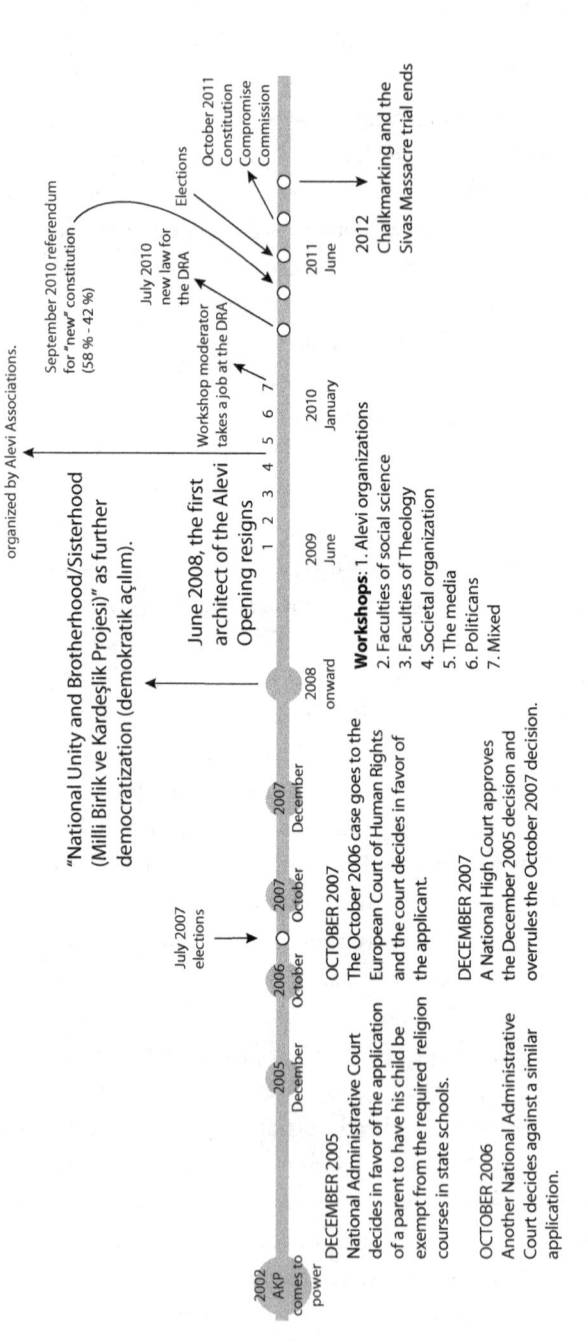

Figure 6.2 Sequence of Events.

in a public statement, "there is only one place of worship in Islam, the mosque. *Cemevi*s are places of *culture.*"[41]

The Immediate Context: Toward the Workshops

In December 2005 an Istanbul Administrative Court decided in favor of a parent having his child exempted from the required religion courses on grounds of being of Alevi faith; nearly a year later another Istanbul Administrative Court decided against a similar request. The latter parent petitioned the European Court of Human Rights[42] and the court decided in the parent's favor. The Turkish State Council approved the decision of the former administrative court and overruled the decision of the latter administrative court in December 2007.[43] According to article 28, paragraph 1, of the Procedures of Administrative Justice Act, these court decisions are binding on the administration and the "administration must implement the acts and take the actions required" within thirty days.[44] The AKP administration never acted on these court decisions. Those parents who also want to benefit from this court decision were asked to present a petition in their own name. Instead of implementing these decisions, the government launched a rewrite of religion and ethics textbooks. A participant in the workshops criticized the government for circumventing the court decisions by advancing with a dialogue project. However, the sequence of events from Çamuroğlu's appointment as consultant to his resignation provides a wider angle on the whole episode. During the interview, Çamuroğlu recalled discussing a couple of times with the minister responsible for the DRA, Said Yazıcıoğlu, that the prime minister did not clarify the "margins" for the Alevi Opening. I asked him how Professor Necdet Subaşı got involved. "It was Yazıcıoğlu's idea," he responded. Yazıcıoğlu argued for taking someone on board for engaging full time on developing the opening project. "I accepted because I knew Subaşı from his publications in the *İslamiyet Journal*, which I found liberal," and he underscored right away how disappointing the final report Subaşı wrote for the Alevi Workshops was. "State seats have this characteristic," he remarked, "they can eat you up like an octopus." Minister Faruk Çelik replaced Yazıcıoğlu as the Minister responsible for the Alevi Opening.[45] The first thing that Çamuroğlu did was to remind Çelik that the "margins" of the project were still unclear and that under such lack of clarity "we will just be passing the ball around. He told me that he never took any position in his political life to pass the ball around." When Çamuroğlu saw the seven-tiered workshop plan, he right away contested that the Alevis would have interlocutors other than the government. In June 2008 he finally resigned from his position as consultant, stating to the media that AKP was not dedicated to ending discrimination against Alevis.[46] AKP carried on with the "opening." Given the final report and the outcomes of the opening, I asked Çamuroğlu if he thought that all was for circumventing the court decisions; he responded that it was election politics, using a well-known Turkish idiom to describe the whole episode: "Dostlar alışverişte görsün."[47] "Imagine," he concluded," "some of the participants came from villages and they had never seen a five-star hotel before. They were hosted, hugged, told 'we are brothers,' and then sent back."

The first of the seven workshops was launched with Alevi organizations on June 3–4, 2009. The other workshops followed with faculties of social science (July 8), faculties of theology (August 19), civil society organizations (September 30), media (November 11), and current and former parliamentarians (December 17). A final three-day workshop was held with certain participants invited from the previous six workshops (January 28–30, 2010).

The "Opening" That Never Comes: The Idea of a Workshop and the Procedural Iron Cage

Başa döndü. (It is back to where we started.)
—PARTICIPANT, WORKSHOP 7

Başa dönen bir şey yok. (Nothing is back to where we started.)
—ANOTHER PARTICIPANT, WORKSHOP 7

Döndü bence. (I think it is back.)
—ANOTHER PARTICIPANT, WORKSHOP 7

The term "workshop" (*çalıştay*) fell into Turkish public discourse as a new practice. It was primarily used in academic circles and known as an academic activity, not as a political activity to mediate the relation between the government and societal organizations. Its emergence resembled the emergence of the term "civil society" (*sivil toplum*) for designating a flourishing phenomenon in the late 1980s during the transition to democracy. Societal organizations, battered as they were by the military takeover in 1980, did exist; yet neither were they designated by the term civil society nor were they flourishing. Yael Navaro-Yashin discusses critically and with examples from certain Islamic movements in the early 1990s how the concept of "flourishing civil society," rather than designating an existing phenomenon, actually preceded and constituted certain political party mobilizations of society.[48] The term workshop also landed in the media as a similar political practice, unleashing a lot of curiosity.

Except for the AKP minister Faruk Çelik's media statement at the end of each workshop, and workshop 5's media participants, the workshops were closed to the media. There were explicit and repeated statements by the minister and the moderator against participants engaging the media. The strongest and clearest one came at the end of workshop 4 from the moderator Necdet Subaşı, ten days before a demonstration for further democratization organized by some Alevi associations that gathered more than 200,000 demonstrators: "We do not discuss in the media or in front of the public . . . because we cannot control [zapt] the subject. . . . An uncontrolled subject can have other tragic outcomes, it can be used for populist or propaganda ends."[49] Even in workshop 5 with media representatives, the participants neither addressed the question of freedom of the press vis-à-vis the government that had already began stifling the media,[50] nor did they problematize the fact that the workshops were taking place closed to the media.

During the workshops there was often not enough time for in-depth discussion of each issue. Toward the end of the second day of the first workshop, discussions were squeezed to accommodate the prescheduled time of the state minister's media statement. There were thirty-six participants in the first workshop, almost all presidents of various Alevi associations. Just before the start of the workshop on June 3, 2009, the word that the government had invited the primary suspect in the Maraş Massacre of Alevis in 1978 to the workshops reverberated in newspapers.[51] The government silence on this rumor left an air of uncertainty around the statement's truth. In workshop 7, the moderator admitted to this invitation and offered the following explanation:

> A criticism concerning . . . [name of person] came, it is time, we have to give an explanation on this. . . . In fact, we were not at the same point of awareness with you on the trauma and deep worries among Alevis. . . . We realized it afterward, this mistake, fault . . . however you

evaluate it, I would like to express this with open-heartedness. But he was invited because he told us that . . . these events [Maraş Massacre] are the manipulation and provocation of a certain community against Alevis . . . , he saw this game, this set-up, [he said] we were used and I would like to declare it.[52]

The president of the Alevi Bektaşi Federation pointed out the absence of European Alevi organizations in the workshop in spite of the fact that "they have succeeded in having Alevi courses taught in Germany."[53] The president of Hacı Bektaş Veli Culture and Promotion Association asked for the inclusion of Alevi organizations in the writing process of the final report,[54] which never materialized. The procedures for the workshops were not shared with the Alevi organizations beforehand, and the organizations were not consulted when participants were invited.

The workshop's minister and moderator repeatedly framed the workshops as an expression of the goodwill of the government and asked the participants to behave properly. The state minister's remarks vacillated between emphasizing difference and unity; at times he framed the workshops as "different beliefs . . . different cultures, different practices . . . have the right to life without the obligation to explain themselves to each other."[55] At other times he framed them in statist-nationalist terms. He opened the first workshop with the following statement: "Instead of wasting our energies with internal struggles, let's use it to take a place in the most advanced and strong league of states. . . . I wish that this workshop will be good for our nation and add to our unity and togetherness."[56]

In his remarks at the end of the first workshop, the moderator summarized its ultimate end as "beneficial to the family. Contributing to the unity and completeness of the state." He concluded that the workshop contributed to diminishing prejudices, the creation of friendships and sincerity, and the diminishing of the distance between the rulers and the ruled of the country (190). He ended with messages of brother/sisterhood and solidarity: "If the will is good, the outcome will also be good. . . . I find it very beneficial that it is known one more time that we sat around the table all together with sincerity and deeply willingly" (268).

The moderator's introduction to the workshop preached to the Alevis to use this opportunity for dialogue correctly. He wished that they would leave aside their internal disagreements and act together (23), and that "if we continue the discussion with respect, public opinion will be positively influenced by the attitude and behavior Alevis portray" (24). The preaching of "correct behavior" peaked on November 8, 2009, when, in between workshops 4 and 5, several Alevi associations participating in the workshops organized a demonstration that gathered more than 200,000 people. The demonstration had been planned before the workshops were launched, but they became an opportunity for some Alevi associations to also express their position on the workshops. The workshops were criticized for seeking solutions behind closed doors and trying to divide Alevis by pushing a discussion on the definition of "Alevilik."[57] Workshop 5 with media on November 11, 2009, started with the AKP minister using a significant part of his opening remarks to address the demonstration. He qualified the demonstration as "radical political" and the government position as "above politics," and he commented that "to call our citizens to the square" is a way of doing politics "that cannot be saved [*iflah olmaz*] and does not benefit anybody for societal peace and conscientious tranquility."[58]

One major mechanism of the workshop model was that the conversations of the first workshop fed into the following workshops as problems to be solved but were mediated by the minister and moderator. For instance, the second workshop (with university faculty members in social science) started with the moderator's remarks, presenting the first workshop as problem-focused and an "emotional" meeting where "Alevis expressed their problems." Some participants, in response to the moderator's remarks, expressed that the results of the previous meeting had not been distributed in writing.[59] And often the procedures of the workshop looked improvised. For instance, toward the end of the second day of workshop 1, one participant asked how it would proceed and whether participants would be contacted again. The moderator responded: "Mainly, we will share the data we gathered here with the participants of the following meetings and ask them proposals for solutions. . . . And naturally I do not have an obligation to present you a report . . . , but me, humanely [*insani olarak*], in every opportunity I find, I will use the phones of the ministry to keep in dialogue with you. Likewise, you can call me whenever you want."[60]

The most visible topic of debate overall, but particularly in workshops 1 and 2, was whether the question at hand was an "Alevi-specific question" or a more general question. The AKP minister had his own take on this debate, which basically turned Alevis from a political subject to the subject of politics in his concluding remarks on workshop 2: "I would like to express with all sincerity that the Alevi-Bektaşi problem is a *societal problem*. . . .

Therefore the solution will be possible after a process in which, Alevi or non-Alevi, everybody will participate. In short, it is the problem of all of us. To keep hand in hand on the way for a solution is a moral obligation for all of us."[61]

By the end of the second workshop, the "Alevi-Bektaşi question" had become a question for the "whole society," and therefore "the whole society" had to decide. In other words, Alevilik could not be left to Alevis. The "opening" had to continue until it recorded the views of "the whole society." But how could one ask "the whole society"? It first had to be called into existence in its bare form—that is, without the media—and, in the words of the minister, with sincerity.

By the end of workshop 5, the radical potential for change in institutions and practices embedded in the promises of further democratization that marked the beginning of the workshop series had become statements on change in "perspective," how we see things.[62] Earlier promises now looked like fancy packaging of old practices in new meanings. The AKP minister, at the end of workshop 5 even defended the DRA and, with the help of lawyers, argued that it is possible to keep the required courses on religion and ethics and, additionally, introduce the optional course on religion suggested in the workshops. This was also the precise conclusion of the Abant platform on religion and ethics courses in state schools on March 13, 2012.[63] The minister remarked on article 24 of the constitution: "If we read article 24 carefully, I think there is a solution there . . . if we split religious education and instruction." On the DRA he commented: "What you call the DRA are state employees. He is an employee, what can he do? He does as told . . . Ha! According to changing world conditions, these persons have to improve themselves and attain a perspective to hug all our people. . . . Let's not forget this institution is a constitutional institution. Its discussion belongs to another terrain."[64]

In the state minister's opening remarks at workshop 6, the preceding workshops slid back to become the "preliminary stages of the Alevi opening" rather than part of the opening. The minister reemphasized that "in order to surpass many problems, we need a language above politics." He also commented on the final workshop:

> We have to do the seventh workshop. It will last one week, discussing within the frame of subjects that has emerged in this workshop. Of course scientific grounds are very important. We will map out a path

with persons who have grown up with Alevi and Sunni values and have accumulated knowledge, on subjects expressed mostly superficially in workshops, but also in demonstrations, meetings, visits on what do these all historically mean and what are some solutions.... I would like you to know that politics here will not be the one which maps out the path. The committee concerned [seventh workshop group] will map out a path on this subject and we will share it with the public.[65]

At the beginning of workshop 7, the minister summarized the first workshop: "If the term is right, we got together with those who know the inside of the home." The other five workshops followed because "we were not of the opinion that the problems voiced by Alevis could be solved only by dialogue with Alevis."[66] He expressed the distinctness of the seventh workshop as an even "deeper" and more solution-oriented discussion (19). "We seek a solution that will hug all of our seventy-two million citizens.... The subject is sensitive and our will is sincere" (20). In his introduction to the final workshop the minister made no remarks on the process to form it. The workshop opened with a participant remarking, before the moderator's introduction, that there were absolutely no women participants in the room (22). Without responding to this particular question, the moderator made his longest framing talk since the first workshop, including the question of how the selection for the seventh workshop was done: "On the subject of who this subject should be debated with, as our minister also underlined, we tried to do a very careful analysis. We compiled a participants' list taking into account interests, knowledge, and missions and of course, thinking it very, very important, public reputation" (22–27).

The question of defining Alevilik, which constituted the majority of the discussion in the first workshop, reemerged in the final workshop. The AKP minister reacted strongly against participants who wanted to put the question of definition aside:

This workshop is very important, very important, very, very important ... please put yourself in our shoes and then make your evaluations ... in fact we are not going to make a decision here ... [name of a person] said that ... [name of another person] expressed that.... This is enough to pass the current item on the agenda.... But if you come up and say, "Let's not talk about this. Then, as the person in charge here, I will also pose the question: "Why shouldn't we talk? What is it that you do not want to talk? What is being hidden? . . . We got to know all parts [on the Alevi question] very well, let me tell you. Therefore an approach of the sort that only those things we like could be spoken is not correct. My knowledge, my habits. . . . A self-centered approach is not correct. If that is the case, *then I represent the state.* (43, 44; italics mine)

Defining and Seeing "Alevis"? The "Goods" State versus the "Rights" Society

Both in national courts and in the European Court of Human Rights, required religion courses have been qualified as a violation of human rights; therefore, the government's move to put this matter for discussion, to say religion courses should also include Alevilik, is an expression of its will to make Alevis a partner to the government disobedience to judicial decisions. And by this means to legitimize the continuity of Sunni religion courses via Alevis. . . . In other words, we are asked to share this space.
—KELIME ATA, PIR SULTAN ABDAL CULTURE ASSOCIATION, WORKSHOP 1

The state minister in his opening remarks to workshop 1 and repeatedly afterward underlined that "as the government we would like to have a reliable, exact and conspicuous Alevi photograph."[67] He called for making human rights sovereign in all spheres of life for societal peace and tranquility, and he suggested seeing "richness in difference and unity in plurality [*çokluk*]" as venues to this goal. He also made references to Turkey's "common identity [*ortak kimliğimiz*]" and "common values [*ortak değerlerimiz*]" (18).

The moderator introduced the first workshop as the framing of problems and opened a discussion on "Alevi experience" and "the definition of Alevilik" and asked, "What are the flaws [*kusur*] of the state, and what are the flaws of the Alevis?" (30). He then made an explicit distinction between laiklik in general and Turkish laiklik and asked, "How do Alevis evaluate the eighty-five years of Turkish laiklik?" (31).

Many participants responded that the question of defining Alevilik should be left to Alevis (5). The president of the Hacı Bektaş Veli Culture and Promotion Association as well as the Pir Sultan Abdal Association underlined that it is not enough just to stop taking a step in the direction of defining Alevilik, that the DRA already had a definition of Alevilik and had to let it go (225). A member of the Pir Sultan Abdal Culture Association summed up that the discussions on "definition" are pulling the matter to a theological terrain and away from the political terrain and the terrain of rights (95, see also 225).

The mayor of Hacıbektaş municipality brought yet another angle to the question of "defining" Alevilik; namely, that some Alevi associations not only refuse to push for a sole definition of Alevilik, they even refuse to be referred to as a "minority." He reminded the group that the European Union progress report on Turkey in 2004 had referred to Alevis as a minority,[68] and this reference was contested at the time by a collective of Alevi associations through media statements and petitions that "Alevis are not a "minority" but a "fundamental element" (*asli unsur*) vis-à-vis the founding of the republic.[69] Post-2004 European Union progress reports still discuss the inegalitarian state practices against Alevis in Turkey but have dropped the term "minority." The president of another association, the Hubyar Sultan Alevi Culture Association, pointed out that Turkish General Chief of Staff reports also define Alevis as a minority (81).

The discussion of definition during the workshop was one of the few times that the moderator intervened strongly and stated that "the state cannot define itself by any religion," a completely ahistorical and acontextual remark given the Turkish context, "but Alevis have to express what they are [religion, belief, culture, etc.]" (72) so that the discussion could proceed as "to the kind of restructuring necessary for opening the way for various lifestyles" (74).

There were two faculty members of theology in the first workshop, and they were particularly keen on keeping the question of defining Alevilik on the agenda even though they did not push a direct link between group definitions and rights. One of them argued that the government could address the demands of Alevilik from the perspective of human rights without the need for a definition of Alevilik but that "this meeting has shown that Alevilik needs a definition" (141). This position was widely criticized. One participant underlined that "Alevilik has many histories, and so does Sunnilik. And so do all beliefs. . . . This is not a matter of objection to the scientific studies on the matter, but rather the purpose of the meeting today is the discussion of some problems and issues between the state and Alevis" (144). The disagreement between the faculty members of theology and presidents of Alevi associations surfaced several times (167, 211, 230). The faculty members defended having written sources of Alevilik documented as opposed to an oral tradition as better. The moderator came to the defense of the faculty members and stated that they are "from within the Alevi society . . . they work in the faculty of theology known as Alevi" (211).

There was strong agreement on the position among participants of workshop 1 that there was no need to define Alevilik, because Alevis have concrete demands and these demands are matters of individual rights and equal citizenship and are even protected under certain articles of the current Turkish constitution (78–81, 158, 225). The president of the Pir Sultan Abdal Culture Association referred to the European Court of Human Rights decision against required religion culture and ethics courses in 2007,[70] the Turkish High Court decision in 2007,[71] and the violation of article 10 of the Turkish constitution (equality before the law and antidiscrimination) in denying legal status[72] to *cemevi*s as a place of worship (82–86).[73] The problems can be solved, he continued, just by applying the court decisions and the constitution, so there is no need for a workshop (see also 226). The references to the violations of law by participants in the workshop often asked the government *not* to do something rather than do something such as ending state mosque-building projects in Alevi villages (260).[74]

On the second day of workshop 1, the moderator made his second intervention on the question of definition, the strongest among all his interventions. He remarked, "It is not acceptable that somebody defines you. But what is more appropriate than Alevis to define themselves."[75] And he continued didactically,

> We should let people talk about us. So that we can answer and our intellectual veins get stronger. Let's discuss and debate, so that issues come up front. . . . If we do not partake in intellectual or emotional grounds, then we will be imprisoned in the language of organization [*örgüt*[76]]. This is a belligerent language . . . as an academician who engages in this issue, I say with ease that if Alevis are disturbed inexorably by the evaluations on themselves, they won't go anywhere.[77]

The question of definition directly translated into a debate on more research or more human rights in the second workshop, with faculties of social science. After various comments to summarize the state of research on Alevilik,[78] the discussion turned to the relation between academic research and politics. Few took the strong position that for solving the problems of Alevi citizens, Alevilik, had to be turned into "an object of research" at all levels, sociological, theological, anthropological, and historical (49). And, one scholar, a member of the DRA's High Council of Religious Affairs (DİYK), called for more theological discussions on the interpretation of Alevi sources

(31–32) and more social-psychological research (37–41). Yet another pointed out that research can at most offer alternative models for institutions, but the solution is in politics (86–87). More speakers formulated the question at hand at the level of rights and equal citizenship, which they saw as distinct and decoupled from the question of the state of current or future research on Alevilik.

After repeated statements on the necessity of differentiating between academic and political problems, the moderator intervened in the discussions and remarked, "Unless objective and true data comes from academia, what are we going to discuss?" (66). A final articulation by one speaker pointed out that the matter at hand was one of human rights, the parties to the dialogue were the Turkish state and Alevi associations, not academics, and Alevi organizations had common demands from the first workshop publicized in the media, which did not look that difficult to solve (66; see also 124, 158).

Among all seven workshops, the push for defining Alevilik could only relatively dominate among the participants of workshop 3, with faculties of theology. The third workshop focused on four issue areas: the state of Alevi studies in faculties of theology; religious pluralism; different interpretations of Islam; religious practices, institutions, and Alevis; and discussions on possible solutions.[79] In this meeting there was strong consensus on not abolishing the DRA, except from maybe one participant, and this position on the DRA went hand in hand with tendencies of antipluralism. Very few made an attempt to decouple the question of fundamental rights and freedoms and questions of theology (48, 116), and even fewer participants argued that Alevis are heterogeneous and therefore cannot be defined (41). Some argued that Alevis have to put forth their theology (45), work together with theologians to make the shift from oral to written tradition,[80] institutionalize (23) to solve their "existential" problem, and make their tradition adapt to modernity (110, 119–22), in order to prevent them from becoming vulnerable to Christian missionaries (119–23). Then the discussion picked up on how to advance research on Alevis in a historical context of how even choosing Alevilik as a research topic had been considered factional (*bölücülük*) (27, 28, 32, 51, 53, 74), and therefore the only faculty members who had relative ease researching Alevis were historians of sects. Still, from the margins of this workshop, one of the most critical statements from of any of the workshops emerged, underlining one of the relations between research and politics. One theology faculty member conveyed the remarks he received from one of his research subjects during his field research in an Alevi village: "Professor, do you make predictions on which villages and towns have Alevis, what is the approximate population. ['Yes']. Do you say how they live? ['Yes']. Do you also give the names of the places? ['Yes']. If what happened before the 1980s repeats, and mobs taking weapons in their hands come to our villages, are you going to save us?" (51).

On the "Alevi Question": The Nonneutral State against Universalist Citizens

A significant number of participants in all workshops reformulated the question from an "Alevi question" to a question of the "nonneutral" Turkish state. In workshop 1, the president of Pir Sultan Abdal 2nd July Culture and Education Foundation pointed out that "the DRA has expressed in writing that *cemevi*s are not places of worship." Such statements and "1980 coup imperialism" that dictated the required religion courses, he pointed out, are against article 10 of the Turkish constitution (equality before the law, antidiscrimination). He argued that there is a clear violation of rule of law and that "a missionary institution" such as the DRA has no place in a real laic state.[81] The state is Sunni and not neutral, and therefore, given this institutional structure, he demanded to know what the government expected from the workshops.[82] The president of the Ehl-i Beyt Foundation gave a brief overview in workshop 1 of the Turkish historical context of violence and discrimination against Alevis, which, he argued, shows that "problems of Alevis" are the problems of all Turkish citizens. The president of the Ankara Hacı Bektaş Culture and Education Association noted that in the Sivas Massacre of 1993 in the Madımak Hotel, "seven Alevis, seven Sunnis, and one Christian burned to death," and he asked why Madımak is an "Alevi problem." Stories of assimilation, discrimination, and racism accumulated throughout the workshops.[83] There was also one story of forced migration in a village.[84]

For the majority of the participants in the second workshop (with faculties of social science) as well, the question was not an Alevi-specific problem[85] but the more general problem of the lack of freedom of religion and consciousness, the lack of universal standards in the institutional relation between state and religion in Turkey, lack of democracy[86] (such as equal citizenship, fundamental rights and freedoms), discrimination, assimilation,[87] the many imprisoned and tortured in Turkey's history, and the lack of freedom of speech from which academic life also suffered.[88] The formulations all were pointing in the same direction; that is, the Alevi question is a particular manifestation of more general questions.[89]

In workshop 4, with civil society organizations, again one main debate was on the formulation of the problem as a specific "Alevi question" or a general "question of equal citizenship and individual rights."[90] There were advances in nuance on the rights and freedoms framework. For instance, one participant made a distinction between the analytical frameworks of freedom of religion and discrimination and underlined the need for more research on the latter. She pointed out a previous insufficient step toward a neutral state: the question of the space for religion in national identity cards. Allowing people to leave the required religion space blank on their national identity cards still creates a stigma for Alevis or atheists who leave it blank. That blank space would become the marker of difference. She also pointed out many citizens in the Turkish context would feel societal pressure to go to the state office and petition for the removal of religion from their identity cards or may feel a similar societal pressure when opting out of courses on religion and ethics.

In response to government "concerns" on the future of Alevi life, one participant in workshop 1 from the Pir Sultan Abdal Culture Association responded that Alevilik is already living. The president of the Hacı Bektaş Veli Culture and Promotion Association criticized the "richness in diversity" talk of government officials, which he argued contributes to the turning of Alevis into an "other," treating them as an attachment or ornament that can always be relinquished. Another participant from the Ankara Hacı Bektaş Culture and Education Association pointed out how reactionary government officials disqualify Alevi organizations' demands as representative of the population with remarks like, "I also have dear Alevi friends, I have spent time and worked with them."[91]

Science and the Religious Brotherhood/Sisterhood against History

With the media present for his closing remarks at the end of the first day of workshop 1, the AKP state minister passed over the history of massacres of Alevis with quick remarks that underlined science:

Science has to be the guide of social events, politics and the politician ... if scientifically-based solutions are sought ... compromise will be easier. But when science is shelved and our personal world, personal expectations, or political ambitions come upfront, neither social nor economic nor other problems, I think, can be solved easily. Turkey has neglected the guidance of science at certain periods, but there is no excuse for neglect anymore.[92]

Similar statements on science and data by the minister and the moderator were scattered through the workshops. In the discussions, arguments from "science" countered arguments from Alevis' own life experiences. To the various contemporary and historical stories of discrimination in workshop 2,[93] the moderator offered a myopic psychological response. He asked whether it is possible that the people narrating their stories of discrimination are actually just trying to find a public reason for their lack of success.[94] The state minister also interfered in the stories of institutional discrimination especially for state jobs and gave an account of the state's neutrality and how it is maintained through the use of new computer-run hiring algorithms. A scholar's mention of the membership records of syndicates showing signs of lack of neutrality went unanswered.

One tendency that the moderator joined in on was to question the representativeness of Alevi organizations with ethnographical authority either by making a distinction between the grassroots and organizations or by portraying the November 8 demonstration as not solely put together by Alevi organizations. The moderator referred to the common demand of Alevi organizations for legal status for *cemevi*s as "mainly the product of their emotional world." His remarks depicted a problematic instance of "ethnographical authority": "I speak as somebody who is very linked with the field, there isn't that much excitement among the Alevis. . . . There is a speech emphasizing *cemevi*, but when you scratch, it comes out as the demanding language of organizations. I think it is up for debate."[95]

History and memory were more directly addressed in workshop 4. Arguments for "forgetting the bad things in the past"[96] and remembering the good things (one speaker explicitly contrasted remembering the war of independence and remembering the Sivas Massacre) went along with turning to the DRA for a solution to the "Alevi problem," emphasizing Muslimness as common ground, an organic language of referring to the workshops as a product of a "we" in emotional brother and sisterhood (58). The representative of the progovernment syndicate, for instance, took such a position. He associated keeping the memory of past massacres alive with a will to revenge (63) and remarked, "This workshop is not a meeting for peace, because we never had quarreled [küstük]" (59).

There was a brief discussion on whether the state pushed for assimilationist policies. An ex-president of religious affairs (1978–1986) during the 1980 military regime insisted that there had been no assimilation during the coup regime (192). A participant who was an eyewitness to the most well-known İmam Hatip school state project from the coup period remarked:

> We did not know what İmam Hatip was at the time. Does it only educate imams? Does the country have such an imam deficit? . . . When we asked our fellow students, they answered: "No, we did not demand it, there are no schools in the villages. We have no chance to get an education, and state tells us, we will take you to a boarding school, and we come to İmam Hatip." When I met this good-willed kid four years later, he started calling me and my friends socialists, you are this, you are that, all just falling short of infidel [kâfir]. (148)

The June 30, 2010, Law of the Directorate of Religious Affairs

The proposal for the Law for the Organization of the DRA, debated in June 2010 and passed on June 30, had absolutely no traces of the Alevi associations' demands. The new DRA law increased the inequalities between urban and rural imams and between religious affairs and administrative affairs personnel, hence giving the institution a more hierarchical structure. A close look at the parliamentary debates on the law shows how the AKP, in the exact military tradition of 1980, mobilized Sunni Islam for assimilation.

During the debates, both the CHP spokesperson and the Peace and Democracy Party (BDP)[97] spokesperson reminded that the proposal for the new law on the organization of the DRA had no traces of the "Alevi opening" and that the law exacerbated income inequality between urban (a 45 percent salary increase) and rural imams (a 10 percent increase) and between personnel for religious affairs and administrative affairs within the DRA.[98] A BDP spokesperson was the only one to mention that in Europe and the United States there is no institution like the DRA, and he reminded that

Turkish-speaking imams lead prayers and give sermons to Kurdish-speaking citizens in the southeast of Turkey:

> [From laiklik] we understand that the state in no way privileges certain religious groups. . . . Unfortunately this is not the case in Turkey. . . . Now, on the one hand, you have entered the free [private] space of people; and intervene in how they will practice their religion and worship, decide on who will be their imam, and, on the other hand, appoint an imam who does not know their language and cannot talk to them.[99]

The AKP spokesperson started his speech by referring to the constitutional place of the DRA (article 136) and presented the DRA as "the reference point in the world and in Turkey for the correct understanding and the correct practice of the religion of Islam," and to mobilize "the accumulated experience and knowledge of Turkey in the field of religion" in order to set an example of humanity to the whole world.[100] He continued with historical accounts from 1920 on the republican sources of the DRA; however, he envisioned a much more extended list of ends for the DRA than had ever been claimed under any version of Kemalist laicism, or for that matter under any government in the history of Turkey. His list covered social, economic, education, and gender questions:

> To enlighten the society on religion . . . without disregarding modern life . . . to provide religious services on the principle of citizenship, without discriminating on schools of jurisprudence, sect, understanding, and application . . . to accept women . . . as the fundamental part of religious services and raise societal consciousness on women rights, honor killings, discrimination against girls, education of girls, and forced marriages, and to put as an indispensable part of religious services to side with our handicapped, homeless, elderly, poor, imprisoned, and in-need-of-support citizens, to help our citizens abroad to maintain their essential identities without being assimilated and at the same time be in harmony with the society.

The AKP spokesperson presented Islam and the tasks of the DRA as beyond the mosque: "The religion of Islam cannot be confined and practiced within the four walls of the mosque, because the religion of Islam puts rules on the whole life of the believer.... Therefore the DRA has to diagnose all kinds of problems of our people and find solutions.... Lack of authority in religious life will produce religious anarchy."[101] And on the mosque beyond Islam: "Mosques are not only places of prayer. In the past, mosques were at the same time places where education in all branches of science, including positive sciences were made, this should also be the case today."

The DRA was an institution of mass education: "In the mosque the *cemaat* [religious community] listens to *khutbah*s [Friday sermons]. With these activities the DRA educates millions of people in religious, national, social, cultural, economic, and similar issues."

The AKP spokesperson further presented the new law for the restructuring and expansion of the DRA as a bulwark against "terrorism" and for reinforcing a monopoly in Islam. He remarked on "terrorism":

> The religion of Islam is the most perfect religion because it is the last religion.... If the divisive terror organization spilling blood for thirty years has not reached its goal, in that our exalted religion's unmatched boundless values strengthening unity, togetherness and brotherhood have played a big role.... Can somebody who enlightens his reason and conscience with the light of Islam pick up a gun and climb mountains?[102]

And on diversity within Islam: "The DRA should consist of enlightened religious leaders who protect the people from theoretical discussions within Islam that are unnecessary and could damage the relation of the people with Islam."[103]

The BDP spokesperson pointed out that the state funds Sunni Islam through the DRA, using everyone's taxes regardless of their religion. For freedom and equality, "the goal should be a DRA not only open to Muslims believing in different religious interpretations but also aim at providing religious rights and freedoms to Alevis, Syrian Orthodox, Jews, Christians, and all religious groups. Therefore, the establishment of a religious organization independent from the state and with its own economic sources would be best."[104]

One proposal for change submitted by six BDP members was on the formation of the High Council of Religious Affairs within the DRA. It asked that some members be "chosen among those who can speak Kurdish at a good level." A BDP member commented on the prohibition of a Kurdish translation of the Koran as a threat to national unity and integrity although the Koran has been translated into many languages and reminded that both translating the Koran into Kurdish and having Kurdish-speaking clerics at all levels of the DRA would contribute to peace and tolerance. Another BDP proposal was "in cities and town where there is a Kurdish majority to appoint the müftü who knows how to speak Kurdish at a good level."[105]

All these proposals concerning Alevis, non-Muslims, and Kurdish-speaking imams were rejected, and the debates ended with a CHP member remarking on the duties of the DRA that "the essence of the religion of Islam is to render the society and the individual moral . . . by fear of God, fear of afterlife, love of God. Moral individual means moral society."[106] An AKP member affirmed the distinction "between the belief and practice aspects of religion" and "the morality aspect of religion" and added that "much falls on the DRA to keep alive our future, our children, our culture, our own values, our own moral life." He argued for the expansion of the policy area of the DRA into social policy, such as "traffic should be the issue of the DRA; paint-thinner-sniffer children, street children . . . street animals . . . prisons, child reform houses, retirement houses."[107]

The new law maintained the exact Kemalist institutional position of the DRA vis-à-vis the state, introduced greater hierarchy to the institution by differentiating in pay among the urban and rural imams, and left the Sunni bias of the institution intact by once again excluding all demands from Alevi organizations and members of parliament from Kurdish regions. The new law even fell short of propositions by the conservative right political theoretician Ali Fuat Başgil (discussed in chapter 5). The new law did not take any steps toward the DRA's autonomy but rather mobilized the state further to strengthen Sunni infrastructure throughout the country, a goal that Başgil had proposed to reach through an autonomous DRA. Yet, as readers will recall, he had prioritized a commitment to the strength of religion in public space over commitment to institutional principles and when necessary had turned to the state for building religion infrastructure.

With the DRA Law of June 30, 2010, the AKP turned the DRA, which just by its institutional positioning within the state can work both as either a brake or a gas pedal on religion, into a gas pedal. Not only that, with the AKP religion has been expanding in its policy areas, putting in danger the institutional principle of differentiation of spheres. The DRA currently has five protocols signed with other state institutions concerning social policy, and four of these were signed under the AKP government: with the Ministry of

Justice on religion courses in prisons (March 30, 2001), with Social Services and Childcare (February 26, 2007) for providing religion personnel to these institutions and to have imams communicate the importance of these institutions to the public, with the Family and Social Research institution (March 13, 2008), and with the Health Ministry (December 14, 2009) on "mother and child health and reproduction health." Another protocol was signed on April 12, 2010, between the state ministry responsible for the DRA and the state ministry responsible for women and family.

The DRA Law of 2010 pretty much went unnoticed because of media attention on the approaching constitutional referendum of September 12, 2010, which was rushed with a generously financed campaign employing all kinds of visual and verbal populist tools touting the AKP's dismantling of 1982 military constitution. The constitutional change package included the restructuring of the judiciary and, in stark contradiction to the presentation of the referendum as dismantling the military constitution, excluded many other possibilities, such as article 24 on required religion and ethics courses in public schools and the article on the DRA, two articles absolutely of military heritage. The amount of money spent on the campaign by political parties was presented as a written question in the parliament two months after the fact, and it was revealed that the AKP had spent more than twice the amount spent by the major opposition party, the CHP.

One aspect of the referendum rush was AKP's huge "emotional" mobilization. Some AKP parliamentarians literally shed tears in parliament for the victims of the September 12, 1980, coup violence, while two years later they were short on "emotions" for the Uludere Incident. Thirty-five civilians, at least half under age twenty, trading across the Iraqi border out of need, were killed by Turkish warplane bombing in Şırnak, Uludere, on December 28, 2011. But not only that, in August 2010, a month before the referendum, in the city of Izmir, a local AKP group opposed the building of a statue of the famous 1970s socialist head of the municipality of Fatsa, who was tortured by the 1980 military government.

The referendum was deemed as a success in the international and national media and was polished with phrases such as "Turkey is passing from the law of the rulers to the rule of law."[108] Actually, evaluated in context of the marks the 1980 military coup left on the bodies and minds of Turkish society, a voter turnout of 77.4 percent (83 percent in 2011, 85.1 percent in 2007) and "No" vote of 42 percent are quite significant for a referendum mobilized against a military coup constitution.

The Elections of 2011 and a New Constitution in a Context of Arbitrary Detentions, Violence, and Violations of Freedom of Speech

The period before and after the June 12, 2011, elections in Turkey proved that elections and violations of freedom of speech, arbitrary detentions, and violence are not mutually exclusive. The military for once was not part of the pre-election scene, but the police showed that they are up to the task of replicating military violence in Turkey against all kinds of antigovernment and nonviolent social movements. Some examples: a teacher who had a heart attack after police tear gassing; a child killed by a police officer in Diyarbakır; many activists and nonactivists taken from their homes by police without needing to provide a reason under terror laws; antisyndicalism propaganda by some imams and gendarmes; a women's rights activist whose hips were broken by the police; and many other, similar incidents.

A demonstration against AKP's election campaign in May 2011 in Hopa, Artvin, in northeastern Turkey protesting against a nationwide government push for hydroelectric dams and increasing tea prices ended with a police gas bomb killing a teacher. This was followed by arrests and a court case opened against protestors, who had their first trial after five months and were released because there was no evidence of any sort. In February 2012 the Justice Medicine Institution[109] and the Turkish Medical Association issued contradictory autopsy reports. The former stated that the person had died not from a gas bomb but from a preexisting heart condition, while the latter stated that the person's heart condition was not advanced enough to cause his death and that he had died from the gas bomb. The court asked for a third opinion. Meanwhile, to a written question in parliament on the use of tear gas, the interior minister belatedly wrote the following answer: "According to the Chemical Weapons Agreement our country has signed in 1997, 'tear-making munition has to meet the condition of not having a lasting effect on human health' and gas munition that has met the condition of not having a lasting effect on human health is being used."[110]

This technical, cold response rocked the Turkish public for a week; many opposition party politicians suggested that the minister should maybe try the gas himself. Turkey had already been convicted at least once at the European Court of Human Rights for arbitrary and reckless use of tear gas. During the May 1 celebrations in 2007, tear gas took another life, and in May 2012 a thirty-year-old man died from tear gas.

In the 2007 and 2011 general elections, minority parties entered elections with independent candidates and not as political parties. Running as independents offers a higher probability of having representation in parliament because of the antiminority electoral system facilitated by the 10 percent national threshold. Part of the BDP's success in the 2011 elections was due to including candidates from marginalized socialists and other groups in its independent lists, and in this election thirty-six independents were elected to parliament.

Yet the security the 10 percent threshold (the highest among European Council member countries) offered to the AKP was apparently not enough. The High Council of Elections' (YSK) decision on April 19, 2011, vetoing twelve out of the sixty-one BDP-supported independent candidates on grounds of having a past "criminal" record showed that the AKP still felt threatened. Some independent candidates who were elected in the June 2011 elections were still in prison four years later. Following the YSK decision, Prime Minister Erdoğan repeated in his election speech on April 30, 2011, in the city of Muş (where in the 2007 general elections an independent candidate had been elected) the motto "single nation, single *patrie*, single flag, and single state," which he had used in December 2007 right after the parliamentary decision to send Turkish troops across the Iraqi border. After protests against the YSK decision during which the police shot a child in Diyarbakır, the YSK rescinded its ruling.

After the elections, some people were seriously injured by police raids on the victory celebrations for the independent candidates for parliament. In one case an elderly woman was beaten with wood planks and had to get 120 stitches. Clearly the AKP had entered and exited the elections with the backing of police violence demobilizing through fear. Many BDP elected mayors, politicians, and activists who were expected to work on the approaching election campaign were labeled as the urban wing of the PKK and taken into custody.

These blows to political rights recall the national referendum of 1987 to end the ban on political rights: whether those politicians banned by the military regime could return to political activity during the transition period from military regime to democracy. The referendum passed with a 50.2 percent "yes" vote nationwide but showed no signs of support for democratization in the hotbeds of religious conservatism. However, Kurdish, Alevi, and workers' cities, which were most harmed by the ban, gave the strongest support to political rights.[111] These referendum results can make us start thinking more critically about the currently widespread turn in the academic literature to "moderately" Islamist actors in Turkey as the agents of democratization.

In announcing the electoral success of the AKP in general, another detail is often overlooked. The parliament represented 53.67 percent of the total voters in 2002, 81.72 percent in 2007, and 88.7 percent in 2011. Not only AKP but all the big parties increased their votes. In other words, the 10 percent threshold probably caused a "lost vote" concern, and small party supporters shifted their support to one of the three major parties, fearing that their small party would not make the threshold.

Arbitrary detentions, violence, violations of freedom of speech, and violent speech by statesmen were not limited to a few instances around election time; they started setting the stage at least a year in advance. The most recent process of constitution writing started in this context with the establishment of a Constitution Compromise Commission (AUK) in October 2011. AUK was dissolved in December 2013 after successive drops in attendance by AKP members because the presidential system they supported faced major disagreement. The previous process of constitution writing under the AKP, which had begun with a draft by professors in 2007, had broken off in 2008 when the AKP reduced the question of a new constitution to one of removing the ban on the veil. Discussion over piecemeal constitutional change and changes in particular laws had replaced the general discussions on the constitution and constitution writing. The Constitutional Court case to close down the AKP, which concluded with a warning and a partial cut of its state budget, listed this agenda in its indictment.

The Constitutional Compromise Commission of 2011 comprised twelve members (eleven of them men): three each from the AKP, the Republican People's Party, the National Action Party, and the Peace and Democracy Party. It was headed by the speaker of the Grand National Assembly (from AKP).[112] In the writing of both the 1961 constitution and the 1982 military constitution, and in the failed attempt for a new constitution in 2008, professors had had a role. The effort in 2011 was the first time that professors took no part in the process. The memoirs of the 1980 military coup leader attest that the 1982 constitution was almost single-handedly dictated by the military with the minimal procedural façade.[113] Yet in the writing of the 1961 constitution, arguably it was the professors' presence that ignited the most interesting debates and hence expanded the discussion.

The task of investigating the Uludere Incident was delegated to a parliamentary commission, and the issue fell from the printed press until an American journalist wrote in the *Wall Street Journal* that intelligence was delivered to the Turkish military by U.S. aircraft before the bombing.[114] The AKP was caught off guard by this return of public discussion, the curtain parted for a split second, and its distaste for antigovernment speech showed one of its clearest and radical expressions: the government wanted silence on arbitrary state violence against civilians. The prime minister cried out, "It can be a mistake. We declared the mistake, we declared an apology, we declared the reparation. But some people are abusing the situation. For the love of God, if it is reparation, here is the reparation. . . . We offered more than the official reparation."[115] The interior minister's public statement had its own distinct flavor. He remarked, "If they had not died, they would have been tried in court for smuggling." The minister of national defense stated, "They are trying to denigrate the Turkish Armed Forces." The precise vocabulary that constituted the Kemalist laicist defense against criticism of state politics now was uttered by an AKP minister. Prime Minister Erdoğan completely changed the public discussion by bursting out in the final meeting of his party that the critics of the government on Uludere were "necrophiles," and "every abortion [*kürtaj*] is an Uludere," setting off the feminist wing of a public mobilizing around the Uludere Incident to now ponder losing abortion rights.

The incident, for which the government was publicly criticized by a wide range of societal organizations and political parties except for the ultranationalists, was the moment when continuous police and judicial attacks on basic rights were replaced by state coercion in its bare military form. In 2011 and 2012 the number of arbitrary and longtime detentions by the police peaked: journalists, lawyers, syndicate leaders, scholars, students, human rights activists, elected representatives. Eight parliamentarians from three opposition political parties were still in prison after being elected in the 2011 elections, and many BDP elected municipal representatives were jailed; another court case against a BDP parliamentarian began in September 2012 and launched a wave of death fasts in prison. The democratic opposition imprisoned and/or on trial by the end of 2012 totaled more than eight thousand custodies and four thousand detentions. Continuous judicial attacks on political rights hindered any possibility of open societal deliberation on a new constitution.

University students were one part of society paying heavy costs for freedom of expression. Two students were detained for displaying a placard demanding "free and public education" during a public speech by the prime minister and were released only after their third trial, having spent nineteen months in prison. They eventually received a sentence of eight and a half years. In another trial of a student who was detained as a "terrorist" just for wearing a *poşu* (a scarf), some police officers admitted that the police report was fabricated. The student was released on March 23, 2012, after twenty-five months in detention and on May 12 was sentenced to eleven years and three months in prison. The ruling was followed by street demonstrations the same day. The Progressive Lawyers' Association (Çağdaş Hukukçular Derneği) found that "the majority of detained students face prosecution under the TPC [Turkish Penal Code] Articles 220 and 314, as well as the Terrorism Prevention Act No. 3713 Article 7/2. One group of students was arrested on the grounds of violating the Demonstrations and Marches Act No. 2911 (TPC Article 265)."[116] These were the precise laws that had not made it to the agenda of the Constitution Compromise Commission.

Artists and journalists also received their share of state-sponsored harassment. A theater actor who staged a one-person play on Karl Marx adapted to the Turkish context, similar to Howard Zinn's *Marx in Soho*, was tried and found guilty for insulting the prime minister with a joke during the play. Applauding the privatization of the state theater, Prime Minster Erdoğan disparaged actors for criticizing the state while on the state payroll.

Two journalists were arrested and charged with being part of the very deep relations they were revealing through their investigation. One was investigating how the Gülen movement was taking over the police force and penned a book entitled *The Army of the İmam*, which was banned prior to publication.[117] The other was investigating the murder of Hrant Dink, editor-in-chief of the only Turkish-language Armenian newspaper, and authored a book entitled *Red Friday: Who Broke Dink's Pen?*[118] They were included in the Ergenekon trials. Mass arrests, which had started after a gunman shot a judge in 2006 (known as the Danıştay Affair), continued with the Ergenekon trials, first against certain factions in the military but later also targeting the civil democratic opposition, and the reappointments of high-ranking military officers. The trials served to restructure the military institution in line with the new bourgeois interests represented by the AKP government. The two journalists had their first trial after eight months in detention and were released only after the eleventh trial, having spent thirteen months in prison. The only evidence was Word documents found on their computers, analyzed by three computer specialist firms—one from the United States—and found to have been placed there by outsiders. After his release, on March 28, 2012, the author of the *Army of the İmam* spoke to the European Parliament underscoring the imprecision of Anti-Terror Laws (last amended in July 2010, right before the 2010 referendum on the constitution), pressures on journalists in the form of imprisonments and layoffs, and a certain religious movement's inroads into the police forces and the military.

One wave of mass arrests included a faculty member who would have had a direct role in the writing of the constitution, as well as a publisher and human rights advocate who joined his son in prison. The International Publishers Association called for the immediate release of the publisher, who was the recipient of the IPA Freedom to Publish Prize in 2008. He was released on April 10, 2012, to continue his trial without pretrial detention after already having spent close to six months in jail. A professor in the Department of Political Science and International Relations at Marmara University who was a BDP member and the faculty member on the BDP's Constitution Commission, was arrested for giving a lecture on her own research in the "politics academy" of the BDP, a party organization that brings academic and field research to the public through open courses taught by volunteers. The meeting place was being tapped by the police, along with many other BDP buildings. Widespread arbitrary and illegal place and phone tapping by the police had made headlines frequently in the past years. The Middle East Studies Association wrote a letter to Prime Minister Erdoğan calling for the immediate release of the professor.[119] Her indictment was prepared after more than five months of detention time.

Diverse examples of violations, all facilitated by the terror laws and the restructuring of the police and the judiciary, can be enumerated. Human Rights Watch reported on some of these detentions, trials, and court sentences. Turkey already had a long record of past witch hunts, and this was just another cycle. According to the Reporters Without Borders (RSF) Press Freedom Index, press freedom has steadily declined during the AKP government. Recent reports on Turkey—for instance, one by RSF entitled *A Book Is Not a Bomb* and another one entitled *Turkey: Set Journalists Free*—compiled collectively by a group of Turkish and European Press Associations laid bare Turkey's race to the bottom in press freedom.[120] The international petition campaign launched right after the wave of mass arrests immediately received more than six thousand signatures.

In this race to the bottom there is no doubt that Turkish society actually hit the bottom with the imprisonment of children. In the city of Diyarbakır, infrastructural insufficiencies, disrupted families, lost economies, and many other dynamics initiated by the state's forced migrations caused a lumpenization of children. Some youth below age eighteen were sentenced under the terror laws to heavy prison terms for protesting. In 2011 the court asked for a twenty-four-year prison sentence for children aged between thirteen and seventeen.

Yet in other trials, the judiciary was not so heavy-handed. In one of the country's biggest corruption cases, a Turkey-based religious charity association involving a Turkish state bureaucrat among the suspects, which shook first Germany (a German judge reported that it was the biggest case Germany had ever seen) and then Turkey, the suspects were tried without being detained. In a rape case of a twelve-year-old girl by more than twenty men, including state employees (a gendarme, a primary school vice-president, neighborhood authorities, a municipal employee), the court lessened the verdict by passing a judgment that the girl had consented. Elsewhere, a police officer who killed a Nigerian professional soccer player in a police station got fewer than five years in prison.

Speech?

These are just some examples of violations of basic human and constitutional rights in Turkey. A further loss of credibility for the Turkish judiciary summed up the situation as of 2012. What was striking is that such facts were easily covered up by academics and journalists who relied heavily and selectively on speeches of government representatives, particularly the speeches by Prime Minister Erdoğan himself, and who sought and often found an international audience that could not weigh these speeches in context. An example was Erdoğan's speech at the Council of Europe Parliamentary Assembly on April 13, 2011, in the midst of the turmoil in Turkey. When a question was posed to him on the banned book *Army of the İmam*, Erdoğan stated that the judiciary in Turkey was independent, and he charged European politicians with discriminating against Turkey:

> It is not me who had the books collected. It is a crime to use a bomb, but it is also a crime to use the ingredients for the making of a bomb. Let's say that there is a denunciation that in a particular place, those ingredients for making a bomb, all of them, from its fuse to other

materials, are present. Don't the security forces go and collect them. This is also a crime so they would go and take them. In this situation as well, if the information previously collected embodies these kind of preparations, justice has made its decision, and asked the security forces to pick and deliver the preparation in question. Hah! This preparation has entered internet websites as a book later on, it is out in the open what its [the book's] content is. Therefore, I think that it is pertinent to see these realities. And this is not an act of the executive, but a decision of the judiciary. I have to say this here: all the time when it suits us we talk about independent judiciary. We defend an independent judiciary everywhere. But when it comes to Turkey, in Turkey you do not want an independent judiciary, ya! You want a judiciary dependent on the executive. There isn't a judiciary dependent on the executive.[121]

The three main aspects of this speech—the claim of an independent Turkish judiciary, the "Europe is discriminating against Turkey" theme, and the "violent" book-bomb analogy—form a distinct synthesis. These are recurring themes that hold clues to Turkish government politics. For instance, in the interview Erdoğan gave to the Italian newspaper *Corriere Della Sera* on May 7, 2012, these themes were present again. He played on how he had been a victim himself—he served time in prison—and therefore appreciated the importance of freedom of speech, but 90 percent of the journalists in jail were there not because of what they wrote but because they had links with terrorist organizations; the British journalists arrested in Britain did not raise a controversy, and everyone picks on Turkey.[122]

The first claim, on the independence of the judiciary, is dubious in terms of the decisions in the examples cited above. The second theme underscores the politics of victimhood that have to be systematically integrated into analytical frameworks for the study of Turkish politics. A recent culmination of such politics was the prime minister declaring all opposition parties in parliament fascistic. The third, the book-bomb analogy, underscores the government party's take on freedom of expression and is just one among many incidents. Erdoğan's defense, in May 2012, of the privatization of the state theater against the critique of intellectuals and actors is worth quoting at length:

We see how despotic intellectuals attempt to advise us and excuse me, maybe it will be a slightly heavy expression, but we pity these poor things.... They began to denigrate and belittle us as well as all conservatives because of a change in the regulation of state theaters [the change allows for a bureaucrat instead of an actor to preside over theaters]. I am asking, look here! Who are you? Is theater in your monopoly in this country? Is art in your monopoly in this country? ... From now on, belittling this nation, scolding this nation, by pointing out your finger with your despotic intellectual attitude remains in the past. Almost in none of the developed countries is there theater by means of the state... We will privatize theaters. With privatization, you are welcome to stage your plays as you like. When necessary, we, as the government, give our sponsorship and support to the plays we want. Here it is! Freedom, stage the plays you want as you like wherever you like. No one will prevent it. But excuse me! In a city theater, you take your wages from the municipality and then criticize the administration as you like. This is nonsense.[123]

Along the same lines, the Ministry of Interior earlier in the year almost coined a concept of "terrorist art." All these statements on intellectuals and artists were just short of the response of 1980 military coup leader General Kenan Evren in 1984 to the famous "intellectuals petitions" for democracy, with 1,260 signatures handed in to the president and the parliament.[124] Evren publicly called all signatories "traitors."[125]

History or Present?

Two cases that put the judiciary and public conscience at odds were the Dink trial and the Sivas Massacre trial. Hrant Dink was the editor-in-chief of the only Turkish-language Armenian weekly and was assassinated on January 19, 2007. The trial concluded in January 2012. The court found no evidence of conspiracy to commit murder and so the convicted got short prison terms, some police officers received only warnings, and the journalist who exposed the state corruption behind the investigation in his book *Red Friday* was imprisoned. The trial for the 1993 Sivas Massacre, the clearest case of religious violence of the past two decades in Turkey, was recently dismissed because of the statute of limitations. In 1993 a mob attacked the Madımak Hotel in the central Anatolian city of Sivas, where the Pir Sultan Abdal Culture Association (an Alevi association) was hosting invited writers and poets for a festival. A religious mob set the hotel on fire and thirty-seven writers and poets were killed. This was neither the first nor the last mob violence against an Alevi or an Alevi-organized activity.

Just before the trial was dismissed, the judiciary had considered via the testimony of a "secret witness" a link between the massacre and "PKK terror." This attempted connection naturally failed because of the numerous accounts and visuals of how religious mob violence was provoked by local authorities. The trajectory of these trials and some of the mass arrests mentioned above revealed one of the most prominent discursive building blocks of antidemocratic politics in Turkey: a politics of memory that makes continuous stabs at the Armenification or Kurdification of all violence.

The 1978 Maraş Massacre was one of the major acts of violence used to precipitate the 1980 military coup. After right-wing provocations pitting Sunnis against Alevis in 1978 in Maraş, 111 left-wing and Alevi citizens, both adults and children, were massacred in their homes by mobs. Many civil society organizations put facing the Maraş Massacre as a necessary condition for dismantling the military heritage in contemporary Turkish politics and for writing a new democratic constitution. Yet on December 24, 2011, the mayor of Maraş—with full support of the interior minister—banned a commemoration protest and mobilized the gendarme to prevent the commemorators from accessing the city center.[126] Just before the Sivas Massacre trials ended, Alevi residences were marked in the city of Adıyaman, later in the city of Izmir, and then in the town of Didim, and written statements calling Alevis to the right path to God were left on their doors. The interior minister refused to acknowledge the situation and declared on March 1, 2012, that the signs were most likely the work of children because they were hung at a low height.

Against History: The Constitution in the Writing?

In this context and given the working principles of the Constitution Compromise Commission, Turkey could have been heading for yet another constitutional change but definitely not for a societally based and well-deliberated democratic constitution writing. According to article 5 of the commission's working principles, it could convene with one member each from three of the four political parties. According to article 7, the commission could decide not to keep records, and no record was to be made public until the commission concluded its task of drafting a new constitution. Arguably, even during the drafting of the military constitution by professors in 1961, for which there were no published minutes, agreements and disagreements during the drafting process were exposed in the media as much as in this failed 2011–2013 episode. According to article 10 of the commission's working principles, commission meetings were closed to the media, and the group, through its head, would make media statements after a meeting only as it saw fit. In October 2012, when the commission expected that the drafting process would not finish before the end of 2012 as originally planned, Prime Minister Erdoğan responded: "This task [the drafting] is either finished by the end of the year, or finished. If not, we will say it has kept us busy too long, and continue our path."[127]

Many associations made public statements on what they wanted from a new constitution, and universities were asked to express their positions in writing. The Constitution Compromise Commission held thirteen outreach meetings with citizens in various cities before starting the drafting process. I tried to attend one of these meetings and was told that I needed to be invited. A couple of days later my Italian doctoral student reported to me with surprise that she had received a phone message inviting her to an outreach meeting. The most comprehensive report was issued by the Constitutional Law Research Association (Anayasa-DER) and presented to the commission on March 20, 2012. The report underlined some criticisms of the content and procedures of the constitution-making process.[128] It presented a list of the laws that violate the rights to freedom of expression, freedom of press, and freedom of association: the Turkish Criminal Code, the Anti-Terror Law, the Radio and Television Establishment and Broadcasting Law, the Information Technologies and Communications Institutions Establishment Law, the law on regulating broadcasting on the Internet and combating crimes committed by these broadcasts, the Meetings and Demonstrations Law, the Police Duties Law, and the Associations Law. These violations have also been noted by many European Union institutions.

The origins of some of these laws and others, such as the Political Parties Law, the Parliamentarians Elections Law, and the Higher Education Law, all dated back to the period between 1980 and 1983 when the National Security Council had the power of legislation. For instance, the often debated 10 percent threshold in the general elections is found in article 33 of the Parliamentarians Elections Law. The report concluded that the 1980 military regime's heritage was in legislation passed between 1980 and 1983, and tackling this legislation was at the top of the list for dismantling the military heritage of Turkish politics and taking steps toward a new constitution.[129]

Yet in a public statement during an academic conference in 2012, one CHP member of the Constitution Compromise Commission remarked that it was precisely this 1980–1983 legislation that the commission was not addressing because of opposition by the AKP:

> That coup spirit is not only in the constitution but it is also in our legislation between September 12, 1980, and December 6, 1983. Approximately 105 coup laws are still in effect. Which laws are these? Political Parties Law, election law, meetings and demonstrations law, police duties laws, 10 percent threshold, syndicate laws . . . we have to change them. In a subcommission of the Constitution Compromise Commission . . . we expressed our will in the direction of a change in coup laws along with the constitution. . . . But government opposes. We insist, but members of the subcommission from the governing party tell us that we [AUK] do not have such authorization.[130]

Dismantling the heritage of the military coup of 1980 may have been the prime motivator for a new constitution, but the examples of what passed for "dismantling" could be described, in my formulation, as "against history." The wills and voices of the actors and associations that suffered after the coup did not bear on the process of "dismantling." For example, the All Teachers Union and Solidarity Association (TÖB-DER) was closed down during the military regime by a military court decision in 1981. It was a strong association in the 1970s and a stronghold against ultranationalists. One key act among the ultranationalist provocations leading up to the Maraş Massacre in 1978 was the murder of two TÖB-DER member teachers. In 2008 TÖB-DER's application to the Ankara mayorship to reopen the association was turned down. TÖB-DER took the matter to court, and in 2010 an Ankara administrative court confirmed that the association could not be reopened. There were many more examples. One striking example along the lines of "against history" was that one of the AKP members of the commission was actually the lawyer of military coup leader General Kenan Evren and defended him against public intellectuals in a court case that concluded in 1990.[131] Aziz Nesin, a famous writer, had opened a court case against Evren when Evren called the 1,260 signatories of the 1984 "intellectuals petition" traitors. Nesin later took the case to the European Court of Human Rights. Both courts turned down the case.

In the parliament emerging from the 2011 elections, the AKP had 326 out of 549 seats, and around 50 of those seats were the effect of the 10 percent threshold. This raised further questions on the legitimacy of that parliament for writing a constitution. On September 19, 2011, twenty-four constitutional law scholars were called in for a meeting with the parliament, and there was a division among them whether a constituent assembly or the parliament should make the new constitution. The parliament decided that it wanted to make the constitution, a typical instance of how starting off with a clean slate is close to impossible in constitution making, for those in power do not want to be bound by any other power. The consultation of law scholars turned into a moment of attempting to elicit legitimacy for the dominant political interests.

Overhaul of Turkey's Education System and Required and Optional Religion Courses

When some members of the CHP appealed to the State Council against the decision of the Higher Council of Education that abolished the national university exam score coefficient disadvantaging students from professional and İmam Hatip high schools, Prime Minister Erdoğan remarked, "CHP does not want that a religious generation is raised."[132] In his speech at the AKP's expanded city representatives meeting on February 1, 2012, the prime minister reiterated his position:

> In my [previous] expression, there isn't [a distinction] between religious and irreligious [persons]. . . . There is [in my expression] raising a religious youth. Yes. (*Applause.*) I say this again, I stand behind this. (*Applause.*) I stand behind this. (*Long applause.*) Sayın Kılıçdaroğlu [leader of the CHP], do you expect from us, AK Party who has a conservative democratic party identity, to raise an atheist generation? (*Applause.*) This can perhaps be your task. It can be your goal. However, we do not have such a goal. We will raise a generation who is conservative and democratic, who embraces the values and principles, principles coming from history, of their nation and *patrie*. We are working for this. (*Applause.*) We are working for this.[133]

In the same speech, the prime minister addressed the question of imprisoned journalists and then mockingly addressed Paul Auster, whose book *Winter Journal* (2012) was published in Turkish and who "refuse[d] to come to Turkey because of imprisoned journalists and writers":[134]

> We explained again and again that, right now, a large majority of suspects and convicts in prison who are presented as journalists, are not incarcerated because of activities of journalism. . . . The majority of those who are presented as imprisoned journalists in Turkey are in fact not journalists, and those who are journalists are not inside because of activities of journalism. Look! Valuable friends, valuable members of the media, I am addressing my dear nation who are right now watching us in front of their screen. There are such suspects who have personally taken part in terror activity, who have engaged in gunned attack, slaughtered policeman, who have been arrested for possession of fire weapons. In their pockets, identity cards of media institutions of the terror organization [PKK] have been found. When these persons are arrested, the terror organization starts a campaign against Turkey saying that journalists have been arrested. Unfortunately, the leader of the main opposition party is also a part of this campaign. He becomes a tool of this campaign. Imagine such a leader that in every country he goes and to every foreigner he meets, he denigrates his country. He denigrates the economy of his country, he claims that journalists are arrested in his country. But even in those places, nobody believes him much. Ha! Doesn't believe, doesn't believe. . . . An American writer, Paul Auster, gives an interview to a newspaper on Sunday, a Turkish newspaper. His statement is exactly this: "I refuse to come to Turkey because of imprisoned writers and journalists. For the same reasons, I also turn down the invitations coming from China." Ah! We were in need of [*muhtaç*] you. (*Laughs in the audience.*) Why didn't you come? (*Applause.*) Aman! Come. Please. What difference does it make if you come or don't come? Ya! Will Turkey lose altitude [*irtifa*]?[135]

A week later the prime minister spoke at the launch of the FATİH education project to upgrade technology in state primary and secondary schools. FATİH is the Turkish acronym for the Movement for Increasing Opportunities in Education and Improving Technology—Eğitimde Fırsatları Artırma ve Teknolojiyi İyileştirme Hareketi—an allusion to Mehmet the Conqueror

(Fatih Sultan Mehmet), who conquered Istanbul from the Byzantine Empire in 1453.[136] In his speech, Erdoğan responded one more time to critics of his previous remarks on raising religious youth: "This country has been prevented from learning its religious, national, and spiritual [manevi] values. . . . Who did this? That well-known CHP mentality. Those who learned and taught those values were arrested as if they committed a crime, followed, subjected to raids and pressures."[137]

After his critique of "well-known CHP mentality," the prime minister rested his case on the Kemalist military constitution's article 24 on required courses on religion, culture, and morality: "Article 24 says that the religion, culture, and morality course is our duty and the state teaches it." Then once more he defended his position on raising religious youth from journalists' criticisms:

I address those who are writing for one week in their columns; do you want these youth to become paint-thinner addicts [tinnerci]?[138] Do you want these youth to become a generation rebellious against their elders? Do you want these youth to become a generation detached from their national and spiritual values, without any direction and cause? We cannot agree with you here, but when you say "a civilized/modern [çağdaş] generation," can't a religious generation be civilized/modern?

On February 19 the prime minister spoke again, this time at the AKP Istanbul City Youth Organization's third congress, where he was introduced with the statement, "The word [söz] is now with the great master [usta]." Erdoğan emphasized one more time: "I am underlining it; I am talking about a modern, religious youth. I am talking about a youth who takes for a cause his/her religion, language, brains, science, chastity [ırzı], home, vengeful hatred [kin], heart."[139] This was an obvious allusion to Necip Fazıl Kısakürek's (1904–1983) work *Gençliğe Hitabe* (Speech to the youth). The prime minister used the name of this conservative novelist and poet playwright in referencing another of his works in his January 31, 2012, speech to parliament.[140] The word *kin* (vengeful hatred) was removed in many media reports but remained in some.[141] Even more striking was what followed in the original text of Necip Fazıl Kısakürek after the section the prime minister quoted. The original text continued with a call for a radically antidemocratic populist mobilization. The next words in the original read: a youth "who believes in God and not in the People, who longs for the maxim 'sovereignty belongs to God' on the wall of the parliament, who finds real justice in this belief and a youth who knows the pure freedom in slavery to God."[142]

This was the background when, on March 30, 2012, the AKP changed the education system and supplemented the existing required courses on the "culture" of religion with two optional courses on religion "as such": one on reading the Koran and the other on the life of the Prophet. One striking argument in defense of this change was that the existing courses were not religion but just culture. This change ignored in-depth discussion on any aspect of laiklik, but even references to the concept of laiklik were scant in the parliamentary debates, suggesting an abating of the depth of discussion and a loss of the focal place the concept has held as the cornerstone of the political field of struggle in Turkey. Only when the constitutional court received a case filed by the CHP after the education law passed parliament was there an attempt to grope for a conceptualization of laiklik. The court imported from France Nicolas Sarkozy's *laïcité positive* for a defense of the new courses.[143] Although these new courses were optional, Prime Minister Erdoğan in his speech to the public on September 2013 explicitly encouraged parents to have their children take them.[144]

The new education law initially lowered the school age to sixty months and but later, after protests and public discussions, raised it to sixty-six months but still allowed children between sixty-one and sixty-six months to register with the written permission of parents.[145] The law claimed to increase the length of obligatory education from eight to twelve years, but in fact by introducing "choice" and "guidance" at the end of the fourth and eighth years, it opened a path for mainly İmam Hatip and professional secondary schooling. The newspaper *Milliyet* reported that there was a quarrel and a physical fight among the education commission drafting the law before it came to parliament and that "approving six articles in six days, the commission accepted the remaining nineteen articles in a half hour without deliberation."[146] The lack of due process in the commission was widely aired by the opposition in parliament, and when the law came up for discussion in parliament on March 28, 2012, street protests just outside parliament in Ankara and in many other cities were countered with police brutality and pepper gas.[147] The opposition in parliament underlined problems with the starting age and with hurrying a law of huge consequences without a pilot project, as well as the lack of order in the commission. They also argued that the law was being guided by economic interests rather than educational principles. They particularly highlighted the economic market opened for the state purchase of the computer equipment demanded by the FATİH project, and that replacing a standard curriculum with an early choice for "guiding" some students to professional secondary schools would create a poorly educated labor force in the interests of capital.

The written justification for the AKP proposal for law referred to EU standards and emphasized that professional education figured much more in the secondary education of European Union countries than it did in Turkey, giving examples from the United States, Britain, Germany, France, and Japan. There was a clear emphasis in the proposal on the relation between economic development and professional schooling at an early age: "Economic competitive power, productivity and efficiency, the firmness of the social fabric, and the liveliness and richness of the fields of culture and art are directly related to the quality of the education system."[148]

The March 27, 2012, parliamentary discussions were mostly on the question of procedural violations. MHP, CHP, and BDP members all pointed out that the draft education law came from a commission meeting where there was a physical fight between AKP and CHP parliamentarians[149] after the AKP head of the commission refused deliberation on proposals, arguing that some of them were the same in content. Where the draft law was not sufficiently deliberated, it could not be brought for discussion in the parliament. The opposition particularly referred to article 46 of the internal regulations of the parliament to call for due process:

> Article 46. If speech is interrupted, there is engagement at the personal level and acts to disrupt order in a commission, the head of the commission keeps order; if necessary he/she suspends the meeting or postpones and reports to the president of the Turkish Grand National Assembly for necessary action.[150]

A CHP parliamentarian stressed:

> The respectful AKP group vice-president stated that the commission spent ninety-one hours in deliberation, implying that the opposition is abusing their rights [to demand further deliberation]. . . . In the year 97, the law proposal for eight-year uninterrupted/continuous required education, consisting of eleven articles, was deliberated for ninety-three hours in the commission. Today, your older brothers [ağabey], the elders of the AKP group, were then parliamentarians from the Welfare Party

and were using their rights to speech. If we are to keep the same standard today, a proposal consisting of twenty-seven articles has to be deliberated 228 hours in total.

During the March 27 parliamentary discussion, tensions rose again with personal comments, mocking, and cursing. The AKP head of the commission advanced the following defense: "The content of a commission report has to address information on the proposal for law decided upon. . . . The scope of the coverage, its level of detail, is at the discretion of the president of the commission."[151] Some AKP members tried to switch the discussion to the level of moralism, tweeting messages such as "4+4+4 [the new education law] hit bars and not schools; all CHP representatives are in the parliament." A BDP member added that given the military heritage in the constitution against language diversity in the country, the education question could not be resolved without a new constitution. The president of parliament asserted, against all opposition grounded on procedure, that there was no violation of internal regulations of parliament and kept the commission's proposal on the parliamentary agenda for discussion.

The discussion on the whole proposal started with the BDP spokesperson taking the floor:

> Just right now, education workers who oppose this proposal for law are on their way to Ankara from various locations in Turkey for a demonstration and all workers . . . have been intercepted by a circular of the minister of interior and instructions from the mayor and [have been] prevented from reaching Ankara. . . . Education is vulnerable to ideology in Turkey because all past governments have shaped this field according to their own political views. . . . We are facing a new proposal for law prepared exactly by such an approach. . . . The prohibition against education in one's mother tongue, compulsory religion courses . . . are the evident proof for that. . . . This proposal is the stage for legalization by the AKP of an assimilationist, pro-exploitation, non-scientific, antidemocratic education. . . . The proposal for law presented as twelve-year obligatory education in fact is not extending the obligatory period of education to twelve years, it is still keeping it at eight. The school life that students continue as obligatory education in the first stage will continue as guidance toward a profession in the second stage. Taking into consideration that ten-year-old children cannot

make healthy choices concerning profession at that age, with this proposal children of poor and uneducated families will be condemned to the same fate as their families. . . . Article 9 [of the proposed law] has been arranged as, "In the primary education second stage schools, optional courses are introduced according to the ability, development, and preferences of students in order to support middle schooling [*ortaöğretim*]." This article also includes a statement that the ministry [of education] determines the curriculum and the optional courses in the second stage of all schools concerned. As the BDP, we are defending that these [optional] courses be determined together by the ministry and local administrations [*yerel yönetimler*, municipalities] according to [local] needs and demands and a clear statement providing the possibility of education in one's mother tongue be added [to the article]. Turkey is a multilingual country where many languages are spoken. Kurdish is at the top of the list, including languages Laz, Circassian, Arabic, Georgian, Hemşin, and others. . . . Education in one's mother tongue is present as a fundamental and inalienable human right in the Universal Declaration of Human Rights and many other international documents and agreements. . . . AKP with this proposal, on the one hand, puts the education system at the service of capital and therefore deepens societal fragmentation; on the other hand, it is telling the poor, handicapped, women, and all other marginalized "to stay wherever you are." . . . This proposal exalts [early] professional education and aims to raise a young, cheap, qualified, supplementary labor force for capital. Since this education system will greatly lower the rate of entrance into the universities, students who have received professional education [*mesleki eğitim*] will be placed at a young age in workshops and textile factories as cheap labor. In this situation, this young section [of society] will be preferred [in employment], the unemployment rate in the unskilled middle age and above section [of society] will rise. In the justification for the law, it is emphasized that eight-year required education prevents the development of professional and technical middle education. Again, [it is emphasized] that professional education is very important, that it has important contributions to the economy, and it is claimed that in European Union countries the ratio is 66 percent while in our country it is 44 percent. I think those who have prepared the text of this law are not aware of the poor condition of education in our country's professional high schools and the poor condition of those who are able to graduate from these schools. Today, graduates of professional high schools are employed in sectors unrelated to their professions at minimum wage, without job security and as cheap labor. . . . I really wonder what percentage of those who appear to defend professional education in fact send their children to such schools. Again, once we consider the proportion of students from rich families in professional schools, guiding [students] to professional education at ten years old is clearly a trap for those children of economically poor and poorly educated families. . . . While the physical infrastructure of schools is highly insufficient, making millions lira worth of technological investment with the FATİH project is [just] opening a huge market to international capital.[152]

The CHP spokesperson, a teacher, took the floor and commented on the police preventing CHP demonstrators against the new law from entering Ankara:

Dear parliamentarians, this is the parliament, the executive is a branch that works under it. . . . There is a document of the Ankara Police Force, coming from . . . the vice mayor, sent to KESK and EĞİTİM-SEN [two syndicates] and warning against demonstrations. The government does not have such a constitutional power . . . a situation even worse. . . . A notification that in case there are individual and collective attempts from our city to join in the demonstration planned in Ankara, no permission will be granted in accordance with the [recent] decision [of the Ankara mayorship] of prohibition. Who is [the signatory?] Manisa [another city around 500 km from Ankara] Police Force. With what right, what power? What power do you have to prevent people who want to travel to Ankara from exiting the city borders of Manisa?

He continued with comments on the content of the proposed law:

I went over the red booklet [on education] our minister had prepared; there isn't a single negative aspect of the [present] eight-year application [in education]. Well, the sources [in the booklet] are from Wikipedia. . . . We know that . . . society and experts were not consulted in the preparation of this proposal [for law]. We know that this proposal was not conceived of in the [government's] development plan, or in the government program, or in the [government's] strategic planning.... The minister of education heard about this proposal almost on the same day as I did, this is a bit too much.... Now, one of your justifications [for the proposed law] is that "it is the state's responsibility toward individuals to guide [them] toward professions at an early age."... Name one country besides Germany, Austria ... and there are two other countries ... that differentiate the education curriculum into different tracks at ten years old, and I will say "yes" to this law.... In the USA, Japan, OECD, and European Union countries, differentiation in the curriculum starts at the age of fifteen.... You are going in front of Germany with [differentiation] at the age of nine.... Now the question of sixty months [as the starting age for primary schooling]. Dear parliamentarians, none of you would send your child or grandchild to school at sixty months.... You do not have a right to declare appropriate something that you do not find appropriate for your own child or grandchild. Didn't twenty-one organizations out of the twenty-four civil society organizations we listened to in the subcommission oppose this? They did. Enough!... One of your justifications is the following: "... Eight-year uninterrupted primary education killed professional high schools."... In 1998, our student ratio in professional technical education is 45.7 percent ... in 1998, the year we passed to eight-year uninterrupted primary education.... Now ... our ratio is 47.9 percent.... This [justification] is also a big lie ... (*an AKP parliamentarian interrupts: "Fear from God!"*). I fear God, but you be careful. (*Applause from CHP rows.*). Now, as the proposal [for law] lacks a pedagogical infrastructure, it also lacks financial and personnel planning.... But you [AKP] are saying: "We will carry on the FATİH project. We will provide smart boards and I-pads [to students].... Now I do not give names but I will tomorrow. You are not aware but the word is already out on who worked in which firms and private sector and later got hired as the vice director of the General Directory of Education Technologies [in the Ministry of Education], on who arranged the patent and license agreements of this project [FATİH].... A friendly warning from me. (*Applause from CHP rows.*)... You did a lot of promoting. It started with big headlines, "Girls to School!"... [followed by] "if we succeed we will hire 110,000 new teachers." Shame! Your own reports says, "130,000 teachers are urgently required now." Why don't you hire the 130,000 teachers stated in the ministry report.... 250,000 teachers are unemployed.... Now, give me one fact showing a shortcoming of the eight years of uninterrupted education, one single [piece of] scientific research, one negative university view, I will vote for [the law]; you cannot give it.... The average education time of the population ... has increased from three-and-a-half to six-and-a-half [years].... In 1997 the schooling percentage was 84 percent, it increases to around 98 percent.... Schooling among girls—you keep doing campaigns—was 78.9; it became 98.2.... There has been a significant decrease in early age marriages among girls.... I speak as an educator and do you know the percentage of education in the consolidated budget now in your term—in 1998, it was 37.3 percent. Eight [percent] ... this is your understanding and approach to education.... You did not do half of what was done in the four years before you. Open up the Ministry of Education Statistical Yearbooks and have a look at them, not at me. (*Applause from CHP rows.*)

The National Action Party (MHP) spokesperson, again a teacher by profession, took the floor:

As the National Action Party we are saying that preschooling has to be mandatory.... Because the main reason for the poverty and inequality bequeathed from generation to generation is preschool education.... Now, there is a form in our hands entitled "Class, Section Counselor Teachers Student Observation Forms.".... Here there are particularly certain section headings, "children's verbal skills, interpersonal skills, logic, and mathematics, observation and spatial, inner world, musical-rhythmic, physical-kinesthetic, and natural skills." There is also [a section on] personal characteristics, "personal characteristics, social characteristics, and general characteristics."... Class teachers from first to fifth grade, branch teachers from six to eighth grade, fill these out and guide [the students]. Did our teachers receive an education for such guidance, [and] how well do they know our children? ... Now, some of our children are guided to professional high schools; as part of this guidance [the parents] of some of our children [are told], "Take your child and have him/her registered in a professional high school. Take your child to an Anatolian high school."... There are already exams....[153] With this practice [of guidance] our children's future is determined.... As the National Action Party we are thinking of one year preschool education, five years in primary school, three years of middle school, three years of high school. . . . I also would like to draw your attention to the optional courses claimed to be given in the 4+4+4 system. At the moment, there is an optional course called "media literacy." . . . Do you have any idea who gives this course? Science teachers give it. . . . In order to fill the [weekly required] hours of teachers, these courses are distributed among them. . . . Let a feasibility study be prepared; determine well which courses and fields, especially in the global conjuncture, are necessary; teachers who are educated in close fields can be educated in these fields [determined by the feasibility study] . . . with a brief training.

An AKP spokesperson also took the floor:

The change in question is not an ideological change as has been the case in the past [before AKP], because while making these changes we researched and examined all the world examples in detail. The change is only a passage to an education with stages. The lawmaker . . . sets the general framework. Of course, here the executor [of the change] is the Ministry [of Education]. . . . The problem which needs to be discussed is the following: "How will the ministry use its power? We don't trust you for that matter." Unfortunately we heard this [statement] many times. Friends, a governing power takes office with elections, it puts forward its acts, its own politics, vision, point of view . . . its class [*zümre*]. . . . The accounts will be settled at the ballot box. (*Applause from AKP rows.*) What we are doing is restoration, meaning to establish what must be, rather than a reform. With this restoration in education, the education system which has been shaped by the intervention of guardian institutions will be returned to normal according to the demands of the nation. (*Applause from AKP rows.*) . . . (A CHP parliamentarian: . . . "According to you, is it democratic that the buses [on their way to Ankara] are stopped?") . . . (Another CHP parliamentarian: "You are limiting the right to travel, you are blocking buses, you are afraid of teachers voicing their rightful demands.") . . . From Germany to the U.K. and the U.S., in all developed countries . . . the education system is structured with stages. . . . In none of the developed countries of the world does the education system have primary education for eight years. Except Ireland and Turkey. . . . Dear parliamentarians, we have no right to imprison students in Turkey in the same space and same program for eight years. We want that our children finishing primary school and stepping into puberty change their space and program according to their physical and psychological changes and their development talents. . . . In this way, let our children live puberty more healthily, let them access a system with multiple options and guidance. . . . We are against all elitist point of views condescending society and excluding its demands. (*Applause from AKP rows.*) The understanding that sees its own point of view as the only truth, considers itself as the master of the nation [*milletin efendisi*], for years tried to civilize [*adam etmek*, literally "to make a man of"] this society. It decided what the individual would believe in, what he/she would think, how to be modern, and imposed these with the hands of the state that is an abstract device. With AKP, state imposition has ended. . . . (A BDP parliamentarian: "You are even silencing the language of the Kurds.") We want that there is a structure that adjusts the system according to persons, and not one that adjusts the persons according to the system. (*Applause from AKP rows.*) The state has to meet the demands of a continuously diversifying and changing society. . . . (An MHP parliamentarian: . . . "Do you yourself believe what you are saying?") . . . In middle school, optional courses will be given to our students so that they discover their own talents and develop their interests; this way, our students will be informed on careers and professions.

Finally, on March 27, the parliament passed from the general discussion to discussion by article with a vote of 289 to 101. All motions for change in the text of the law were turned down in the March 28, 2012, parliamentary session.[154] In that session the BDP spokesperson underlined that the proposed law was aiming to raise religious youth in the service of capital, and the MHP spokesperson said, "A human being who is lacking either in national or religious values is in fact not a full human being."[155] He defended an explicit statement in article 9 of the law "making the learning of Koran, life of the Prophet, courses on how to memorize the Koran [*hafızlık*], knowledge of Islam" optional. In the March 29 session, three motions concerning the proposed law's article 9 on optional courses were read back to back.[156] The first motion by the BDP on education in one's mother tongue was rejected. The second motion was by the MHP and the third by the AKP, both on the introduction of optional courses on the Koran and the life of the Prophet. This session was marked by the struggle between the MHP and AKP for claiming to be the authors of the idea of optional religion courses and with the dearth and poverty of references to laiklik. There was a significant amount of cursing, personal mocking, and insults, and the demand for apologies. Somebody attacked the speaker on the floor of the parliament, cursing the CHP. The moment these two motions made it to the agenda and the president of the assembly was reading them, a CHP parliamentarian interrupted and remarked that they were against the constitution's article 24:

> Dear President [of the Assembly] . . . this motion is against constitutional article 24. You cannot process it. . . . With this motion, the laic republic is completely annulled, [and] a religious state is being established. . . . When you were taking office, you swore an oath of loyalty to the Constitution and to laiklik. . . . According to article 24 of the Constitution, there is a religion culture and morality course; in what this [the motion at hand] brings there is the basis of a religious state.

Another CHP parliamentarian commented:

> With these motions for the first time in the history of the Turkish Republic an arrangement of the school curriculum concerning courses is being made [by the parliament]. Maybe some of you might step forward and say "with the 1982 constitution some courses were put into practice." However, let's not forget that that was a military coup constitution. Today, the holy book of our exalted [*yüce*] religion, Koran, has been turned into a tool in politics for the sake of votes. It looks like the AKP and its followers from this moment onward would like to create a polarization in society around holy books of religion. Dear parliamentarians, the state does not differentiate among citizens with respect to religion and beliefs. . . . The duty of the state is to remove the impediments in the way of the citizens living their faiths and religions in freedom. This is not only a definition of the laic state; at the same time, it is the definition of a freedom defending democratic state. Today, AKP . . . has demonstrated that they do not have an understanding [of a freedom defending democratic government]. . . . Come, let's talk all

together at which point society and students need religious education and arrange for it. It is absolutely wrong to draw such a frame polarizing citizens with motions . . . distributed to opposition parties just five minutes ago and not seeking compromise. This is even contrary to the fundamentals of our religion. The fundamental principle of Islam is to eliminate injustice within the frame of the principle of oneness of God [*tevhit*] . . . to arrange for property and sovereignty relations, to reveal that these belong to the people. You put all these aside, [and there is] in this proposal . . . a twenty billion dollar bid. . . . You are bringing together a holy book, Kur'an-ı Kerim, embodying the concept of *helal* with a *haram* bid. (*Bravo from CHP rows, clapping.*)

An MHP parliamentarian commented:

What we are doing is the following: we are turning into law the education of a country's, a 99 percent Muslim nation's, children in the sources of their own beliefs and values. It is time that we make peace between our nation and the republic. . . . The fundamental source of our belief values, Kur'an-ı Kerim and the life of its best practitioner, the Prophet, and . . . the catechism [*ilmihal*]—this is where AKP is lacking—must be taught. . . . In a little while, the AKP motion will be read—of course we would like that you support our motion. . . . Our [motion] is better developed. . . . We, as the National Action Party, will vote "yes" to your [AKP] motion and the article in question. . . . Nobody should think that this arrangement is against the republic, against Atatürk. Even great Atatürk says: "Teach religion in schools." . . . To teach Muslimness from its sources to children is in no way against the republic or laiklik or the principles of Atatürk.

This MHP motion was rejected by the AKP majority parliament, upon which an MHP parliamentarian remarked, "Will it be said 'no' when *kelimeişehadet*[157] comes from here [these rows of parliament] and 'yes' when it comes from there?" The AKP motion was read and the AKP parliamentarian in charge of the motion took the floor:

Yes, with this motion, a demand, a wish, a longing which our nation has been waiting for a long time will *inşallah* [God willing] be realized with the approval of the exalted parliament. In this respect today is really a historical day (*Applause from AKP rows, noise from CHP rows.*) (A CHP parliamentarian: "It is a historical day, because you destroyed the Turkish Republican state!") . . . Dear friends, this is not only an order of our nation. . . . It is at the same time the order of constitutional article 24. (An MHP parliamentarian: "Here it is! This is how we bring it [a motion]!" . . . Another: "Why are you doing it by yourself?" . . . Another: "I wish you had not blocked it in the commission!") . . . A moment ago MHP said that they would support, has MHP changed its mind, I do not know! . . . (A CHP parliamentarian: "What happened, [you had said] it was a military coup constitution?") . . . The system permits whomever wants to give his/her children an education in his/her religion, whatever religion he/she professes, this can be done in the form of an optional course. . . . (A CHP parliamentarian: "You will not be able to destroy this republic!" . . . An MHP parliamentarian: "Why can't you show the courage to say that you did it because MHP asked for it? Have courage; say thank you.")

The tension rose again when a CHP parliamentarian took the floor:

Shame! Instead of discussing here the Internet, computers, schools, [we are discussing] who is the better Muslim. What kind of a discussion is this? What a pity! This is a sin, sin, sin (*Applause from CHP rows.*) . . . You are using the Kur'an-ı Kerim in order to get votes. (*Applause and "Bravo" from CHP rows.*) . . . For arrangements concerning the Kur'an-ı Kerim, I want here 550 out of 550 parliamentarians to participate in the vote. (*Applause from AKP rows.*). We have to do this together. All your action is about those computers, those billions of dollars, you are trying to cover them up with the Kur'an, to cover up *haram* with the Kur'an! (*Applause from CHP rows.*) . . . You are Muslims, and we are not?

An MHP parliamentarian interrupted: "Dear President [of the assembly] . . . we also have a motion. Dear . . . [CHP parliamentarian] expressed that a motion concerning the Koran has been given in order to collect votes. I am embarrassed. These values of ours are not the kind for abusing in return for votes. These are values, we all and together have to claim. Therefore it is not possible for us to accept this evaluation. (*Applause from MHP and AKP rows*.)." Another MHP parliamentarian intervened; "Our objection is the following . . . if you had let us speak in the commission, we were going to give this motion there and this discussion would end there, but you did not permit."

A CHP parliamentarian took the floor:

> Dear President [of the assembly], the president and any representative of the Council of Education and Instruction (Talim Terbiye Kurulu)[158] has to get up from his/her seat and leave the general assembly now. I demand it, because to lay out the curriculum of primary education, to develop courses is the task of Talim Terbiye Kurulu. . . . If we are undertaking this task here, the president and any representative of the Talim Terbiye Kurulu has no business here. . . . By processing this motion [of] MHP's or AKP's, despite motions on its contrariness to the Constitution, you [president of the assembly] have violated the Constitution.

The AKP motion on article 9 was the first motion after two days of discussion that the commission and the government declared support for. And this was the first motion out of two accepted by the parliament by a vote of 306 to 85. The law passed on March 30 with a vote of 295 to 91 while the police took many persons under custody in Ankara.[159] On September 26, 2013, the media reported that the Ankara prosecutor of the republic had opened cases against 502 people who had participated in the demonstrations.[160]

The Constitutional Court turned down the CHP's appeal. The court's decision is worth quoting at length, for it embodies a reconceptualization of laiklik radically different from previous Constitutional Court decisions concerning laiklik.[161] The decision started out with an institutionalist approach to laiklik: "Laiklik is an attribute of neither the individual nor society, but of the state" (65). It articulated two types of laiklik, one of which was the same as Sarkozy's *laïcité positive* and was also visible in the writing of the 1961 constitution:

> According to rigid [*katı*] laiklik, religion only has a place in the individual conscience and should not step out into societal and public space. On the other hand, the more flexible and freedom-defending interpretation of laiklik stems from ascertaining that religion has a societal

dimension besides its individual dimension. This understanding of laiklik does not imprison religion to the inner world of the individual, [but rather] sees it [religion] as an important element of both individual and collective identity [and] allows for its societal visibility. In a laic political system, individual preferences on religious matters and lifestyles shaped by them are free from the intervention of the state; yet they are [at the same time] under its protection. In this meaning, the principle of laiklik is the guarantee of freedom of religion and conscience. (65)

Then the decision addressed sociological diversity and traced positive laiklik to the Kemalist constitution of 1982:

It is a historical and sociological fact that societies are diverse with regard to religion and belief; different beliefs, religions, or unbeliefs in society. Therefore one of the fundamental goals of the democratic and laic state is, by protecting societal diversity, to construct political orders where individuals with their beliefs can live together in peace. Laiklik is a constitutional principle providing for state's impartiality toward religion and beliefs, designating the state's legal status [*hukuki konumu*], duties, and powers and its limits. The laic state does not have an official religion, it has an equidistant stance toward religion and beliefs, it provides a legal order where individuals can freely learn and live their religious beliefs in peace, it ensures freedom of religion and conscience. The separation of state and religion is necessary for the freedom of religion and conscience but also necessary for protecting religion from political interventions and for continuing its independence. Laic states protect those who profess different religious beliefs or who do not profess a belief. In fact, the justification for article 2 [declaring Turkey a laic state] reads, "Laiklik never means a lack of religion [*dinsizlik*], it means that each individual can profess and practice the belief and sect [*mezhep*] they want, and not be treated differently from other citizens because of his/her religious beliefs." The state has to take the necessary precautions for preparing the environment for the realization of the freedom of religion and conscience. Laiklik in this meaning obliges the state with positive and negative responsibilities. Negative responsibility requires that the state does not embrace officially any religion or belief and does not interfere in individuals' freedom of religion and conscience unless there are necessary reasons. Positive responsibility, on the other hand, requires that the state remove the barriers in front of freedom of religion and conscience, that it provides for the appropriate environment and necessary opportunities for individuals to be able to live as they believe. The source of the positive responsibilities laiklik obliged the state are articles 5 and 24. (65–66)

Then the court decision turned to an evaluation of the October 9, 2007, judgment of the European Court of Human Rights on Turkey and underscored that in this judgment the ECHR also had a comparative evaluation of law, and that many European countries have some form of religion courses in the curriculum (66). The decision evaluated the act of putting in the curriculum an optional course on the life of the Prophet and the Koran. The evaluation started out in light of the definitions of laiklik articulated previously and then rested its back on the law of majorities and an interpretation of constitutional article 10 on equality before the law in the form of an Aristotelian notion of "proportional equality":

> On the other hand, the preference of the lawmaker for the title of "The Life of Our (Hz.) Prophet" does not necessarily result in the establishment of a relation of belonging between the religion of Islam and the state. Before anything else, what is introduced with the new rule is an optional course based on choice. The course addresses the students who will opt for it. Therefore the name of the course has been determined by taking into consideration those who will choose it. Second, as in the case of the other optional course, the "Kur'an" course where the exalting adjective "Kerim" has been added, the use of the title "The Life of Hz. Prophet," rather than specifying a belonging, expresses respect for the sacred [items] of the members of that religion. . . . Last but not least, viewed in its totality, it cannot be said that the principle of laiklik in Turkey absolutely excludes an institutional relation between the state and the religion of Islam at the constitutional level and in application. Although the constitution does not include an official religion, it does preconceive official mechanisms toward meeting the needs, such as belief, practice, and education, of the majority religion via constitutional article 136 [the Directorate of Religious Affairs]. . . . In conclusion, the constitution sees religious services as a social need and obliges the state to meet these needs. (66–67) . . .

In the petition for the case [initiated by the CHP], it is claimed that constitutional article 10 on equality before the law has been violated, because the rule in question gives place to an optional course from which only members of one religion can benefit and leaves optional courses regarding members of other religions to the discretion of the ministry. The principle of equality protected in the constitution requires that similar rules are applied to those in a similar situation; different rules are applied to those in different situations. A law on the teaching of optional courses comprising knowledge on the religion of Islam's—of which the majority of society is a member of—holy book Koran and the life of the Prophet does not mean that other holy books and the life of other prophets cannot be taught as optional courses. (67)

"In the case of an emerging social need in this direction, there is no legal impediment to the Ministry" (67) in establishing such courses. The decision continues with a blatant claim, normalizing the law of majorities: "Education and instruction in religion in almost all countries give a weight to the dominant religion and provide some priorities to the members of the majority religion against other religions." It continued with references to European Court of Human Rights decisions on Italy and Turkey.

Among the judges who opposed the decision, two of them explicitly addressed the optional courses and underlined overall a violation of equality before the law and the principle of impartiality. I quote one at length:

As the state cannot have a religion, it also cannot have a prophet. . . . Providing a legal guarantee only for courses for the learning of the religion of Islam among optional courses will lead to discrimination among citizens belonging to different religions and obviously damages the principle of laiklik. . . . That the great majority of society belongs to the religion of Islam cannot be accepted as a reason for the discrimination put in practice. Contemporary democracies are not majoritarian [çoğunlukçu] but pluralist [çoğulcu] regimes. In benefiting from the rights recognized by the constitution, one cannot differentiate between citizens according to whether they constitute the majority or not. . . . Moreover, the case by case decisions of the European Court of Human Rights on countries showing differences in the place and effect of religion in society cannot be generalized to explicate a content for the principle of laiklik. (85–86)

On February 22, 2013, Erdoğan publicly stated that Alevilik is not a religion but a culture.[162] These institutional changes in education were followed by a bill guaranteeing freedom to wear the headscarf in all state institutions in September 2014. The conceptual and practical contradictions produced by the Constitutional Court decisions were continued in the discussion and decisions of the Nineteenth National Education Congress on December 2–5, 2014, suggesting an advance in religion infrastructure without any "principled distance."[163] The congress discussed religion courses for first, second, and third graders as well as for kindergarteners. It finally dismissed the latter but agreed on the former.[164]

This chapter has offered analyses of significant moments during the AKP's terms in government, paying attention to primary sources on the specific arguments advanced for and against the institutional changes on the relation between state and religion in question. The chapter has shown that AKP does not stand for some kind of a liberal alternative to the Kemalist establishment. The liberal arguments were rather to be found among societal organizations and some of the opposition in parliament. The AKP stuck to the "law of majorities" and "utility of religion" frameworks in its institutional politics, which were the common marks of most of the various Kemalist institutionalist positions covered in chapter 5, oscillating between anticlericalism and what I called "state-civil religionism." However, these Kemalist institutionalist positions also had in common abstracting Islam as culture from Islam as such, although they almost never reached a level of abstraction as far as religion as a general category; that is, a category that does not designate any particular religious tradition as the socialists in the Third French Republic did. Rather, the Kemalist institutional positions fell sometimes close to those of *Républicains opportunistes* and other times to those of *Républicains progressistes* of the Third French Republic. The crucial differences in AKP institutional politics of religion from the Kemalist lines is that AKP de-abstracted and pushed toward Islam as such from Islam as culture, and it worked against the institutional differentiation of spheres, deepening state-civil religionism by "layering" existing institutions; and all that by often mobilizing the idea of a Europe strong in religious institutions or a Europe diverse enough to accommodate the Turkish version of state-religion relations, or the threat of missionaries from Europe. Their position shares quite a bit with the political Catholics of the Third French Republic covered in chapter 3. The party's most loudly advertised democratic projects took place either in the context of violation of basic human and constitutional rights or through made-up procedures and violation of existing procedures that aimed to enhance the party's hegemony.

Conclusion

In this book I have built a critique of sociocultural and ideational approaches by mapping out the political field of potential institutional change where ideas of secularism and religion and sociology were discussed and negotiated comparatively. I have resituated Kemalist laicism vis-à-vis the different types of Republicanism in the French Third Republic, the Justice and Development Party (AKP) vis-à-vis Kemalist laicism, and the Union for a Popular Movement (UMP) and AKP vis-à-vis each other and the French Third Republic. The book also opens up further debates on the limits of secular politics when it locates some of the antisecularist arguments of the political Catholics in the French Third Republic presented in defense of alternative conceptualizations of secularism in contemporary France and Turkey.

The comparisons I have offered not only recast some of the research questions specific to Turkey and France but also address larger theoretical discussions on the question of *traveling*. The hermeneutical turns *claimed* under the multiple modernities approach once more recast differences across countries as matters of *(re)interpretation*, or struggles within countries over institutional relations between the state and religions as struggles between different *understandings* of secularism. First, I have shown that not all the arguments in debates on the institutional relations between the state and religions are arguments from secularism. That is precisely why the struggles in France and Turkey cannot be reduced to a struggle over the *meaning* of secularism. There are also arguments on the importance of having a religious society, and some of the actors who advance such arguments have made the effort to convincingly or unconvincingly redefine secularism; others have not made an effort. I found the latter group only among the political Catholics in Third Republic France and among AKP parliamentarians in Turkey.

Second, the multiple modernities approach in fact calls for a focus on interaction and relaxing the assumption of the boundedness of each single modernity project. I have shown that interaction and unboundedness are the rule rather than the exception when one takes a close look at moments of potential institutional change, even in the case of France, which holds the position of one of the most self-referential cases in the academic literature. With such a microlevel focus on the politics of institutions, it also becomes quite impossible to stick to a Hegelian-inspired "imaginaries" or Weberian "Verstehen" approach. The sovereignty these approaches attribute to ideas simply becomes unconvincing in the face of the lack of isomorphism between ideas and institutions—the coterminous and diachronic competing claims on ideas of secularism and religion prevailing in the political field of institution making.

Third, this book shows that in all these moments of struggle in France and Turkey, three political ends were present in the numerous arguments—from or against secularism—in defense of institutions: mobilizing religion, demobilizing religion, or institutional neutrality; in other words, three distinct institutionalist political currents: civil religionism, anticlericalism, and liberalism.

This is not to say that ideas are unimportant. In a book with such meticulous documentation of political arguments, such a statement would be a contradiction in terms. But I want to underscore that a hermeneutical turn in itself suffices neither to constitute a critique of the teleology of modernization theory nor to pin down and account for trajectories of secularism. A quick look at Daniel Lerner's *The Passing of Traditional Society: Modernizing the Middle East*, the classic statement of modernization theory after the Second World War, shows that Lerner had as his central claim a focus on meaning and self-descriptions against macroeconomic perspectives. Lerner was taking such a hermeneutical turn in response to the Huntingtonians of his time, modernist-orientalists who would take a macro(economic) perspective and argue that the Middle East could not modernize. Although the book's argument relies on survey data, its main thesis has been conveyed by the more ethnographical part of the book on the Grocer and the Chief from a Turkish village. There is no doubt that Lerner's historicism[1] put the Middle East in the "waiting room of history";[2] that is, the Middle East had to be patient and acknowledge the longtime historical development the West passed through to reach its current stage. In *Provincializing Europe: Post-Colonial Thought and Historical Difference*, Dipesh Chakrabarty precisely addresses "the divide between analytical and hermeneutic tradition in the social sciences,"[3] what he calls the "breach" between "secular narratives" and "the politics of human belonging and diversity." A "breach" of the same sort is precisely what lies at the backbone of Lerner's book as well. Against "secular narratives" that described the Middle East in what it lacks vis-à-vis the secular West, Lerner claimed a focus on "transformation of lifeways," "on the personal meaning of social change," on "their habits and preferences with regard to the mass media of communication, their attitudes toward foreigners and foreign countries, their general outlook on life, as well as certain features of their daily life."[4] It is stunning to note how close some of his language is to the "multiple modernity" discussion of today.[5] His analytical framework of modernity was "a sharper conception of modernity as a behavioral system, a comprehensive interlocking of life ways,"[6] and posed explicitly as a critique of macrosociological and macroeconomic approaches. And David Riesman's remark in his introduction to Lerner's book that "Mr. Lerner shows that every encounter with another people is a confrontation with ourselves"[7] recalls Clifford Geertz's statement that "all ethnography is part philosophy, and a good deal of the rest is confession,"[8] though one can hardly mistake Lerner for Geertz.

Despite his orientalist descriptions—such as "Anatolian black eyes," "strangling in the throat that Anatolian talk sometimes has," Lerner's narratives of the Chief and the Grocer of a village near the capital city of Ankara were the parts of the book where he actually made an attempt to lay out the world of meaning he encountered. The conceptual world of the Grocer (*Bakkal*) and the Chief (*Muhtar*), underdeveloped as they are, still leaves a snail trail to follow with regard to rethinking what actually constitutes a methodological shortcoming of this book.

The shortcoming is not as simple as some hermeneutical critique of modernization theory would like to have it; namely, that Lerner's conceptual-analytical world straightjackets the Turkish experience, or, in Charles Taylor's distinction, it is an "acultural" rather than a "cultural" look at modernity.[9] Lerner had covered himself better in this respect than some are willing to look closely at and admit. He located modernization not in macro-socioeconomic processes imposed by an analytical framework defined by him on the Middle East but in the world of meaning expressed by persons in the Middle East.[10] In other words, there were modernist "desires" in the Middle East, and therefore what was going on there could still be understood in reference to the Western model. This sounds very close to the multiple modernities approach. The goal of Lerner's book, he explains, is "to locate these diverse figures in the modernizing Middle East" who have received the modernist virus.[11] These "diverse figures," if I may, have "double-consciousness,"[12] and they have stepped out of the *isomorphic* mode. They permanently negotiate as a way of being the relation between the "modern" and conflicting contextual ways of life. Lerner focuses on behavior and searches for the "desiring" and "mobile personality." His question was again that of "traveling": can modernity (equated with secularism) travel from the West to the Middle East? The answer was yes, through the "diverse figures," double-conscious, "empathetic," mobile, and desiring modern Middle Eastern. The "breach" between the modernist narrative and human diversity is "mended" in Lerner by finding evidence for the modernist-secular narrative in the self-descriptions of the Middle Eastern. Such "mending" was not hermeneutically insensitive—although it was limited given Lerner's ethnographical skills and his frequent use of intermediaries—but, more important, it completely overlooked the political sphere.

The interesting point is that such overlooking of the political is also present in some of the critiques of Lerner's modernist teleology; namely, Nilüfer Göle's *The Forbidden Modern: Civilization and Veiling*, the book that Shmuel Eisenstadt relies on in designating Turkey as an example of his multiple modernities approach. Göle cites Lerner's book when she remarks: "The phenomenon of modernization is generally assumed to follow a unilateral path of evolution different from that of traditional attachments and religious belief systems, toward the transition to modern society."[13] Writing at the dawn of the "clash of civilizations" orientalist wave, Göle criticizes the taking of veiling as the manifestation of a total project called Islamism, against another total project called modernity, and calls for attention to context and how specific persons elaborate their life and veiling. Göle "argues that contemporary Islamism cannot be adequately understood in isolation from the local constructs of Western modernity in which women have an edificatory role."[14] *The Forbidden Modern* puts forth a critique of the modernity-Islam distinction presented as mutually exclusive by precisely giving a voice to veiled university students through interviews. The comparisons, deliberations, negotiations, and synthesis between often mutually exclusively placed worldviews of modernity and Islam that these women articulate, in other words these "diverse figures," double-conscious women, not only question established boundaries of modernity and Islam but also put the agency of women on the social map.[15] The interesting point of comparison is that the answer in both Lerner and Göle is these diverse and complex figures who live change as the normal state of affairs and whose self-descriptions disrupt some of the analytical distinctions erected in politics and academics. This line of critique is very common in postcolonial studies and literature, finding some of its best expressions in novels such as Salman Rushdie's *Midnight's Children*.[16] Yet what is forgone in both accounts of traveling, which run self-descriptions against macro accounts, is the political sphere.

The analytical distinction present in almost all research questions on secularism—rigid forms of secularism versus the challenges of diversity— also requires further critical reflection. This book has taken a step in that direction. Many scholars labeling France and Turkey as ardent followers of comprehensive doctrines, and laïcité and laiklik as religion, would reduce Third Republic France and Kemalist laicism to Combisme and ignore the main architects of the *Loi du 9 Décembre 1905*, the socialists that chapter 3 argues aimed in the direction of posing a general doctrine against comprehensive doctrines, and would overlook the similarities between Kemalist laicism and Républicains opportunistes and Républicains progressistes. It does not suffice to leave laïcité as an amorphous object, a field of some sort, a "narrative framework"[17] from which each political actor in contemporary public debates remembers according to his or her politics. This kind of relativism ignores the powerful arguments from "neutrality" and "diversity" of the socialists in the parliament during the deliberation of the separation law of 1905 as well as Républicains opportunistes in defending the March 28, 1882, law on obligatory primary education. Diversity was not a challenge to the institutions of laïcité in the Third French Republic; to the contrary, it was a constitutive premise of these institutions. And "neutrality" in institutions was not just another comprehensive doctrine incomprehensible to those who did not endorse it. Even Albert de Mun, the political Catholic leader, understood it quite well—he just did not "believe at all in the neutral state in matters of religion."[18]

The exclusive focus on the headscarf question—a question of accommodating behavior—in describing and comparatively mapping political fields across countries and through time has truly misguided the assessment of comparative trajectories of secularism and contributed to refusing any autonomy to the political field of struggle over institutions from a question of behavior. For instance, it is no coincidence that Ahmet Kuru and many others who focus on the headscarf question and put the challenge of a moderate political Islam to Kemalism as a liberal challenge in the Turkish context miss the debate between Jean Baubérot and Jean-Paul Willaime, and also miss that some public intellectuals who disagree on the headscarf ban in fact agree on the teaching of religious facts in the public school curriculum in the French context. Moreover, by mapping political Islamists in the Turkish context onto anti-Combistes in the French context without further qualification, they risk taking political Islamists in the Turkish context for French socialists in the Third Republic.

In all the moments of struggle in France and Turkey addressed here, three political ends were behind the numerous arguments from or against secularism: mobilizing religion, demobilizing religion, and institutional neutrality. However, I have also shown the lack of isomorphism between the set of institutional options and these political ends; both institutional separation and state participation in religious affairs can serve the purposes of mobilizing or demobilizing religion depending on the context and how the particular terms of the institutional arrangement are negotiated. The close attention given to documenting the arguments for institutions showed that the struggle over institutions was a multidimensional, transnational struggle of evaluating institutions in other countries. This book has offered a unique map of the references Europe (France in particular) receives in Turkey, the United States received in the French Third Republic, and Turkey receives in contemporary France. The undeniable presence of comparisons as part of the institutional politics of secularism is better described as "mutually interactional modernities" rather than multiple modernities. Modernity does not necessarily multiply out of one historical origin through reinterpretations but rather through mutual interactions. The interpretation of other countries varies across competing political interests and also changes through history with changing political interests; therefore one cannot really talk about "being modeled after" but perhaps rather of taking as a reference point and as a battlefield. One striking thread in both France and Turkey is the struggle over sociological and institutional interpretations of secularism in other countries. The referenced countries partially frame the discussions and set the battleground. This may seem like stating the obvious; however, the issue is theoretically much more significant than it sounds. One important point is that through the "bounded" take on multiple modernities, a post-Huntingtonian culturalism sneaks back in, while the multiple modernities approach was precisely meant to take us in another direction. Focusing on the interactions reveals an unbounded transnational space of discussion filtered through contextual political ends. Talal Asad once advanced a critique of the argument for multiplicity in Western modernity:

> Many critics have now taken the position that "modernity" (in which *secularism* is centrally located) is not a verifiable project. They argue that contemporary societies are heterogeneous and overlapping, that they contain disparate, even discordant, circumstances, origins, values, and so forth. My response is that these critics are right (although the heuristic value of looking for necessary connections should not be forgotten) but that what we have here is not a simple cognitive error. *Assumptions about the integrated character of "modernity" are themselves part of practical and political reality. They direct the way in which people committed to it act in critical situations. These people aim at "modernity," and expect others (especially in the non-West) to do so too. This fact doesn't disappear when we simply point out that the "West" isn't an integrated totality, that many people in the West contest secularism or interpret it in different ways, that the modern epoch in the West has witnessed many arguments and several irreconcilable aspirations.*[19]

As much as I find Asad's intervention very important, the material of this book first shows that the multiplicity of Western modernity is part of the narrative of Turkey's "aim at modernity." The moments this book documents have various non-European images of European secularity (reversing a title from an earlier work by Asad[20]). And the declining of references to European secularisms in the past years among AKP parliamentarians is also a politically significant development, raising questions on whether European secularism is ceasing to be the battleground or not. Moreover, the Third French Republic struggles over the interpretation of the United States, and some references to Turkey in contemporary discussions in France, just add other twists to the debate and suggest "mutually interacting modernities" as an alternative approach. This, I would say, is a novel way of *Provincialing Europe*[21] as well as Turkey.

The book has fleshed out state-civil religionism—state mobilization of religion as the cement of society—which is not only left out of other comparisons of the two countries but also largely ignored in the emerging literature on secularism and religion. Focusing on state-civil religionism is important for a fuller account of the institutional outcomes in France and Turkey, but it is also theoretically significant because it has its own way of articulating the boundary between the secular and the religious. This articulation at times resonates with antisecular movements as well, and by focusing on them it becomes possible to investigate the limits of secular politics. State-civil religionists emerged from the ranks of anticlericals, as was the case with Kemalism in late 1940s and with Républicains progressistes at the end of the nineteenth century in France, but they could also emerge from ex-monarchists, as was the case with political Catholics at the end of the nineteenth century in France. At different degrees and with different arguments, they both demanded the state play a role in maintaining or promoting religion (a majority religion only or pulling minority religions along) as the cement of society as an end in itself or as a means to various ends of governance. In the case of these actors, studying the anomaly of promoting religion in the name of secularism takes on a new significance. How such political actors negotiate this position and what kind of new meanings they create to render the anomaly "normal" also become part of the politics over secularism. These pragmatic utilitarians are a transition point, a vessel for some religious actors. This path is visible in Turkish politics, especially contemporary Turkish politics, and with lesser intensity in contemporary France, and this proactive utilitarian approach to institutions is precisely what ended in the separation of churches and state in the Third French Republic. The political fields laid out also show that the current literature on secularism and religion has still not broken with the assumption that the fields of the "secular" and the "religious" are autonomous. It is precisely for this reason that the state-civil religionists this book has empirically located at multiple occasions in the political field in France and Turkey fall between the cracks or are reduced to "anomalies." Particularly, the utilitarian approach to religion that some of these political actors take exposes religion as less than an autonomous field and rather as a battlefield.

State-civil religionism also calls for a critical reflection on the popular distinction between moderate and radical religion. This distinction often has been articulated according to the content of religious tradition, its theology, practices, and so forth. Instead, this book's findings call for an attention to the level—society, state institutions, constitution—at which this content has been expressed, and to what I call the direction of abstraction vis-à-vis religion in general, rather than to the specific religious tradition in question. For instance, when the Turkish military officers who instituted required Sunni religion courses in the public school curriculum with the constitution of 1982 in the name of secularism, the argument in the National Security Council was one of abstracting religion as culture from religion as such on grounds of utility of religion as a cement of society. As in Third Republic France, where Henri de Lacretelle was abstracting a general notion of religion from religion as such and aiming to "improve the moral physiognomy of the republic" for obedience and war, and Agénor Bardoux for fighting "an excess of taste for material well-being," the makers of the 1982 constitution were abstracting a general notion of religion from religion as such in order to fight the left, whereas Erdoğan's AKP was de-abstracting from religion as a general notion or as culture, to the specific religious tradition in its practices and theology.

I have shown that the direction of these processes of abstraction is a significant variable in assessing (de)secularization and the difference between radical and moderate religion and radical and moderate secularism. The institutional level at which religion finds an expression is more important than its theology in assessing what is moderate and radical, for this level is directly related to the one common element of democracy and secularism pronounced across the board: differentiation of spheres. The Turkish military put religion as culture in the 1982 constitution. Fethullah Gülen—for some time praised as a leader of moderate Islam—commended the military at that time and on their act of writing into the constitution a compulsory course on religion as culture in public schools is reported to have remarked, "Revolutionaries [the military] did what republican governments could not do."[22] On March 30, 2012, when the AKP attempted to change the education system and supplement the already existing required courses on "culture" of religion with two optional courses on religion "as such," their precise argument was that the existing courses were not religion but merely culture. There was almost no or minimal reference to secularism in the parliamentary debates; only when the Constitutional Court received a case filed by the CHP did they defend the new courses, importing from France Nicolas Sarkozy's *laïcité positive*. Which one of these positions deserves to be called moderate?

Notes

Preface

1. Antonio Gramsci, *Selections from the Prison Notebooks*, ed. and trans. Quintin Hoare and Geoffrey Nowell Smith (New York: International Publishers, 1971), 243–44.
2. Niccolò Machiavelli, *Selected Political Writings* (Indianapolis: Hackett, 1994).
3. Max Weber, *The Protestant Ethic and the Spirit of Capitalism*, trans. Talcott Parons (New York: Routledge, 1992 [1930]), 30, italics in original, bolding mine.
4. Charles Taylor, *Modern Social Imaginaries* (Durham, N.C.: Duke University Press, 2004).
5. Charles Taylor, "Interpretation and the Sciences of Man," in *Interpretive Social Science: A Second Look*, ed. Paul Rabinow and William M. Sullivan (Berkeley: University of California Press, 1987). This article was first published in 1971 in the journal *Review of Metaphysics*.
6. Judith N. Shklar, "Squaring the Hermeneutical Circle," *Social Research* 53, no. 3 (1986): 662, 677.

1. Traveling Through Analytical and Hermeneutical Approaches

1. Charles Taylor, "Modes of Secularism," in *Secularism and Its Critics*, ed. Rajeev Bhargava (New Delhi: Oxford University Press, 1998), 31.

2. Alfred Stepan, "The Multiple Secularisms of Modern Democratic and Non-Democratic Regimes," in *Rethinking Secularism*, ed. Craig Calhoun, Mark Juergensmeyer, and Jonathan VanAntwerpen (Oxford: Oxford University Press, 2011).
3. Dilip Parameshwar Gaonkar, "On Alternative Modernities," in "Alter/Native Modernities," ed. Dilip Parameshwar Gaonkar, special issue, *Public Culture* 11, no. 1 (1999): 1–18.
4. José Casanova, "A Secular Age Dawn or Twilight," in *Varieties of Secularism in a Secular Age*, ed. M. Warner, J. VanAntwerpen, and C. Calhoun (Cambridge, Mass.: Harvard University Press, 2010); José Casanova, "Public Religions Revisited," in *Religion Beyond the Concept*, ed. Hent de Vries (New York: Fordham University Press, 2008); Peter J. Katzenstein, "Multiple Modernities as Limits to Secular Europeanization," in *Religion in an Expanding Europe*, ed. Timothy A. Byrnes and Peter J. Katzenstein (Cambridge: Cambridge University Press, 2006); Shmuel Noah Eisenstadt, "Multiple Modernities," *Daedalus* 129, no. 1 (2000): 1–29; Ira Katznelson and Gareth Stedman Jones, "Introduction: Multiple Secularities," in *Religion and the Political Imagination*, ed. Ira Katznelson and Gareth Stedman Jones (Cambridge: Cambridge University Press, 2010).
5. For an overview of the literature, see José Casanova, *Public Religions in the Modern World* (Chicago: University of Chicago Press, 1994).
6. Samuel Huntington, *The Clash of Civilizations: Remaking of the World Order* (New York: Touchstone, 1997).
7. Francis Fukuyama, "The End of History?," *National Interest* (Summer 1989): 3–18.
8. Casanova, *Public Religions*.
9. Karl Marx, *The 18th Brumaire of Louis Bonaparte* (New York: International Publishers, 1998), 43.
10. Nancy L. Rosenblum, ed., *Obligations of Citizenship and Demands of Faith: Religious Accommodation in Pluralist Societies* (Princeton, N.J.: Princeton University Press, 2000); Jürgen Habermas, "Religion in the Public Sphere," *European Journal of Philosophy* 14, no. 1 (2006): 1–25.
11. Jean Michel Gaillard in *Jules Ferry* (Paris: Fayard, 1989), 449, quotes Jules Ferry, the architect of the laic education laws, declaring in parliament in 1881: "We wanted the anti-clerical struggle, but never, never the anti-religious struggle." George Jacob Holyoake, the Englishmen who coined the term "secularism," also conceptualized it with a distance to atheism. See George Jacob Holyoake and Charles Albert Watts, *English Secularism and the Progress of Society: Two Papers Read at the Brussels International Congress . . . 1880* (London, 1880), 2.
12. *Alliance of Civilizations: Report of the High-Level Group* (New York: United Nations, November 13, 2006).
13. For univocal, see Huntington, *Clash of Civilizations*; for multivocal, see Alfred Stepan, "The World's Religious Systems and Democracy: Crafting the 'Twin Tolerations,'" in *Arguing Comparative Politics* (Oxford: Oxford University Press, 2001).

14. Saba Mahmood, "Secularism, Hermeneutics, and Empire: The Politics of Islamic Reformation," *Public Culture* 18, no. 2 (2006): 329.
15. Talal Asad, *Formations of the Secular: Christianity, Islam, Modernity* (Stanford, Calif.: Stanford University Press, 2003); Talal Asad, *Genealogies of Religion: Discipline and Reasons of Power in Christianity and Islam* (London: Johns Hopkins University Press, 1993).
16. Hent de Vries and Lawrence E. Sullivan, eds., preface to *Political Theologies: Public Religions in a Post-Secular World* (New York: Fordham University Press, 2006); Hent de Vries, "Introduction: Before, Around and Beyond the Theologico-Political," in ibid.; Andrew Davison, *Secularism and Revivalism in Turkey: A Hermeneutical Approach* (New Haven, Conn.: Yale University Press, 1998).
17. John Locke, "A Letter Concerning Toleration," in *The Works of John Locke*, 9 vols., 12th ed. (London: Rivington, 1824), 5:26, http://oll.libertyfund.org/titles/764.
18. See John Stuart Mill, "Utility of Religion," in *Three Essays on Religion* (1874; New York: Prometheus Books, 1998), and the chapter on civil religion in Jean Jacques Rousseau, *The Social Contract* (1762; London: Penguin Books, 1968).
19. The institutional and sociological aspects of religion's power discussed by John Stuart Mill in the "Utility of Religion" do not receive sufficient attention. Mill underscores that religion is powerful because it has power over early education, and early education is powerful for being "early" and not for being religious.
20. Talal Asad does address this question. He poses the research question, "how does (religious) power create (religious) truth?" in "The Construction of Religion as an Anthropological Category," in *Genealogies of Religion*, 33.
21. Charles Taylor, "Why We Need a Radical Redefinition of Secularism," in *The Power of Religion in the Public Sphere*, ed. Eduardo Mendieta and Jonathan VanAntwerpen (New York: Columbia University Press, 2011), 53.
22. For an overview see Casanova, *Public Religions*.
23. Robert Audi, "The Separation of Church and State and Obligations of Citizenship," *Philosophy and Public Affairs* 18, no. 3 (1989): 259–96; Bhargava, *Secularism and Its Critics*; Taha Parla and Andrew Davison, "Secularism and Laicism in Turkey," in *Secularisms*, ed. Janet R. Jacobsen and Ann Pellegrini (Durham, N.C.: Duke University Press, 2008).
24. Asad, *Formations of the Secular*; Yael Navaro-Yashin, *Faces of the State: Secularism and Public Life in Turkey* (Princeton, N.J.: Princeton University Press, 2002); Taha Parla and Andrew Davison, *Corporatist Ideology in Kemalist Turkey* (Syracuse, N.Y.: Syracuse University Press, 2005); İştar Tarhanlı, *Müslüman Toplum, "Laik" Devlet: Türkiye'de Diyanet İşleri Başkanlığı* [Muslim society, "laik" state: Directorate of Religious Affairs in Turkey] (Istanbul: Afa Yayınları, 1993); Stepan, "Multiple Secularisms"; Stepan, "The World's Religious Systems"; Ahmet T. Kuru and Alfred Stepan, eds., *Democracy, Islam, and Secularism in Turkey* (New York: Columbia

University Press, 2012); Hans Joas and Klaus Wiegandt, eds., *Secularization and the World Religions* (Liverpool: Liverpool University Press, 2009).

25. Taylor, "Modes of Secularism," 37. See also Charles Taylor, "Can Secularism Travel?," in *Beyond the Secular West*, ed. Akeel Bilgrami (New York: Columbia University Press, 2016). The question of traveling is also the benchmark question addressed by those aiming to write postorientalist histories, although the focus is not necessarily secularism. See Partha Chatterjee, *Nationalist Thought and the Colonial World: A Derivative Discourse?* (Minneapolis: University of Minnesota Press, 1986), and *The Nation and Its Fragments: Colonial and Postcolonial Histories* (Princeton, N.J.: Princeton University Press, 1992). See also Gyan Prakash, "Writing Post-Orientalist Histories of the Third World: Perspectives from Indian Historiography," *Comparative Studies in Society and History* 32, no. 2 (1990): 383–408.

26. Paul Rabinow and William M. Sullivan, eds., *Interpretive Social Science: A Second Look* (Berkeley: University of California Press, 1987); Davison, *Secularism and Religious Revivalism in Turkey*; Eisenstadt, "Multiple Modernities"; Shmuel Noah Eisenstadt and Wolfgang Schluchter, "Introduction: Paths to Early Modernities—a Comparative View," *Daedalus* 127, no. 3 (1998): 1–18.

27. Charles Taylor, *A Secular Age* (Cambridge, Mass.: Belknap Press of Harvard University Press, 2007), 22.

28. Daniel Lerner, *The Passing of Traditional Society: Modernizing the Middle East* (Glencoe, Ill.: Free Press, 1958); Samuel Huntington, "The Clash of Civilizations?," *Foreign Affairs* 72, no. 3 (1993): 22–49.

29. Nilüfer Göle, *The Forbidden Modern: Civilization and Veiling* (Ann Arbor: University of Michigan Press, 1996).

30. Just some examples are Geoffrey Brahm Levey and Tariq Modood, eds., *Secularism, Religion and Multicultural Citizenship* (Cambridge: Cambridge University Press, 2008); Jocelyn Maclure and Charles Taylor, *Secularism and Freedom of Conscience* (Cambridge, Mass.: Harvard University Press).

31. Ahmet T. Kuru, *Secularism and State Policies Toward Religion: The United States, France, and Turkey* (Cambridge: Cambridge University Press, 2009).

32. Jon Elster, *Nuts and Bolts for the Social Sciences* (Cambridge: Cambridge University Press, 1989).

33. Clifford Geertz, "Ritual and Social Change: A Javanese Example," *American Anthropologist* 59, no. 1 (1957): 32–54.

34. Peter van der Veer, *Imperial Encounters: Religion and Modernity in India and Britain* (Princeton, N.J.: Princeton University Press, 2001).

35. Giovanni Capoccia and R. Daniel Kelemen, "The Study of Critical Junctures: Theory, Narrative, and Counterfactuals in Historical Institutionalism," *World Politics* 59, no. 3 (2007): 341–69.

36. For "institutional layering," see Kathleen Thelen, "How Institutions Evolve: Insights From Comparative Historical Research," in *Comparative Historical*

Analysis in the Social Sciences, ed. James Mahoney and Dietrich Rueschemeyer (Cambridge: Cambridge University Press, 2006), 226.
37. Alevis are an Islamic group in Turkey. The majority of Muslims in Turkey are Sunni. The population statistics on the Alevis are highly politicized, but they run between twelve and twenty million. The total population in Turkey is more than seventy-eight million.

2. Accounting for Institutional Outcomes and Trajectories

1. Charles Taylor, "Modes of Secularism," in *Secularism and Its Critics*, ed. Rajeev Bhargava (New Delhi: Oxford University Press, 1998); Charles Taylor, "Can Secularism Travel?," in *Beyond the Secular West*, ed. Akeel Bilgrami (New York: Columbia University Press, 2016); Charles Taylor, "Two Theories of Modernity," *Public Culture* 11, no. 1 (1999); Charles Taylor, *Modern Social Imaginaries* (Durham, N.C.: Duke University Press, 2004), 1–2, 195; Charles Taylor, *A Secular Age* (Cambridge. Mass.: Belknap Press of Harvard University Press, 2007).
2. Charles Taylor, "Interpretation and the Sciences of Man," in *Interpretive Social Science: A Second Look*, ed. Paul Rabinow and William M. Sullivan (Berkeley: University of California Press, 1987).
3. Charles Taylor, "The Hermeneutics of Conflict," in *Meaning and Context: Quentin Skinner and His Critics*, ed. James Tully (Princeton, N.J.: Princeton University Press, 1988), 221, 224.
4. Ibid., 226, 227.
5. Max Weber, *The Protestant Ethic and the Spirit of Capitalism*, trans. Talcott Parsons (1930; New York: Routledge, 1992), 30; italics in original, bolding mine.
6. Kathleen Thelen, "How Institutions Evolve: Insights from Comparative Historical Research," in *Comparative Historical Analysis in the Social Sciences*, ed. James Mahoney and Dietrich Rueschemeyer (Cambridge: Cambridge University Press, 2006); James Mahoney and Kathleen Thelen, "A Theory of Gradual Institutional Change," in *Explaining Institutional Change: Ambiguity, Agency, and Power*, ed. James Mahoney and Kathleen Thelen (New York: Cambridge University Press, 2009).
7. Clifford Geertz, "Ritual and Social Change: A Javanese Example," *American Anthropologist* 59, no. 1 (1957): 33; italics mine.
8. Charles Taylor, *Dilemmas and Connections: Selected Essays* (Cambridge, Mass.: Harvard University Press, 2011), 306.
9. For a detailed empirical analysis of this subject, see Sandrine Bertaux, "Towards the Unmaking of the French Mainstream: The Empirical Turn in Immigrant Assimilation and the Making of Frenchness," *Journal of Ethnic and Migration Studies* 42, no. 9 (2016): 1496–1512.

10. In Nicolas Sarkozy, *La République, les religions, l'espérance* (Paris: Cerf, 2004), 16, Sarkozy explained: "I believe in *laïcité positive*, that is to say a *laïcité* which guarantees the right to live one's religion like a fundamental personal right. *Laïcité* isn't the enemy of religions. Quite the contrary. *Laïcité* is the guarantee for each to be able to believe and live his/her faith."
11. John R. Bowen, *Why the French Don't Like Headscarves: Islam, the State, and Public Space* (Princeton, N.J.: Princeton University Press, 2007), 3, 32, 33, 156, 249.
12. Joan W. Scott, *The Politics of the Veil* (Princeton, N.J.: Princeton University Press, 2007), 13.
13. See Cécile Laborde, "Secular Philosophy and Muslim Headscarves in Schools," *Journal of Political Philososphy* 13, no. 3 (2005): 305–29; Riva Kastoryano, "Religion and Incorporation: Islam in France and Germany," *International Migration Review* 38, no. 3 (2004): 1236.
14. For further discussion of the French exception thesis, see Jean Baubérot, "Laïcité, Laïcisation, Sécularisation," in *Pluralisme religieux et laïcité dans l'Union européenne*, ed. Alain Dierkens (Brussels: Editions de l'Universite de Bruxelles, 1994), 12.
15. M. Hakan Yavuz, "Introduction: The Role of the New Bourgeoisie in the Transformation of the Turkish Islamic Movement," in *The Emergence of a New Turkey: Democracy and the AK Parti*, ed. M. H. Yavuz (Salt Lake City: University of Utah Press, 2006), 2–3; M. Hakan Yavuz, *Secularism and Muslim Democracy* (Cambridge: Cambridge University Press, 2009); Ahmet T. Kuru, *Secularism and State Policies Toward Religion: The United States, France, and Turkey* (Cambridge: Cambridge University Press, 2009).
16. Thelen, "How Institutions Evolve," 226.
17. Kuru, in *Secularism and State Policies Toward Religion*, 164, offers the distinction between "passive" and "assertive" secularism to capture the precise terms of the struggle. "The Kemalists have defended assertive secularism, which aims to eliminate Islam, in particular, and religion, in general, from the public sphere, whereas the conservatives have tried to replace it with passive secularism, which allows the public visibility of religion."
18. Ibid., 11.
19. Ibid., 164.
20. The most recent reference to a parliamentary record in Kuru's bibliography is 1965. There is no analysis of parliamentary discussions during the interim of the AKP.
21. Ibid., 178–79.
22. Ibid., 229.
23. Régis Debray, "L'enseignement du fait religieux dans l'école laïque," Rapport à monsieur le ministre de l'éducation nationale (February 2002).
24. Jean-Paul Willaime, "Teaching Religious Issues in French Public Schools: From Abstentionist *Laïcité* to a Return of Religion to Public Education," in *Religion*

and *Education in Europe: Developments, Contexts, and Debates*, ed. Robert Jackson et al. (Berlin: Waxman Münster, 2007), 95.
25. Jean Baubérot, "Existe-t-il une religion civile républicaine?," *French Politics, Culture & Society* 25, no. 2 (2007): 6, 8.
26. Jean-Paul Willaime, "1905 et la pratique d'une laïcité de reconnaissance sociale des religions," 50e année, no. 129, La République ne reconnaît aucun culte, *Archives de Sciences Sociales des Religions* 129 (2005): 69.
27. Jean-Paul Willaime, "The Cultural Turn in the Sociology of Religion in France," *Sociology of Religion* 65, no. 4 (2004): 380; Jean Baubérot, "La laïcité, le chêne et le roseau," *Libération*, December 15, 2003.
28. Partha Chatterjee, "Secularism and Tolerance," in *Secularism and Its Critics*, ed. Rajeev Bhargava (New Delhi: Oxford University Press, 1998).
29. Binnaz Toprak, "The State, Politics and Religion in Turkey," in *State, Democracy and the Military: Turkey in the 1980s*, ed. Metin Heper and Ahmet Evin (New York: De Gruyter, 1988); Erik J. Zurcher, *Turkey a Modern History* (New York: I. B. Tauris, 1997), 195. See also the literature review in Andrew Davison, *Secularism and Revivalism in Turkey: A Hermeneutical Approach* (New Haven, Conn.: Yale University Press, 1998).
30. Niyazi Berkes, *The Development of Secularism in Turkey* (Montreal: McGill University Press, 1964).
31. Hıfzı Veldet Velidedeoğlu, "Din, Halk ve Devlet" [Religion, people and the state], *Cumhuriyet*, April 16, 1952; Bülent Daver, *Türkiye Cumhuriyetinde Lâyiklik* [Laiklik in the Republic of Turkey] (Ankara: Son Havadis, 1955).
32. Çetin Özek, *Türkiye'de Laiklik: Gelişim ve Koruyucu Ceza Hükümleri* [Laiklik in Turkey: Development and the protective penal code] (Istanbul: Baha Matbaası, 1962).
33. Dilip Parameshwar Gaonkar, "On Alternative Modernities," in "Alter/Native Modernities," ed. Dilip Parameshwar Gaonkar, special issue, *Public Culture* 11, no. 1 (1999): 1–18.
34. Chatterjee, "Secularism and Tolerance," 358, 365.
35. Nikki R. Keddie, "Secularism and the State: Towards Clarity and Global Comparison," *New Left Review* 226 (November/December 1997), 21.
36. For instance, Charles Tilly has suggested that we compare past European societies with current non-European societies. This book actually does some of that, but that is not the gist of my point here.
37. Turkey State Ministry, *Alevi Workshop 2* (2009; Ankara: Devlet Bakanlığı, 2011), 169.
38. Turkey State Ministry. *Alevi Workshops*, 7 vols. (Ankara: Devlet Bakanlığı, 2011).
39. Deniz Ekşioğlu, "The Politics of Religion in the United States Federal Context: The Faith-Based Initiative," PhD dissertation, Boğaziçi University, 2011.

40. Saba Mahmood, "Secularism, Hermeneutics, and Empire: The Politics of Islamic Reformation," *Public Culture* 18, no. 2 (2006): 331; Cheryl Benard, *Civil and Democratic Islam: Partners, Resources, Strategies* (Pittsburgh: RAND Corporation, 2003).
41. Commission de réflexion sur l'application du principe de laïcité dans la République, *Rapport au président de la République* (Paris: La Documentation Française, 2003); Projet de loi: encadrant, en application du principe de *laïcité*, le port de signes ou de tenues manifestant une appartenance religieuse dans les écoles, collèges et lycées publics, Sénate 66; Ralph Grillo and Prakash Shah, "Reasons to Ban? The Anti-Burqa Movement in Western Europe," MMG Working Paper 12–05 (2012), 18.
42. Jocelyn Maclure and Charles Taylor, *Secularism and Freedom of Conscience* (Cambridge, Mass.: Harvard University Press), 41, 3, 29. See also Charles Taylor, "What Does Secularism Mean?" in *Dilemmas and Connections: Selected Essays* (Cambridge, Mass.: Harvard University Press, 2011), 314.
43. Charles Taylor, "Why We Need a Radical Redefinition of Secularism," in *The Power of Religion in the Public Sphere*, ed. Eduardo Mendieta and Jonathan VanAntwerpen (New York: Columbia University Press, 2011), 36. See also Charles Taylor, "What Is Secularism?" in *Secularism, Religion and Multicultural Citizenship*, ed. Geoffrey Brahm Levey and Tariq Modood (Cambridge: Cambridge University Press, 2008).
44. Maclure and Taylor, *Secularism and Freedom of Conscience*, 10–11.
45. John Rawls, *Political Liberalism* (New York: Columbia University Press, 1993), 13. "A moral conception is general if it applies to a wide range of subjects, and in the limit to all subjects universally. It is comprehensive when it includes conceptions of what is of value in human life, and ideals of personal character, as well as ideals of friendship and of familial and associational relationships, and much else that is to inform our conduct, and in the limit to our life as a whole. A conception is fully comprehensive if it covers all recognized values and virtues within one rather precisely articulated system; whereas a conception is only partially comprehensive when it comprises a number of, but by no means all, nonpolitical values and virtues and is rather loosely articulated. Many religious and philosophical doctrines aspire to be both general and comprehensive."
46. Maclure and Taylor, *Secularism and Freedom of Conscience*, 24–25, 27, 31.
47. Charles Taylor, "The Politics of Recognition," in *Multiculturalism*, ed. A. Gutmann (Princeton, N.J.: Princeton University Press, 1994).
48. Maclure and Taylor, *Secularism and Freedom of Conscience*, 67, 50, 51.
49. Ibid., 76, 79–80; Brian Barry, *Culture and Equality: An Egalitarian Critique of Multiculturalism* (Cambridge, Mass.: Harvard University Press, 2002); Brian Barry, "Second Thoughts—and Some First Thoughts Revived," in *Multiculturalism Reconsidered*, ed. Paul Kelly (Cambridge: Polity, 2002); Brian Barry, "The Muddles of Multiculturalism," *New Left Review* 8 (March/April 2001): 50.

50. Cécile Laborde, "Secular Philosophy and Muslim Headscarves in Schools," *Journal of Political Philosophy* 13, no 3 (2005): 314.
51. Barry, *Culture and Equality*, 54–62, 319–20.
52. Ibid., 62.
53. For an article that problematizes Barry's defense of the students donning religious symbols to attend school, see Steve On, "Brian Barry and the Headscarf Case in France," *Contemporary Political Theory* 5, no. 2 (2006): 176–92. On's is one of the few articles that notices Barry's defense of students donning religious symbols to attend school; yet he presents this defense as Barry's allowance for "exemptions" in his theory. On is right about some of the shortcomings in the way Barry deals with certain real cases in the book, and Barry is sometimes less than articulate on the relation of the general law and exemption. However, Barry's theory is about setting a normative framework for evaluating laws with three principles: freedom, equality, and generality. He therefore works with a distinction between laws-as-is and laws as they should be. And in the case of the headscarf, his point, as I understand it, is that a law on clothing is discriminatory and intervenes with the right to education. In other words, he does not call for an exemption but calls into question the existence of a law.
54. Will Kymlicka, *Liberalism, Community, and Culture* (Oxford: Oxford University Press, 1989); for further discussion see Murat Akan, "Contextualizing Multiculturalism," *Studies in Comparative International Development* 38, no. 2 (2003): 57–75; Will Kymlicka, *Multicultural Citizenship* (Oxford: Clarendon Press, 1995), chap. 8; Will Kymlicka and Magdalena Opalski, *Can Liberal Pluralism be Exported?: Western Political Theory and Ethnic Relations in Eastern Europe* (New York: Oxford University Press, 2001), 49.
55. This is different from "institutionalizing dualism" in Bruno Palier and Kathleen Thelen, "Institutionalizing Dualism: Complementarities and Change in France and Germany," *Politics and Society* 38, no. 1 (2010): 119–48.
56. Thelen, "How Institutions Evolve," 228.

3. The Institutional Politics of Laïcité in the French Third Republic

1. See entry in Pierre Larousse, *Grand dictionnaire universel du XIXe siècle: Français, historique, géographique, mythologique, bibliographique* (Paris: Administration du Grand Dictionnaire Universel, 1866–1877); see also Jean-Marie Mayeur and Madeleine Rebérioux, *The Third Republic from Its Origins to the Great War, 1871–1914* (Cambridge: Cambridge University Press, 1984), 72.
2. The Concordat was a bilateral agreement of the Catholic Church with a nation-state for managing the place of Catholicism within the law and borders of

national sovereignty. The separation law did not apply in the departments of Algeria.
3. The law passed with 341 votes for and 233 against. See Mayeur and Rebérioux, *The Third Republic*, 230.
4. Larousse, *Grand dictionnaire universel du XIXe siècle*, vol. 5, defines *culte* as "religious homage given to God or to certain creatures considered to have some supernatural power.... By extension. Religion, set of dogmas and practices proper to a religious association." Napoléon established the Administration des Cultes on October 7, 1801. See P. F. Pinaud, "L'Administration des Cultes de 1800 à 1815," *Revue de l'Institut Napoléon* 132 (1976): 31–39. Its main task was to monitor and act as an intermediary between Rome and the French state especially on these two issues, nomination and salaries of religion personnel. As Maurice Larkin, historian of state-church relations in France, explains in "The Church and the French Concordat, 1891 to 1902," *English Historical Review* 81, no. 321 (1966): 721, "French *Direction des Cultes* maintained a list of suitable candidates which it based on the various recommendations it had received from civil servants, members of parliament and certain of the more Republican bishops." The Reformed and Lutheran clergy in April 1802 and the Jewish Rabbis in February 1831 also went on state salaries, hence becoming civil officials. See Maurice Larkin, *Church and State After the Dreyfus Affair* (New York: Harper & Row, 1973), 35; C. T. McIntire, "Changing Religious Establishments and Religious Liberty in France Part I: 1787–1879," in *Freedom and Religion in the Nineteenth Century*, ed. Richard Helmstadter (Stanford, Calif.: Stanford University Press, 1997), 257–58. In 1881 a decree extended state salaries to the Muslim religion personnel of Algeria as well. See C. T. McIntire, "Changing Religious Establishments and Religious Liberty in France Part II: 1879–1908," in Helmstadter, *Freedom and Religion in the Nineteenth Century*. In 1876 there were 55,000 priests on state salaries, and the *budget des cultes* was up to 52,000,000 francs from 45,500,000 francs in 1868. See Evelyn Martha Acomb, *The French Laic Laws 1879–1889* (New York: Columbia University Press, 1941), 16; John McManners, *Church and State in France, 1870–1914* (New York: Harper & Row, 1972), xviii.
5. Service de la statistique générale de France, *Annuaire statistique de la France*, vol. 1: Paris [etc.] (1878), 480, 481; vol. 2 (1879); vol. 4 (1881); vol. 7 (1884); vol. 9 (1886), 594, 595; vol. 15 (1894), 561, 563; vol. 16 (1896), 451, 452.
6. *Journal officiel de la République française*. Débats parlementaires. Chambre des députés, December 5, 17, 22, 26, 1880; July 24, 25, 1881; Sénat, July 3, 5, 13, 1881.
7. Karl Marx, *The 18th Brumaire of Louis Bonaparte* (New York: International Publishers, 1998).
8. Acomb, *The French Laic Laws 1879–1889*, 18.
9. Paul Bert, *La loi de l'enseignement primaire (Proposition Barodet): Rapport présenté à la Chambre des députés* (Paris: G. Masson, Éditeu, 1880), 7, 15–31.

10. Frédéric Salmon, *Atlas électoral de la France 1848–2001* (Paris: Éditions du Seuil, 2001), 21–22, graphically portrays how the monarchist versus republican cleavage was still dominant in the 1877 legislative elections. Republican votes totaled 4,327,000 and monarchist votes totaled 3,648,000 (xii). However, with the 1881 elections, monarchist votes declined to 1,756,000, and with declining regime threat from monarchists, the republicans started splitting among themselves. See also Mayeur and Rebérioux, *The Third Republic*, 72. Salmon refers to Extrême gauche, Gauche radicale, and Opportunistes. Opportunistes were also fragmented. They were constituted by two major groups, Union républicaine and Gauche républicaine. Jean-Marie Mayeur, *La vie politique sous la Troisième République 1870–1940* (Paris: Éditions du Seuil, 1984), 72, mentions Centre gauche, Extrême gauche, Gauche républicaine, and Union républicaine. The web archives of the French parliament have the following leftist group affiliations for those who were parliamentarians in the chamber in December 1880: Gauche radicale, Centre gauche, Extrême gauche, Gauche républicaine, and Gauche démocratique.
11. Bert, *La loi de l'enseignement primaire*, 122, 131. Subsequent references are cited in the text. All translations from French throughout this book are mine, and capitalization is as given in the original text.
12. The commune is the smallest administrative division in France.
13. The group memberships are taken from the website of the National Assembly of France, http://www.assemblee-nationale.fr, accessed between December 10, 2012, and March 5, 2013.
14. *Journal officiel de la République française*. Débats parlementaires. Chambre des députés, December 17, 1880, 12430. Subsequent references are cited in the text.
15. Duruy was minister of public instruction under the Second Empire (1863–1869). He accepted this position on the condition that the Ministry of Public Instruction be separated from the Ministry of Cultes.
16. *Journal officiel*, December 19, 1880, 12525–26. Subsequent references are cited in the text.
17. Larousse, *Grand dictionnaire universel du XIXe siècle*, vol. 4, 1001, defines a *consistoire* as an "assembly of pastors and elderly of a protestant communion, gathered on the subject of the affairs of their Church." In vol. 8, *conseils de fabrique* are defined as a "group of persons officially appointed for administering church funds."
18. *Journal officiel*, December 21, 1880, 12610.
19. Ibid., 12612.
20. Ibid., 12614.
21. Mayeur and Rebérioux, *The Third Republic*, 75.
22. *Journal officiel*, December 21, 1880, 12614. Subsequent references are cited in the text.

23. Ibid., December 22, 1880, 12676.
24. Mayeur and Rebérioux, *The Third Republic*, 152; James E. Ward, "The Algiers Toast: Lavigerie's Work or Leo XIII's?," *Catholic Historical Review* 51, no. 2 (1965): 173–91.
25. Ward, "The Algiers Toast."
26. *Journal officiel*, December 22, 1880, 12676. Subsequent references are cited in the text.
27. See entry in Larousse, *Grand dictionnaire universel du XIXe siècle*.
28. *Journal officiel*, December 24, 1880, 12791. Subsequent references are cited in the text.
29. Ultramontane Catholicism had its primary allegiance to the Vatican rather than the French Republic.
30. Jean Baubérot, "La séparation et son contexte sociohistorique," in *De la séparation des Églises et de l'État à l'avenir de la laïcité*, ed. Jean Baubérot and Michel Wieviorka (France: Éditions de l'Aube, 2005), 69–70.
31. *Journal officiel de la République française*. Débats parlementaires. Sénat, July 5, 1881, 1031; Baubérot, "Le cas français ou l'impossible religion civile," in *Les nouvelles manières de croire: Judaïsme, christianisme, islam, nouvelles religiosities*, ed. Leïla Babès (Paris: Les Éditions de l'Atelier/Éditions Ouvrières, 1996), 187.
32. Baubérot, "La séparation et son contexte sociohistorique," 70.
33. Mayeur and Rebérioux, *The Third Republic*, 89.
34. Jacqueline Lalouette, *La séparation des Églises et de l'État: Genèse et développement d'une idée 1789–1905* (Paris: Éditions du seuil, 2005), 298–304.
35. Jules Simon, *La liberté de conscience* (Paris: Hachette, 1857).
36. Jules Ferry, *Discours et opinions de Jules Ferry. Le second Empire, la guerre et la Commune / publiés avec commentaires et notes, par Paul Robiquet*, 7 vols. (Paris: A. Colin, 1893), 1:191.
37. Jules Ferry quoted in Jean Michel Gaillard, *Jules Ferry* (Paris: Fayard, 1989), 449.
38. *Journal officiel de la République française*. Débats parlementaires. Chambre des députés, May 29, 1881, 1046. *Césarisme* is a monarchical type of rule.
39. Ibid., 1047.
40. Ibid. A *desservant* is a priest who serves in a parish or a chapel.
41. Bernard Ardura, *Le Concordat entre Pie VII et Bonaparte, 15 Juillet 1801: Bicentenaire d'une réconciliation* (Paris: Cerf, 2001), 74.
42. Articles 12, 13, and 14 were part of the bargain. See Acomb, *The French Laic Laws 1879–1889*, 13.
43. See declaration of 1682 for Gallican liberties, which proposed a clerical council superior to the pope, that the French king's sovereignty was independent of the pope, and that French clerics' superior was the king. See ibid., 14.
44. Jean Baubérot, "The Two Thresholds of Laicization," in *Secularism and Its Critics*, ed. Rajeev Bhargava (New Delhi: Oxford University Press, 1998), 102.

45. McIntire, "Changing Religious Establishments and Religious Liberty in France Part I," 259; Pinaud, "L'Administration des Cultes de 1800 à 1815."
46. Larkin, "The Church and the French Concordat," 721.
47. Larkin, *Church and State*, 35; McIntire, "Changing Religious Establishments and Religious Liberty in France Part I," 257–58.
48. See McIntire, "Changing Religious Establishments and Religious Liberty in France Part II," 275.
49. Alexander Sedgwick, *The Ralliement in French Politics 1890–1898* (Cambridge, Mass.: Harvard University Press, 1965), 88.
50. Ward, "The Algiers Toast."
51. Sedgwick, *The Ralliement*, 4.
52. http://w2.vatican.va/content/leo-xiii/en/encyclicals/documents, accessed December 4, 2016.
53. Sedgwick, *The Ralliement*, 121.
54. Maxime Le Comte, *Les Ralliés: Histoire d'un parti (1886–1898)* (Paris: Ernest Flammarion, 1898), vi.
55. Adrien Dansette, *Religious History of Modern France*, 2 vols. (New York: Herder and Herder, 1961), 2:153.
56. Ibid., 160.
57. Ibid., 151: "The ralliement had divided the beaten conservative army into two main bodies. One remained faithful either to Bonapartism or to Orleanism and the other accepted the established authorities and looked forward in consequence to co-operation with the republicans."
58. Emile Zola, *The Dreyfus Affair: 'J'accuse' and Other Writings*, ed. Alain Pagès (New Haven, Conn.: Yale University Press, 1996); Michael Burns, *France and the Dreyfus Affair: A Documentary History* (New York: Bedford/St. Martin's, 1999), 195. Captain Alfred Dreyfus, a Jewish French military officer, was imprisoned on October 15, 1894, on charges of treason after the discovery of a handwritten note he was accused of having written that supposedly revealed French military secrets to Germany. The incident ignited a public debate on whether a Jew can serve the French state, and French politics realigned one more time along the old line of republicans versus political Catholics. The discovery on August 13, 1898, that the handwriting was forged and the following acquittal of Captain Dreyfus concluded a political victory for the Dreyfusards and were influential in marking the end of the New Spirit.
59. Benjamin F. Martin Junior, "The Creation of the Action Libérale Populaire: An Example of Party Formation in Third Republic France," *French Historical Studies* 9, no. 4 (1976): 661.
60. Malcolm O. Partin, *Waldeck-Rousseau, Combes, and the Church: The Politics of Anti-Clericalism, 1899–1905* (Durham, N.C.: Duke University Press, 1969).
61. Jules Ferry quoted in Gaillard, *Jules Ferry*, 434.

62. Nancy Fitch, "Mass Culture, Mass Parliamentary Politics, and Modern Anti-Semitism: The Dreyfus Affair in Rural France," *American Historical Review* 97, no. 1 (1992): 55–95.
63. Sedgwick, *The Ralliement*, 88.
64. Larkin, *Church and State*, 83.
65. Jean-Marie Mayeur, *La séparation de l'Église et de l'État (1905)* (Paris: René Julliard, 1966), 21–22.
66. Dansette, *Religious History of Modern France*, 2:191, 192, 193.
67. Mayeur and Rebérioux, *The Third Republic*, 228.
68. Jean-Claude Bardout, *L'histoire étonnante de la loi 1901* (Lyon: Editions Juris, 2000), 250, 253–54.
69. Ibid., 254. The Falloux law of 1850 had allowed religious orders to take a more active role in education. See Partin, *Waldeck-Rousseau, Combes, and the Church*, 20–44.
70. Partin, *Waldeck-Rousseau, Combes, and the Church*, 79.
71. Larkin, *Church and State*, 129.
72. Ibid., 129.
73. Partin, *Waldeck-Rousseau, Combes, and the Church*, 145–46.
74. Dansette, *Religious History of Modern France*, 2:197, 202, 204.
75. Quoted in ibid., 205.
76. Maurice Larkin. "Loubet's Visit to Rome and the Question of Papal Prestige," *Historical Journal* 4, no. 1 (1961): 97–103.
77. Larkin, *Church and State*, 2.
78. http://www2.assemblee-nationale.fr/decouvrir-l-assemblee/histoire. Partin, in *Waldeck-Rousseau, Combes, and the Church*, 129, gives the composition of the chamber as 228 Radicals and Radical socialists, 45 Socialists, 48 Ministerial republicans, 140 Progressistes, 50 Ralliés, 45 Nationalists, and 33 Conservatives. Mayeur, in *La vie politique sous la troisième république*, 185–86, gives 48 Socialistes, more than 200 Radicaux, fewer than 100 followers of Waldeck-Rousseau, 127 Républicains progressistes, 35 Action libérale populaire, 43 Nationalistes, and 41 Conservateurs de tradition monarchiste.
79. "Nouvelles des jour," *Le Temps* (Paris), 2; André Daniel, *L'année politique* (Paris: Librairie Académique Didier, 1903), 132.
80. Larkin, *Church and State*, 103.
81. Ibid., 105.
82. Jean Jaurès, "La séparation et l'Union démocratique," *l'Humanité*, June 1, 1904.
83. For full text of the law, see Larkin, *Church and State*, appendix.
84. "Ecclesiastical revenues" in Larousse, *Grand dictionnaire universel du XIXe siècle*, digital ed.
85. Paul Sabatier, *Disestablishment in France*, trans. Robert Dell (London: T. F. Unwin, 1906), 141–42.

86. Larkin, *Church and State*, 171.
87. Mayeur and Rebérioux, *The Third Republic*, 230.
88. McManners, *Church and State in France*, 149.
89. Mayeur and Rebérioux, *The Third Republic*, 230.
90. "Aux règles d'organisation générale du culte elles se proposent d'assurer l'exercice." *Journal officiel*, April 20, 1905.
91. McManners, *Church and State in France*, 150.
92. Mayeur, *La séparation de l'Église et de l'État*, 61.
93. Ibid., 62.
94. Larkin, *Church and State*, 172.
95. Albert de Mun, *Contre la séparation* (Paris: Librairie Vve CH. Poussielgue, 1905); Albert de Mun, *Contre la séparation: De la rupture à la condamnation* (Paris: Librairie Vve CH. Poussielgue, 1906).
96. Albert de Mun, "De la rupture à la séparation: Séance du 22 octobre 1904," in *Contre la séparation*, 56–57; my italics.
97. *Journal officiel*, July 3, 1905, 1260.
98. Mun, *Contre la séparation*, 71.
99. Ibid., 72, 73.
100. Maurice Larkin, "The Vatican, French Catholics, and the Associations Cultuelles," *Journal of Modern History* 36, no. 3 (1964): 298–317. According to Larkin, the Vatican's major concern between 1870 and 1929 was its international reputation. Recognition from France was particularly important because it set an example for its Concordats with other states. On the other hand, some of the clergy, for instance, Mgr. Maurice d'Hulst, rector of the Institut Catholique de Paris and deputy for Brest (Royalist), saw the Concordat as a humiliation for the Catholic Church.
101. Ronald J. Ross, "The Kulturkampf: Restrictions and Controls on the Practice of Religion in Bismarck's Germany," in *Freedom and Religion in the Nineteenth Century*, ed. Richard Helmstadter (Stanford, Calif.: Stanford University Press, 1997), 174, 194.
102. Mun, *Contre la séparation*, 77, 73.
103. Ibid., 69.
104. Mun, "L'apostasie officielle," in *Contre la séparation*, 99–100.
105. Mun, "Une entreprise sans exemple en Europe," in *Contre la séparation*, 106–7.
106. Mun, *Contre la séparation*, 78
107. *Journal officiel*, February 11, 1905, 275. Subsequent references are cited in the text.
108. Mun, *Contre la séparation*, 68–69.
109. *Journal officiel*, March 22, 1905, 986.
110. Briand, *La séparation des Églises et de l'État*, 97.
111. Dansette, *Religious History of Modern France*, 1:207.
112. Briand, *La séparation des Églises et de l'État*, 98, 100.

113. Joan L. Coffey, "The Aix Affair of 1891: A Turning Point in Church-State Relations Before the Separation," *French Historical Studies* 21, no. 4 (1958): 543–59.
114. Mun, "Une entreprise sans exemple en Europe," 112.
115. Albert de Mun, "Une entreprise sans exemple en Amérique," in *Contre la séparation*, 113.
116. Ibid., 76–77.
117. Mun, "De la rupture a la séparation: Séance du 22 octobre 1904," 58–59.
118. Mun, "Une entreprise sans exemple en Amérique," 113–14.
119. Mun, *Contre la séparation*, 75–76, 63.
120. Ibid., 76.
121. Mun, "Le nouvel article 4," in *Contre la séparation*, 215.
122. This criterion of "generality" emerging in the Third Republic chamber deliberations on institutional separation is highly significant for theoretical discussions on the relation between the modern concept of law and liberalism. See H.L.A. Hart, *The Concept of Law* (1961; Oxford: Oxford University Press, 2012); Brian Barry, *Culture and Equality: An Egalitarian Critique of Multiculturalism* (Cambridge, Mass.: Harvard University Press, 2002).
123. Briand, *La séparation des Églises et de l'État*, 3; italics mine. Subsequent references are cited in the text.
124. "Projet de loi relatif à la séparation des Églises et de l'État," in Émile Combes, *Une deuxième campagne laïque: Vers la séparation* (Paris: G. Bellais, 1905), 542, 539.
125. Briand, *La séparation des Églises et de l'État*, 250, 251, 253.
126. Larkin, *Church and State*, 143.
127. Partin, *Waldeck-Rousseau, Combes, and the Church*, 15.
128. *Journal officiel*, April 20, 1905, 1607; Gabriel Bertrand, "A la chambre: La séparation des Églises et de l'État, un important débat sur l'article 4," *L'Humanité*, April 21, 1905, 1.
129. *Journal officiel*, April 20, 1905, 1607. Subsequent references are cited in the text.
130. "Ensemble des personnes nommeés officiellement pour administrer les fonds d'une église," Larousse, *Grand dictionnaire universel du XIXe siècle*.
131. *Journal officiel*, April 21, 1905, 1627. Subsequent references are cited in the text.
132. Member of *conseil de fabrique* responsible for administering church goods at the parish level under the ancient regime and concordat. From Larousse, *Grand dictionnaire universel du XIXe siècle*, digital ed.
133. *Journal officiel*, April 22, 1905, 1658. Subsequent references are cited in the text.
134. The role of socialists is insufficiently theorized in the current literature on secularism, religion, and democracy. For instance, in the comparative historical account of Stathis N. Kalyvas, *The Rise of Christian Democracy in Europe* (Ithaca, N.Y.: Cornell University Press, 1996), covering six European countries, France is the only case of failure. Kalyvas does not provide a comparative account of

the relative power of socialists in each country in order to weigh and evaluate whether this power had any impact on the rise and fall of Christian democracy across the six cases.

4. The Politics of *Laïcité Positive* and Diversity in Contemporary France

1. Murat Akan, "Laïcité and Multiculturalism: The Stasi Report in Context," *British Journal of Sociology* 60, no. 2 (2009): 237–56, lays out and discusses only a "double movement."
2. Nicolas Sarkozy, *La République, les religions, l'espérance* (Paris: Cerf, 2004), 16; italics mine.
3. "Discours de Nicolas Sarkozy au Palais du Lateran le 20 décembre 2007," *Le Monde*, December 21, 2007; "Discours de Nicolas Sarkozy à Riyad le 14 janvier 2008," *Le Monde*, April 24, 2008.
4. Patrice de Beer, "Sarkozy and God," *Open Democracy*, February 6, 2008; Magdi Abdelhadi, "Sheikh Sanctions Headscarf Ban," *BBC*, December 30, 2003.
5. http://www.diplomatie.gouv.fr/en/spip.php?page=rubrique_imprim&id_rubrique=6735, accessed 1 March 1, 2013.
6. In the Second French Republic, the Falloux law of 1850 encouraged Catholic education as a source of public morality.
7. Pope Benedict's speech at Elysée Palace, Paris, September 12, 2008, http://www.vatican.va, accessed March 2, 2013.
8. "Discours de Nicolas Sarkozy à Riyad le 14 janvier 2008."
9. Jean Baubérot, *La laïcité expliquée à M. Sarkozy . . . et à ceux qui écrivent ses discours* (Paris: Éditions Albin Michel, 2008).
10. Jean Baubérot, "Existe-t-il une religion civile républicaine?," *French Politics, Culture & Society* 25, no. 2 (2007): 16.
11. Jean Baubérot, "Identité nationale: Pour une laïcité de sang-froid," *Le Monde*, December 22, 2009; italics in original.
12. *Projet de Loi: encadrant, en application du principe de laïcité, le port de signes ou de tenues manifestant une appartenance religieuse dans les écoles, collèges et lycées publics*. Sénate 66, adopted March 3, 2004.
13. Commission de réflexion sur l'application du principe de laïcité dans la République, *Rapport au président de la République* (Paris, December 11, 2003), 20.
14. Karen Barkey, "Rethinking Ottoman Management of Diversity: What Can We Learn for Modern Turkey," in *Democracy, Islam and Secularism in Turkey*, ed. Ahmet T. Kuru and Alfred Stepan (New York: Columbia University Press, 2012).
15. Commission, *Rapport au président*, 17–18. Subsequent references are cited in the text.

16. Conseil d'État, Avis du Conseil d'État sur le port de signes religieux dans les établissements scolaires no. 346893, 27 novembre 1989; emphasis added. One of the discussions in the Stasi Commission was whether to ban *signes religieux ostentatoires* or *signes religieux ostensibles*. The threshold for the exclusion of religious symbols from public space in this decision of the State Council is proselytism, and the choice of adjective for describing proselytic religious symbols, as underlined in the passage, is *ostentatoire*. The Stasi Commission's choice for *ostensibles*—simply meaning "visible"—over *ostentatoire* (ostentatious) strongly suggests a lowering of the threshold of exclusion, since banning the headscarf as a religious symbol by qualifying it as *ostentatoire* would directly contradict the vocabulary of the State Council's decision in 1989 and, more significantly, would assume that wearing a headscarf is in itself proselytic, or, more generally, that Islam is proselytic in itself.
17. Charles Taylor, "Modes of Secularism," in *Secularism and Its Critics*, ed. Rajeev Bhargava (New Delhi: Oxford University Press, 1998), 33.
18. Commission, *Rapport au président*, 63; italics mine.
19. Ibid., 64.
20. For further discussion, see Murat Akan, "Contextualizing Multiculturalism," *Studies in Comparative International Development* 38, no. 2 (2003): 57–75.
21. Elisabeth Badinter, Régis Debray, Alain Finkielkraut, Elisabeth de Fontenay, and Catherine Kintzler, "Profs, ne capitulons pas!," *Le Nouvel Observateur*, October 27, 1989.
22. Mohamed Harbi, Haylham Manna, Homa Nategh, Nasser Pakdaman, Mustaph Merchaoui, Fawzia Ghouzlanh, and Bahman Nirumand, "Ne laissons pas la parole aux fanatiques!," *Le Nouvel Observateur*, October 27, 1989.
23. Joëlle Brunerie-Kaufmann et al., "Pour une laïcité ouverte," *Politis*, November 9–15, 1989.
24. Here the reference is to the right-wing political party Front National currently led by Marine Le Pen.
25. Régis Debray, *Rapport à Monsieur le Ministre de l'Éducation nationale: L'enseignement du fait religieux dans l'école laïque* (February 2002).
26. "Discours de Monsieur Nicolas Sarkozy Ministre de l'Intérieur, de la sécurité intérieure et des libertés locales Audition devant la 'Commission Stasi,'" October 7, 2003, French Ministry of Interior, http://www.interieur.gouv.fr/Archives/.
27. "'Interventions de Monsieur Nicolas Sarkozy, ministre de l'intérieur' 20ème rassemblement annuel de l'UOIF," April 2003, French Ministry of Interior, http://www.interieur.gouv.fr. The UOIF, or Federation of Muslim Civil Society Organizations, was established in 1983.
28. Sarkozy, *La République, les religions, l'espérance*, 23–25.
29. Abdelhadi, "Sheikh Sanctions Headscarf Ban"; "En Egypte, M. Sarkozy fait 'le service après-vente' de la loi sur la laïcité," *Le Monde*, December 31, 2003.

30. Jean Baubérot, "La Commission Stasi vue par l'un de ses membres," *French Politics, Culture & Society* 22, no. 3 (2004): 139.
31. Alain Touraine, "Modernité et convictions," *Libération*, January 7, 2004.
32. Jean Baubérot, "La laïcité, le chêne et le roseau," *Libération*, December 15, 2003.
33. Michel Debré, *Gouverner mémoires 1958–1962*, vol. 3 (Paris: Éditions Albin Michel, 1988), 52.
34. S. Hazareesingh, *Political Traditions in Modern France* (Oxford: Oxford University Press, 1994), 118.
35. S. Tippett-Spirtou, *French Catholicism* (New York: St. Martin's Press, 2000), 52.
36. Nicholas Beattie, "Yeast in the Dough? Catholic Schooling in France 1981–95," in *Catholicism, Politics and Society in Twentieth-Century France*, ed. Kay Chadwick (Liverpool: Liverpool University Press, 2000), 205.
37. The list of signatories can be found at http://lmsi.net/, accessed May 26, 2015.
38. Pierre Tévanian, "Banning the Hijab: Say No to Racial Discimination," *Le Monde Diplomatique*, February 2004; Pierre Tévanian, *Le voile médiatique. Un faux débat: "L'affaire du foulard islamique"* (Paris: Éditions Raisons D'agir, 2005).
39. Étienne Balibar, "Dissonances Within *Laïcité*," *Constellations* 11, no. 3 (2004): 353–67.
40. The chief rabbi of France, Joseph Sitruk, wrote against a law in *Le Monde* on May 19, 2003. *Le Monde* reported that the Reformed Church of France made a statement against a law on May 31, 2004. The archbishop of Paris, Cardinal Lustiger, warned Chirac against a change in the 1905 law. Monsignor Ricard, president of the Bishop's Conference of France, took a position against the law on November 10, 2003, in *Le Monde*.
41. "LAÏCITÉ: des enseignants du collège Rémy-Faesch de Thann (Haut-Rhin) ont observé une grève," *Le Monde*, March 11, 2004.
42. Patrick Weil, "A Nation in Diversity: France, Muslims and the Headscarf," *Open Democracy*, March 25, 2004, 4.
43. "France Gets First Private Muslim Lycée," *BBC*, July 11, 2003.
44. Reuters, March 31, 2005.
45. I. Chouder, M. Latrèche, and P. Tévanian, *Les filles voilées parlent* (Paris: La fabrique éditions, 2008).
46. Alexis de Tocqueville, *Democracy in America*, 2 vols. (1835 and 1840) (New York: Harper & Row Publishers, 1966), 292.
47. Sarkozy, *La République, les religions, l'espérance*, 7.
48. Tocqueville, *Democracy in America*, 292, 12.
49. Sarkozy, *La République, les religions, l'espérance*, 19, 20.
50. Tocqueville, *Democracy in America*, 295.
51. In Marseille renting state land for a symbolic amount of money to build a mosque has been critized as a state subsidy to religion.

52. Sarkozy, *La République, les religions, l'espérance*, 23–25.
53. Ruth Berins Collier and David Collier, "Inducements Versus Constraints: Disaggregating: Corporatism," *American Political Science Review* 73, no. 4 (1979): 967–86.
54. "Interview with Dounia Bouzar," *Algérie News*, June 10, 2008.
55. Communiqué from CFCM, October 11, 2003.
56. "Entre inquiétude et satisfaction, syndicats d'enseignants et autorités religieuses sont divisés," *Le Monde*, December 19, 2003.
57. "Dalil Boubakeur hostile aux manifestations," *Le Monde*, January 8, 2004.
58. Philippe Joutard, *Rapport de la mission de réflexion sur l'enseignement de l'histoire la géographie et les sciences sociales* (Paris: La Documentation Français, 1989).
59. Debray, *Rapport à monsieur le ministre*, 3, 4. Subsequent references are cited in the text.
60. *Journal officiel de la République française*. Débats parlementaires. Sénat, January 23, 2003, 280.
61. As I will discuss in chapter 5, this is similar to a political position maintained, more or less, in Turkey by the military regime during 1980–1989. The constitution of 1982 had put a required religion course on culture and ethics in primary and secondary public schools, while in 1989 military president Kenan Evren opened a court case against headscarves in schools. Ahmet T. Kuru, *Secularism and State Policies Toward Religion: The United States, Frances, and Turkey* (Cambridge: Cambridge University Press, 2009), 166, refers to such moments as simply "contradictory" and "inconsistent."
62. "Interview de M. Xavier Darcos, ministre délégué à l'enseignement scolaire à 'France 2' le 20 janvier 2004, sur le débat sur l'école, notamment les programmes scolaires, la vie et la violence scolaires, la question des signes religieux," http://discours.vie-publique.fr/, accessed June 16, 2015.
63. René-Samuel Sirat, Philippe Capelle, Dalil Boubakeur, and Philippe Joutard, *L'enseignement des religions à l'école laïque* (Paris: Éditions Salvator, 2003).
64. René-Samuel Sirat, "Enseigner les religions: quel ton juste au pays de la laïcité?." in ibid., 13, 14, 15, 22, 20.
65. Philippe Capelle, "Laïcité, religion, école," in ibid., 39, 40, 41, 42, 43, 47–49.
66. Dalil Boubakeur, "L'Islam et l'enseignement des religions dans l'école de la République," in ibid., 53, 57, 59, 60–62.
67. Philippe Joutard, "L'enseignement du fait religieux à l'école laïque," in ibid., 79–80, 81, 83, 88.
68. Jean-Paul Willaime, "Teaching Religious Issues in French Public Schools: From Abstentionist Laïcité to a Return of Religion to Public Education" in *Religion and Education in Europe: Developments, Contexts, and Debates*, ed. Robert Jackson, Siebren Miedema, Wolfram Weisse, and Jean-Paul Willaime (Berlin: Waxman Münster, 2007), 96.

69. *Journal officiel de la République française.* Débats parlementaires. Chambre des députés, December 22, 1880, 12683; December 17, 1880, 12433–34.
70. John Stuart Mill, "Utility of Religion," in *Three Essays on Religion* (New York: Prometheus Books, 1998), 69–122.

5. The Institutional Politics of Laiklik in Kemalist Turkey

1. *Journal officiel de la République française.* Débats parlementaires. Chambre des députés, December 22, 1880, 12683.
2. Ibid., December 17, 1880, 12433–34.
3. *Milli Güvenlik Konseyi Tutanak Dergisi,* vol. 7, 118th meeting, October 18, 1982, 340; italics mine.
4. *Danışma Meclisi Tutanak Dergisi,* vol. 9, 1st year, 140th meeting, September 1, 1982, 275.
5. Faruk Mercan, *Fethullah Gülen* (Istanbul: Doğan Egmont, 2008), 113.
6. Mustafa Kemal, *Nutuk-Söylev* (1927; Ankara: Türk Tarih Kurumu Basımevi, 1999), 348–49.
7. Binnaz Toprak, *Islam and Political Development in Turkey* (Leiden: E. J. Brill, 1981), 50.
8. C.H.P. *Yedinci Kurultay Tutanağı* [Records of the Republican People's Party Seventh Congress] (Ankara, 1948), 448.
9. *Journal of Minutes,* 2nd year, 22nd meeting, 8th term, December 24, 1946, 428.
10. Mete Tunçay, *Türkiye Cumhuriyeti'nde Tek-Parti Yönetiminin Kurulması (1923–1931)* [The establishment of the single-party rule in the Turkish republic (1923–1931)] (Istanbul: Cem Yayinevi, 1981); Taha Parla, *Türkiye' de Siyasal Kültürün Resmi Kaynakları III: Kemalist Tek-Parti Ideolojisi ve CHP'nin Altı Ok'u* [Official sources of political culture in Turkey III: Kemalist single-party ideology and CHP's six arrows] (Istanbul: Iletişim Yayınları, 1992); Çağlar Keyder, *State and Class in Turkey: A Study in Capitalist Development* (London: Verso, 1987).
11. Taha Parla and Andrew Davison, *Corporatist Ideology in Kemalist Turkey* (Syracuse: Syracuse University Press, 2005), 110.
12. "Türkiye Devletinin dini, Dini İslamdır," in Suna Kili and Şeref Gözübüyük, *Türk Anayasa Metinleri (Sened-i Ittifaktan Günümüze)* [The texts of Turkish constitutions] (Istanbul: Türkiye İş Bankası Kültür Yayınları, 2000), 112.
13. Kemal, *Nutuk-Söylev,* 955-56.
14. Ibid., 348–49. See *Journal of the Minutes of the Turkish Grand National Assembly,* vol. 7, 2nd year, 2nd meeting, 2nd term, March 3, 1924, 27–69. The laws of March 3, 1924, aimed to appropriate all religious property and place it under the control of the Directorate of Religious Affairs established by the same law. The directorate was defined as an institution of the republic (article 1). The head of

the directorate would be appointed by the president upon the recommendation of the prime minister (article 3). The directorate and its budget were attached to the prime ministry (article 4).

15. *Journal of the Minutes*, vol. 7, 2nd year, 2nd meeting, 2nd term, March 3, 1924, 50, 55, 60.
16. Ibid., vol. 3, 1st year, 59th meeting, 3rd term, April 9, 1928, 117.
17. Halide Edib Adıvar, "Dictatorship and Reforms in Turkey," *Yale Review* 19 (1929): 27–44. Halide Edib (1884–1964) was a novelist, university lecturer, advocate of women's rights, and at times critical of Mustafa Kemal Atatürk's politics.
18. *Journal of the Minutes*, vol. 3, 1st year, 59th meeting, 3rd term, April 9, 1928, 2.
19. It is a matter of debate in the literature whether *inkılap* corresponds to revolution, reform, or transformation.
20. *Journal of the Minutes*, vol. 3, 1st year, 59th meeting, 3rd term, April 9, 1928, 2.
21. Adıvar, "Dictatorship and Reforms in Turkey," 37–38.
22. See Kili and Gözübüyük, *Türk Anayasa Metinleri*, 136. In the constitution of 1924 article 75 read: "Nobody can be criticized/blamed for the religion, religious sect [*mezhep*], religious order [*tarikat*] of which she/he is a member or for the philosophical opinion which he/she holds. Unless contrary to order, public rules of good manners, and laws, all kinds of religious ceremonies [*ayin*] are permitted." After revision in 1937 it read: "Nobody can be criticized/blamed for the philosophical opinion she/he holds, or the religion or religious sect to which he/she belongs. Unless contrary to order, public rules of good manners, and laws, all kinds of religious ceremonies are permitted."
23. *Journal of the Minutes*, vol. 16, 2nd year, 33rd meeting, 5th term, February 5, 1937, 61.
24. Ibid., 62.
25. Ömer Okutan, "Din Eğitimi [Religious instruction]," in *Cumhuriyet Döneminde Eğitim* (Istanbul: Milli Eğitim Basimevi, 1983), 409–25.
26. Ruşen Çakır, İrfan Bozan, and Balkan Talu, *İmam Hatip Liseleri: Efsaneler ve Gerçekler* (Istanbul: Tesev Yayınları, 2004), 57.
27. Jean Baubérot, "D'une comparaison laïcité française, laïcité turque," in *Turquie, Les mille visages: Politique, religion, femmes, immigration*, ed. Isabelle Rigoni (Paris: Éditions Syllepsse, 2000), 35–36; Baubérot, "Existe-t-il une religion civile républicaine?," *French Politics, Culture & Society* 25, no. 2 (2007):7. Baubérot qualifies Combisme as the second of the two "civil religion" movements in France: "la 'cléricale' croyances communes—et l'"anticlérical'—religion civique."
28. *Turkish Dictionary* (Istanbul: Cumhuriyet Basımevi, 1945), 153. The Turkish Language Association is a state institution established in 1932.
29. Quoted in Evelyn Martha Acomb, *The French Laic Laws 1879–1889* (New York: Columbia University Press, 1941), 237.

30. The CHP party programs in 1931 and 1935 contained the following statement on the relation among religion, politics, and affairs of the world: "The Party has approved as a principle, adherence to the latest fundamentals of science and technique and adherence to the necessities of the century/times in the making ... of all laws, regulations, and procedures. Because religion is a matter of conscience, the Party accepts keeping religion separate from affairs of the world and from the affairs of the state as one of the leading/fundamental conditions for the progress of our nation on the path toward contemporary civilization." Quoted in Parla, *Türkiye' de Siyasal Kültürün Resmi Kaynakları III*, 39, 116.
31. Eric Zürcher, *Turkey: A Modern History* (London: I. B. Tauris, 2004), 213.
32. "Seçimin Umumi neticesi," *Cumhuriyet*, July 24, 1946.
33. "Seçimlerin neticesi Sabaha karşı belli oldu," *Cumhuriyet*, May 17, 1950.
34. *Demokrat Parti Tüzük ve Programı* [Democrat party regulations and program] (Ankara: Güneş Matbaacılık, 1952), 50. For the 1946 program see "Yeni Partinin Programı," *Cumhuriyet*, January 8, 1946, 2.
35. Bernard Lewis, "Islamic Revival in Turkey," *International Affairs* 28, no. 1 (1952): 41.
36. "C.H.P. Meclis Gurubu: Eğitim Bakanlığı, İmam, Hatip gibi din elemanları yetiştirmek üzere kurslar açacak," *Ulus*, May 21, 1948.
37. *Journal of Minutes*, 2nd year, 22nd meeting, 8th term, December 24, 1946.
38. "Mecliste Hadiseli bir Gün," *Cumhuriyet*, December 19, 1946; "Demokratların Meclise Yarın İştirakı Umuluyor," *Cumhuriyet*, December 24, 1946.
39. *Journal of Minutes*, 2nd year, 22nd meeting, 8th term, December 24, 1946, 428. Subsequent references are cited in the text.
40. "General Sadık Aldoğan'ın Yeni İki Nutku," *Cumhuriyet*, September 28, 1947.
41. *C.H.P. Yedinci Kurultay Tutanağı*, 451–52. Subsequent references are cited in the text.
42. The six arrows of Kemalism are *Milliyetçilik* (nationalism), *Cumhuriyetçilik* (republicanism), *Laiklik* (laicism), *Halkçılık* (populism), *Devletçilik* (statism), and *İnkılapçılık* (translated as transformationism, reformism, or revolutionism).
43. A *müftü* is the person responsible for religious affairs at the city well.
44. Village institutes were built as part of the Kemalist modernization project in the late 1930s and lasted until the early 1950s. See M. Asım Karaömerlioğlu, "The Village Intitutes Experience in Turkey," *British Journal of Middle Eastern Studies* 25, no. 1 (1998): 47–73.
45. "Din Tedrisatı Meselesi Dün C.H.P. Grubunda Görüşüldü," *Cumhuriyet*, February 20, 1948.
46. "İlkokullarda Din Dersleri," *Cumhuriyet*, November 5, 1950; "Din Derslerine dair Tebliğ," *Zafer*, November 5, 1950.
47. Ali Fuad Başgil, *İlmin Işığında Günün Meseleleri* (Istanbul: Yağmur Yayınları, 2006), 91.

48. "Decision e. number 952/186, k. number 53/73," in *Devlet Şurası Kararlar Dergisi* 17, no. 60 (April 1953–June 1953): 54; *Devlet Şurası Kararları Dergisi, yıl*: 17, *Nisan* 1953–Hazieran 1953 *sayı* 60, 53–54. I thank Evren Çelik Wiltse for helping me retrieve the State Council decision from the National Library.
49. *Beşinci Milli Eğitim Şûrası 5–14 Şubat 1953* [Fifth National Education Congress 5–14 February 1953] (Ankara: Maarif Vekâleti Yayın Müdürlüğü, 1954), 370–437.
50. Ibid., 373–74, 380–82. Subsequent references are cited in the text. The UK Education Act is covered in R.J.K. Freathy, "Ecclesiastical and Religious Factors Which Preserved Christian and Traditional Forms of Education for Citizenship in English Schools 1934–1944," *Oxford Review of Education* 33, no. 3 (2007): 367–77.
51. "Diyanet İşleri ve Din Tedrisatı Meselesi," *Milliyet*, June 17, 1950.
52. "Diyanet İşleri Bütçesi Tartışmalara Yol Açtı," *Milliyet*, February 23, 1951; *Journal of the Minutes*, 1st year, 48th meeting, 9th term, February 22, 1951.
53. *Journal of the Minutes*, 1st year, 48th meeting, 9th term, February 22, 1951, 427. Subsequent references are cited in the text.
54. "Prof. Toynbee Ankarada," *Cumhuriyet*, November 2, 1948.
55. Ali Fuad Başgil, "Dördüncü Kurultay Münasebetiyle," *Siyasal Bilgiler*, no. 50 (May 1935): 2, 3, 4.
56. Ali Fuad Başgil, *Din ve Laiklik* [Religion and laiklik] (Istanbul: Sönmez Neşriyat ve Matbaacılık, 1954), 184.
57. *Dördüncü Milli Eğitim Şûrası*, August 22–31, 1949 [Fourth National Education Congress] (Ankara: Maarif Vekâleti Yayın Müdürlüğü, 1949), 47–76.
58. Ali Fuad Başgil, *Yakın Maziden Hatıra Kırıntıları* [Crumbs of memories from the recent past] (Istanbul: Yağmur Yayınevi, 2007); Başgil, *Başgil'den Mektuplar* [Letters from Başgil] (Istanbul: Yağmur Yayınevi, 2007); Başgil, *Din ve Laiklik*; Başgil, *İlmin Işığında Günün Meseleleri* [Issues of the day in light of science] (1960; Istanbul: Yağmur Yayınevi, 2006); Başgil, *Hukukun Ana Meseleleri ve Müesseleri: Konferanslar* [The main issues and institutions of law: conferences] (Istanbul: Yağmur Yayınevi, 2008); Başgil, *Demokrasi Yolunda* [On the way to democracy] (1961; Istanbul, Yağmur Yayınevi, 2006); Başgil, *Gençlerle Başbaşa* [Together with the youth] (1949; Istanbul: Yağmur Yayınevi, 2007); Başgil, *Türkçe Meselesi* [The question of Turkish] (1948; Istanbul, Yağmur Yayınevi, 2006); Başgil, *27 Mayıs İhtilali ve Sebepleri* [The May 27 Revolution and its causes] (Istanbul: Çeltüt Matbaacılık, 1966); Başgil, *Esas Teşkilat Hukuku Dersleri* [Constitutional law lectures] (Istanbul: İnkılap Kitabevi, 1940), and many news articles.
59. Deniz Bölükbaşı, *Türk Siyasetinde Anadolu Fırtınası: Osman Bölükbaşı* [Anatolian storm in Turkish politics: Osman Bölükbaşı] (Istanbul: Doğan Kitap, 2005), 283.
60. Başgil, *Yakın Maziden Hatıra Kırıntıları*, 45.
61. Başgil, *Din ve Laiklik*; Başgil, *Yakın Maziden Hatıra Kırıntıları*; "A.F. Başgil, iki günde üç defa fikir değiştirdi: Başbakanlığa çağrılan Başgil, girerken 'adayım'

çıkarken 'değilim' dedi," *Vatan*, October 25, 1961; "Başgil, Senatodan aniden istifa etti," *Vatan*, October 26, 1961.
62. Başgil, *Din ve Laiklik*, 10. Subsequent references are cited in the text.
63. Başgil, *Yakın Maziden Hatıra Kırıntıları*, 25–26.
64. Başgil, *Din ve Laiklik*, 95–96.
65. Başgil, *Yakın Maziden Hatıra Kırıntıları*, 28.
66. Ali Fuad Başgil, "Mekteplerde Mecburi Din Dersleri Meselesi," *Zafer*, October 30, 1950.
67. Ali Fuad Başgil, "Mekteplerde Mecburi Din Dersleri," *Zafer*, November 5, 1950.
68. Interview with Vakur Versan, Istanbul, October 29, 2009.
69. Sıddık Sami Onar, *İdare Hukukunun Umumi Esasları* [General principles of administrative law], 3 vols. (1952; Istanbul: İsmail Akgün Matbaası, 1960), 1:590–92. For analysis of the content of the 1961 constitution, see Bülent Tanör, *İki Anayasa, 1961–1982* [Two constitutions, 1961–1982] (Istanbul: Beta Basım, 1986); Taha Parla, *Türkiye'de Anayasalar* [Constitutions in Turkey] (Istanbul: İletişim Yayınları, 2002). For a recent political and sociological analysis of the 1960 coup d'état, see İsmet Akça, "Ordu, Devlet ve Sınıflar: Mayıs 27, 1960, Darbesi Örneği Üzerinden Alternatif Bir Okuma Denemesi," [Military, state and classes: An alternative perspective from the example of the May 27, 1960, coup] in *Türkiye'de Ordu Devlet ve Güvenlik Siyaseti* [Military, state and politics of security in Turkey], ed. Evren Balta Paker and İsmet Akça (Istanbul: Bilgi Üniversitesi Yayınları, 2010).
70. Interview with Vakur Versan, Istanbul, October 29, 2009.
71. Kazım Öztürk, *Türk Anayasası* [Records of the Turkish constitution], 3 vols. (İstanbul: İş Bankası Yayınları, 1966), 1:28. Italics mine.
72. Ibid., 2:1342–1466.
73. Ibid., 2:1377.
74. Hıfzı Veldet Velidedeoğlu, *Türkiye' de Üç Devir Var* [There are three epochs in Turkey] (Istanbul: Sinan Yayınları, 1972). The newspaper *Akşam* covered on July 7, 1960, a meeting of teachers with military officers in government and reported that "teachers will explain in villages that laiklik is not irreligion [*dinsizlik*]."
75. Alevis are an Islamic group in Turkey. The majority of Muslims in Turkey are Sunni. The population statistics on the Alevis are highly politicized, but they number between twelve and twenty million. The total population of Turkey is more than seventy million.
76. "Anayasa Komisyonuna Garip Bir Müracaat: Aleviliğin Devletçe Tanınması için 'Alevi Grubu' Tarafından Anayasa Komisyonuna Başvuruldu," *Dünya*, July 26, 1960. See also *Türk Basınında Anayasa Tartışmaları 1960–1961 Bibliyografya* [Constitution debates in the Turkish media 1960–1961: A bibliography] (Ankara: TBMM Basımevi, 1981).
77. "Alevilerin Anayasa Komisyonuna Müracaatları," *Cumhuriyet*, July 27, 1960.

78. For a discussion on difference-blind liberalism and group-specific rights, see Murat Akan, "Contextualizing Multiculturalism," *Studies in Comparative International Development* 38, no. 2 (2003): 57–75.
79. There is significant variaton among the reporting of newspapers. For instance, "Dini İnanışlara Müdahele Yok: Milli Birlik Komitesi Dini Konularda Zor Kullanılmayacağını Bildirdi," *Milliyet*, July 26, 1960, reports Alevis demanding the abolishment of the state budget for the DRA and representation for Bektaşilik within the DRA.
80. Isaah Berlin, "Two Concepts of Liberty," in *Four Essays on Liberty* (Oxford: Oxford Paperbacks, 1969)
81. Öztürk, *Türk Anayasası*, 2:1361.
82. Ibid., 3:3826–27.
83. "Gürsel'in Seçeceği 10 Temsilciden 6 sı Belli Oldu," *Milliyet*, December 26, 1960; "Bir Temsilci CHP'ye Girdi," *Milliyet*, February 19, 1961.
84. Öztürk, *Türk Anayasası*, 2:1357.
85. Ibid., 2:1451.
86. Ibid., 2:1067.
87. Ibid., 2:1386.
88. "Kurucu Meclis Seçimleri Tamamlandı: Gayri Resmi Tasnife Göre 142 CHP'li 85 Müstakil ve 25 CKMP li seçildi," *Milliyet*, December 31, 1960.
89. Velidedeoğlu, *Türkiye' De Üç Devir Var*, 187.
90. Kadircan Kaflı, "Evet mi Hayır mı? . . . ," *Tercüman*, June 1, 1961.
91. This distinction has also been highlighted as a central analytical one for an anthropology of religion. As Asad underlines, all religions strike a balance between ortho-'doxy' and ortho-'praxy.' See Talal Asad, "The Idea of an Anthropology of Islam," Occasional Paper Series, Center for Contemporary Area Studies, Georgetown University, March 1986, 15.
92. For example, see Robert Audi, "The Separation of Church and State and Obligations of Citizenship," *Philosophy and Public Affairs* 18, no. 3 (1989): 256–96.
93. Öztürk, *Türk Anayasası*, 2:1399.
94. İştar B. Tarhanlı, *Müslüman Toplum, "Laik" Devlet: Türkiye'de Diyanet İşleri Başkanlığı* (Istanbul: Afa Yayınları, 1993), 29–30.
95. Öztürk, *Türk Anayasası*, 2:967.
96. Osman Bölükbaşı, " '27 Mayıs' ve Beklediğimiz Nizam," *Kudret*, October 12, 1960.
97. Kadircan Kaflı, "Evet mi Hayır mı? . . . ," *Tercüman*, June 1, 1961.
98. Kadircan Kaflı, "Dinde Reform Tasarısı . . . ," *Tercüman*, May 8, 1961.
99. Öztürk, *Türk Anayasası*, 2:1348.
100. Ibid., 2:1349.
101. For historicism and modernity, see Dipesh Chakrabarty, *Provincializing Europe: Postcolonial Thought and Historical Difference* (Princeton, N.J.: Princeton University Press, 2000).

102. Öztürk, *Türk Anayasası*, 2:1381.
103. Ibid., 2:1384.
104. See Timothy Mitchell, *Rule of Experts: Egypt, Techno-Politics, Modernity* (Berkeley: University of California Press, 2002), on modernity, colonization, and expertise.
105. Öztürk, *Türk Anayasası*, 2:1412. Soysal misquotes the numbers in the report. The original text of the report, in Albert Malche, *Istanbul Üniversitesi Hakkında Rapor* [Report on Istanbul University] (Istanbul: Devlet Basımevi, 1939), 52, reads "thirteen teachers and three students." Note also the foreword to the report by Hasan Ali Yücel, v–vi. Malche, from the University of Geneva, was invited by Mustafa Kemal to act as a consultant to the Turkish National Ministry of Education. He completed his report on the University of Istanbul on May 29, 1932. Also see his lectures addressed to the new state teachers of Turkey in February and March 1934, Albert Malche, *Yeni Terbiyenin Prensipleri* [Principles of contemporary education], trans. Sabri Esat Siyavuşgil (Istanbul: Arkadaş Matbaası, 1939).
106. Öztürk, *Türk Anayasası*, 1:172–73.
107. Ibid., 2:1370–72.
108. Ibid., 2:1372.
109. This approach has its roots in the Western republican and liberal traditions. The best examples are Niccolò Machiavelli in his republican writings, *Selected Political Writings* (Indianapolis: Hackett, 1994), 114–18, and John Stuart Mill, "Utility of Religion," in *Three Essays on Religion* (New York: Prometheus Books, 1998), 69–122.
110. Öztürk, *Türk Anayasası*, 2:1357–58. Subsequent references are cited in the text.
111. "Istanbul'da 100 Yere Bombalı Pankart Asıldı," *Milliyet*, September 12, 1980.
112. Eric J. Zürcher, *Turkey: A Modern History* (New York: I. B. Tauris, 1997), 294.
113. "Toplu Sözleşme Uzadığı için İşçiler Direniş Yaptı," *Milliyet*, September 9, 1980; "Sözleşme Olmazsa Ataş ta Bugün Greve Başlıyor," *Milliyet*, September 12, 1980.
114. "53 bin İşçinin Grevi Sürüyor," *Milliyet*, September 6, 1980.
115. "100 bin İşçiyi Kapsayan Toplu Pazarlık Görüşmelerinde Sonuç Alınamadı," *Milliyet*, September 7, 1980.
116. "80 bin İşçi Greve Hazır," *Milliyet*, September 10, 1980.
117. "Cam İşkolunda Grevler 100 Günü Aştı," *Milliyet*, September 11, 1980.
118. Notification number 7, http://www.belgenet.com, accessed in December 14, 2010. For political economic developments until 1980, see Çağlar Keyder, "The Political Economy of Turkish Democracy," *New Left Review* 115 (May/June 1979). Notification 7 asked leaders of DİSK and MİSK to turn themselves in by 6 p.m. on September 16, 2010. With notification number 8, the National Security Council blocked the bank accounts of DİSK, MİSK, and HAK İŞ and required that all documents at their headquarters would be documented in detail by the martial law. See "Disk ve Misk'e Bağlı Sendikaların Yönetici ve Baştemsilcilerinin Hemen Teslim Olması İstendi," *Milliyet*, September 23, 1980.

119. "Türk-İş'e Bağlı Sendikaların 148'nin Faaliyeti Durduruldu," *Milliyet*, September 19, 1980; "Çalışma Bakanlığı Çalışmaları men Edilen 84 Sendikayı Açıkladı," *Milliyet*, September 18, 1980.
120. Paul W. Drake, *Labour Movements and Dictatorship: The Southern Cone in Comparative Perspective* (London: Johns Hopkins University Press, 1996).
121. "İstanbul'da Türk-İş'e Bağlı Sendikaların Tümü Açıldı," *Milliyet*, September 25, 1980.
122. " 'Tek Sendika' İçin Çalışmalar Sürdürülüyor," *Milliyet*, November 6, 1980.
123. "Emsal Sözleşmeler Hazırlanıyor," *Milliyet*, November 23, 1980.
124. "Toplu Sözleşmeler Hızla Sonuçlandırılacak," *Milliyet*, November 14, 1980; "Çalışma Bakanı: 'Açıkta Kalan 30 bin Sendikalının Durumları İncelenecek,' " *Milliyet*, September 27, 1980.
125. Dankwart A. Rustow and Metin Heper evaluate these shorter terms of military rule in Turkey as a sign of the military's commitment to democracy. See Dankwart A. Rustow, "Turkish Democracy in Historical and Comparative Perspective," in *Politics in the Third Turkish Republic*, ed. Metin Heper and Ahmet Evin (Boulder, Colo.: Westview Press, 1994), 3; Metin Heper, "Transition to Democracy in Turkey: Toward a New Pattern," in ibid., 13. Stephan Haggard and Robert Kaufman make the distinction between "ruling" and "corrective" authority in comparing the Latin American militaries with the Turkish military. See Stephan Haggard and Robert R. Kaufman, *The Political Economy of Democratic Transitions* (Princeton, N.J.: Princeton University Press, 1995), 97.
126. See *Diyarbakır 5 Nolu Cezaevi*, documentary film by Çayan Demirel. A headline on September 14 in *Milliyet* read, "Life Is Back to Normal," and a small news article on the front page was entitled "In Samsun Prison Convicts and Arrested from Right and Left Movements Made Peace."
127. "İngiltere'de Türkiye'yi Protesto Eden 3 Kişi Açlık Grevine Başladı," *Milliyet*, May 9, 1982; "Turkish Hunger Strike," *Financial Times*, June 4, 1982; "Uncertain Role of Religion" *Financial Times*, May 17, 1982; "Trials Without Dignity," *Financial Times*, May 17, 1982.
128. Ruşen Çakır, *Ayet ve Slogan: Türkiye'de İslami Oluşumlar* [Verse and slogan: Islamic formations in Turkey] (Istanbul: Metis, 1990), 92.
129. The Democrat Party (overthrown by the 1960 military intervention), the Justice Party (warned by the military in 1971 and overthrown by the military intervention in 1980), and the True Path Party (in a coalition government with the Welfare Party when the military issued a warning in 1997).
130. Bekir Berk, "Ordumuzun Sesi," *Yeni Asya*, February 10, 1971.
131. Nihal Mete, "Fethullah Hoca Çiller'i Savundu," *Milliyet*, April 7, 1995.
132. "Asker," *Sızıntı* 1, no. 5 (June 1979).
133. "Son Karakol," *Sızıntı* 2, no. 2 (October 1980).

134. Çakır, *Ayet ve Slogan*, 103–4.
135. Faruk Mercan, *Fethullah Gülen* (Istanbul: Doğan Egmont, 2008), 113.
136. Çakır, *Ayet ve Slogan*, 106–7.
137. The postcoup academic and media discussions on democratization give a significant place to Islam as a constitutive element of civil society in Turkey. Çağlar Keyder argues that Islamic activism of the 1990s is a potential modernization from below in "Whither the Project of Modernity? Turkey in the 1990s," in *Rethinking Modernity and National Identity in Turkey*, ed. Sibel Bozdoğan and Reşat Kasaba (Seattle: University of Washington Press, 1997). Nilüfer Göle places postcoup Islamist activism within what she calls "autonomization of civil society" in "Toward an Autonomization of Politics and Civil Society in Turkey," in Heper and Evin, *Politics in the Third Turkish Republic*. For a critique of this literature, see Yael Navaro-Yashin, "Uses and Abuses of 'State and Civil Society' in Contemporary Turkey," *New Perspectives on Turkey* 18 (1998): 1–22.
138. *Birinci Kültür Şurası (23–27 Ekim 1982): Genel Kurul Görüşmeleri* [The first culture congress (October 23–27, 1982): general council meetings] (Ankara: Kültür ve Turizm Bakanlığı Yayınları, 1983).
139. İrfan Bozan, *Devlet ile Toplum Arasında Bir Okul: İmam Hatip Liseleri . . . Bir Kurum: Diyanet İşleri Başkanlığı* [A school between state and society: imam hatip schools . . . an institution: directorate of religious affairs] (Istanbul: TESEV, 2006).
140. "Evren: 'Medeniyet Milletlerarası, Kültür Millidir,'" *Milliyet*, October 24, 1982.
141. "Alevilere Sunni İmam," *Milliyet*, February 19, 1989.
142. *Danışma Meclisi Tutanak Dergisi*, 273, 275, 292.
143. Kenan Evren, *Kenan Evren'in Anıları* [Memoirs of Kenan Evren], 3 vols. (Istanbul: Milliyet Yayınları, 1991), 3:276.
144. *Türkiye Cumhuriyeti Anayasa Tasarsı Ve Anayasa Komisyonu Raporu* [Republic of Turkey constitution draft and constitution commission report] (Ankara, 1982), 91.
145. Ibid., 78.
146. *Danışma Meclisi Tutanak Dergisi*, 269. Subsequent references are cited in the text.
147. A saying or action of the Prophet Muhammad.
148. *Milli Güvenlik Konseyi Tutanak Dergisi*. Subsequent references are cited in the text.
149. For further discussion on the relevance of the empirical findings from the 1961 constitution-writing episode for the academic literature on Turkey, see Murat Akan, "Infrastructural Politics of Laiklik in the Writing of the 1961 Turkish Constitution," *Interventions: International Journal of Postcolonial Studies* 13, no. 2 (2011): 190–211. For a more general theoretical and methodological discussion, see Murat Akan, "A Politics of Comparative Conceptualizations and Institutions: Two Non-European Images on European Secularity in the Writing of the 1961 Turkish Constitution," Max Planck Institute Working Paper 13–02 (2013): 1–34.

6. The Sincere Government (*Samimi Hükümet*), the Institutional Politics of Religion, and Diversity in Contemporary Turkey

1. An international project led by Spain and Turkey to produce alternatives to the "clash of civilizations" perception of world politics, originally popularized by Samuel Huntington.
2. *Yargıtay Cumhuriyet Başsavcılığı Vs Refah Partisi*, 1997 (decided on January 16, 1998), Constitutional Court, *Anayasa Mahkemesi Kararlar Dergisi*; Case of *Refah Partisi (The Welfare Party) and Others vs. Turkey*, European Court of Human Rights, February 13, 2003.
3. José Casanova, "Religion, European Secular Identities, and European integration," in *Religion in an Expanding Europe*, ed. Timothy Byrnes and Peter J. Katzenstein (Cambridge: Cambridge University Press, 2006), 91–92. For similar lines of argument on the AKP, see also Daniel Philpott and Timothy Samuel Shah, "Faith and Federation: the Role of the Religious Ideas and Institutions in European Political Convergence," in ibid.; and Monica Duffy Toft, Daniel Philpott, and Timothy Samuel Shah, *God's Century: Resurgent Religion and Global Politics* (New York: W. W. Norton, 2011). Jocelyn Maclure and Charles Taylor, *Secularism and Freedom of Conscience* (Cambridge, Mass.: Harvard University Press, 2011), also assume the AKP to be pushing a liberal line against Kemalism.
4. "Din Çimentomuz," *Radikal*, December 12, 2005.
5. *Journal of the Minutes*, 4th year, 35th meeting, 22nd term, December 18, 2005.
6. Ibid.
7. Ibid.
8. For further discussion on AKP's politics of the DRA in light of Alfred Stepan's "twin tolerations" and "organic statism," see Murat Akan, "Twin Tolerations or Siamese Twins: Kemalist Laicism and Political Islam in Turkey," in *Institutions and Democracy: Essays in Honor of Alfred Stepan*, ed. Douglas Chalmers and Scott Mainwaring (Notre Dame, Ind.: University of Notre Dame Press, 2012).
9. *Journal of the Minutes*, 4th year, 30th meeting, 21st term, December 4, 2001; "Diyanet Kaldırılsın mı?," *Milliyet*, May 6, 2006.
10. This comparative point calls for a reevaluation of the question of continuity and discontinuity between AKP and previous parties of political Islam. The empirical evidence challenges the common narrative of the AKP break from the previous parties of political Islam toward a more moderate position. See Binnaz Toprak, "Islam and Democracy in Turkey," *Turkish Studies* 6, no. 2 (2005): 167–86, for an example of such an analysis.
11. "Diyanet Bütçesi 37 Kurumu Solladı," *Hürriyet*, October 24, 2006.

12. *Journal of the Minutes*, 4th year, 35th meeting, 22nd term, December 18, 2005.
13. *Refah Partisi'nin "Anayasa Uzlaşma Teklifi"* [Proposal for compromise on constitutional change by the Welfare Party] (Ankara: Semih Ofset, 1994), 25–37.
14. Necmettin Erbakan, *Milli Görüş* [National perspective] (Istanbul: Dergah Yayınları, 1975), 9–10.
15. Murat Akan, "Governing Religious Difference or Differentiating Governance Religiously?," paper presented at the ECPR Joint Sessions, Lisbon, 2009.
16. "Politics, Not Religion, at the Heart of Growing Muslim-West Divide, New Report Argues," Alliance of Civilizations press release, Fourth High-Level Group Meeting, November 12–13, 2006.
17. Alliance of Civilizations, *Report of the High-Level Group*, November 13, 2006, 6.
18. *Journal of the Minutes*, 4th year, 35th meeting, 22nd term, December 18, 2005.
19. Ibid., 3rd year, 30th meeting, 21st term, December 13, 2000.
20. Ibid.
21. Ibid.
22. *Journal of the Minutes*, 2nd year, 31st meeting, 20th term, December 12, 1996.
23. "Orgeneral Büyükanıt 'Kuzey Irak'a Girmeliyiz' Deyip Topu Hükümete Attı," *Radikal*, April 13, 2007; "Büyükanıt Cumhurbaşkanı Adayını Tariff Etti," *Radikal*, April 13, 2007.
24. This term misrepresents the military warning in 2007 as completely discontinuous with the past tradition of military takeovers and warnings in Turkey.
25. http://www.tsk.mil.tr/, accessed April 28, 2007.
26. "Gül: Artık Diplomatlar Değil, Asker Konuşacak," *Radikal*, November 7, 2007. See also "Devletin Tepesinde Sağırlar Diyaloğu," *Radikal*, June 1, 2007.
27. "Erdoğan Fena Patladı," *Internet Haber*, December 27, 2007.
28. "Demokrasi Kararlılığı," *Milliyet*, June 1, 1997; italics mine.
29. "Adalete 'Kılıç' Saplandı," *Birgün*, April 26, 2012.
30. *Soruları ve Cevaplarıyla Demokratik Açılım Süreci: Milli Birlik ve Kardeşlik Projesi* [With questions and answers the Democratic Opening Process: National Unity and Brotherhood/Sisterhood Project] (January 2010, AKP Tanıtım ve Medya Başkanlığı). For brotherhood and sisterhood, there is only one gender-free term in Turkish, *kardeşlik*.
31. Interview with Reha Çamuroğlu, Ankara, January 16, 2016.
32. "Ak Parti'den Alevi Açılımı," *CNN Türk*, November 21, 2007.
33. The following minutes were published in 2011 in Ankara by Devlet Bakanlığı: *First Alevi Workshop, 3–4 June 2009, Ankara; Second Alevi Workshop, 8 July, Ankara; Third Alevi Workshop, 19 August, Ankara; Fourth Alevi Workshop, 30 September, Ankara; Fifth Alevi Workshop, 11 November, Ankara; Sixth Alevi Workshop, 17 December, Ankara;* and *Seventh Alevi Workshop, 28–29–30 January 2010, Ankara*. The *Alevi Workshops Final Report* was published in 2010.
34. Oral Çalışlar, "Alevi Önraporu'ndaki Sorunlar," *Radikal*, February 12, 2010.

35. Talha Köse, *Alevi Opening and the Democratization Opening in Turkey* (Ankara: SETA Policy Report, 2010).
36. *First Alevi Workshop*, 5, 6.
37. "Alevi Örgütleri Beş Talepte Uzlaştı," *Bianet*, June 5, 2009; "Alevi Çalıştayı'nda Alevilere Hakaret Edildi," *Bianet*, July 13, 2009.
38. In 1993 a mob attacked the Madımak Hotel in Sivas, a central Anatolian city, where the Pir Sultan Abdal Culture Association (an Alevi association) was hosting invited writers and poets for a festival the association was organizing. The mob set the hotel on fire, and more than thirty writers and poets were killed.
39. See *First Alevi Workshop*, 41, 176, 195–200, 252, for discussion and disagreement among different Alevi representatives on this question.
40. *Journal of the Minutes*, 1st year, 54th meeting, 22nd term, March 24, 2003.
41. "Alevilik Din Değil; Ali ile Alakaları Yok," *Radikal*, February 22, 2013; italics mine.
42. *Hasan and Eylem Zengin v. Turkey*, no. 1448/04 (Sect. 2), ECHR 2007-XI, October 9, 2007.
43. Danıştay Sekizinci daire yer 207, decision no 7481, December 28, 2007.
44. Law number 2577, "Procedure of Administrative Justice Act."
45. "Aleviler İçin Genel Müdürlük Kurulacak," *Sabah*, November 13, 2008; "Hükümet Açılım İçin Çalışmaları Hızlandırdı," *Radikal*, November 27, 2008.
46. "AKP'de Alevi Sıkıntısı," *Milliyet*, June 13, 2008.
47. It would literally translate as "let friends see us at shopping." It means to do something for appearance's sake.
48. Yael Navaro-Yashin, "Uses and Abuses of 'State and Civil Society' in Contemporary Turkey," *New Perspectives on Turkey* 18 (1998): 1–22. Also see chapter 5 of this book.
49. *Fourth Alevi Workshop*, 189.
50. E.g., *Reporters Without Borders* notes that out of 179 countries, ranked Turkey 101st in 2007, 102nd in 2008, 122nd in 2009, 138th in 2010, and 148th in 2011.
51. The Maraş Massacre of December 19–24, 1978, was one of the major events in Turkish history. Right-wing groups massacred 111 left-wing and Alevi citizens, adults as well as children in their homes. See Emma Sinclair-Webb, "Sectarian Violence, the Alevi Minority and the Left: Kahramanmaraş 1978," in *Turkey's Alevi Enigma: A Comprehensive Overview*, ed. Paul J. White and Joost Jongerden (Leiden: Brill, 2003).
52. *Seventh Alevi Workshop*, 139.
53. *First Alevi Workshop*, 32.
54. Ibid., 94.
55. *Third Alevi Workshop*, 16.
56. *First Alevi Workshop*, 18; Subsequent references are cited in the text.
57. "Ali Balkız'ın Kadıköy 'deki Alevi Mitinginde Yaptığı Konuşma," *Bianet*, November 9, 2009.

58. *Fifth Alevi Workshop*, 15–16.
59. *Second Alevi Workshop*, 20, 16, 47.
60. *First Alevi Workshop,* 233. 234.
61. *Second Alevi Workshop*, 169; italics mine.
62. See also the framing in the report *Alevi Workshops Final Report*, 1–2.
63. The Abant platform is a regularly meeting discussion forum of the Journalists and Writers Association known to be part of the Gülen movement. The forum brings together intellectuals and decision makers. "Abant'tan Zorunlu Din Dersi Çıktı," *Birgün*, March 13, 2012.
64. *Fifth Alevi Workshop,* 199–201.
65. *Sixth Alevi Workshop*, 15, 180, 78–79.
66. *Seventh Alevi Workshop*, 28. Subsequent references are cited in the text.
67. *First Alevi Workshop*, 17, statement repeated on p. 30. Subsequent references are cited in the text.
68. Commission of the European Communities, *Regular Report for Turkey's Progress Toward Accession 2004*, 44–45, 54.
69. *First Alevi Workshop*, 68. Subsequent references are cited in the text.
70. *Hasan and Eylem Zengin v. Turkey*.
71. Danıştay Sekizinci daire yer 207, decision no 7481, December 28, 2007.
72. Many speakers also articulated further the concrete daily problems issuing from the lack of legal status for Cemevi, such as that they cannot be constructed on land spared for places of worship because the law specifies only mosques, churches, and synagogues. See *First Alevi Workshop*, 123, 183–84. They cannot benefit from a 2008 law (5784) covering the electricity expenses of places of worship under the state budget. The lack of legal status leads to closed dervish lodges (*dergah*), or radical instances such as the AKP Istanbul City Organization building being built on Karaağaç Bektaşi Dervish Lodge (120–21). One speaker pointed out that the prevailing definition of a village in Turkey includes a mosque, according to which many Alevi villages do not qualify as villages (137).
73. See related discussion on p. 176. The vice president of the DRA insisted that the Koran specifies the mosque as the place of worship, and a participant pointed out that in the Koran there is place of worship (*mescit*), but *cami* or *cemevi* is not specified.
74. A participant pointed out that despite a petition against a mosque with five hundred signatures in a village, the state built the mosque.
75. *First Alevi Workshop*, 203.
76. The word *örgüt* literally means organization, but the statist language in Turkey uses the term pejoratively and even moralistically and dehumanizingly to designate any range of collective activity it sees as in opposition to the state.
77. *First Alevi Workshop*, 204.

78. *Second Alevi Workshop*, 28–29, 43–44, 48–49, 45, 58, 59, 63, 99, 156, 159. Subsequent references are cited in the text.
79. *Third Alevi Workshop*, 19–20. Subsequent references are cited in the text.
80. The Alevi Encyclopedia Project of the DRA was part of the state/government politics of turning Alevilik into a written and more institutionalized tradition.
81. *First Alevi Workshop*, 47, 48.
82. The misperception of neutrality of the Turkish state vis-à-vis religion and how this misperception informs general theoretical discussions on secularism are striking. See particularly comparative comments on Turkey and France in Maclure and Taylor, *Secularism and Freedom of Conscience*, 2, 14.
83. *First Alevi Workshop*, 112, 116–18, 126, 149–50, 221; *Second Alevi Workshop*, 63–65, 71–72, 101, 123.
84. *First Alevi Workshop*, 127.
85. For example, see *Second Alevi Workshop*, 17–18, 24, 25, 105–7, 124, 144, 148. Many pointed to the articles 24 and 136 of the constitution or the political parties law, article 89.
86. Ibid., 115, 127.
87. One participant gave two examples to underscore that the problem is not one of further research: one on the hardship of building *cemevi*s (63–65), and another a municipality where an Alevi-populated neighborhood is named after an Ottoman sultan who massacred Alevis. Despite the fact that the locals went to the head of the AKP municipality with a petition containing eleven thousand signatures, they were literally kicked out.
88. *Second Alevi Workshop*, 75–79, 84, 86, 143.
89. Ibid., 85, 130–33.
90. *Fourth Alevi Workshop*, 28, 39, 106, 128, 134, 140, 176, 179, 194, 199.
91. *First Alevi Workshop*, 225–26, 96, 111.
92. Ibid., 189–90.
93. *Second Alevi Workshop*, 71–72, 101, 123.
94. Ibid., 100.
95. *Fifth Alevi Workshop*, 78, 134, 117, 37.
96. *Fourth Alevi Workshop*, 136, 185, 214. Subsequent references are cited in the text.
97. BDP members, Kurdish and socialist, entered parliament as independents and formed a party group in parliament afterward.
98. *Journal of the Minutes*, 4th year, 124th meeting, 23rd term, June 25, 2010.
99. Ibid.
100. Ibid.
101. The presentation of the role of religion here casts serious doubt on the argument of Yavuz against AKP being a religious actor. Hakan Yavuz, *Secularism and Muslim Democracy in Turkey* (Cambridge: Cambridge University Press, 2009).
102. *Journal of the Minutes*, 4th year, 126th meeting, 23rd term, June 30, 2010.

103. Ibid.
104. *Journal of the Minutes*, 4th year, 125th meeting, 23rd term, June 29, 2010.
105. Ibid.
106. *Journal of the Minutes*, 4th year, 127th meeting, 23rd term, July 1, 2010.
107. Ibid., 4th year, 126th meeting, 23rd term, June 30, 2010.
108. From a pamphlet distributed in the streets.
109. The Justice Medicine Institution operates under the Ministry of Justice and carries out all medical reports necessary for courts.
110. Turkey Grand National Assembly, answer to written question, 24th term, 2nd legislative year, March 29, 2012, no: B.05.1.EGM.0.12.48287 (91250) 2082-2650/71423.
111. Turkey Statistical Institution (Tüik), Referendum on the Political Rights, 1987. In religiously conservative cities, 61 to 71 percent of voters were against raising restrictions on political rights, while among the top six cities saying "yes" to political rights were Tunceli, homeland of Kurdish Alevis (78.7%); Mardin, a southeastern city (67.1%); Hakkari, also a southeastern city (63.4%); and Zonguldak, a city of miners (61.9%).
112. Turkish Grand National Assembly, https://yenianayasa.tbmm.gov.tr, accessed January 2, 2012.
113. Kenan Evren, *Kenan Evren'in Anıları* [Memoirs of Kenan Evren] (Istanbul: Milliyet Yayınları, 1991), 276.
114. Adam Entous and Joe Parkinson, "Turkey's Attack on Civilians Tied to U.S. Military Drone," *Wall Street Journal*, May 16, 2012.
115. "Allah Aşkına Tazminatsa Tazminat," *Radikal*, May 22, 2012. The state paid a certain amount of money to the families of the deceased; however, most of them refused it.
116. Progressive Lawyers Association, *Detained Students Report*, October 2011, 2.
117. Ahmet Şık et al., *Oookitap: Dokunan Yanar* [That book: Whoever touches burns] (Istanbul: Postacı Kitabevi, 2011).
118. Nedim Şener, *Kırmızı Cuma: Dink'in Kalemini Kim kırdı* [Red Friday: Who broke Hrant Dink's pen?] (Istanbul: Doğan Kitapçılık, 2011).
119. Middle East Studies Association, letters on Turkey, letter written on November 21, 2011.
120. Reporters Without Borders, *A Book Is Not a Bomb! Media and Justice in Turkey, Mistrust and Repression, Investigation Report*, 2011; International Press Freedom Mission to Turkey, *Final Report Turkey: Set Journalists Free*, 2011.
121. Tayyip Erdoğan, speech at the Parliamentary Assembly of the Council of Europe, April 14, 2011.
122. "Erdogan: 'Siamo stati pazienti, ma se la Siria continua a sconfinare la Nato dovrà reagire,'" *Corriere Della Sera*, May 7, 2012.
123. "Gidin Başka Yerde Oynayın!," *Bianet*, May 2, 2012.

124. "Aydınlar Dilekçesi ile İlgili İfade İşlemi Devam Ediyor," *Milliyet*, May 24, 1984.
125. "Aziz Nesin Dava Dilekçesini Verdi: Cumhurbaşkanı da Benim Gibi Yurttaş," *Milliyet*, February 6, 1987.
126. "Maraş Katliamı Protestosu Engellendi," *Bianet*, December 24, 2011.
127. "Önümüzde Üç Dönüm Noktası Var," *NTV*, October 2, 2012.
128. Constitutional Law Research Association (Anayasa-Der), *Report on the Constitution* (Istanbul: Legal Yayincilik, 2012).
129. Ibid., 27.
130. From author's notes at the conference, "Constitutional Processes in the Mediterranean Basin," hosted by Marmara University Constitution Law Faculty.
131. "Nesin-Evren Davasına Ret," *Milliyet*, June 20, 1990.
132. Kılıçdaroğlu, "Senden Önceki Nesil Dinsiz Miydi," *Hürriyet Gündem*, January 31, 2012; "Dindar Nesil Polemiği," *Haberturk*, Feburary 2, 2012.
133. "Dindar Gençlik Yetiştirmek İstiyoruz," *Bianet*, February 1, 2012; https://www.youtube.com/watch?v=AnKDiG7cLvk, accessed March 27, 2015.
134. "Paul Auster Refuses Turkey Visit Over Jailed Scribes," *Hürriyet Daily News*, January 29, 2012.
135. "Dindar Gençlik Yetiştirmek İstiyoruz"; https://www.youtube.com/watch?v=AnKDiG7cLvk.
136. FATİH is a project for state investment to widely introduce computers, the Internet, and technology in education.
137. "Erdoğan: Gençlik Tinerci mi Olsun?," *NTV*, February 6, 2012.
138. A drug addiction seen mostly among the lumpen youth.
139. "Seçilmişleri Atanmışlara Etmeyiz," *CNN Türk*, February 19, 2012.
140. https://www.youtube.com/watch?v=Kz2o5AGsBUI, accessed December 12, 2014. For further discussion on Necip Fazıl Kısakürek, see Umut Azak, *Islam and Secularism in Turkey: Kemalism, Religion and the Nation-State* (London: I. B. Tauris 2010).
141. "Bahçeli: Maksatları Arızalı ve Marazlı," *Milliyet*, March 5, 2012.
142. Necip Fazıl Kısakürek, *Hitâbeler* (Istanbul: B. D. Yayınları, 1997), 215.
143. Such a conceptualization of laiklik was not new in Turkey. It was defended by the CKMP in the writing of the 1961 constitution (see chap. 5), although it was not coined as such.
144. "Başbakan Recep Tayyip Erdoğan'dan Seçmeli Ders Uyarısı," *Hürriyet*, September 23, 2013; "Başbakan Erdoğan'dan Velilere Seçmeli Ders Uyarısı," *T24 Bağımsız Internet Gazetesi*, September 22, 2013.
145. http://www.meb.gov.tr/duyurular/duyurular2012/12yil_soru_cevaplar.pdf, accessed December 13, 2014.
146. "4+4+4 Büyük Kavgayla Komisyondan Geçti," *Milliyet*, March 11, 2012.
147. http://www.hurriyet.com.tr/gundem/20235384.asp, http://www.hurriyet.com.tr/gundem/20221595.asp, accessed December 13, 2014.

148. Proposal for Law, no. 199, *Journal of the Minutes*, 2nd year, 24th term, 6, 4.
149. "Komisyonda Yumruk Yumruğa Kavga," *NTV*, March 8, 2012.
150. http://www.tbmm.gov.tr/ictuzuk/ictuzuk.htm, accessed January 15, 2014.
151. *Journal of the Minutes*, 2nd year, 83rd Meeting, 24th term, March 27, 2012.
152. Ibid.
153. The Turkish education system has central exams at the end of the sixth, seventh, and eighth years for placement in high schools. The guidance in question in the making of this law is a supplementary practice.
154. The High Council of Education had identified plagiarism in an academic book of the AKP minister of education, who had a PhD. This issue came up for discussion again during the parliamentary debates on the new education law, and the minister responded: "That person posing a question on my plagiarism, first should give an account of the sources of his own wealth, before asking me questions." The defense of corruption hit bottom when, during the larger debates on AKP corruption starting in December 2013, one AKP member talked about the "right to sin." See http://www.bianet.org /bianet/siyaset/153987 -metin-kulunk-un-17-aralik-i-aklayan-akli-gunah-isleme-ozgurlugu, accessed December 14, 2014.
155. *Journal of the Minutes*, 2nd year, 84th meeting, 24th term, March 28, 2012.
156. Ibid., 2nd year, 85th meeting, 24th term, March 29, 2012.
157. The words recited on becoming a Muslim.
158. A council under the Ministry of Interior responsible for designing curricula.
159. "Kesk Eylemcilerine Sert Müdahele," *CNN Türk*, March 28, 2012.
160. "KESK'in 4+4+4 Eylemi Nedeniyle 502 Kişi Yargılancak," *T24 Bağımsız Internet Gazetesi*, September 26, 2013.
161. "Constitutional Court Decision," *Official Gazette*, no. 2012/65, April 18, 2013, decision no. 2012/128, September 20, 2012. Subsequent references are cited in the text.
162. "Alevilik Din Değildir; Ali ile Alakaları Yok," *Radikal*, February 22, 2013.
163. Rajeev Bhargava, "What Is Secularism For?," in *Secularism and Its Critics*, ed. Rajeev Bhargava (New Delhi: Oxford University Press, 1998), 493.
164. http://www.bianet.org/bianet/egitim/160505-din-dersi-1-siniflara-demo krasi-dersi-sosyal-bilgilerin-icine.

Conclusion

1. Daniel Lerner, *The Passing of Traditional Society: Modernizing the Middle East* (Glencoe, Ill.: Free Press, 1958), 43.
2. Dipesh Chakrabarty, *Provincializing Europe: Post-Colonial Thought and Historical Difference* (Princeton, N.J.: Princeton University Press, 2000), 8.

3. Ibid., 18.
4. Lerner, *The Passing of Traditional Society*, viii, ix, vii.
5. Lerner's mention of modernization reaching lower levels of society also resembles post-1990 evaluations of political Islam in Turkey. See Çağlar Keyder, "Whither the Project of Modernity? Turkey in the 1990s," in *Rethinking Modernity and National Identity in Turkey*, ed. Sibel Bozdoğan and Reşat Kasaba (Seattle: University of Washington Press, 1997), 37– 51.
6. Lerner, *The Passing of Traditional Society*, viii.
7. Ibid., 13.
8. Clifford Geertz, "The Cerebral Savage: On the Work of Claude Levi-Strauss," in *The Interpretation of Cultures* (New York: Basic Books, 1973).
9. Charles Taylor, "Two Theories of Modernity," *Public Culture* 11, no. 1 (1999), 154.
10. Lerner, *The Passing of Traditional Society*, 46–47. Lerner writes: "Taking the Western model of modernization as a baseline is forced upon us, moreover, by the tacit assumption and proclaimed goals which prevail among Middle East spokesmen. . . . Their own declared policies and programs set our criteria of modernization. . . . The West is still a useful model. . . . But these societies-in-a-hurry have little patience with the historical *pace* of Western development; what happened in the West over centuries, some Middle Easterners now seek to accomplish in years. Moreover, they want to do it their 'own way.'"
11. Ibid., 43–44.
12. W. E. B. Du Bois, *The Souls of Black Folk* (1903; New York: Dover Publications 1994), 2, "double-conscousness"; and Yael Navaro-Yashin, "Introduction: Semiconscious States: The Political and the Psychic in Urban Public Life," in *Faces of the State: Secularism and Public Life in Turkey* (Princeton, N.J.: Princeton University Press, 2002), 15, "semi-consciousness" comes to my mind for further comparison.
13. Nilüfer Göle, *The Forbidden Modern: Civilization and Veiling* (Ann Arbor: University of Michigan Press, 1996), 97.
14. Ibid., 2.
15. Ibid., 131.
16. Salman Rushdie, *Midnight's Children* (London: Vintage Books, 1995).
17. John R. Bowen, *Why the French Don't Like the Headscarves: Islam, the State, and Public Space* (Princeton, N.J.: Princeton University Press, 2007), 32.
18. Albert de Mun, "De la rupture à la séparation: Séance du 22 octobre 1904," in *Contre la séparation* (Paris: Librairie Vve CH. Poussielgue, 1905), 57.
19. Talal Asad, *Formations of the Secular: Christianity, Islam, Modernity* (Stanford, Calif.: Standord University Press, 2003), 13; italics mine.
20. Talal Asad, "Two European Images on Non-European Rule," in *Anthropology & the Colonial Encounter*, ed. Talal Asad (New York: Humanities Press, 1973).
21. Chakrabarty, *Provincializing Europe*.
22. Faruk Mercan, *Fethullah Gülen* (Istanbul: Doğan Egmont, 2008), 113.

Bibliography

Acomb, Evelyn Martha. *The French Laic Laws 1879–1889*. New York: Columbia University Press, 1941.

Adıvar, Halide Edib. "Dictatorship and Reforms in Turkey." *Yale Review* 19 (1929): 27–44.

Akan, Murat. "Contextualizing Multiculturalism." *Studies in Comparative International Development* 38, no. 2 (2003): 57–75.

——. "Governing Religious Difference or Differentiating Governance Religiously?" Paper presented at the ECPR Joint Sessions, Lisbon, 2009.

——. "Infrastructural Politics of Laiklik in the Writing of the 1961 Turkish Constitution." *Interventions: International Journal of Postcolonial Studies* 13, no. 2 (2011): 190–211.

——. "Laïcité and Multiculturalism: The Stasi Report in Context." *British Journal of Sociology* 60, no. 2 (2009): 237–56.

——. "A Politics of Comparative Conceptualizations and Institutions: Two Non-European Images on European Secularity in the Writing of the 1961 Turkish Constitution." Max Planck Institute Working Paper 13–02 (2013): 1–34.

——. "Twin Tolerations or Siamese Twins: Kemalist Laicism and Political Islam in Turkey." In *Institutions and Democracy: Essays in Honor of Alfred Stepan*, edited by Douglas Chalmers and Scott Mainwaring, 381–423. Notre Dame, Ind.: University of Notre Dame Press, 2012.

Akça, İsmet. "Ordu, Devlet ve Sınıflar: 27 Mayıs 1960 Darbesi Örneği Üzerinden Alternatif Bir Okuma Denemesi." In Balta and Akça, *Türkiye'de Ordu Devlet ve Güvenlik Siyaseti*, 351–406.

Ardura, Bernard. *Le Concordat entre Pie VII et Bonaparte, 15 Juillet 1801: Bicentenaire d'une réconciliation*. Paris: Cerf, 2001.

Asad, Talal, ed. *Anthropology & the Colonial Encounter*. New York: Humanities Press, 1973.

——. "The Construction of Religion as an Anthropological Category." In Asad, *Genealogies of Religion: Discipline and Reasons of Power in Christianity and Islam*, 27–54.

——. *Formations of the Secular: Christianity, Islam, Modernity*. Stanford, Calif.: Stanford University Press, 2003.

——. *Genealogies of Religion: Discipline and Reasons of Power in Christianity and Islam*. London: John Hopkins University Press, 1993.

——. "The Idea of an Anthropology of Islam." Occasional Paper Series, Center for Contemporary Area Studies, Georgetown University, March 1986.

——. "Two European Images on Non-European Rule." In Asad, *Anthropology & the Colonial Encounter*.

Audi, Robert. "The Separation of Church and State and Obligations of Citizenship." *Philosophy and Public Affairs* 18, no. 3 (1989): 256–96.

Azak, Umut. *Islam and Secularism in Turkey: Kemalism, Religion and the Nation-State*. London: I. B. Tauris, 2010.

Babès, Leïla, ed. *Les nouvelles manières de croire: Judaïsme, christianisme, islam, nouvelles religiosities*. Paris: Les Éditions de l'Atelier/Éditions Ouvrières, 1996.

Balibar, Étienne. "Dissonances Within *Laïcité*." *Constellations* 11, no. 3 (2004): 353–67.

Balta Paker, Evren, and İsmet Akça, eds. *Türkiye'de Ordu Devlet ve Güvenlik Siyaseti*. Bilgi Üniversitesi Yayınları, 2010.

Bardout, Jean-Claude. *L'histoire étonnante de la loi 1901*. Lyon: Editions Juris, 2000.

Barkey, Karen. "Rethinking Ottoman Management of Diversity: What Can We Learn for Modern Turkey." In Kuru and Stepan, *Democracy, Islam and Secularism in Turkey*, 12–31.

Barry, Brian. *Culture and Equality: An Egalitarian Critique of Multiculturalism*. Cambridge, Mass.: Harvard University Press, 2002.

——. "The Muddles of Multiculturalism." *New Left Review* 8 (March/April 2001): 49–71.

——. "Second Thoughts-and Some First Thoughts Revived." In Kelly *Multiculturalism Reconsidered*, 204–38.

Başgil, Ali Fuad. *Başgil'den Mektuplar*. Istanbul: Yağmur Yayınevi, 2007.

——. *Demokrasi Yolunda*. Istanbul: Yağmur Yayınevi, 2006.

——. *Din ve Laiklik*. Istanbul: Sönmez Neşriyat ve Matbaacılık, 1954.

——. "Dördüncü Kurultay Münasebetiyle," *Siyasal Bilgiler*, no. 50 (May 1935): 1–5.

——. *Esas Teşkilat Hukuku Dersleri*. Istanbul: İnkilap Kitabevi, 1940.

——. *Gençlerle Başbaşa*. Istanbul: Yağmur Yayınevi, 2007.

——. *Hukukun Ana Meseleleri ve Müesseleri: Konferanslar*. Istanbul: Yağmur Yayınevi, 2008.

——. *İlmin Işığında Günün Meseleleri*. Istanbul: Yağmur Yayınevi, 2006.

———. *Türkçe Meselesi*. Istanbul: Yağmur Yayınevi, 2007.
———. *27 Mayıs İhtilali ve Sepebleri*. Istanbul: Çeltüt Matbaacılık, 1966.
———. *Yakın Maziden Hatıra Kırıntıları*. Istanbul: Yağmur Yayınevi, 2007.
Baubérot, Jean. "Le cas français ou l'impossible religion civile." In *Les nouvelles manières de croire: Judaïsme, christianisme, islam, nouvelles religiosities*, edited by Leila Babès, 177–89.
———. "La Commission Stasi vue par l'un de ses membres." *French Politics, Culture & Society* 22, no. 3 (2004): 135–41.
———. "Existe-t-il une religion civile républicaine?" *French Politics, Culture & Society* 25, no. 2 (2007): 3–18.
———. *La laïcité expliquée à M. Sarkozy . . . et à ceux qui écrivent ses discours*. Paris: Éditions Albin Michel, 2008.
———. "Laïcité, laïcisation, sécularisation." In Dierkens, *Pluralisme religieux et laïcité dans l'Union européenne*, 9–19.
———. "La laïcité, le chêne et le Roseau." *Libération*, December 15, 2003.
———. "La séparation et son contexte sociohistorique." In Baubérot and Wieviorka, *De la séparation des Églises et de l'État à l'avenir de la laïcité*, 61–74.
———. "The Two Thresholds of Laicization." In Bhargava, *Secularism and Its Critics*, 94–136.
———. "D'une comparaison laïcité française, laïcité turque." In Rigoni, *Turquie, Les mille visages: Politique, religion, femmes, immigration*, 35–40.
Baubérot, Jean, and Michel Wieviorka, eds. *De la séparation des Églises et de l'État à l'avenir de la laïcité*. France: Éditions de l'Aube, 2005.
Beattie, Nicholas. "Yeast in the Dough? Catholic Schooling in France 1981–95." In Chadwick, *Catholicism, Politics and Society in Twentieth-Century France*, 197–218.
Berkes, Niyazi. *The Development of Secularism in Turkey*. Montreal: McGill University Press, 1964.
Bertaux, Sandrine. "Towards the Unmaking of the French Mainstream: The Empirical Turn in Immigrant Assimilation and the Making of Frenchness." *Journal of Ethnic and Migration Studies* 42, no. 9 (2016): 1496–1512.
Bhargava, Rajeev, ed. *Secularism and Its Critics*. New Delhi: Oxford University Press, 1998.
Bilgrami, Akeel, ed. *Beyond the Secular West*. New York: Columbia University Press, 2016.
Bölükbaşı, Deniz. *Türk Siyasetin Anadolu Fırtınası: Osman Bölükbaşı*. Istanbul: Doğan Kitap, 2005.
Boubakeur, Dalil. "L'Islam et l'enseignement des religions dans l'École de la République." In Sirat, Capelle, Boubakeur, and Joutard, *L'enseignement des religions à l'école laïque*, 51–76.
Bowen, John R. *Why the French Don't Like Headscarves: Islam, the State, and Public Space*. Princeton, N.J.: Princeton University Press, 2007.

Bozan, İrfan. *Devlet ile Toplum Arasında Bir Okul: İmam hatip Liseleri . . . Bir Kurum: Diyanet İşleri Başkanlığı*. Istanbul: TESEV, 2006.

Bozdoğan, Sibel, and Reşat Kasaba, eds. *Rethinking Modernity and National Identity in Turkey*. Seattle: University of Washington Press, 1997.

Burns, Michael. *France and the Dreyfus Affair: A Documentary History*. New York: Bedford/St. Martin's, 1999.

Byrnes, Timothy, and Peter J. Katzenstein, eds. *Religion in an Expanding Europe*. Cambridge: Cambridge University Press, 2006.

Çakır, Ruşen, İrfan Bozan, and Balkan Talu. *İmam Hatip Liseleri: Efsaneler ve Gerçekler*. Istanbul: Tesev Yayınları, 2004.

Calhoun, Craig, Mark Juergensmeyer, and Jonathan VanAntwerpen, eds. *Rethinking Secularism*. Oxford: Oxford University Press, 2011.

Capelle, Philippe. "Laïcité, religion, école." In Sirat, Capelle, Boubakeur, and Joutard, *L'enseignement des religions à l'école laïque*, 27–49.

Capoccia, Giovanni, and R. Daniel Kelemen. "The Study of Critical Junctures: Theory, Narrative, and Counterfactuals in Historical Institutionalism." *World Politics* 59, no. 3 (2007): 341–69.

Casanova, José. *Public Religions in the Modern World*. Chicago: University of Chicago Press, 1994.

———. "Public Religions Revisited." In *Religion Beyond the Concept*, ed. Hent De Vries. New York: Fordham University Press, 2008.

———. "Religion, European Secular Identities, and European Integration." In Byrnes and Katzenstein, *Religion in an Expanding Europe*, 65–92.

———. "A Secular Age Dawn or Twilight?" In Warner, VanAntwerpen, and Calhoun, *Varieties of Secularism in a Secular Age*, 265–81.

Chadwick, Kay, ed. *Catholicism, Politics and Society in Twientieth-Century France*. Liverpool: Liverpool University Press, 2000.

Chakrabarty, Dipesh. *Provincializing Europe: Post-Colonial Thought and Historical Difference*. Princeton, N.J.: Princeton University Press, 2000.

Chalmers, Douglas, and Scott Mainwaring, eds. *Institutions and Democracy: Essays in Honor of Alfred Stepan*. Notre Dame, Ind.: University of Notre Dame Press, 2012.

Chatterjee, Partha. *Nationalist Thought and the Colonial World: A Derivative Discourse*. Minneapolis: University of Minnesota Press, 1986.

———. *The Nation and Its Fragments: Colonial and Postcolonial Histories*. Princeton, N.J.: Princeton University Press, 1992.

———. "Secularism and Tolerance." In Bhargava, *Secularism and Its Critics*, 345–79.

Chouder, Ismahane, Malika Latrèche, and Pierre Tévanian. *Les filles voilées parlent*. Paris: La fabrique éditions, 2008.

Coffey, Joan L. "The Aix Affair of 1891: A Turning Point in Church-State Relations Before the Separation." *French Historical Studies* 21, no. 4 (1958): 543–59.

Collier, Ruth Berins, and David Collier. "Inducements Versus Constraints: Disaggregating: Corporatism." *American Political Science Review* 73, no. 4 (1979): 967–86.

Combes, Émile. *Une deuxième campagne laïque: Vers la séparation.* Paris: G. Bellais, 1905.

Daniel, André. *L'année politique.* Paris: Librairie Académique Didier, 1903.

Dansette, Adrien. *Religious History of Modern France.* 2 vols. New York: Herder and Herder, 1961.

Daver, Bülent. *Türkiye Cumhuriyetinde Layiklik.* Ankara: Son Havadis, 1955.

Davison, Andrew. *Secularism and Revivalism in Turkey: A Hermeneutical Approach.* New Haven, Conn.: Yale University Press, 1998.

Debré, Michel. *Gouverner mémoires 1958–1962*, vol. 3. Paris: Éditions Albin Michel, 1988.

Dierkens, Alain, ed. *Pluralisme religieux et laïcité dans l'Union européenne.* Brussels: Editions de l'Universite de Bruxelles, 1994.

Drake, Paul W. *Labor Movements and Dictatorship: The Southern Cone in Comparative Perspective.* London: John Hopkins University Press, 1996.

Du Bois, W. E. B. *The Souls of Black Folk.* New York: Dover Publications, 1994.

Eisenstadt, Shmuel Noah. "Multiple Modernities." *Daedalus* 129, no. 1 (2000): 1–29.

Eisenstadt, Shmuel Noah, and Wolfgang Schluchter. "Introduction: Paths to Early Modernities—A Comparative View." *Daedalus* 127, no. 3 (1998): 1–18.

Elster, Jon. *Nuts and Bolts for the Social Sciences.* Cambridge: Cambridge University Press, 1989.

Erbakan, Necmettin. *Milli Görüş.* Istanbul: Dergah Yayınları, 1975.

Ekşioğlu, Deniz. "The Politics of Religion in the United States Federal Context: The Faith-Based Initiative." PhD dissertation, Boğaziçi University, 2011.

Fitch, Nancy. "Mass Culture, Mass Parliamentary Politics, and Modern Anti-Semitism: The Dreyfus Affair in Rural France." *American Historical Review* 97, no. 1 (1992): 55–95.

Freathy, R.J.K. "Ecclesiastical and Religious Factors Which Preserved Christian and Traditional Forms of Education for Citizenship in English Schools 1934–1944." *Oxford Review of Education* 33, no. 3 (July 2007): 367–77.

Fukuyama, Francis. "The End of History?" *National Interest* (Summer 1989): 3–18.

Gaonkar, Dilip Parameshwar. "On Alternative Modernities." In Gaonkar, "Alter/Native Modernities." 1–18.

———, ed. "Alter/Native Modernities." Special issue, *Public Culture* 11, no. 1 (1999).

Geertz, Clifford. "The Cerebral Savage: On the Work of Claude Levi-Strauss." In Geertz, *The Interpretation of Cultures*, 345–59.

———. *The Interpretation of Cultures.* New York: Basic Books, 1973.

———. "Ritual and Social Change: A Javanese Example." *American Anthropologist* 59, no. 1 (1957): 32–54.

———. "Thick Description: Toward an Interpretive Theory of Culture." In Geertz, *The Interpretation of Cultures*, 3–30.

Göle, Nilüfer. *The Forbidden Modern: Civilization and Veiling.* Ann Arbor: University of Michigan Press, 1996.

———. "Toward an Autonomization of Politics and Civil Society in Turkey." In Heper and Evin, *Politics in the Third Turkish Republic*, 213–22.

Gramsci, Antonio. *Selections from the Prison Notebooks.* Edited and translated by Quintin Hoare and Geoffrey Nowell Smith. New York: International Publishers, 1971.

Grillo, Ralph, and Prakash Shah. "Reasons to Ban? The Anti-Burqa Movement in Western Europe." MMG Working Paper 12–05 (2012).

Habermas, Jürgen. "Religion in the Public Sphere." *European Journal of Philosophy* 14, no. 1 (2006): 1–25.

Haggard, Stephan, and Robert R. Kaufman. *The Political Economy of Democratic Transitions.* Princeton, N.J.: Princeton University Press, 1995.

Hart, H.L.A. *The Concept of Law.* Oxford: Oxford University Press, 2012.

Hazareesingh, S. *Political Traditions in Modern France.* Oxford: Oxford University Press, 1994.

Helmstadter, Richard, ed. *Freedom and Religion in the Nineteenth Century.* Stanford, Calif.: Stanford University Press, 1997.

Heper, Metin. "Transition to Democracy in Turkey: Toward a New Pattern." In Heper and Evin, *Politics in the Third Turkish Republic*, 13–20.

Heper, Metin, and Ahmet Evin, eds. *Politics in the Third Turkish Republic.* Boulder, Colo.: Westview Press, 1994.

———. *State, Democracy and the Military: Turkey in the 1980s.* New York: De Gruyter, 1988.

Holyoake, George Jacob, and Charles Albert Watts. *English Secularism and the Progress of Society: . . . Two Papers Read at the Brussels International Congress . . . 1880.* London, 1880?

Huntington, Samuel. "The Clash of Civilizations?" *Foreign Affairs* 72, no. 3 (1993): 22–49.

———. *The Clash of Civilizations: Remaking of the World Order.* New York: Touchstone, 1997.

Jackson, Robert, Siebren Miedema, Wolfram Weisse, and Jean-Paul Willaime, eds. *Religion and Education in Europe: Developments, Contexts, and Debates.* Berlin: Waxman Münster, 2007.

Jacobsen, Janet R., and Ann Pellegrini, eds. *Secularisms.* Durham, N.C.: Duke University Press, 2008.

Joas, Hans, and Klaus Wiegandt, eds. *Secularization and the World Religions.* Translated by Alex Skinner. Liverpool: Liverpool University Press, 2009.

Joutard, Phillippe. "L'enseignement du fait religieux à l'école laïque." In Sirat, Capelle, Boubakeur, and Joutard, *L'enseignement des religions à l'école laïque*, 77–88.

Kalyvas, Stathis N. *The Rise of Christian Democracy in Europe.* Ithaca, N.Y.: Cornell University Press, 1996.

Karaosmanoğlu, Yakup Kadri. *Yaban.* Istanbul: İletişim Yayınları, 2008.
Karaömerlioğlu, M. Asım. "The Village Institutes Experience in Turkey." *British Journal of Middle Eastern Studies* 25, no. 1 (1998): 47–73.
Kastoryano, Riva. "Religion and Incorporation: Islam in France and Germany." *International Migration Review* 38, no. 3 (2004):1234–55.
Katzenstein, Peter J. "Multiple Modernities as Limits to Secular Europeanization." In Byrnes and Katzenstein, *Religion in an Expanding Europe,* 1–33.
Katznelson, Ira, and Gareth Stedman Jones. "Introduction: Multiple Secularisities." In Katznelson and Jones, *Religion and the Political Imagination,* 1–22.
———, eds. *Religion and the Political Imagination.* Cambridge: Cambridge University Press, 2010.
Keddie, Nikki R. "Secularism and the State: Towards Clarity and Global Comparison." *New Left Review* 226 (November/December 1997): 21–40.
Kelly, Paul, ed. *Multiculturalism Reconsidered.* Cambridge: Polity, 2002.
Kemal, Mustafa. *Nutuk-Söylev.* Ankara: Türk Tarih Kurumu Basimevi, 1999.
Keyder, Çağlar. "The Political Economy of Turkish Democracy." *New Left Review* 115 (May/June 1979): 3–44.
———. *State and Class in Turkey: A Study in Capitalist Development.* London: Verso, 1987.
———. "Whither the Project of Modernity? Turkey in the 1990s." In Bozdoğan and Kasaba, *Rethinking Modernity and National Identity in Turkey,* 37–51.
Kili, Suna, and Şeref Gözübüyük. *Türk Anayasa Metinleri (Sened-i Ittifaktan Günümüze).* Istanbul: Türkiye İş Bankası Kültür Yayınları, 2000.
Kısakürek, Necip Fazıl. *Hitabeler.* Istanbul: B. D. Yayınları, 1997.
Kuru, Ahmet T. *Secularsim and State Policies Toward Religion: The United States, Frances, and Turkey.* Cambridge: Cambridge University Press, 2009.
Kuru, Ahmet T., and Alfred Stepan, eds. *Democracy, Islam, and Secularsim in Turkey.* New York: Columbia University Press, 2012.
Kymlicka, Will. *Liberalism, Community, and Culture.* Oxford: Oxford University Press, 1989.
———. *Multicultural Citizenship.* Oxford: Clarendon Press, 1995.
Kymlicka, Will, and Magdalena Opalski. *Can Liberal Pluralism be Exported?: Western Political Theory and Ethnic Relations in Eastern Europe* New York: Oxford University Press, 2001.
Laborde, Cécile. "Secular Philosophy and Muslim Headscarves in Schools." *Journal of Political Philosophy* 13, no 3 (2005): 305–29.
Lalouette, Jacqueline. *La séparation des Églises et de l'État: Genèse et développement d'une idée 1789–1905.* Paris: Éditions du seuil, 2005.
Larkin, Maurice. *Church and State After the Dreyfus Affair.* New York: Harper & Row, 1973.
———. "The Church and the French Concordat, 1891 to 1902." *English Historical Review* 81, no. 321 (1966): 717–39.

———. "Loubet's Visit to Rome and the Question of Papal Prestige." *Historical Journal* 4, no. 1 (1961): 97–103.

———. "The Vatican, French Catholics, and the Associations Cultuelles." *Journal of Modern History* 36, no. 3 (1964): 298–317.

Le Comte, Maxime. *Les Ralliés: Histoire d'un parti (1886–1898)*. Paris: Ernest Flammarion, 1898.

Lerner, Daniel. *The Passing of Traditional Society: Modernizing the Middle East*. Glencoe, Ill.: Free Press, 1958.

Levey, Geoffrey Brahm, and Tariq Modood, eds. *Secularism, Religion and Multicultural Citizenship*. Cambridge: Cambridge University Press, 2008.

Locke, John. "Letter Concerning Toleration." In *The Works of John Locke*. 9 vols. 12th ed. (London: Rivington, 1824). http://oll.libertyfund.org/titles/764.

Machiavelli, Niccolò. *Selected Political Writings*. Indianapolis: Hackett, 1994.

Maclure, Jocelyn, and Charles Taylor. *Secularism and Freedom of Conscience*. Translated by Jane Marie Todd. Cambridge, Mass.: Harvard University Press, 2011.

Mahmood, Saba. "Secularism, Hermeneutics, and Empire: The Politics of Islamic Reformation." *Public Culture* 18, no. 2 (2006): 323–47.

Martin, Benjamin F., Jr. "The Creation of the Action Liberale Populaire: An Example of Party Formation in Third Republic France." *French Historical Studies* 9, no. 4 (1976): 660–89.

McIntire, C. T. "Changing Religious Establishments and Religious Liberty in France Part I: 1787–1879." In Helmstadter, *Freedom and Religion in the Nineteenth Century*, 233–72.

———. "Changing Religious Establishments and Religious Liberty in France Part II: 1879–1908." In Helmstadter, *Freedom and Religion in the Nineteenth Century*, 273–302.

Mahoney, James, and Dietrich Rueschemeyer, eds. *Comparative Historical Analysis in the Social Sciences*. Cambridge: Cambridge University Press, 2006.

Mahoney, James, and Kathleen Thelen. *Explaining Institutional Change: Ambiguity, Agency, and Power*. New York: Cambridge University Press, 2009.

———. "A Theory of Gradual Institutional Change." In Mahoney and Thelen, *Explaining Institutional Change: Ambiguity, Agency, and Power*, 1–37.

Malche, Albert. *Istanbul Üniversitesi Hakkında Rapor*. Istanbul: Devlet Basımevi, 1939.

———. *Yeni Terbiyenin Prensipleri*. Translated by Sabri Esat Siyavuşgil. Istanbul: Arkadaş Matbaası, 1939.

Marx, Karl. *The 18th Brumaire of Louis Bonaparte*. New York: International Publishers, 1998.

Mayeur, Jean-Marie. *La séparation de l'Église et de l'État (1905)*. Paris: René Julliard, 1966.

———. *La vie politique sous la Troisième République 1870–1940*. Paris: Éditions du Seuil, 1984.

Mayeur, Jean-Marie, and Madeleine Rebérioux. *The Third Republic from Its Origins to the Great War, 1871–1914*. Translated by J. R. Foster. Cambridge: Cambridge University Press, 1984.

McManners, John. *Church and State in France, 1870–1914*. New York: Harper & Row, 1972.

Mendieta, Eduardo, and Jonathan VanAntwerpen, eds. *The Power of Religion in the Public Sphere*. New York: Columbia University Press, 2011.

Mercan, Faruk. *Fethullah Gülen*. Istanbul: Doğan Egmont, 2008.

Mill, John Stuart. *Three Essays on Religion*. New York: Prometheus Books, 1998.

———. "Utility of Religion." In Mill, *Three Essays on Religion*, 69–122.

Mitchell, Timothy. *Rule of Experts: Egypt, Techno-Politics, Modernity*. Berkeley: University of California Press, 2002.

Mun, Albert de. "L'apostasie officielle." In *Contre la séparation*, 96–105.

———. *Contre la séparation*. Paris: Librairie Vve CH. Poussielgue, 1905.

———. *Contre la séparation: De la rupture à la condamnation*. Paris: Librairie Vve CH. Poussielgue, 1906.

———. "De la rupture à la séparation: Séance du 22 octobre 1904." In *Contre la séparation*, 52–61.

———. "Le nouvel article 4." In *Contre la séparation*, 213–20.

———. "Une entreprise sans exemple en Amérique." In *Contre la séparation*, 113–21.

———. "Une entreprise sans exemple en Europe." In *Contre la séparation*, 106–12.

Navaro-Yashin, Yael. *Faces of the State: Secularism and Public Life in Turkey*. Princeton, N.J.: Princeton University Press, 2002.

———. "Introduction: Semiconscious States: The Political and the Psychic in Urban Public Life." In *Faces of the State: Secularism and Public Life in Turkey*, 1–16.

———. "Uses and Abuses of State and Civil Society in Contemporary Turkey." *New Perspectives on Turkey* 18 (Spring 1998).

Okutan, Ömer. "Din Eğitimi." In *Cumhuriyet Döneminde Eğitim*. Istanbul: Milli Eğitim Basimevi, 1983, 409–25.

On, Steve. "Brian Barry and the Headscarf Case in France." *Contemporary Political Theory* 5, no. 2 (2006): 176–92.

Onar, Sıddık Sami. *İdare Hukukunun Umumi Esasları*. 3 vols. Istanbul: İsmail Akgün Matbaası, 1960.

Özek, Çetin. *Türkiye'de Laiklik: Gelişim ve Koruyucu Ceza Hükümleri*. Istanbul: Baha Matbaası, 1962.

Öztürk, Kazım. *Türk Anayasası*. Istanbul: İş Bankası Yayınları, 1966.

Palier, Bruno, and Kathleen Thelen. "Institutionalizing Dualism: Complementarities and Change in France and Germany." *Politics and Society* 38, no. 1 (2010): 119–48.

Parla, Taha. *Türkiye'de Anayasalar*. Istanbul: Iletişim Yayınları, 2002.

———. *Türkiye' de Siyasal Kültürün Resmi Kaynakları III: Kemalist Tek-Parti İdeolojisi ve CHP'nin Altı Ok'u*. Istanbul: Iletişim Yayınları, 1992.

Parla, Taha, and Andrew Davsion. *Corporatist Ideology in Kemalist Turkey*. Syracuse, N.Y.: Syracuse University Press, 2005.

——. "Secularism and Laicism in Turkey." In Jacobsen and Pellegrini, *Secularisms*, 58–75.

Partin, Malcolm O. *Waldeck-Rousseau, Combes and the Church: The Politics of Anti-Clericalism, 1899–1905*. Durham, N.C.: Duke University Press, 1969.

Philpott, Daniel, and Timothy Samuel Shah. "Faith and Federation: the Role of the Religious Ideas and Institutions in European Political Convergence." In Byrnes and Katzenstein, *Religion in an Expanding Europe*, 34–64.

Pinaud, P. F. "L'administration des Cultes de 1800 à 1815." *Revue de l'Institut Napoléon* 132 (1976): 31–39.

Prakash, Gyan. "Writing Post-Orientalist Histories of the Third World: Perspectives from Indian Historiography." *Comparative Studies in Society and History* 32, no. 2 (1990): 383–408.

Rabinow, Paul, and William M. Sullivan, eds. *Interpretive Social Science: A Second Look*. Berkeley: University of California Press, 1987.

Rawls, John. *Political Liberalism*. New York: Columbia University Press, 1993.

Riesman, David. "Introduction." In Daniel Lerner, *The Passing of Traditional Society: Modernizing the Middle East*. Glencoe, Ill.: The Free Press, 1958.

Rigoni, Isabelle, ed. *Turquie, Les mille visages: Politique, religion, femmes, immigration*. Paris: Éditions Syllepsse, 2000.

Rosenblum, Nancy L., ed. *Obligations of Citizenship and Demands of Faith: Religious Accommodation in Pluralist Societies*. Princeton, N.J.: Princeton University Press, 2000.

Ross, Ronald J. "The Kulturkampf: Restrictions and Controls on the Practice of Religion in Bismarck's Germany." In Helmstadter, *Freedom and Religion in the Nineteenth Century*, 172–95.

Rousseau, Jean Jacques. *The Social Contract*. Translated by M. Cranston. London: Penguin Books, 1968.

Rushdie, Salman. *Midnight's Children*. London: Vintage Books, 1995.

Rustow, Dankwart A. "Turkish Democracy in Historical and Comparative Perspective." In Heper and Evin, *Politics in the Third Turkish Republic*, 3–12.

Sabatier, Paul. *Disestablishment in France*. Translated by Robert Dell. London: T. F. Unwin, 1906.

Salmon, Frédéric. *Atlas électoral de la France 1848–2001*. Paris: Éditions du Seuil, 2001.

Sarkozy, Nicolas. *La République, les religions, l'espérance*. Paris: Cerf, 2004.

Scott, Joan W. *The Politics of the Veil*. Princeton, N.J.: Princeton University Press, 2007.

Sedgwick, Alexander. *The Ralliement in French Politics 1890–1898*. Cambridge, Mass.: Harvard University Press, 1965.

Şener, Nedim. *Kırmızı Cuma: Dink'in Kalemini Kim kırdı*. Istanbul: Doğan Kitapçılık, 2011.

Shklar, Judith N., "Squaring the Hermeneutical Circle." *Social Research* 53, no. 3 (1986).
Şık, Ahmet, et al. *Oookitap: Dokunan Yanar*. Istanbul: Postacı Kitapevi, 2011.
Simon, Jules. *La liberté de conscience*. Paris: Hachette, 1857.
Sinclair-Webb, Emma. "Sectarian Violence, the Alevi Minority and the Left: Kahramanmaraş 1978," In White and Jongerden, *Turkey's Alevi Enigma: A Comprehensive Overview*, 215–35.
Sirat, René-Samuel. "Enseigner les religions: Quel ton juste au pays de la laïcité?" In Sirat, Capelle, Boubakeur, and Joutard, *L'enseignement des religions à l'école laïque*, 7–26.
Sirat, René-Samuel, Philippe Capelle, Dalil Boubakeur, and Philippe Joutard. *L'enseignement des religions à l'école laïque*. Paris: Éditions Salvator, 2003.
Stepan, Alfred. *Arguing Comparative Politics*. Oxford: Oxford University Press, 2001.
——. "The Multiple Secularisms of Modern Democratic and Non-Democratic Regimes." In Calhoun, Juergensmeyer, and Van Antwerpen, *Rethinking Secularism*, 114–44.
——. "The World's Religious Systems and Democracy: Crafting the 'Twin Tolerations.'" In Stepan, *Arguing Comparative Politics*, 213–53.
Tanör, Bülent. *İki Anayasa, 1961–1982*. Istanbul: Beta Basım, 1986.
——. *Osmanlı-Türk Anayasal Gelişmeleri (1789–1980)*. Istanbul: Yapı Kredi Yayınları, 2000.
Tarhanlı, İştar B. *Müslüman Toplum, "Laik" Devlet: Türkiye'de Diyanet İşleri Başkanlığı*. Istanbul: Afa Yayınları, 1993.
Taylor, Charles. "Can Secularism Travel?" In Bilgrami, *Beyond the Secular West*, 1–27.
——. *Dilemmas and Connections: Selected Essays*. Cambridge, Mass.: Harvard University Press, 2011.
——. "Foreword. What Is Secularism?" In Levey and Modood, *Secularism, Religion and Multicultural Citizenship*, xi–xxii.
——. "The Hermeneutics of Conflict." In Tully, *Meaning and Context: Quentin Skinner and His Critics*, 218–28.
——. "Interpretation and the Sciences of Man." In Rabinow and Sullivan, *Interpretive Social Science: A Second Look*, 33–81.
——. *Modern Social Imaginaries*. Durham, N.C.: Duke University Press, 2004.
——. "Modes of Secularism." In Bhargava, *Secularism and Its Critics*, 31–53.
——. "The Politics of Recognition." In *Multiculturalism*, ed. A. Gutmann. Princeton, N.J.: Princeton University Press, 1994.
——. *A Secular Age*. Cambridge, Mass.: Belknap Press of Harvard University Press, 2007.
——. "Two Theories of Modernity." *Public Culture* 11, no. 1 (1999).
——. "What Does Secularism Mean?" In *Dilemmas and Connections: Selected Essays*, 303–25.

———. "Why We Need a Radical Redefinition of Secularism." In Mendieta and VanAntwerpen, *The Power of Religion in the Public Sphere*, 34–59.

Tévanian, Pierre. *Le voile médiatique. Un faux débat: "l'affaire du foulard islamique."* Paris: Éditions Raisons D'agir, 2005.

Thelen, Kathleen. "How Institutions Evolve: Insights from Comparative Historical Research." In Mahoney and Rueschemeyer, *Comparative Historical Analysis in the Social Sciences*, 208–40.

Tippett-Spirtou, S. *French Catholicism*. New York: St. Martin's Press, 2000.

Tocqueville, Alexis de. *Democracy in America*. New York: Harper & Row, 1966.

Toft, Monica Duffy, Daniel Philpott, and Timothy Samuel Shah. *God's Century: Resurgent Religion and Global Politics*. New York. W. W. Norton, 2011.

Toprak, Binnaz. "Islam and Democracy in Turkey." *Turkish Studies* 6, no. 2 (2005): 167–86.

———. *Islam and Political Development in Turkey*. Leiden: E. J. Brill, 1981.

———. "The State, Politics and Religion in Turkey." In Heper and Evin, *State, Democracy and the Military: Turkey in the 1980s*, 119–36.

Tully, James, ed. *Meaning and Context: Quentin Skinner and His Critics*. Princeton, N.J.: Princeton University Press, 1988.

Tunçay, Mete. *Türkiye Cumhuriyeti'nde Tek-Parti Yönetiminin Kurulması (1923–1931)*. Istanbul: Cem Yayinevi, 1981.

Türk Basınında Anayasa Tartışmaları 1960–1961 Bibliyografya. Ankara: TBMM Basımevi, 1981.

Van der Veer, Peter. *Imperial Encounters: Religion and Modernity in India and Britain*. Princeton, N.J.: Princeton University Press, 2001.

Velidedeoğlu, Hıfzı Veldet. *Türkiye' De Üç Devir Var*. Istanbul: Sinan Yayınları, 1972.

Vries, Hent de. "Introduction: Before, Around and Beyond the Theologico-Political." In Vries and Sullivan, *Political Theologies: Public Religions in a Post-Secular World*, 1–88.

———, ed. *Religion Beyond the Concept*. New York: Fordham University Press, 2008.

Vries, Hent de, and Lawrence E. Sullivan, eds. *Political Theologies: Public Religions in a Post-Secular World*. New York: Fordham University Press, 2006.

———. "Preface." In *Political Theoloies: Public Religions in a Post-Secular World*, ix–xii.

Ward, James E. "The Algiers Toast: Lavigerie's Work or Leo XIII's?" *Catholic Historical Review* 51, no. 2 (1965): 173–91.

Warner, M., J. VanAntwerpen, and Craig Calhoun, eds. *Varieties of Secularism in a Secular Age*. Cambridge, Mass.: Harvard University Press, 2010.

Weber, Max. *The Protestant Ethic and the Spirit of Capitalism*. Translated by Talcott Parsons. New York: Routledge, 1992.

White, Paul J., and Joost Jongerden, eds. *Turkey's Alevi Enigma: A Comprehensive Overview*. Leiden: Brill, 2003.

Willaime, Jean-Paul. "The Cultural Turn in the Sociology of Religion in France." *Sociology of Religion* 65, no. 4, (2004): 380.

———. "1905 et la pratique d'une laïcité de reconnaissance sociale des religions." 50e année, no. 129, La République ne reconnaît aucun culte. *Archives de Sciences Sociales des Religions* 129 (2005): 67–82.

———. "Teaching Religious Issues in French Public Schools: From Abstentionist *Laïcité* to a Return of Religion to Public Education." In Jackson, Miedema, Weisse, and Willaime, *Religion and Education in Europe: Developments, Contexts, and Debates*, 87–102.

Yavuz, M. Hakan, ed. *The Emergence of a New Turkey: Democracy and the AK Parti*. Salt Lake City: University of Utah Press, 2006.

———. *Secularism and Muslim Democracy in Turkey*. Cambridge: Cambridge University Press, 2009.

Zola, Émile. *The Dreyfus Affair: 'J'accuse' and Other Writings*. Edited by Alain Pagès, translated by Eleanor Levieux. New Haven, Conn.: Yale University Press, 1996.

Zürcher, Eric J. *Turkey: A Modern History*. New York: I. B. Tauris, 1997.

Biographies and Memoirs

Başgil, Ali Fuad. *Yakın Maziden Hatıra Kırıntıları* [Crumbs of memories from the recent past]. Istanbul: Yağmur Yayınevi, 2007.

Evren, Kenan. *Kenan Evren'in Anıları* [Memoirs of Kenan Evren]. 3 vols. Istanbul: Milliyet Yayınları, 1991.

Ferry, Jules. *Discours et opinions de Jules Ferry. Le second empire, la guerre et la commune / publiés avec commentaires et notes, par Paul Robiquet*. 7 vols. Paris: A. Colin, 1893.

Gaillard, Jean Michel. *Jules Ferry*. Paris: Fayard, 1989.

Hıfzı Veldet Velidedeoğlu. *Türkiye' de Üç Devir Var* [There are three epochs in Turkey]. 2 vols. Istanbul: Sinan Yayınları, 1972.

Court Decisions

"Constitutional Court Decision," *Official Gazette*, April 18, 2013, no. 2012/65, decision no. 2012/128, September 20, 2012.

Danıştay Sekizinci daire yer 207, decision no. 7481, December 28, 2007.

Devlet Şurası Kararlar Dergisi, year 17 no. 60, April 1953–June 1953, 54. Devlet Surasi Kararlari Dergisi, yil: 17, nisan 1953—Hazirna 1953 sayi 60.

Hasan and Eylem Zengin v. Turkey, no. 1448/04 (Sect. 2), ECHR 2007-XI (October 9, 2007).
Yargıtay Cumhuriyet Başsavcılığı vs. Refah Partisi, 1997 (decided on January 16, 1998). Constitutional Court, *Anayasa Mahkemesi Kararlar Dergisi*. Case of *Refah Partisi (Welfare Party) and Others vs. Turkey, European Court of Human Rights*, February 13, 2003.

Dictionaries and Encyclopedias

Larousse, Pierre. *Grand dictionnaire universel du XIXe siècle: Français, historique, géographique, mythologique, bibliographique*, vol. 5, CONTRE-CZYZ. Paris: Administration du Grand Dictionnaire Universel, 1866–1877.
Turkish Dictionary. Istanbul: Cumhuriyet Basimevi, 1945.

Interviews (by Author)

Reha Çamuroğlu, AKP parliamentarian 2007–2011, Ankara, January 16, 2016.
Vural Savaş, general prosecutor of the Supreme Court of Cassation 1997–2001, Ankara, 2003.
Vakur Versan, one of the ten professors who drafted the 1961 constitution, Istanbul, October 28, 2009.
Mehmet Nuri Yılmaz, head of the Directorate of Religious Affairs 1992–2003, Ankara, 2003.

Minutes and Decisions

Beşinci Milli Eğitim Şûrası 5–14 Şubat 1953 [Fifth National Education Congress February 5–14, 1953]. Ankara: Maarif Vekâleti Yayın Müdürlüğü, 1954.
Birinci Kültür Şurası (23–27 Ekim 1982): Genel Kurul Görüşmeleri. Ankara: Kültür ve Turizm Bakanlığı Yayınları, 1983.
Conseil d'État. Avis du Conseil d'État sur le port de signes religieux dans les établissements scolaires no. 346893, 27 novembre1989.
Danışma Meclisi Tutanak Dergisi. 23 vols.
Devlet Bakanlığı. *Alevi Çalıştayları*.
"Discours de Monsieur Nicolas Sarkozy Ministre de l'Intérieur, de la sécurité intérieure et des libertés locales audition devant la 'Commission Stasi,'" October 7, 2003, French Ministry of Interior. http://www.interieur.gouv.fr/Archives/.

Dördüncü Milli Eğitim Şûrası, 22–31 August 1949 [Fourth National Education Congress]. Ankara: Maarif Vekâleti Yayın Müdürlüğü, 1949.

French Ministry of Interior. http://www.interieur.gouv.fr/Archives/.

Journal officiel de la République française. Débats parlementaires. Chambre des députés.

Journal officiel de la République française. Débats parlementaires. Sénat.

Milli Güvenlik Konseyi Tutanak Dergisi. 11 vols.

Öztürk, Kazım. *Türk Anayasası* [Records of the Turkish constitution]. 3 vols. Istanbul: İş Bankası Yayınları, 1966.

Türkiye Büyük Millet Meclisi (TBMM). *Tutanak Dergisi* [Journal of the minutes of the Turkish Grand National Assembly].

Turkey State Ministry. *Alevi Workshops*. 7 vols. Ankara: Devlet Bakanlığı, 2011.

National Statistics

Service de la statistique générale de France. *Annuaire statistique de la France*. 107 vols. Vols. 1, 2, 4, 7, 9, 15, 16. Paris [etc.], 1878, 1879, 1881, 1884, 1886, 1894, 1896.

Turkey Statistical Institution (Tüik). 1987. *Referendum on the Political Rights*. http://www.turkstat.gov.tr/.

Turkey Statistical Institution (Tüik). *Turkey's Statistical Yearbooks*. http://www.turkstat.gov.tr/.

Newspapers, Journals, Broadcasting Channels

English: *BBC, Financial Times, Open Democracy, Wall Street Journal*

French: *Algérie News, La Croix, Le Figaro, Le Gaulois, L'Humanité, Libération, Le Monde, Le Monde Diplomatique, Le Nouvel Observateur, Politis,* http://discours.vie-publique.fr

Italian: *Corriere Della Sera*

Turkish: *Akşam, Bağımsız Internet Gazetesi, Bianet, Birgün, CNN Türk, Cumhuriyet, Dünya, Haberturk, Hürriyet, Hürriyet Daily News, Hürriyet Gündem, Internet Haber, Kudret, Milliyet, Radikal, Sabah, Sızıntı, Ntvmsnbc, T24, Tercüman, Ulus, Yeni Asya, Vatan, Zafer*

Political Party Publications

Refah Partisi'nin. "Anayasa Uzlaşma Teklifi." Ankara: Semih Ofset, 1994.

Soruları ve Cevaplarıyla Demokratik Açılım Süreci: Milli Birlik ve Kardeşlik Süreci. January 2010, AKP Tanıtım ve Medya Başkanlığı.

Reports

Alevi Workshops Final Report. Ankara: Devlet Bakanlığı, 2010.

Alliance of Civilizations. *Report of the High-Level Group*, November 13, 2006. New York: United Nations.

Benard, Cheryl. *Civil and Democratic Islam: Partners, Resources, Strategies*. Pittsburgh: RAND Corporation, 2003.

Bert, Paul. *La loi de l'enseignement primaire (Proposition Barodet): Rapport présenté à la Chambre des députés*. Paris: G. Masson, Éditeu, 1880.

Briand, Aristide. *La séparation des Églises et de l'État: Rapport fait au nom de la commission de la Chambre des députés, suivi des pièces annexes / Aristide Briand député*. Paris: E. Cornély, 1905.

Commission de réflexion sur l'application du principe de laïcité dans la République. *Rapport au président de la République*. Paris: La Documentation Française, December 2003.

Constitutional Law Research Association (Anayasa-Der). *Report on the Constitution*. Istanbul: Legal Yayincilik, 2012.

Debray, Régis. "L'enseignement du fait religieux dans l'école laïque." *Rapport à monsieur le ministre de l'éducation nationale* (February 2002).

Joutard, Philippe. *Rapport de la mission de réflexion sur l'enseignement de l'histoire la géographie et les sciences sociales*. Paris: La Documentation Française, 1989.

Köse, Talha. *Alevi Opening and the Democratization Opening in Turkey*. Ankara: SETA Policy Report, 2010.

Progressive Lawyers Association. *Detained Students Report*. October 2011.

12 Yil Zorunlu Eğitim Sorular—Cevaplar. Ankara, 2012. http://www.meb.gov.tr/duy urular/duyurular2012/12yil_soru_cevaplar.pdf.

Index

Abant platform, 230, 319n63
Açanal, Necdet, 171
Acomb, Evelyn Martha, 31, 70
Action libérale populaire (ALP, France), 53, 57; and 1905 separation law, 58, 59, 62–73, 95
Adıvar, Halide Edib, 141, 308n17
Administrative Justice Act (Turkey), 225
AKP. *See* Justice and Development Party
Aksoy, Muammer, 179–80, 185, 194
Aldıkaçtı, Orhan, 202, 204
Alevi Bektaşi Federation, 228
"Alevi-Bektaşi Question," 24, 229–30
Alevilik, 183, 223, 237; defining, 229, 231–36; Erdoğan on, 223, 225, 274; religious institutions of, 223
Alevis: about, 291n37, 311n75; and AKP, 212, 222–223, 225, 226; assimilationist policies toward, 236, 239; and CHP, 183, 211–12, 216; constitution nondiscrimination clause on, 182, 183; demands of, 183, 223; discrimination against, 169; and DRA, 183, 211–12, 223, 230, 232, 235, 236, 241, 320n80; in Germany, 25; history of, 235, 236, 320n80, 320n87; massacres of, 227–28, 236, 237, 238, 252–53, 318n51; mass demonstration by, 229; and Sunni mosque-building projects, 200, 223, 234, 319nn72–74
Alevi Workshops, 222–25; Alevilik definition discussed at, 231–36; on Alevi question as societal issue, 229–30; on history and memory, 227–28, 237–39; laiklik as main issue of debate in, 223, 232, 236–37; organizing of, 225–26; procedures in, 228–29
Algeria, 35–36, 52, 294–95n2
Allard, Maurice, 93
Alliance of Civilizations meeting (2006), 2, 209, 216
All Teachers Union and Solidarity Association (TÖB-DER), 255
Alpaslan, Tevfik Fikret, 202
alternative modernities approach, 1, 3, 17, 23, 103, 235, 276

[341]

anticlericalism: Catholic Church alliance with, 10, 31; CHP's past, 12, 137; French Chamber discussion of (1883), 10, 31, 44, 49; French Chamber discussion of (1905), 62, 76; Kemalism and, 12, 135–36, 143, 275, 284; as not antireligious, 16, 49, 144, 207, 288n11; and state-civil religionism, 7, 8, 10–11, 12, 135, 207–8, 275, 278
antipluralism, 35, 38, 212, 235
anti-Semitism, 54, 299n58
Anti-Terror Laws (Turkey), 249, 254
Arkoun, Mohammed, 102
Army of the İmam, The, 248, 250
Asad, Talal: genealogical approach of, 2, 9; on modernity, 283; on religion, 289n20, 312n91
assimilationism, 20, 236, 239
associations cultuelles, 85, 88, 89, 90–91, 93
Assumptionists, 54–55
Ata, Kelime, 232
atheism, 26, 44, 288n11
Auster, Paul, 257
autonomy: DRA and, 166, 214, 223, 242; moral, 22, 26, 27
Ayanoğlu, Nurettin, 202–3
Aydın, Mehmet, 216

Baha Pars, Muhittin, 146
Balibar, Étienne, 116
Bardoux, Agénor, 36–37, 47, 133, 285
Barlas, Cemil Sait, 154–55
Barodet, Jean, 41, 47–48
Barry, Brian, 25, 27, 28, 295n53
Barthou, Louis, 59, 77, 84
Başgil, Ali Fuad, 171–79, 214, 242
Başkaynak, Muzaffer, 205, 206
Baubérot, Jean, 21, 48, 51, 102; on Combisme, 143, 308n27; on headscarf ban, 22, 114–16, 129, 282; on laïcité, 22, 101, 115

Bayrou, François, 107
BDP. *See* Peace and Democracy Party
Beaussire, Émile, 47
Belgium, 34, 47, 153, 155, 159, 161
Benedict, Pope, 100
Bepmale, Jean, 85
Bert, Paul, 32, 38, 39, 44, 47
Bert Report, 32–34, 37, 42
Bienvenu-Martin, Jean-Baptiste, 92–93
Bishop's Conference of France, 117, 305n40
Bismarck, Otto von, 64, 155
Bölükbaşı, Osman, 169–70, 172, 189
Book Is Not a Bomb, A, 249
Bora, Arslan, 183–84
Bos, Charles, 92
Bouamama, Saïd, 116
Boubakeur, Dalil, 120, 122, 123, 131
Bousquet, Victor, 47–48
Bouzar, Dounia, 122
Bowen, John, 19–20
Boyer, Ferdinand, 37–39
Boztepe, Feyzi, 165–66, 169
Brazil, 75
Briand, Aristide, 60–61, 69, 72, 101; in debate on 1905 law, 78–81, 82–84, 91–92
Briand Report, 73–77
Broglie, Albert de, 65
Bryce, James, 75
budget des cultes, 31, 55–56; Briand Report on, 74, 76; debate over, 49, 69, 89; establishment of, 51–52, 296n4; suppression of, 37, 59–60, 86, 91
Buisson, Ferdinand, 65, 67
Büyükanıt, Yasar, 219, 220

Çağlar, Behçet Kemal, 155–56
Caillaux, Joseph, 92
Çakır, Ruşen, 199
Çamuroğlu, Reha, 222, 225–26

Canada, 74–75
Capelle, Philippe, 130–31
capitalism, 213–14
Casanova, José, 210
Catholicism: anticlericalism's alliance with, 10, 31; Başgil on, 174–75; Briand Report on, 73; as bulwark against socialism and communism, 10, 31, 174–75; as cement of society, 10, 95, 99; and Concordat, 30, 50–51, 89, 295–96n2; and democracy, 53; and ecclesiastical property, 76, 92; and *laïcité positive*, 98–99, 100; lower vs. upper clergy in, 86; and morality, 34, 99; Mun on, 64–65, 71; nationalizing, 48, 51; and Ralliement, 41, 52; as religion of French majority, 30, 38, 41, 46, 78, 85, 99; and religious orders and associations, 54, 61, 80–81, 89; and republicanism-monarchism schism, 52, 77; Stasi Report on, 104; ultramontane, 47, 69–70, 73, 298n29. *See also* Vatican
Çelik, Faruk, 225, 227
cemevis, 320n87; and legal status question, 223, 225, 234, 236, 238, 319n72
Cha'are Shalom ve Tsedek against France (European Court of Human Rights case), 103
Chakrabarty, Dipesh, 279
Chalamet, Arthur, 35–36
Chatterjee, Partha, 9, 23–24
Cherifi, Hanifa, 102–3
Chernière, Ernest, 107
Chevènement, Jean-Pierre, 118, 120
Chirac, Jacques, 102, 124, 127–28, 130, 131–32
CHP. *See* Republican People's Party
Christian missionaries, 213, 235
Church and State after the Dreyfus Affair (Larkin), 60
Churchill, Winston, 152, 168

civil society, 20, 199, 253; Alevi Workshops as dialogue with, 222–23, 237; and French headscarf ban, 97, 120; Islamist, 199, 226–27, 315n137
CKMP. *See* Republican Peasant Nation Party
"Clash of Civilizations, The," (Huntington), 4
Collier, David, 122
Collier, Ruth Berins, 122
Combes, Émile, 10, 21, 55–56, 72; and 1905 separation law, 30, 54, 76
Combisme, 10, 11; Baubérot on, 143, 308n27; and Opportunistes, 143–44
communism, 147, 148, 152, 154, 167, 174, 199; CHP on, 12–13, 138, 168
communitarianism, 110, 122, 127, 130, 132, 144
conciliatory civil religion, 48
Concordat, 30, 48, 69, 95–96; about, 50–51, 295–96n2; Briand on, 91; Ferry on, 49–50, 54; Jaurès on, 87, 88; Larkin on, 51–52, 64, 296n4, 301n100; Mun on, 63–64, 65, 71
Confederation of Nationalist Workers' Syndicates (MİSK), 197, 313–14n118
Confederation of Revolutionary Workers' Syndicates (DİSK), 197, 313–14n118
Conseil Français du Culte Musulman (CFCM), 97; on headscarf question, 123; Sarkozy and, 112, 114, 118, 120–22
conseils de fabrique, 38, 82, 297n17
Constitutional Court (Turkey), 221; annulment of elections by, 220, 268; on education law, 271–74, 285
constitutional referendum (Turkey, 2010), 221, 223, 243
Constitution Compromise Commission (AUK, Turkey), 246, 255; working principles of, 253–54

constitution of 1928 (Turkey), 140–41, 308n22; 1937 revision of, 141–42, 308n22
constitution of 1961 (Turkey), 179–87, 246; defense of laiklik in, 181–83; DRA reference in, 180; on religious minorities, 181
constitution of 1982 (Turkey), 199, 200–205; article 10 of, 234, 236, 273; article 24 of, 199, 200, 201–6, 258, 268; article 102 of, 220; article 136 of, 199, 200, 240; and laiklik, 196–99, 272–73; National Security Council deliberations over, 205–7
Contre la séparation (Mun), 62–63
corporatism, 122
Corriere Della Sera, 251
corruption, 250, 323n154
Costa-Lascoux, Jacqueline, 102
critical junctures concept, 12–13, 137, 138, 144, 179. *See also* institutional change moments
Cuba, 75
culturalism, x–xi, 191, 192, 193–94, 283
Culture and Equality (Barry), 27, 28
Cumhuriyet, 148, 183

Dahlab against Switzerland (European Court of Human Rights case), 103
Danıştay affair, 221, 248
Dansette, Adrien, 56, 70
Darcos, Xavier, 113, 128, 131–32
Dauzon, Philippe, 67
Davison, Andrew, 23
Dayıbaş, Vehbi, 149–50
Debray, Régis, 102, 106, 113, 128; and headscarf issue, 107–8, 129; and teaching of religion as fact, 21, 110, 123–26, 129, 131–32

Debray Report (*The Teaching of Religious Fact in the Laic School*), 21, 110, 123–26, 129–30, 131; critique of, 130–31
Debré, Michel, 115
Debré law, 115
Dedelik schools, 223
de La Biliais, Henri Le Loup, 35
Delebarre, Michel, 102–3
Demirel, Süleyman, 196
democracy, 168, 205, 210, 236, 252; American, 16, 70, 120, 121; and Catholicism, 53; and laiklik, 158, 176; and morality, 189, 190; and secularism, 210, 285; Turkey's transition to, 172, 209, 226, 245
Democracy in America (Tocqueville), 120, 121
Democratic Left Party (Turkey), 216, 217, 218
Democratic Opening: National Unity and Brotherhood/Sisterhood Project, 24, 209, 222–39. *See also* Alevi Workshops
Democratic Society Party (Turkey), 221
Democrat Party (DP, Turkey), 12–13, 137, 145, 172, 314n129; and DRA budget, 138, 166–68, 169; founding of, 144–45
Denmark, 216
Deschanel, Paul, 53, 59, 63, 77
d'Hulst, Maurice, 301n100
Dink, Hrant, 248, 252
Directorate of Religious Affairs (DRA, Turkey): and AKP, 211–20, 239, 240–43; and Alevis, 183, 211–12, 223, 230, 232, 235, 236, 241, 320n80; and autonomy, 166, 214, 223, 242; budget of, 145, 165–71, 173–74, 179, 214–15, 216, 217, 218, 219; and CHP, 137, 149, 168–69, 171, 216, 242; constitution of 1961 on, 180; constitution of 1982 on, 200; and diversity within Islam, 241;

[344] INDEX

establishment of, 136, 139, 142, 307–8n14; High Council of Religious Affairs within, 213, 234, 241, 323n154; as institution of education, 156, 241; international responsibilities of, 215; and laiklik, 165–66, 168–69, 170, 192–93, 240; law of 2010 on, 223, 239–43; state-salaried imams administered by, 135, 136; structure and personnel of, 151, 210, 213, 217–18; Sunni Islam privileged by, 212–13

Directorate of Religious Endowments, 149, 151, 167

"Dissonances within *Laïcité*" (Balibar), 116

diversity: as challenge to laïcité, 11, 33, 104, 110, 132–33, 281; and debate on 1882 French law, 10, 11, 34–35, 96, 281; and debate on 1905 French law, 73, 78, 96, 281; Debray Report on, 124; and French headscarf ban, 18–19, 101–2, 109, 132, 133; within Islam, 241; and laiklik, 13, 272; and law of majorities, 94, 137; Lerner on, 280; and neutrality, 11, 26, 94, 132; politics of, 13, 101, 211, 276; religious, 11, 14, 26, 206, 211, 272, 281; Sarkozy on, 99, 100–101, 102; and secularism, 4, 19, 22, 26, 94, 279, 281; Stasi Report on, 104; Turkish Constitutional Court on, 272; Turkish debates on, 13, 206, 211, 237, 241, 261, 272, 276

Dreyfus affair, 53, 54, 299n58

Dumont, Charles, 82, 84, 85

Dünya, 183

Duruy, Jean Victor, 36, 41, 397n15

education law (Turkey, 2012): background to, 256–59; Constitutional Court on, 271–74; opposition to, 259–60; parliamentary discussion of, 260–67; passage of, 267–68, 271; provisions of, 259

education system (France): closing of religious schools, 55–56; Debré law on, 115; distinction between public and private, 115–16; and optional religious instruction, 23, 32–33, 34, 35, 36, 40, 47; provisions of 1882 law on, 23, 30; teaching religion "as fact" in, 19, 21, 110, 112–13, 123–28, 129–30, 131–32, 133. *See also Loi du 28 Mars 1882 sur l'enseignement primaire obligatoire*; religious instruction (France)

education system (Turkey): 1924 law on, 136, 139; constitution on, 180–81, 201–5, 258; exams in, 265, 323n153; law of 2012 on, 259–68, 271; National Education Congres debate over, 157–65. *See also* religious instruction (Turkey)

Ehl-i Beyt Foundation, 236

18th Brumaire of Louis Bonaparte, The (Marx), 31

Eisenstadt, Shmuel N., 4, 280

England. *See* United Kingdom

Erbakan, Necmettin, 197, 215

Erdoğan, Recep Tayyip, 2, 220, 222, 247, 248, 254; on Alevilik, 223–25, 274; book-bomb analogy by, 250–51; on education system, 256–58; on freedom of expression, 251–52; on laiklik, 211, 221; on Turkey as single nation, 221, 245

Ergenekon trials, 221, 248–49

Esen, Bülent Nuri, 157, 158–59, 161

European Court of Human Rights, 103, 244–45; and banning of Islamic party, 210, 216; and Turkish education law, 225, 232, 234, 273, 274

European Institute of Religious Sciences, 127–28

European Union, 210, 215, 233, 254, 260, 262
Evren, Kenan, 200, 201, 206, 252, 306n61
Explaining Institutional Change (Mahoney and Thelen), 9

Falloux law, 31, 55, 99, 300n69, 303n6
FATİH project, 257–58, 259–60, 263, 264
Ferry, Jules, 48, 53, 56, 143; and 1905 separation law, 30; on anticlericalism as not antireligious, 16, 49, 144, 207, 288n11; on Concordat, 49–50, 54; on neutrality, 45–46; on religious education, 39–40
Ferry, Luc, 113, 126–27, 131–32
Financial Times, 198
Finland, 167
First National Culture Meeting (Turkey, 1982), 199, 200
Fitch, Nancy, 54
Forbidden Modern, The (Göle), 4, 280–81
Formations of the Secular (Asad), 9
Foucault, Michel, 18
France, 9–12, 30–96, 97–133; *budget des cultes* in, 31, 37, 49, 51–52, 55–56, 59–60, 69, 74, 76, 86, 89, 91, 296n4; as Catholic-majority country, 30, 38, 41, 46, 78, 85, 99; Concordat in, 48, 49–52, 63–64, 65, 69, 71, 91, 95–96; contemporary debates over, 17–20; Debré law in, 115; Dreyfus affair in, 53, 54, 299n58; Falloux law in, 31, 55, 99, 300n69, 303n6; freedom of conscience in, 33–34, 37, 39–40, 44–45, 48–49, 71–72, 81, 104, 105, 110; and Gallican liberties, 298n43; generality of law in, 73, 302n22; and headscarf issue, 5, 6, 11, 12, 14, 18–19, 22, 25, 28, 101–2, 105, 107–12, 114–18, 120–21, 123, 129, 281–82, 295n53; Jews and Protestants in, 33, 52, 54, 76, 117, 296n4, 299n58, 305n40; judicial system in, 82–84, 89–90, 92–93; law public education (1882) in, 9–10, 31–50, 95, 96, 133, 281; Law of Associations in, 54, 55; law on separation (1905) in, 6, 9–10, 52–94, 95, 96, 281; moments of institutional change in, 30, 94, 98, 118, 132, 278; monarchists vs. republicans in, 32, 297n10; Muslim organizations and infrastructure in, 12, 19, 97, 112, 114, 118–23; Opportunistes vs. Combistes in, 143–44; passive and assertive secularism in, 21–22; religion infrastructure in public space in, 12, 19, 98, 118, 121, 132; "religious fact" teaching in, 19, 21, 110, 112–13, 123–28, 129, 131–32, 133; religious orders in, 31–32, 54–56, 143, 150; Stasi Commission and Report in, 102–7, 110–11, 113, 114, 119, 304n16; state-civil religionism in, 8, 10–12, 32, 36–37, 43–44, 95, 132–33, 135, 207–8; Turkey comparisons to, 22–23, 136, 137, 162, 175, 195–96, 207, 216, 275, 276, 281, 284. See also laïcité; *Loi du 9 Décembre 1905 concernant la séparation des églises et de l'État*; *Loi du 28 Mars 1882 sur l'enseignement primaire obligatoire*; separation, religion-state
freedom of conscience: in contemporary France, 104, 105, 110; in French Third Republic, 33–34, 37, 39–40, 44–45, 48–49, 71–72, 81; in Turkey, 141–42, 158, 159, 164, 176, 190. See also religious freedom
freedom of speech and expression, 105, 236, 244, 246, 247, 251–52, 254
French Declaration of Human Rights, 120
French Laic Laws 1879–1889 (Acomb), 31

French Revolution, 37, 147
Freppel, Bishop Charles-Émile, 41–43, 45, 46–47

Gaspard, François, 116
Gauche radical (France), 57, 82, 85, 89–90, 93–94, 95, 96
Gayraud, Hippolyte, 66–68
Geertz, Clifford, 1, 8, 18, 279
Genç, Kamer, 203–4
George VI (king of England), 178
Germany, 64, 153, 215, 250, 264; and religious education, 25, 161, 216, 228, 266, 268
Göksel Paşa, İhsan, 202, 204–5
Göle, Nilüfer, 4, 280–81, 315n137
Gramsci, Antonio, ix
Greece, 216
Guedj, Nicole, 102–3
Gül, Abdullah, 219, 220
Gülen movement, 119, 198–99, 248, 285, 319n63
Güney, Abdulkadir, 150
Gürkan, Ahmet, 167

Hacı-Bektaş Dergahı, 223
Hacı Bektaş Veli Culture and Promotion Association, 228, 232, 236, 237
Haggard, Stephan, 314n125
Hanafi denomination, 183
headscarf ban (France), 5, 12, 281–82; Baubérot on, 22, 114–16, 129, 282; court decision on, 105; debate over, 6, 19, 22, 28, 107–10, 114–17, 295n53; Debray on, 107–8, 129; expulsions and disciplining over, 117–18, 120, 123; letters supporting and opposing, 107–10; Muslim council position on, 123; petition opposing, 116–17; radicalization of students over, 120–21; Sarkozy on, 111, 112, 128–29

headscarf issue (Turkey), 5, 20, 281–82; ban on, 210, 306n61; bill granting freedom to wear, 5, 14, 274–75
Hegel, G. W. F., x
hermeneutical approach, 22–23, 132; vs. analytical framework, xi, 23, 279; by Taylor, 17–18; turns toward, x–xi, 3–4, 6, 17, 94, 277, 278
"Hermeneutics of Conflict, The" (Taylor), 17–18
High Council of Elections (YSK, Turkey), 245
High Islam Institutes, 198
historicism, 191–92, 193–94, 278–79
Hitler, Adolf, 156
Holyoake, George Jacob, 288n11
Hubbart, Mr., 84–85
Hudson, Ghislaine, 102–3, 114
human rights, 26, 232, 234, 235
Human Rights Watch, 249
Huntington, Samuel, 4

İdare Hukukunun Umumi Esasları (Onar), 180
İğneciler, Asım, 204
İmam Hatip schools, 154, 239, 256; decline and closure of, 143, 154; establishment of, 142–43, 199–200; reopening of, 145, 259
imams, state-salaried, 6, 12, 135, 136, 138, 207, 239
immigrants, 101–2
Imperial Encounters: Religion and Modernity in India and Britain (van der Veer), 9
India, 23–24
institutional change moments, 9, 17, 29, 277; about, 4–5; in France, 30, 94, 98, 118, 132, 278; in Turkey, 12, 13, 135, 138, 211, 223, 274–75. *See also* critical junctures concept
institutional dualism, 29

interactional histories, 9
International Publishers Association (IPA), 249
Iraq, 219, 221, 245
Ireland, 74, 75, 266
Islam: all-encompassing nature of, 192, 241; as cement of Turkish society, 136, 137, 144, 199, 200, 207, 211, 217–18, 276; and Christianity, 175; as culture, 136, 203, 207, 275, 285; diversity within, 241; and fight against communism, 138, 147–48, 167, 168; in France, 12, 19, 97, 112, 114, 118–23; fundamentalist, 109, 110, 114, 115, 126, 151, 166, 167, 170; as grounded in love, 217; importance of education for, 193–94; Kemal on, 136–37, 138–39; and mosques, 212, 240–41; privileging of Sunni, 212–13; and religious sects, 202, 203, 204; and spirituality, 139–40, 175; and terrorism, 241. *See also* Directorate of Religious Affairs; laiklik; religion; religious instruction
Islamism, 19, 136, 246, 280; and civil society activism, 199, 282, 315n137; and Kemalism, 21, 172, 182–83, 282
İslamiyet Journal, 225
İsmet Paşa, 16, 140
Istanbul University theology faculty, 191–92
Italy, 161, 215

Jaurès, Jean, 21; in debate in 1905 law, 83, 87–89, 93; "The Separation and the Union démocratique," 59, 63
Jesuits, 32, 54, 143, 155
Jews: in France, 33, 52, 54, 76, 117, 299n58, 305n40; in Turkey, 151, 164, 176–77, 241. *See also* anti-Semitism
Jospin, Lionel, 107–8, 123–24
Joutard, Philippe, 106, 128, 129, 131–32

Justice and Development Party (AKP, Turkey), 6, 14, 21, 247, 281; and Alevis, 212, 222–23, 225, 226; and DRA, 211–20, 239, 240–43; and education law, 124, 259, 260–61, 266–67, 269–70, 271, 285; in elections, 209, 245, 246, 256; and Kemalist continuity, 21, 173, 212, 214, 316n10; and liberalism, 14, 275; and military establishment, 219–21; state-civil religionism of, 210, 211, 275
Justice Medicine Institution, 244, 321n109
Justice Party (Turkey), 314n129

Kaflı, Kadircan, 187, 190, 191
Kalaç against Turkey (European Court of Human Rights case), 103
Kalüstyan, Hermine, 183, 184
Kalyvas, Stathis N., 302–3n134
Karaduman against Turkey (European Court of Human Rights case), 103
Karaosmanoğlu, Yakup Kadri, 1
Kaufman, Robert, 314n125
Keddie, Nikki R., 24
Keller, Émile, 40–41
Kemal Atatürk, Mustafa, 146, 217; on education and religion, 136–37, 192, 202–3, 204; on Islam as state religion, 138–39; on religious orders, 150, 202
Kemalism, 8, 211, 216; AKP and, 21, 173, 212, 214, 316n10; and anticlericalism, 12, 135–36, 143, 275, 284; Baubérot on, 143; French similarities to, 136, 137, 175, 207, 275, 276, 281, 284; and Islamism, 21, 172, 182–83, 282; six arrows of, 150, 204, 309n42; and state-civil religionism, 207, 275; utilitarian framework of, 137–38, 146, 165, 194–95, 207
Kepel, Gilles, 102

Keyder, Çağlar, 315n137
Kılıçdaroğlu, Sayın, 256
Kılıçoğlu, Hakkı, 142
Kısakürek, Necip Fazıl, 258
Kişioğlu, Yeredoğ, 168–69
Koran (Kur'an-ı Kerim), 113, 130, 140, 168, 183, 204, 205–6, 268, 319n73; call for wide distribution of, 217; Kurdish translation prohibited, 241–42; optional school courses on, 20, 210, 259, 267–68, 269, 270, 273, 274; Turkish constitution on, 267
Kudret, 189
Kurdish question, 220, 240, 241–42
Kurdistan Workers' Party (PKK), 221
Kuru, Ahmet, 20–21, 282, 292n17
Kymlicka, Will, 28

Laborde, Cécile, 27
Lacordaire, Jean-Baptiste, 73
Lacretelle, Henri de, 43–44, 133, 285
La Croix, 54, 68, 72, 117, 196
laïcité: and assertive, passive secularism, 21; Baubérot on, 22, 101, 115; Chirac on, 130; Debray Report on, 125–26; and diversity, 11, 33, 104, 110, 132–33, 281; in Europe, 36, 74–75; and headscarf issue, 14, 19, 22, 27, 97–98, 102, 104, 105, 107, 108–9, 110, 114–15, 116, 123, 133; and law of 1882, 31, 35, 37–38, 39; literature and studies on, 4, 5, 18–20, 21, 27; and multiculturalism, 20, 27; and public instruction of religion, 35, 37–38, 39, 125–27, 131–32; and separation law of 1905, 63, 74, 75; Stasi Report on, 106. *See also* France; secularism; separation, religion-state
La laïcité expliqué e à M. Sarkozy . . . et à ceux qui écrivent ses discours (Baubérot), 101

laïcité positive, 98–102, 132; Sarkozy view of, 19, 98–101, 110–14, 133, 159, 187, 259, 285, 292n10; as state-civil religionism, 133; Turkey's laiklik and, 187, 259, 285
laiklik: and AKP, 209, 211, 221; Alevi Workshop debate on, 223, 232, 236–37; Başgil on, 173, 176, 177–78; CHP discussion of, 144, 145, 149–56, 240; and CKMP, 189, 190, 322n143; conceptualizations of, 185, 187, 190–91, 194, 259, 271, 322n143; and constitutional change of 1937, 140–42; Constitutional Court on, 271–74; and constitution of 1961, 179–85; and constitution of 1982, 196–99, 272–73; and debates on religious education, 157–61, 204–5, 259, 268, 269, 271–74; and democracy, 158, 176; and diversity, 13, 272; and DRA, 165–66, 168–69, 170, 192–93, 240; and DRA budget, 165–66, 168, 170–72, 193–94; Erdoğan on, 211, 221; and headscarf question, 20, 210; of Kemal, 138–39, 204; and *laïcité positive*, 187, 259, 285; literature and studies on, 4, 5, 20–21, 22–23; and neutrality, 160; Savcı on, 192–93; and separation of religion and state, 160, 180, 189, 190, 204. *See also* secularism; separation, religion-state; Turkey
Lamennais, Felicité Robert de, 70, 73
L'Année Politique, 57–58
Lang, Jack, 21, 124, 131
La République, les religions, l'espérance (Sarkozy), 98, 99–100, 118, 121
Larkin, Maurice, 59, 60, 70; on Concordat, 51–52, 64, 296n4, 301n100
La séparation de l'église et de l'Etat (Mayeuer), 61–62
Laskaris, Kaludi, 183

Lausanne Treaty, 150, 206
L'Avenir, 69
Lavigerie, Cardinal Charles, 52
Law of Associations (France, 1901), 54, 55, 74
law of majorities: and contemporary France, 130, 137, 158; in French Third Republic, 33–35, 38, 41, 42, 94, 95; Turkish debates' premise of, 165, 169, 179, 207, 273, 274, 275
Le Figaro, 62–63, 65, 70, 71
Le Gaulois, 63–64, 65, 70–72
Le Monde, 114, 118, 123, 173
Le Nouvel Observateur, 107, 108–9
L'enseignement des religions à l'école laïque, 129
Leo XIII, Pope, 52
Lerner, Daniel, 4, 278–80, 324n10
Les filles voilées parlent, 119
Le Temps, 57–58
Letter Concerning Toleration (Locke), 3
Le voile médiatique. Un faux débat (Tévanian), 116
Levraud, Léonce, 86
Lévy, Catherine, 116
Leygues, Georges, 85–87, 93
L'Humanité, 59, 63
liberalism, 7, 12, 32, 278; of Brian Barry, 27; compatibility of with religion courses, 138, 164–65
Libération, 114–15, 117
La Liberté de conscience (Simon), 48–49
liberty, religious. *See* freedom of conscience; religious freedom
Ligue Française de l'Enseignement, 173
Locke, John, 3
Lockroy, Edouard, 49, 50
Loi du 9 Décembre 1905 concernant la séparation des églises et de l'État, 6, 10, 23, 30–31, 281; Action libérale populaire and, 58, 59, 62–73, 95; article 1 of, 59–60; article 4 of, 59, 60–62, 77–94; article 10 of, 55; article 13 of, 55; article 14 of, 55; and *associations cultuelles*, 60, 61–62, 80–81, 82, 86, 91; Baubérot on, 22; Bempale on, 85; Briand on, 78–81, 82–83, 84, 91–92, 93–94; Caillaux on, 92; civil courts and, 82–84, 89–90, 92–93; Dumont on, 82, 85; Hubbart on, 84–85; Jaurès on, 87–89; Leygues on, 85–87, 93; Martin on, 92–93; Noulens on, 89–91; politics of, 54, 57–62, 95, 96; Ribot on, 77–78, 81, 83, 93; Sarkozy view of, 98, 110, 133; and state-civil religionism, 11, 95; Vazeille on, 81–82
Loi du 28 Mars 1882 sur l'enseignement primaire obligatoire, 31–50; Bardoux on, 36–37, 47; and Bert Report, 32–34, 37, 42; Boyer on, 37–39; Briand Report on, 74; Chalamet on, 35–36; and diversity, 34, 96; Ferry on, 39–40, 45–46; and freedom of conscience, 37, 39–40, 44–45; Freppel on, 41–43, 47; Keller on, 40; Lacretele on, 43–45; and neutrality issue, 30, 34–35, 36, 37, 38, 42–43, 44–45, 46, 47, 96, 281; and optional religious instruction, 23, 32–33, 34, 35, 36, 40, 47; political ends in debate on, 95–96; provisions of, 23, 30; Ribot on, 47; Stasi Report on, 104; and state-civil religionism, 36–37, 43–44, 95, 133
Long, Marceau, 102–3
Lustiger, Cardinal Jean-Marie, 117, 305n40
Luther, Martin, 155

Machiavelli, Niccolò, ix–x
Maclure, Jocelyn, 26–27, 28
Madımak Hotel incident, 223, 236, 252–53, 318n38

Mahmood, Saba, 2, 25
Mahoney, James, 9
Maigne, Jules, 44–45
Malche, Albert, 192, 313n105
Maraş Massacre, 227–28, 252, 318n51
Marx, Karl, 1, 31, 42, 248
Mayeur, Jean-Marie, 48, 60–62, 297n10
McManners, John, 61
Mehmet the Conqueror, 257–58
Méline, Jules, 53
Menderes, Adnan, 166, 169, 170
Middle East Studies Association, 249
Midnight's Children (Rushdie), 281
Mill, John Stuart, 289n19
Milliyet, 165, 187, 197, 259
Minghetti, Marco, 75
modernization: from above and from below, 23, 315n137; Asad on, 283; Lerner on, 4, 278–80, 324n10; outside West, 23–24, 208; Taylor on, 279–80; and traveling, 103, 165, 276, 280. *See also* alternative modernities approach; multiple modernities approach
modernization-secularization thesis, 3
moments of institutional change. *See* institutional change moments
Montalembert, Charles Forbes René de, 69, 73
morality: and Christianity, 34, 99; CKMP emphasis on, 189–90; and democracy, 189, 190; Rawlsian view of, 26, 294n45; and religion, 37, 40, 43, 75, 94, 99–100, 146, 147, 148, 152–53, 170–71, 195, 242; Turkish constitution on, 190, 203, 258, 268; Turkish military's promotion of, 199
mosques: in Alevi villages, 200, 223, 234, 319nn72–74; in France, 122, 305n51; and Islam, 212, 240–41
multiculturalism, 20, 26–27, 28, 97, 102
"Multiple Modernities" (Eisenstadt), 4

multiple modernities approach, 3, 4, 279; boundedness of, 278, 283; hermeneutical turn of, 17, 277; interactional focus of, 7, 9, 278
Mun, Albert de, 16, 53, 281; on liberty and religion, 64–65, 71–73; on separation law, 62–64, 65, 68, 70–71
Mussolini, Benito, 172
mutually interactional modernities, 7–8, 282

Napoléon Bonaparte, 50, 51
National Action Party (MHP, Turkey), 169–70, 246; and education law, 260, 265–66, 267–68, 269–70
National Center for Distance Learning (CNED), 120
National Education Congress (Turkey): in 2014, 275; in 1953, 13, 138, 157–65
National Front (France), 109, 304n24
Nationalist Thought and the Colonial World (Chatterjee), 9
National Security Council (MGK, Turkey), 221, 254, 285; and 1982 constitution, 200, 201, 202, 205–7; initial deeds of, 197
Nation Party (NP, Turkey), 145, 166, 169
Navaro-Yashin, Yael, 227
Nayman, Şükrü, 149, 152–53
Nesin, Aziz, 255–56
neutrality: critiques of, 94, 95; and debate on 1882 law, 30, 34–35, 36, 37, 38, 42–43, 44–45, 46, 47, 96, 281; and debate on 1905 law, 30, 63, 68, 75, 95, 96; and diversity, 11, 26, 94, 132; French Muslim council on, 120; Sarkozy on, 110–11, 112; and secularism, 19, 94; Stasi Report on, 104, 106; and state nonneutrality, 27; and Turkish state, 124, 160, 236, 238, 320n82
New Spirit, 53, 77, 299n58
Norway, 161, 167, 216

Noulens, Joseph, 89–91
Nursi, Said, 198

Olin, Nelly, 102–3
Onar, Sıddık Sami, 180
Onat, Burhanettin, 168
Open Democracy, 119
Özal, Turgut, 196

Paris Commune, 37, 39
Partin, Malcolm O., 55
Passing of Traditional Society, The (Lerner), 4, 278–80, 324n10
Peace and Democracy Party (BDP, Turkey), 245, 246, 249, 320n97; and DRA law, 239–40, 241–42; and education law, 261–63, 267
Peker, Recep, 144, 147–48
Pena-Ruiz, Henri, 21, 102
Pétain, Henri-Philippe, 115
Petek, Gaye, 102–3
Piou, Jacques, 53
Pir Sultan Abdal 2nd July Culture and Education Foundation, 236
Pir Sultan Abdal Culture Association, 232–33, 234, 237
Pius VII, Pope, 50
pluralism, 26, 32, 35, 86, 203
"Politics of Recognition, The" (Taylor), 26
Politics of the Veil (Scott), 20
Politis, 107, 109
Prince, The (Machiavelli), ix–x
Progressive Lawyers' Association (Turkey), 248
proselytism, 105, 304n16
Protestant Ethic and the Spirit of Capitalism, The (Weber), x
Protestants, 33, 37–38, 42, 46, 67, 74, 76, 109
Proudhon, Pierre-Joseph, 37, 42
Provincializing Europe (Chakrabarty), 279

Quebec, 26–27
Quenet, Maurice, 102–3
Quinet, Edgar, 173

racism, 112, 169, 184, 236
Radical socialistes, 48, 56, 57; and debate over 1905 law, 58, 81–82, 84–85, 95, 96
Ralliement, 41, 52–53, 54, 299n57
Ramel, Fernand de, 84
Rawls, John, 26, 294n45
Rebérioux, Madeleine, 48, 60–61
Red Friday: Who Broke Dink's Pen? (Dink), 248, 252
Refah Party and others against Turkey (European Court of Human Rights case), 103
Reformed Church of France, 67, 68, 117, 305n40
religion: Alliance of Civilization meeting on, 2, 216; Asad on, 289n20, 312n91; Başgil on, 174–75; and capitalism, 213–14; as cement of society, 7, 8, 10, 11, 13, 29, 48, 72, 95, 118, 133, 137, 144, 199, 200, 211, 217–18, 276; CHP and, 12, 137, 144, 145–47, 149, 150, 155–56, 242, 309n30; civic function of, 48, 110–11; conciliatory civil, 48; as culture, 112–13, 118, 123–32, 133, 136, 203, 207, 285; as fact, 19, 21, 110, 112–13, 123–32; and faith, 146–47; to fight communism and socialism, 10, 31, 131, 138, 152, 167, 168, 174; freedom of conscience in, 33–34, 37, 39–40, 44–45, 48–49, 71–72, 81, 104, 105, 110, 141–42, 158, 159, 164, 176; as general category, 60, 68, 94, 95, 275; Lacretelle on, 133, 285; as matter of practice, 187, 312n91; moderate vs. radical, 2, 284–85; and morality, 37, 40, 43, 75, 94, 99–100, 146, 147, 148,

[352] INDEX

152–53, 170–71, 195, 242; Mun on, 64–65, 71–73; and nation, 160, 203; and pluralism, 86, 203; as political tool, 2–3, 145, 211, 278, 282; power of, 73, 215, 289nn19–20; Sarkozy on, 99, 100–101, 110–11, 112–13, 121, 124; and science, 164; as social necessity, 147–48, 158, 203–4, 218–19, 273, 274; state funding of, 31, 37, 49, 51–52, 55–56, 59–60, 69, 74, 76, 86, 89, 91, 145, 165–71, 173–74, 179, 214–15, 216, 217, 218, 219; Tocqueville on, 120; in United States, 25, 70–71, 75, 81, 82, 88, 96, 152, 153, 168, 196, 208, 219, 260; utilitarian approach to, 3, 12, 137–38, 146, 165, 194–95, 207, 275, 284, 289n20. *See also* Catholicism; Islam; laïcité; *laïcité positive*; laiklik; separation, religion-state; state-civil religionism

religion infrastructure: Başgil on, 177, 242; CHP on, 148–56, 168–69, 171; in French public space, 12, 19, 98, 118, 121, 132; lack of independent, 162; for Muslim organizations in France, 12, 97, 98, 112, 114, 118–23; and religious freedom, 187, 190, 195; Sarkozy support for, 113, 122; state funding for in Turkey, 148–49, 167–69, 200; Turkey comparisons with abroad on, 152, 153–54, 161, 168; Turkish Constituent Assembly discussion of, 187, 190–91, 194–96; Turkish Constitutional Court on, 275

religious freedom, 100, 145, 184; defending, 189–90; and religion infrastructure, 187, 190, 195; Turkish constitutions on, 164, 181, 183, 184. *See also* freedom of conscience

Religious History of Modern France (Dansette), 70

religious instruction (France): 1882 law on, 23, 32–33, 34, 35, 36, 40, 47. *See also* education system (France)

religious instruction (Turkey): Alevis and, 223, 225, 236, 237; Başgil on, 171–72, 175–79; constitution of 1961 on, 180–81; constitution of 1982 on, 200, 201–6, 230, 243, 258, 268; decision of 1948 on, 156, 176; DRA as institution of, 156, 241; DRA law of 2010 on, 243; Erdoğan on, 256–58; European Court of Human Rights on, 232, 234, 273, 274; and Islam, 130, 193–94; and Kemalism, 150; law of 2012 on, 259–68, 271; as national culture, 203; National Education Congress on, 157–65; optional vs. required, 14, 32, 124, 159, 163, 195, 210, 259; Savcı on, 192, 193; separation from education in 1924, 136, 139; Sirat on, 130; Welfare Party support for, 218–19. *See also* education system (Turkey)

religious orders: in France, 31–32, 54, 55–56, 80–81, 143; in Turkey, 150, 202

religious symbols. *See* headscarf ban

Rémond, René, 102

Reporters without Borders (RSF), 249

Républicains opportunistes (France), 30, 32, 96, 137; and Combistes, 143–44; and Concordat, 48–50; divisions among, 39; Kemalist similarities to, 136, 137, 275; renamed Républicains progressistes, 58, 137, 143–44

Républicains progressistes (France), 57, 58; and 1905 separation law, 59, 63, 66, 72–73, 77–78, 80, 95, 96; and Catholic Church, 66, 80, 95; emergence of, 58, 137, 143–44; and Kemalism, 175, 207, 275, 281, 284; and socialists, 53, 68; state-civil religionism of, 8; and Union démocratique, 59, 68

INDEX [353]

Republican Peasant Nation Party
(CKMP, Turkey), 169, 172; and
conceptualization of laiklik, 189, 190,
322n143; in Constituent Assembly of
1961, 179, 187, 191–92
Republican People's Party (CHP, Turkey):
and Alevis, 183, 211–12, 216;
antisocialism and anticommunism of,
137, 145; in Constituent Assembly 1961
debates, 179, 181, 187, 190, 191–92;
and Constitutional Compromise
Commission, 246, 255; and DRA
budget debate, 145, 146, 154–55,
168–69, 171; and education law, 208,
260–61, 263–65, 268–69, 270, 271;
French republicans' similarity to, 136,
138–44, 207; party programs of, 144,
309n30; and religion-state separation,
137, 155–56, 172, 189, 190; and religious
infrastructure debate, 148–56; turn
toward religion by, 12, 137, 145–47, 242
Rerum Novarum, 41, 52
Réveillaud, Eugène, 93–94
Ribot, Alexandre, 47, 59; in debate in
1905 law, 77–78, 81, 83–84, 93; Mun
on, 72–73
Richard, Cardinal François-Marie-
Benjamin, 54–55
Riesman, David, 1, 279
"Ritual and Social Change" (Geertz), 8
Roosevelt, Franklin, 152, 168
Roosevelt, Theodore, 70–71
Rousseau, Jean-Jacques, 97
Rushdie, Salman, 281
Russia, 147, 153, 177

Safa, Peyami, 164
Salmon, Frédéric, 297n10
Saltau, Roger, 31
Sarkozy, Nicolas: and French Muslim
Council, 112, 114, 118, 120–22, 133;
and headscarf ban, 111, 112, 128–29;
laïcité positive of, 19, 98–101, 110–14,
133, 159, 187, 259, 285, 292n10;
politics of, 133; on religion as culture,
112–13, 133; *La République, les religions,
l'espérance,* 98, 99–100, 118, 121; speech
at Lateran, 98–99, 132, 133; speech at
Riyad, 100–101; speech at Union des
Organisations Islamiques de France,
111–12; on teaching religious facts,
112–13
Şarlan, Hamdi, 171
Savcı, Bahri, 192–94
Schwartz, Rémy, 102
science, 164, 237–38
Scott, Joan, 20
Secular Age, A (Taylor), 17
secularism: from above and from below, 23;
and democracy, 210, 285; and diversity, 4,
19, 22, 26, 94, 279, 281; hermeneutical
approach to study of, 17–23, 132, 277,
278, 279; "independent ethic" version
of, 106; and institutional options, 5, 8,
25–29, 30–31, 277–78, 282; Keddie on,
24; multiple modernities approach to,
3, 17, 277, 280, 282; and neutrality, 19,
94; as not antireligious, 2, 16, 49, 144,
207, 288n11; passive and assertive,
20–22, 292n17; promoting religion in
name of, 23–24, 38, 284, 285; Western
vs. non-Western, 3–4, 22–25, 293n36.
See also laïcité; laiklik
Secularism and Freedom of Conscience
(Maclure and Taylor), 26–27
Secularism and Revivalism in Turkey
(Davison), 23
"Secularism and the State" (Keddie), 24
Secularisms and State Policies toward Religion
(Kuru), 20–21, 292n17
separation, religion-state: Başgil on,
171–72, 174–75; and CHP, 137,

155–56, 172, 189, 190; and DRA, 165, 168–69, 192; Ferry defense of, 49; "for more religion," 13, 132, 138; French law of 1905 on, 52–94; laiklik as, 160, 180, 189, 190, 204; limits of, 189–90; Paris Commune call for, 37; Sarkozy view of, 121–22; Turkish constitutions on, 140–41, 191, 194, 272; Western model of, 22–23. See also *Loi du 9 Décembre 1905 concernant la séparation des églises et de l'État*

Seyid B., Adliye Verkili, 139–40
Shari'a law, 209, 216
Shklar, Judith, x
Simon, Jules, 48–49, 72
Sirat, René-Samuel, 130
Sitruk, Joseph, 117, 305n40
Sivas Massacre, 236, 238, 252–53
Sızıntı, 198, 199
Skinner, Quentin, 17–18
socialists, 52, 302n134; Catholic Church as bulwark against, 10, 31; and diversity, 11, 281; and Républicains progressistes, 53, 68; Socialistes parlementaires, 57, 78, 96; in Turkey, 145
Soubie, Raymond, 102–3
Spain, 161, 316n1
Spuller, Eugène, 53
Stasi, Bernard, 102
Stasi Commission, 119, 304n16; composition of, 102–3; opposition to religious symbols ban in, 113, 114; Sarkozy speech to, 110–11
Stasi Report, 102–7, 119; on "Implementation of Existing Texts Concerning Chaplaincies," 107; on "Teaching of Religious Facts at School," 106
state-civil religionism, 7, 11–12, 95, 135, 278, 284–85; and AKP, 210, 211, 275; and anticlericalism, 7, 8, 10–11, 12, 135,

207–8, 275; in contemporary France, 131–33; and French 1882 law, 32, 36–37, 43–44, 95, 133; and French 1905 law, 11, 95; and Kemalism, 207, 275; and moderate-radical religion distinction, 284–85. See also laïcité; laiklik

Stepan, Alfred, 9
Subaşı, Necdet, 225, 227
Şürü Kaya, V., 141–42
Sweden, 161, 167
Switzerland, 36, 74, 153, 159, 174, 177–78
Syllabus of Errors, 32, 34, 49, 73–74

Tanrıöver, Hamdullah Suphi, 146–47, 153–54, 168; replies to, 154–56
Tantaoui, Mohamed Sayyed, 113–14
Taylor, Charles, 21, 279; criticisms of, 27, 28; on France and laïcité, 18, 19–20; on secularism, 17, 26–27, 106; works: "The Hermeneutics of Conflict," 17–18; "The Politics of Recognition," 26; *A Secular Age*, 17; *Secularism and Freedom of Conscience*, 26–27
Tekelioğlu, Sinan, 150–52, 166–67
Tercüman, 190
terrorism, 219, 241, 251, 252
Tévanian, Pierre, 116
Thelen, Kathleen, 9, 29
Third Republic from Its Origins to the Great War 1871–1914, The (Mayeuer and Rebérioux), 60–61
Tilly, Charles, 293n36
Tocqueville, Alexis de, 37, 70, 120, 121
Tokbey, Sadettin, 190
tolerance, 33, 53, 112, 127, 130, 131, 213–14
Touraine, Alain, 102, 107, 110, 114–15
Toynbee, Arnold Joseph, 168
traveling, 3–4, 6–7, 215, 277, 290n25; of modernity, 103, 165, 276, 280

INDEX [355]

True Path Party (Turkey), 314n129
Tümer, Nejat, 206–7
Turkey, 12–14, 135–208, 209–76; Alevi question in, 24, 183, 211–12, 216, 222–39, 291n37, 311n75; antidemocratic laws in, 254–55; caliphate abolished in, 139, 307–8n14; closing of religious schools in, 142–43; comparisons to Europe and U.S., 22–23, 152, 153–54, 161–62, 163, 167, 168, 174–75, 177–78, 195–96, 208, 215–16, 219, 264, 266, 276; constitutional revision of 1937 in, 141–42, 308n22; Constitution of 1928 in, 140–41, 308n22; Constitution of 1961 in, 179–87, 246; Constitution of 1982 in, 13, 136, 196–206, 220, 234, 236, 240, 258, 268, 273, 306n61; contemporary debates over, 20–21; corruption in, 250, 323n154; coup of 1960 in, 13, 179; coup of 1980 in, 12, 135, 196, 197–98, 243, 313–14n118; coup of 1982 in, 20; Democratic Opening project in, 24, 222–39; democratic transition in, 172, 209, 226, 245; and DRA budget, 145, 165–71, 173–74, 179, 214–15, 216, 217, 218, 219; election of 2001 in, 209, 244–46; election of 2007 in, 209, 219–220; European Court of Human Rights cases about, 103; fight against communism in, 12–13, 131, 138, 152, 167, 168; foreign schools in, 206; freedom of conscience in, 141–42, 158, 159, 164, 176, 190; headscarf issue in, 5, 20, 210, 306n61; Jews and Christians in, 151, 164, 176–77, 241; judiciary in, 221, 250, 252–53; Kurdish question in, 220, 240, 241–42; law on DRA in, 223, 239–43; laws of 1924 in, 139–40, 307–8n14; massacres of Alevis in, 227–28, 236, 237, 238, 252–53, 318n51; military establishment in, 219–21; moments of institutional change in, 12, 13, 135, 138, 211, 223, 274–75; as multilingual country, 262; multiparty system created in, 136; national culture in, 200; National Education Congresses in, 13, 138, 157–65; political repression and violence in, 145, 196, 243, 244–45, 246, 247–48, 249–52, 253, 259; and public school religion courses, 6, 12, 21, 124, 156, 175–79, 256–75, 306n61; referendum of 1987 in, 245–46, 321n111; secularization of, 139–40, 307–8n14; state-civil religionism in, 8, 135, 207, 210, 211, 275; state-salaried imams in, 6, 12, 135, 136, 138, 207, 239; workers' strikes in, 197. *See also* Directorate of Religious Affairs; Kemalism; laiklik
Turkey: Set Journalists Free, 249
Turkish Medical Association, 244
Turkish Socialist Party, 145
Turkish Socialist Workers and Peasants Party, 145

Uludere Incident, 243, 247, 321n15
UNESCO, 130, 164
Union démocratique (France), 57–58; and 1905 separation law, 77, 84, 85–87, 92, 96; and Républicains progressistes, 59, 68
Union des Droites (France), 37, 38–39, 40, 41, 50
Union des Organisations Islamiques de France (UOIF), 97, 111
Union for a Popular Movement, (UMP, France), 11–12, 19, 103, 118, 277, 281
Union of Education Law (Turkey), 124–25, 136

Union of Lyon Muslim Sisters, 120
Union of National Civil Society Organizations (Turkey), 219
Union républicaine (France), 47–48
United Kingdom, 36, 152, 178, 216; Education Act in, 158, 164
United States: debate over sphere of religion in, 25; French comparative references to, 70–71, 75, 81, 82, 88, 96; Turkish comparative references to, 152, 153, 168, 196, 208, 219, 260; and Uludere Incident, 247
Universal Declaration on Human Rights, 158, 161, 262
utilitarian framework, 3, 12, 275, 284; Kemalist, 137–38, 146, 165, 194–95, 207

Valsamis against Greece (European Court of Human Rights case), 103
van der Veer, Peter, 9
Vatican, 32, 54, 61, 64, 301n100; and Doctrine of Infallibility, 32, 49, 53, 74; French government relations with, 51, 56, 66, 73; and Ralliement, 41, 52; Sarkozy speech at Lateran, 98–99, 132, 133. *See also* Catholicism
Vazeille, Albert, 66, 81–82
Velidedeoğlu, Hıfzı Veldet, 181, 187

Versan, Vakur, 179–80
Verstehen approach, 8, 17, 20, 21, 278
Virtue Party (Turkey), 217–18

Waldeck-Rousseau, Pierre, 53, 54–55, 56
Wall Street Journal, 247
Weber, Max, x, 18
Weil, Patrick, 102–3, 118–19
Welfare Party (RP, Turkey): banning of, 210, 216; in government, 215–16, 218
White House Office of Faith-Based and Neighborhood Partnerships, 25
Why the French Don't Like Headscarves (Bowen), 19–20
Willaime, Jean-Paul, 21, 22, 282
Winter Journal (Auster), 257
"World's Religious Systems and Democracy, The" (Stepan), 9

Yakın Maziden Hatıra Kırıntıları (Başgil), 174
Yazıcıoğlu, Said, 225
Yeni Asya, 198

Zafer, 176–77
Zapatero, José Luis Rodríguez, 2
Zinn, Howard, 248
Zürcher, Eric, 196

RELIGION, CULTURE, AND PUBLIC LIFE
Series Editor: Katherine Pratt Ewing

After Pluralism: Reimagining Religious Engagement, edited by Courtney Bender and Pamela E. Klassen

Religion and International Relations Theory, edited by Jack Snyder

Religion in America: A Political History, Denis Lacorne

Democracy, Islam, and Secularism in Turkey, edited by Ahmet T. Kuru and Alfred Stepan

Refiguring the Spiritual: Beuys, Barney, Turrell, Goldsworthy, Mark C. Taylor

Tolerance, Democracy, and Sufis in Senegal, edited by Mamadou Diouf

Rewiring the Real: In Conversation with William Gaddis, Richard Powers, Mark Danielewski, and Don DeLillo, Mark C. Taylor

Democracy and Islam in Indonesia, edited by Mirjam Künkler and Alfred Stepan

Religion, the Secular, and the Politics of Sexual Difference, edited by Linell E. Cady and Tracy Fessenden

Boundaries of Toleration, edited by Alfred Stepan and Charles Taylor

Recovering Place: Reflections on Stone Hill, Mark C. Taylor

Blood: A Critique of Christianity, Gil Anidjar

Choreographies of Shared Sacred Sites: Religion, Politics, and Conflict Resolution, edited by Elazar Barkan and Karen Barkey

Beyond Individualism: The Challenge of Inclusive Communities, George Rupp

Love and Forgiveness for a More Just World, edited by Hent de Vries and Nils F. Schott

Relativism and Religion: Why Democratic Societies Do Not Need Moral Absolutes, Carlo Invernizzi Accetti

The Making of Salafism: Islamic Reform in the Twentieth Century, Henri Lauzière

Mormonism and American Politics, edited by Randall Balmer and Jana Riess

Religion, Secularism, and Constitutional Democracy, edited by Jean L. Cohen and Cécile Laborde

Race and Secularism in America, edited by Jonathon S. Kahn and Vincent W. Lloyd

Beyond the Secular West, edited by Akeel Bilgrami

Pakistan at the Crossroads: Domestic Dynamics and External Pressures, edited by Christophe Jaffrelot

Faithful to Secularism: The Religious Politics of Democracy in Ireland, Senegal, and the Philippines, David T. Buckley

Holy Wars or Holy Alliances: The Return of Religion Onto the Global Political Stage, Manlio Graziano